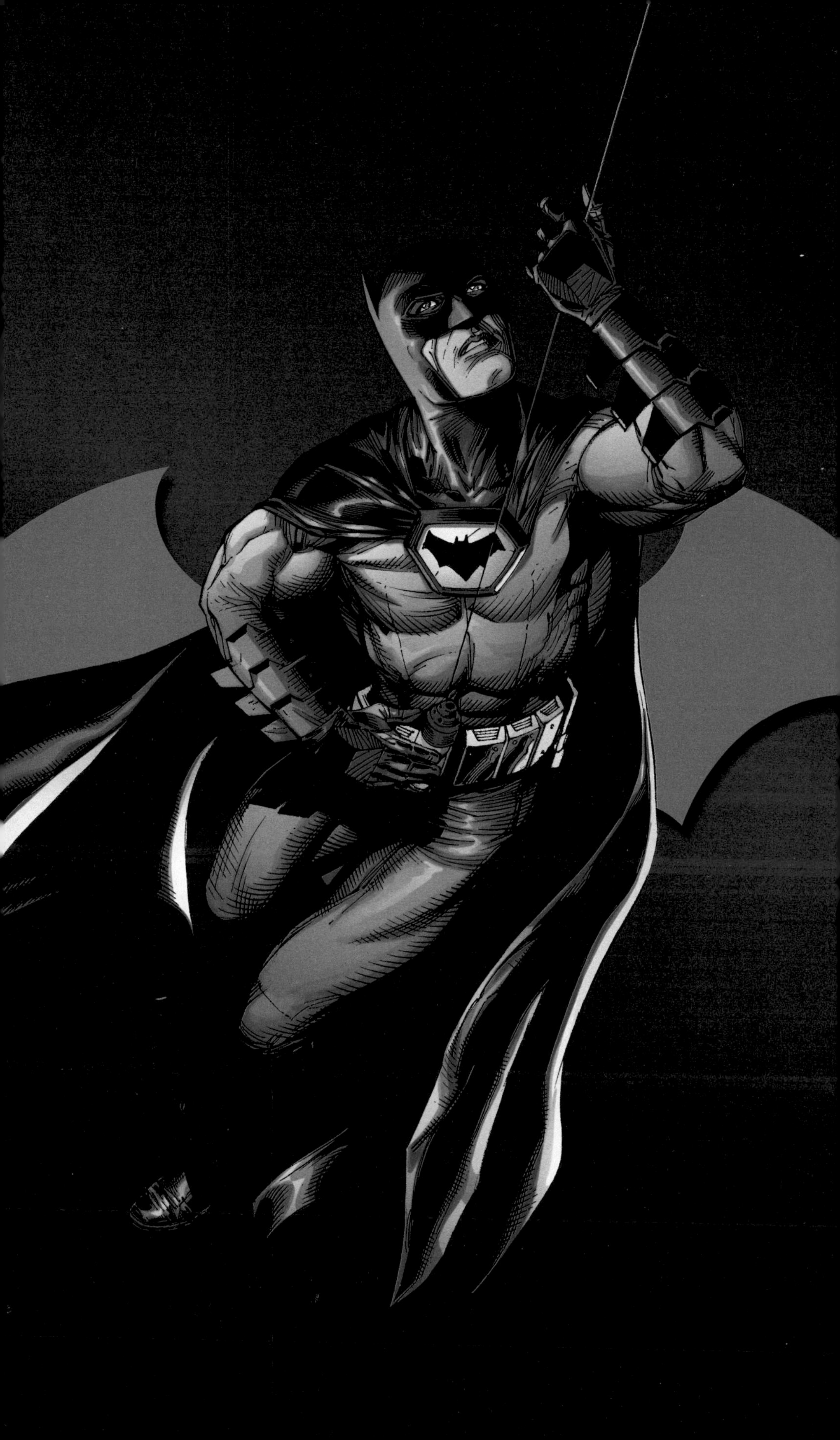

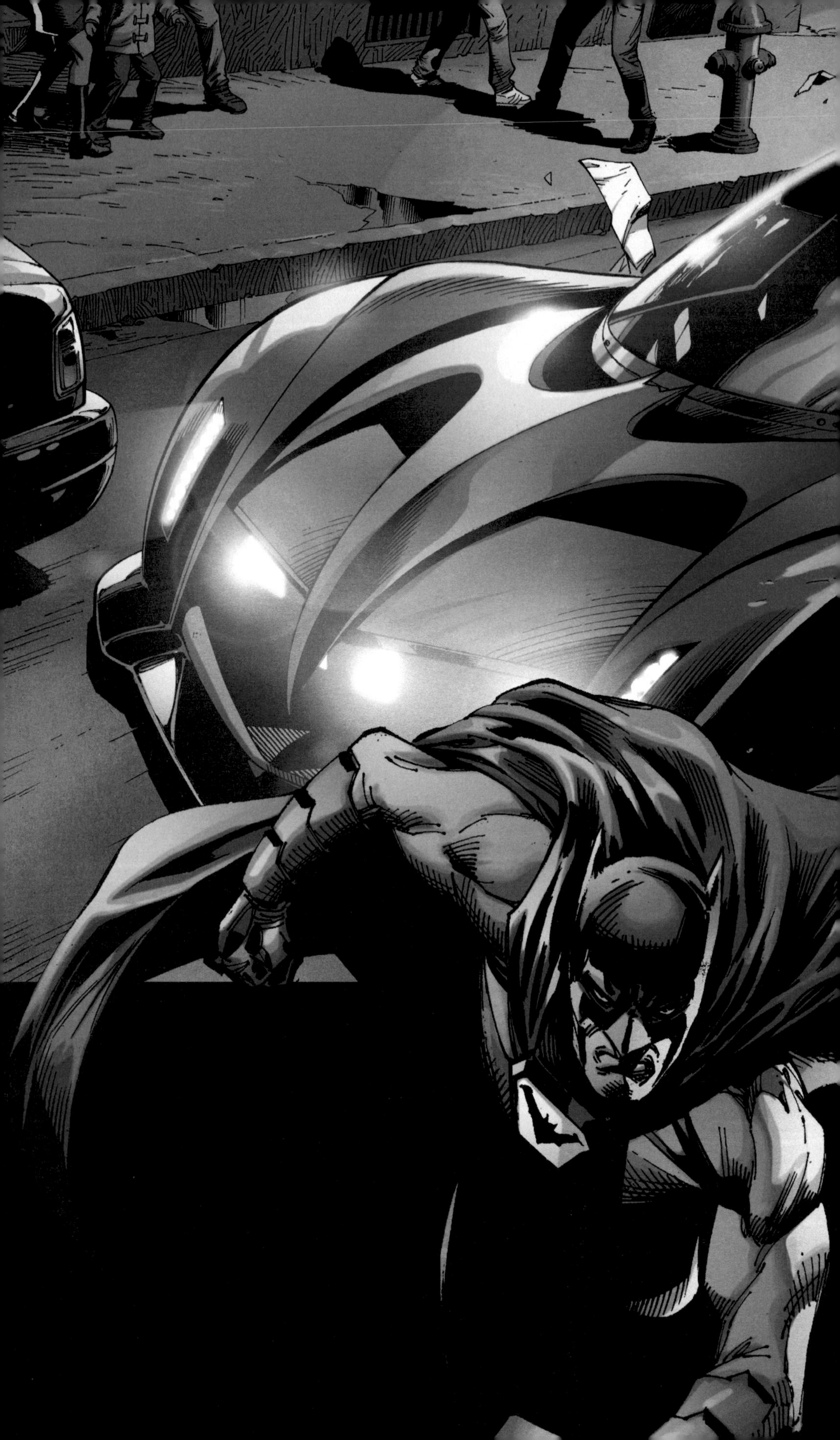

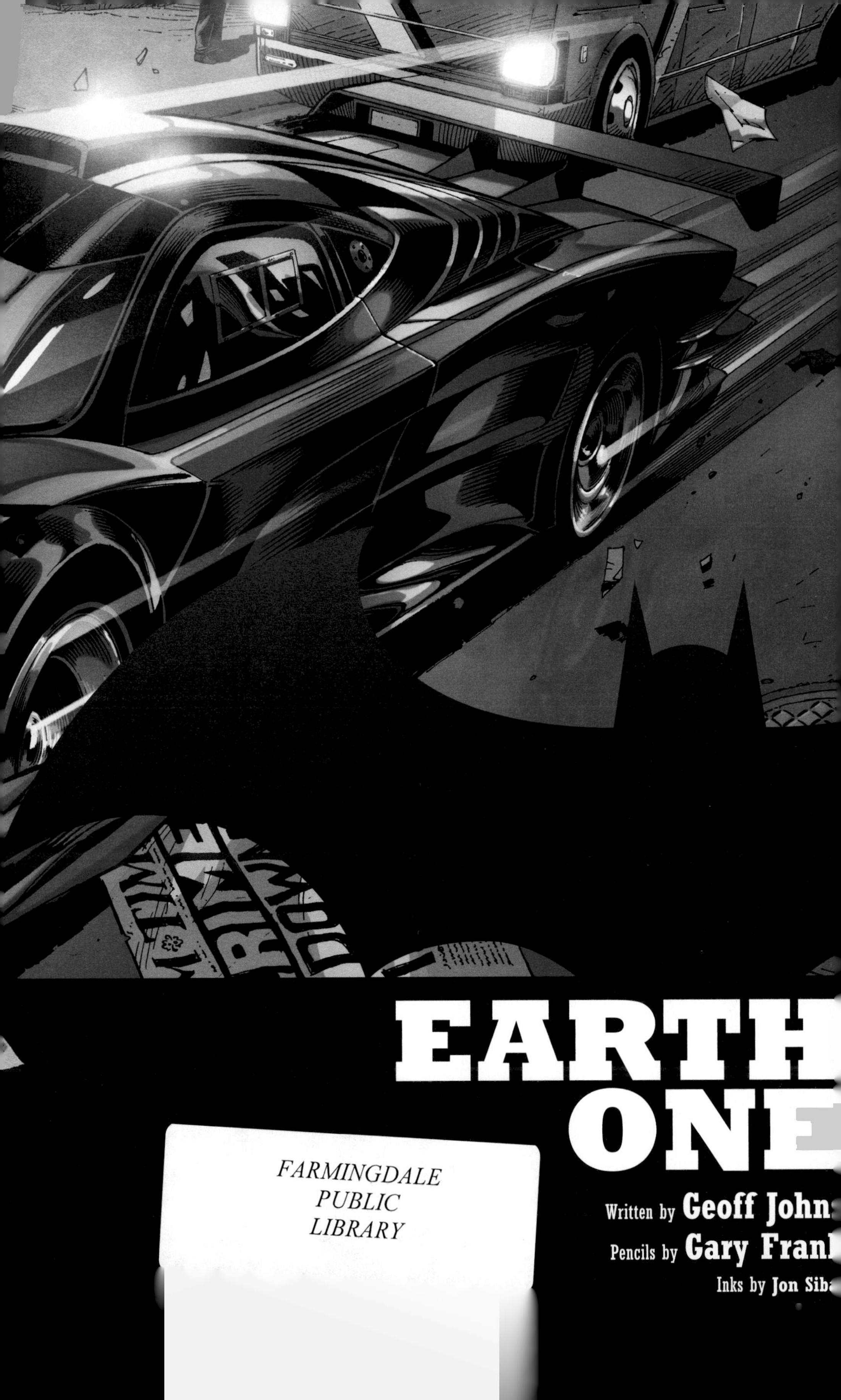

EARTH ONE

Written by Geoff John

Pencils by Gary Fran

Inks by Jon Sib

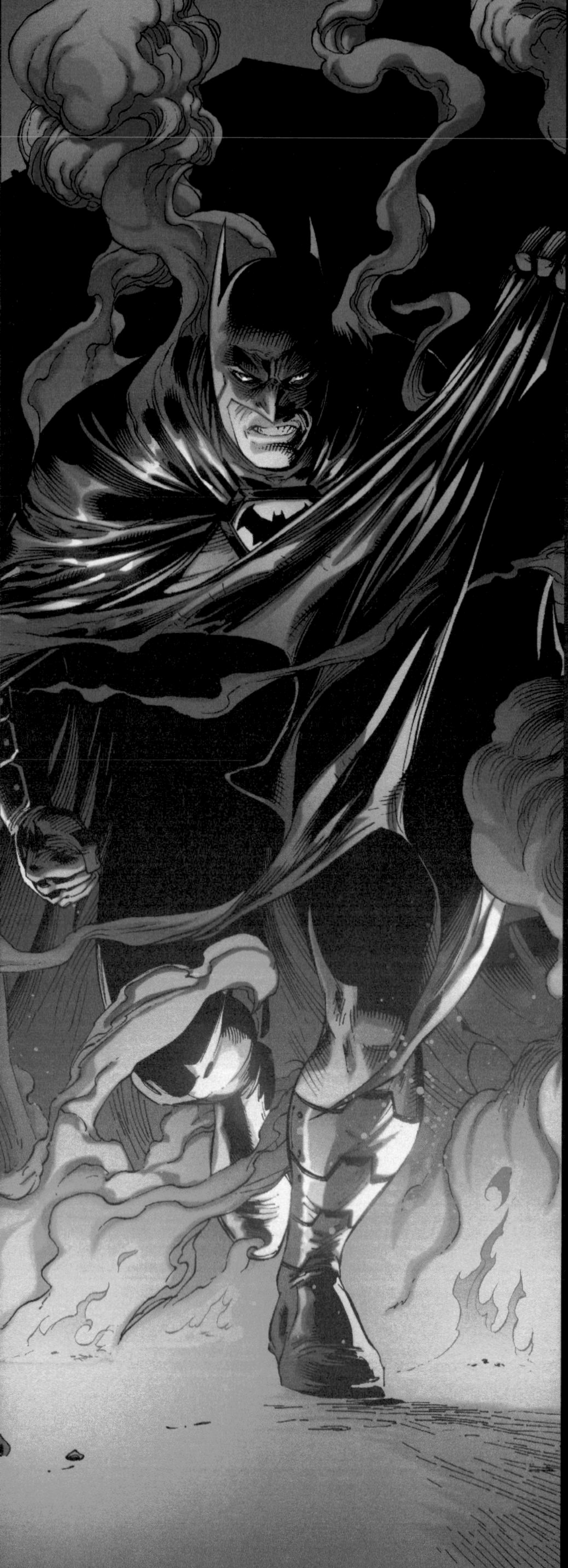

Brian Cunningham Editor
Amedeo Turturro Associate Editor
Steve Cook Design Director – Books
Curtis King Jr. Publication Design
Sandy Alonzo Publication Production

Marie Javins Editor-in-Chief, DC Comics

Daniel Cherry III Senior VP – General Manager
Jim Lee Publisher & Chief Creative Officer
Joen Choe VP – Global Brand & Creative Services
Don Falletti VP – Manufacturing Operations & Workflow Management
Lawrence Ganem VP – Talent Services
Alison Gill Senior VP – Manufacturing & Operations
Nick J. Napolitano VP – Manufacturing Administration & Design
Nancy Spears VP – Revenue

BATMAN: EARTH ONE VOLUME THREE

DC Comics, 2900 West Alameda Ave., Burbank, CA 91505
Printed by LSC Communications, Willard, OH, USA. 4/30/21.
First Printing. ISBN: 978-1-4012-5904-4

Library of Congress Cataloging-in-Publication Data is available.

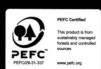

PEFC Certified
This product is from sustainably managed forests and controlled sources
PEFC
PEFC/29-31-337
www.pefc.org

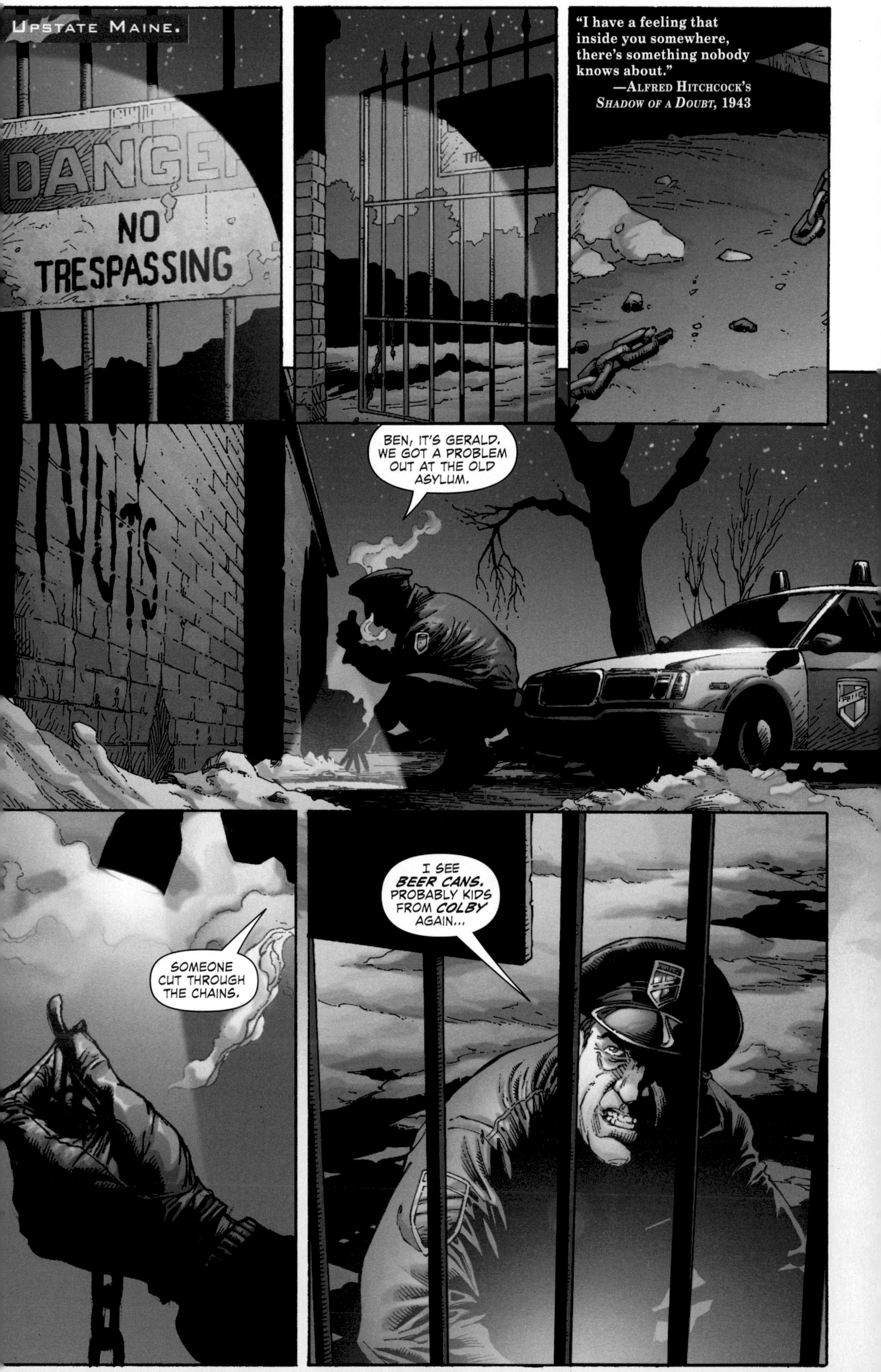
UPSTATE MAINE.
DANGER
NO TRESPASSING
"I have a feeling that inside you somewhere, there's something nobody knows about."
—ALFRED HITCHCOCK'S SHADOW OF A DOUBT, 1943
BEN, IT'S GERALD. WE GOT A PROBLEM OUT AT THE OLD ASYLUM.
SOMEONE CUT THROUGH THE CHAINS.
I SEE BEER CANS. PROBABLY KIDS FROM COLBY AGAIN...

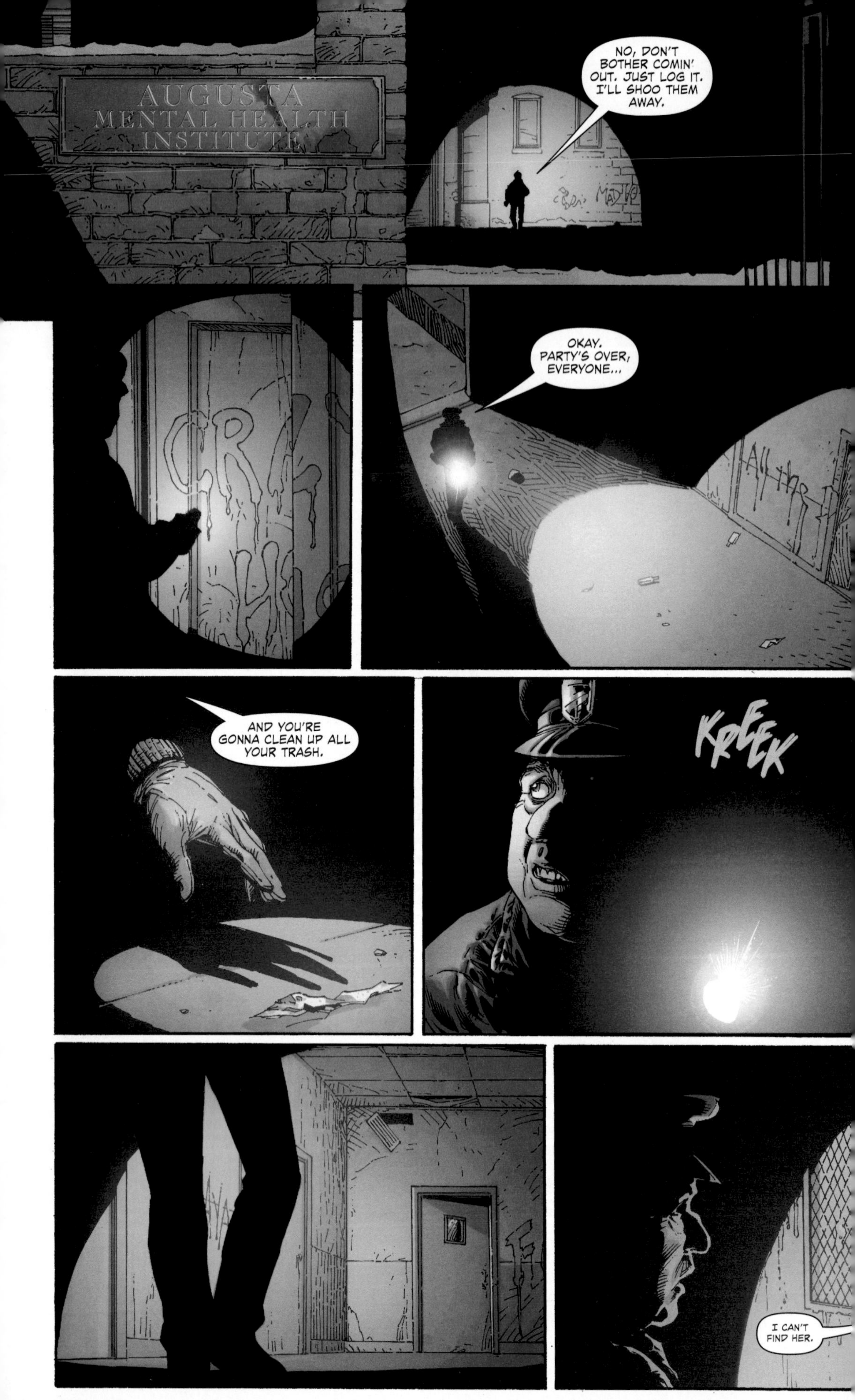
AUGUSTA
MENTAL HEALTH
INSTITUTE
NO, DON'T BOTHER COMIN' OUT. JUST LOG IT. I'LL SHOO THEM AWAY.
OKAY. PARTY'S OVER, EVERYONE...
AND YOU'RE GONNA CLEAN UP ALL YOUR TRASH.
KREEEK
I CAN'T FIND HER.

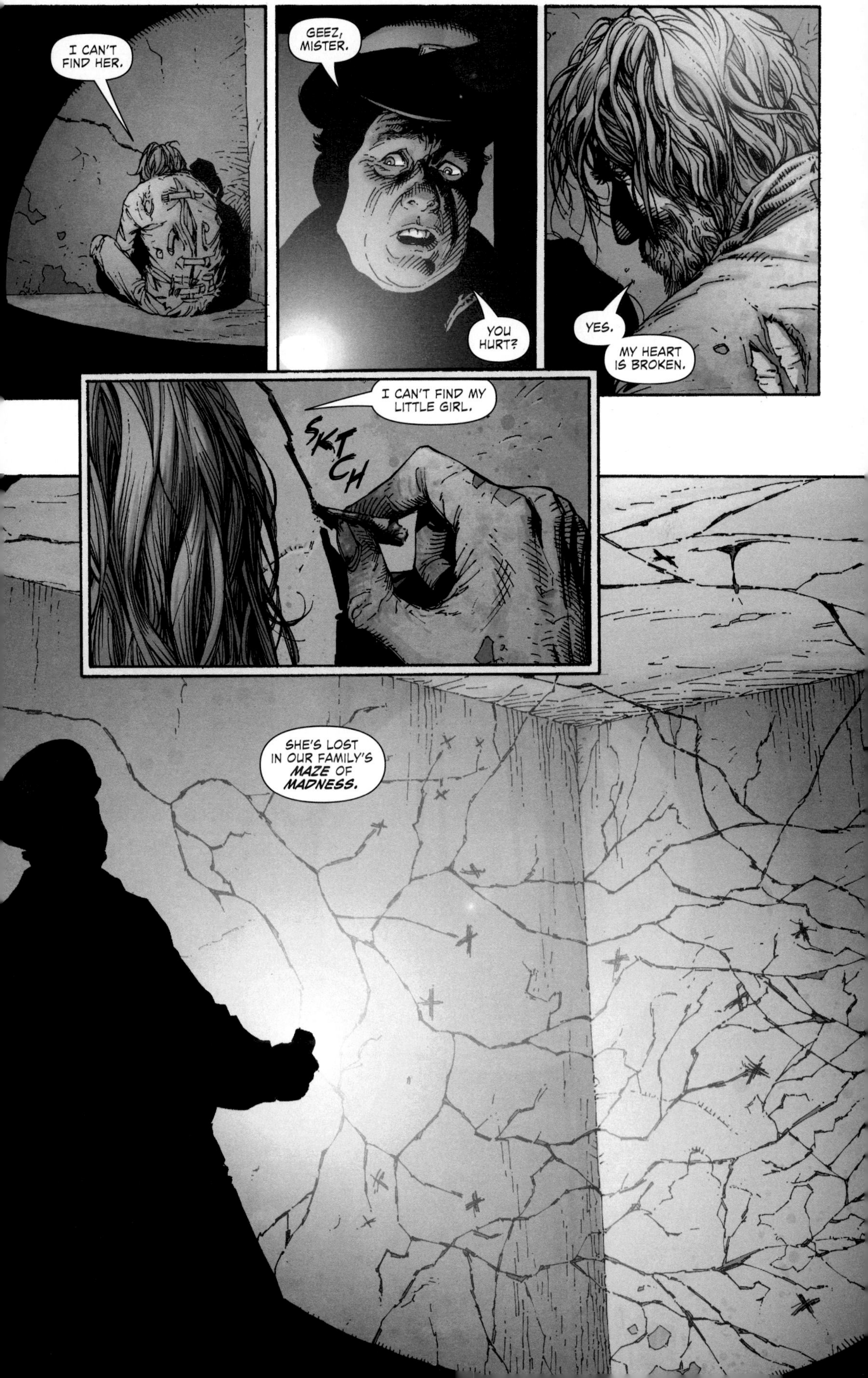
I CAN'T FIND HER.
GEEZ, MISTER.
YOU HURT?
YES.
MY HEART IS BROKEN.
I CAN'T FIND MY LITTLE GIRL.
SKTCH
SHE'S LOST IN OUR FAMILY'S *MAZE* OF *MADNESS.*

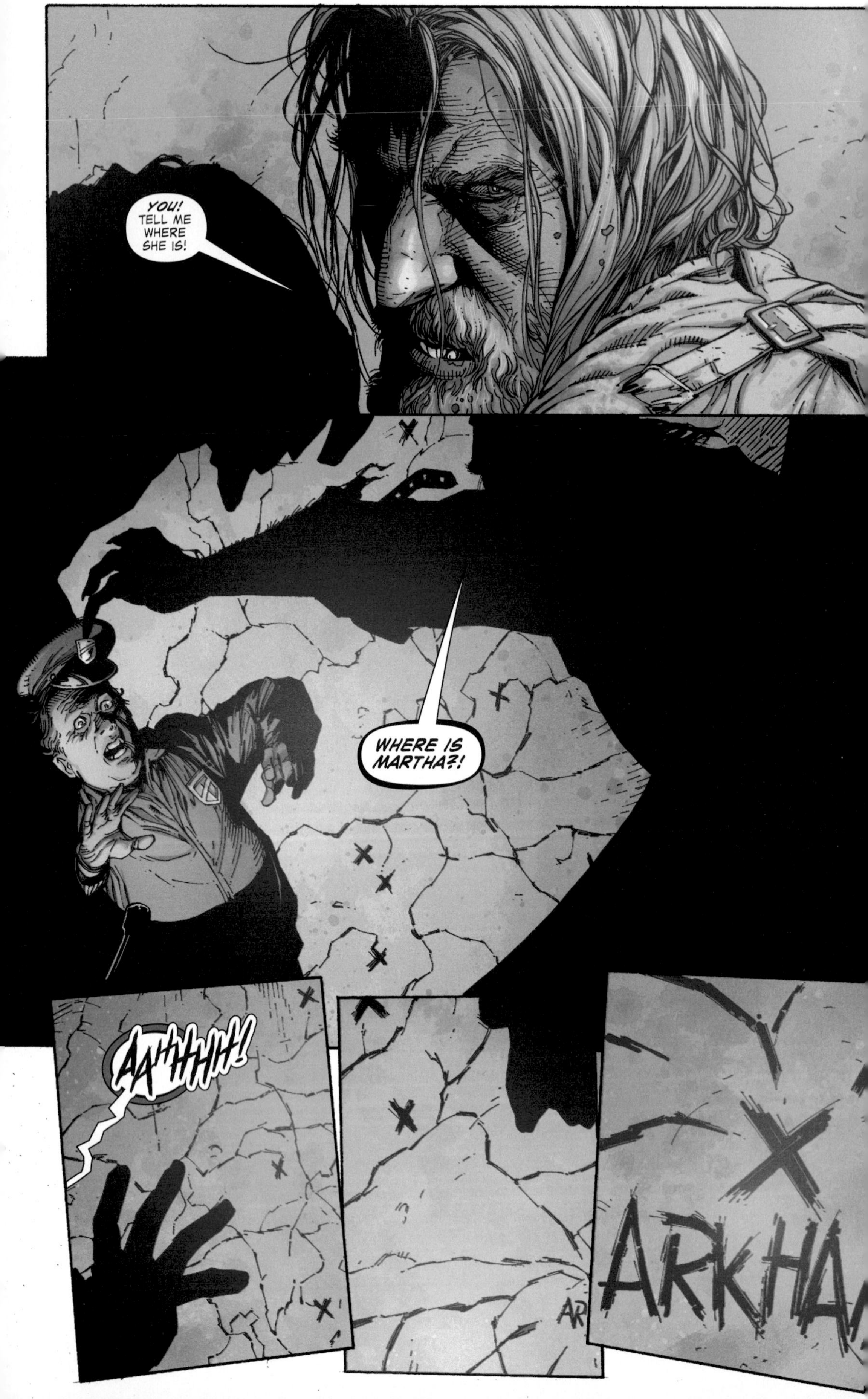
YOU! TELL ME WHERE SHE IS!
WHERE IS MARTHA?!
AAHHHH!
ARKHA

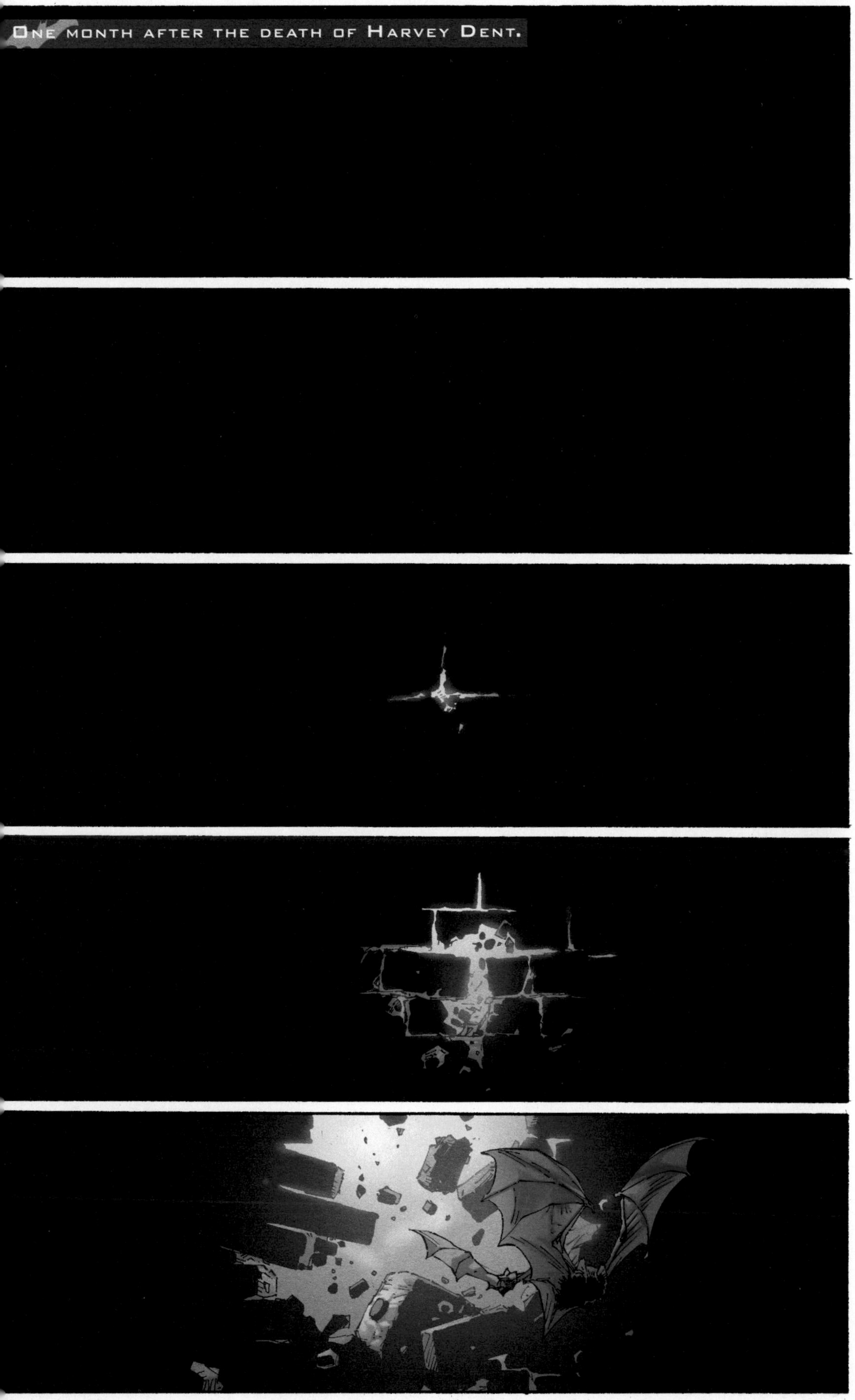
ONE MONTH AFTER THE DEATH OF HARVEY DENT.

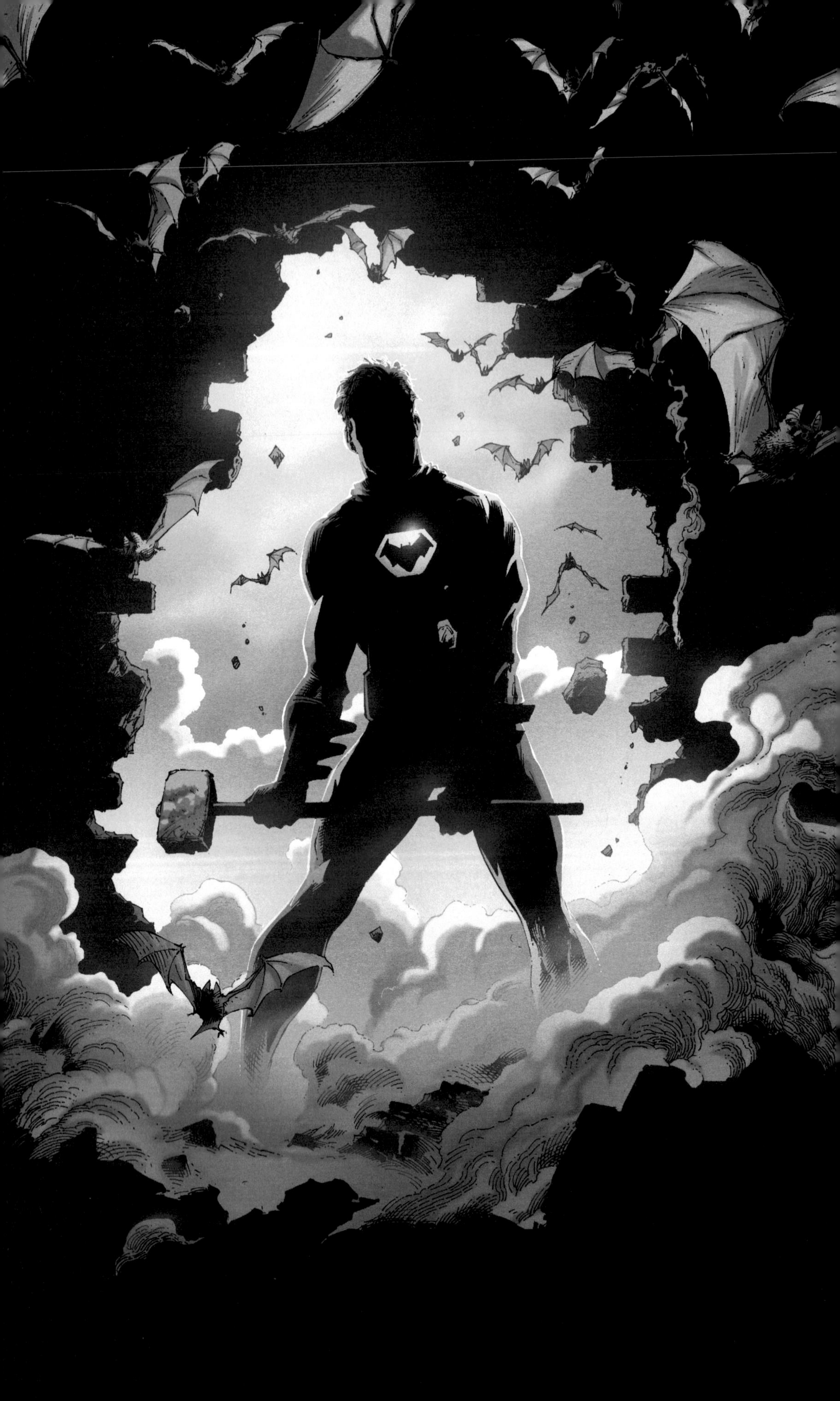

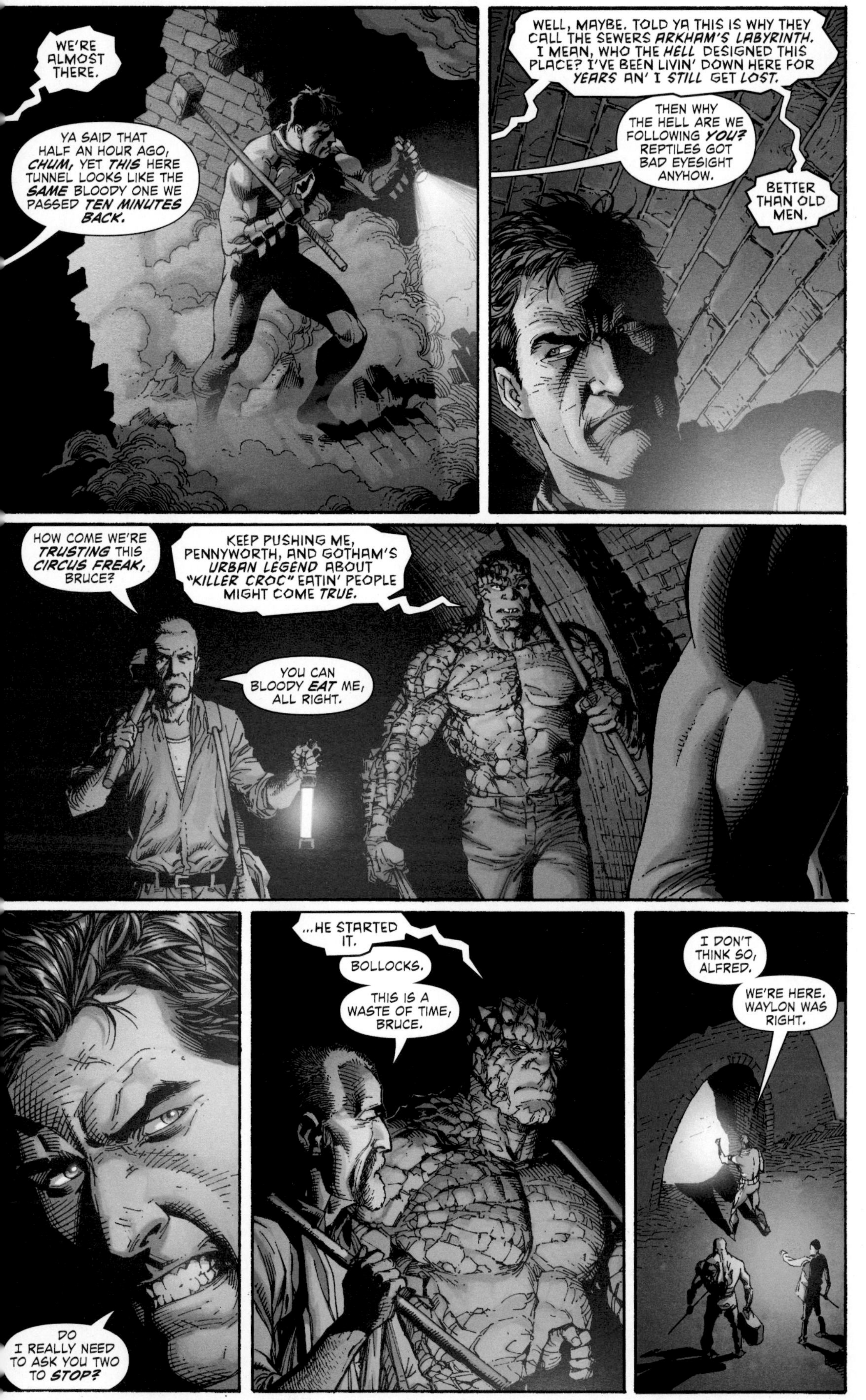

WE'RE ALMOST THERE.
YA SAID THAT HALF AN HOUR AGO, CHUM, YET THIS HERE TUNNEL LOOKS LIKE THE SAME BLOODY ONE WE PASSED TEN MINUTES BACK.
WELL, MAYBE. TOLD YA THIS IS WHY THEY CALL THE SEWERS ARKHAM'S LABYRINTH. I MEAN, WHO THE HELL DESIGNED THIS PLACE? I'VE BEEN LIVIN' DOWN HERE FOR YEARS AN' I STILL GET LOST.
THEN WHY THE HELL ARE WE FOLLOWING YOU? REPTILES GOT BAD EYESIGHT ANYHOW.
BETTER THAN OLD MEN.
HOW COME WE'RE TRUSTING THIS CIRCUS FREAK, BRUCE?
KEEP PUSHING ME, PENNYWORTH, AND GOTHAM'S URBAN LEGEND ABOUT "KILLER CROC" EATIN' PEOPLE MIGHT COME TRUE.
YOU CAN BLOODY EAT ME, ALL RIGHT.
DO I REALLY NEED TO ASK YOU TWO TO STOP?
...HE STARTED IT.
BOLLOCKS.
THIS IS A WASTE OF TIME, BRUCE.
I DON'T THINK SO, ALFRED.
WE'RE HERE. WAYLON WAS RIGHT.

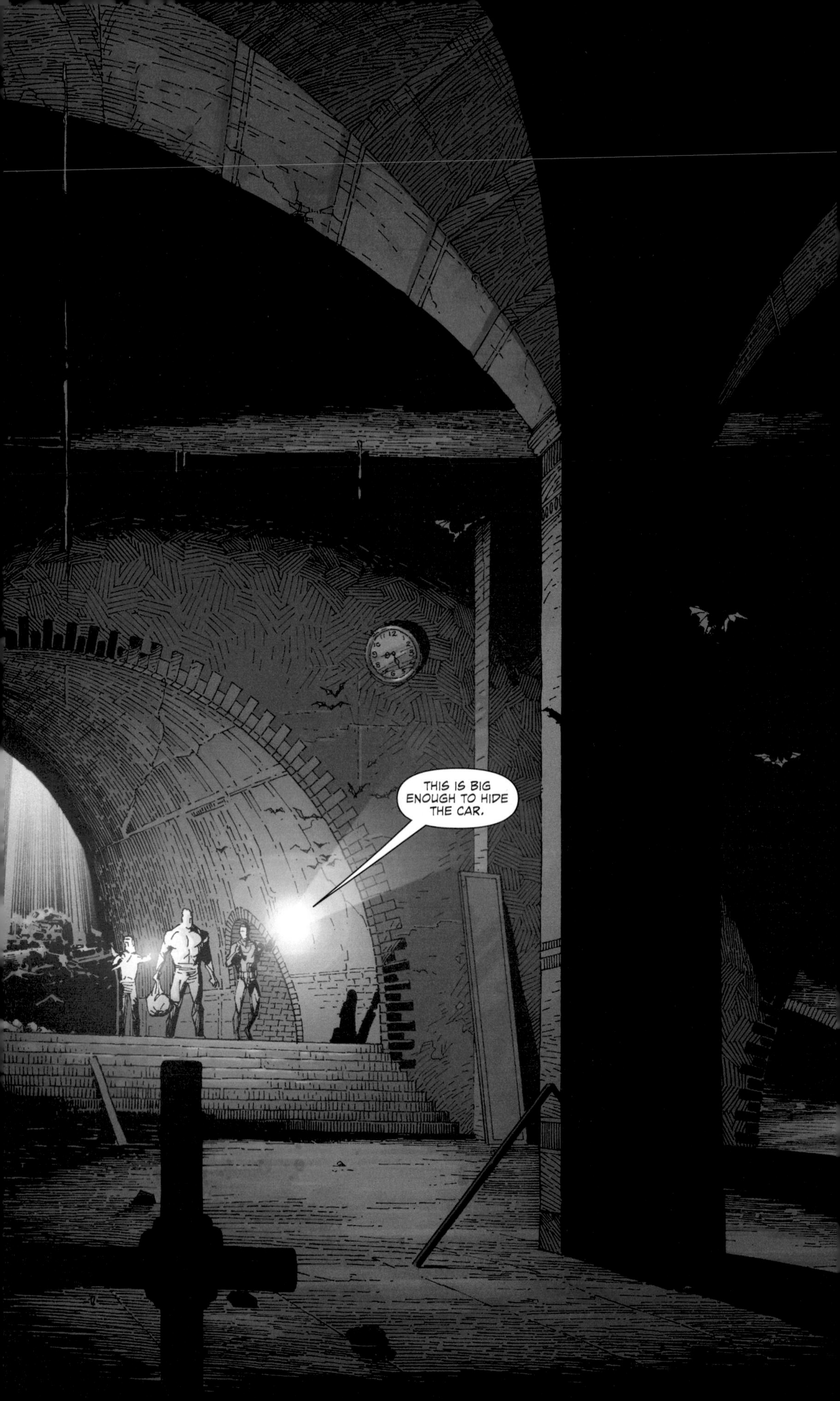
THIS IS BIG ENOUGH TO HIDE THE CAR.

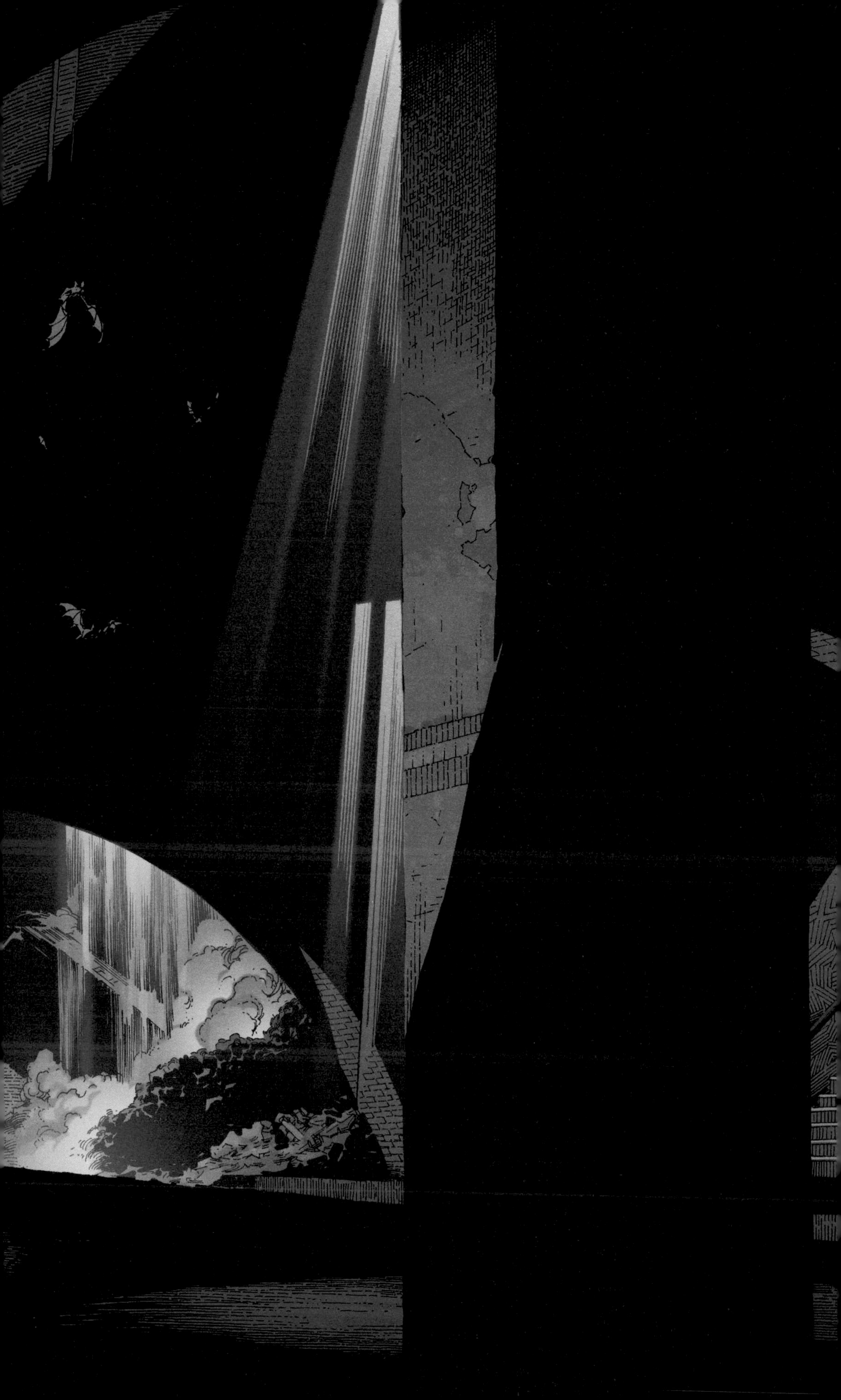

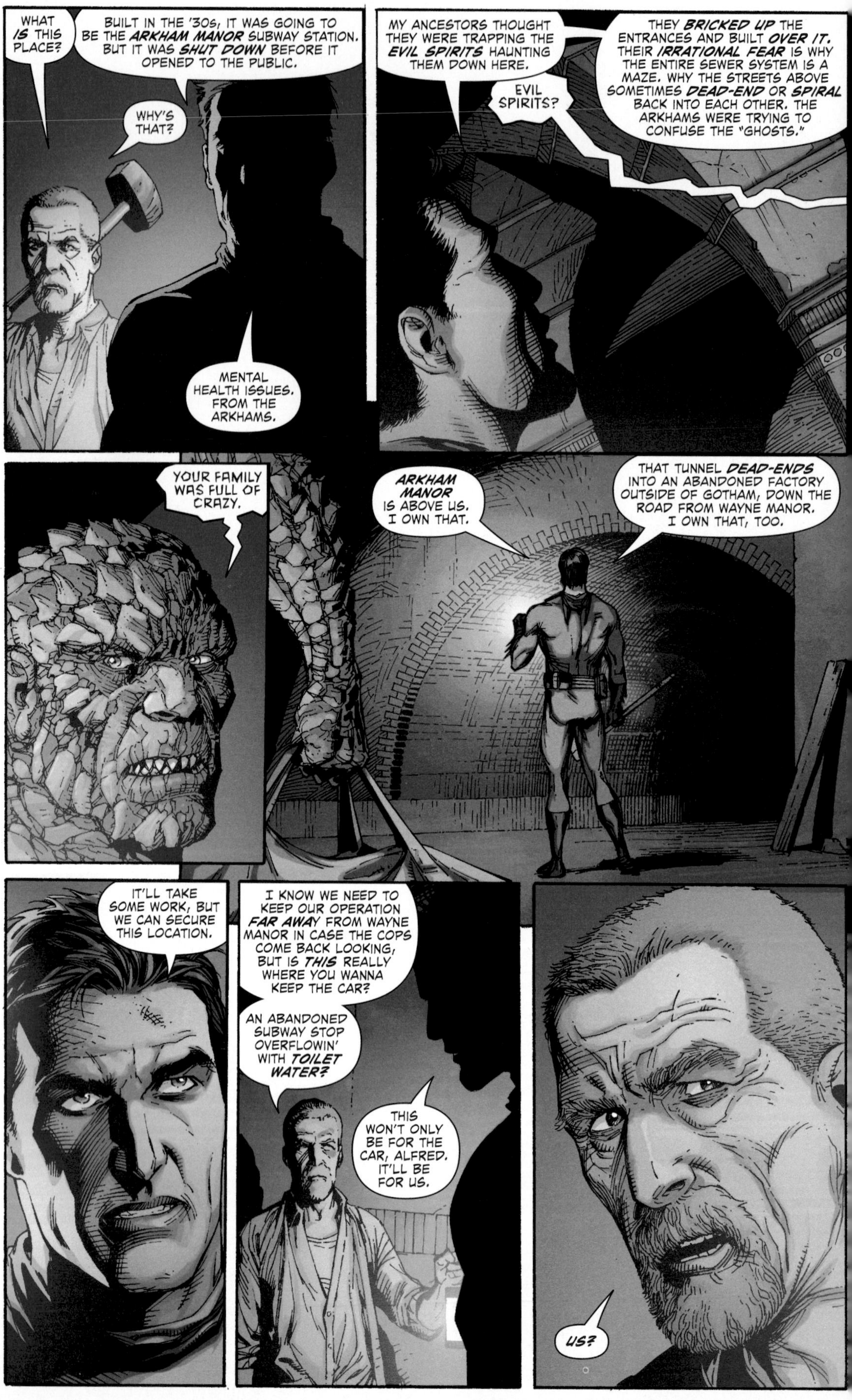
WHAT IS THIS PLACE?
BUILT IN THE '30s, IT WAS GOING TO BE THE ARKHAM MANOR SUBWAY STATION. BUT IT WAS SHUT DOWN BEFORE IT OPENED TO THE PUBLIC.
WHY'S THAT?
MENTAL HEALTH ISSUES. FROM THE ARKHAMS.
MY ANCESTORS THOUGHT THEY WERE TRAPPING THE EVIL SPIRITS HAUNTING THEM DOWN HERE.
EVIL SPIRITS?
THEY BRICKED UP THE ENTRANCES AND BUILT OVER IT. THEIR IRRATIONAL FEAR IS WHY THE ENTIRE SEWER SYSTEM IS A MAZE. WHY THE STREETS ABOVE SOMETIMES DEAD-END OR SPIRAL BACK INTO EACH OTHER. THE ARKHAMS WERE TRYING TO CONFUSE THE "GHOSTS."
YOUR FAMILY WAS FULL OF CRAZY.
ARKHAM MANOR IS ABOVE US. I OWN THAT.
THAT TUNNEL DEAD-ENDS INTO AN ABANDONED FACTORY OUTSIDE OF GOTHAM, DOWN THE ROAD FROM WAYNE MANOR. I OWN THAT, TOO.
IT'LL TAKE SOME WORK, BUT WE CAN SECURE THIS LOCATION.
I KNOW WE NEED TO KEEP OUR OPERATION FAR AWAY FROM WAYNE MANOR IN CASE THE COPS COME BACK LOOKING, BUT IS THIS REALLY WHERE YOU WANNA KEEP THE CAR?
AN ABANDONED SUBWAY STOP OVERFLOWIN' WITH TOILET WATER?
THIS WON'T ONLY BE FOR THE CAR, ALFRED. IT'LL BE FOR US.
US?

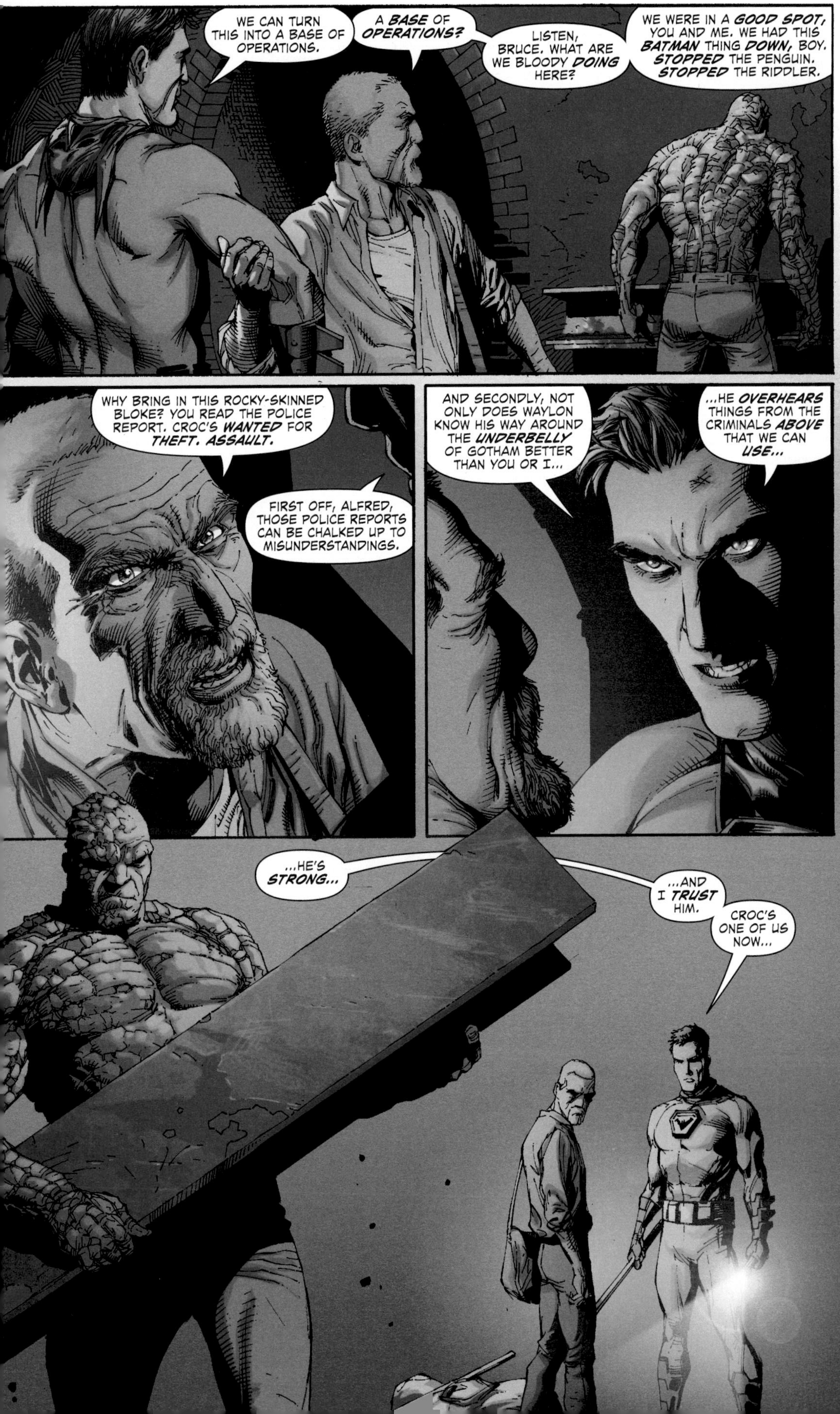
WE CAN TURN THIS INTO A BASE OF OPERATIONS.
A *BASE* OF *OPERATIONS?*
LISTEN, BRUCE. WHAT ARE WE BLOODY *DOING* HERE?
WE WERE IN A *GOOD SPOT,* YOU AND ME. WE HAD THIS *BATMAN* THING *DOWN,* BOY. *STOPPED* THE PENGUIN. *STOPPED* THE RIDDLER.
WHY BRING IN THIS ROCKY-SKINNED BLOKE? YOU READ THE POLICE REPORT. CROC'S *WANTED* FOR *THEFT. ASSAULT.*
FIRST OFF, ALFRED, THOSE POLICE REPORTS CAN BE CHALKED UP TO MISUNDERSTANDINGS.
AND SECONDLY, NOT ONLY DOES WAYLON KNOW HIS WAY AROUND THE *UNDERBELLY* OF GOTHAM BETTER THAN YOU OR I...
...HE *OVERHEARS* THINGS FROM THE CRIMINALS *ABOVE* THAT WE CAN *USE...*
...HE'S *STRONG...*
...AND I *TRUST* HIM.
CROC'S ONE OF US NOW...

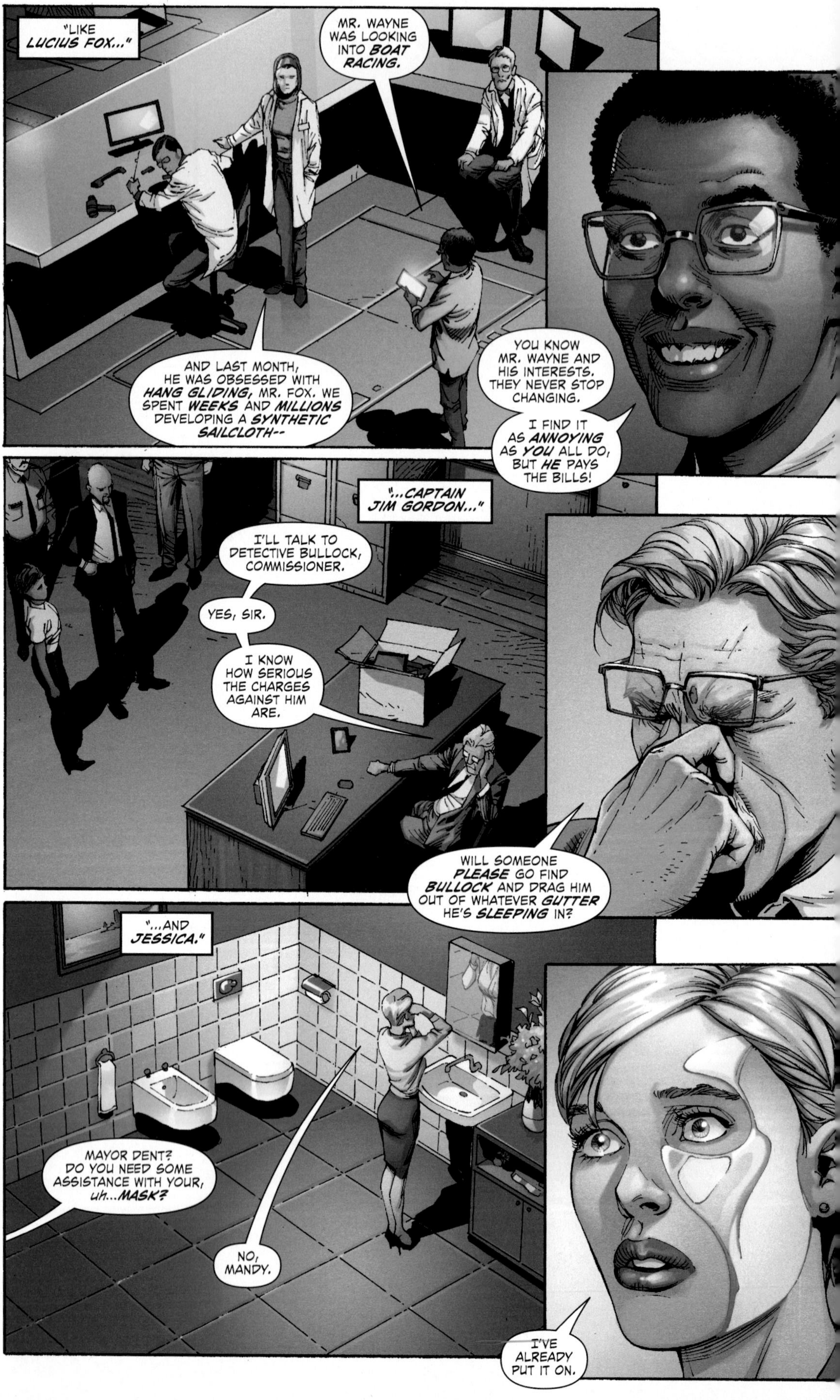
"LIKE LUCIUS FOX..."
MR. WAYNE WAS LOOKING INTO BOAT RACING.
AND LAST MONTH, HE WAS OBSESSED WITH HANG GLIDING, MR. FOX. WE SPENT WEEKS AND MILLIONS DEVELOPING A SYNTHETIC SAILCLOTH--
YOU KNOW MR. WAYNE AND HIS INTERESTS. THEY NEVER STOP CHANGING.
I FIND IT AS ANNOYING AS YOU ALL DO, BUT HE PAYS THE BILLS!
"...CAPTAIN JIM GORDON..."
I'LL TALK TO DETECTIVE BULLOCK, COMMISSIONER.
YES, SIR.
I KNOW HOW SERIOUS THE CHARGES AGAINST HIM ARE.
WILL SOMEONE PLEASE GO FIND BULLOCK AND DRAG HIM OUT OF WHATEVER GUTTER HE'S SLEEPING IN?
"...AND JESSICA."
MAYOR DENT? DO YOU NEED SOME ASSISTANCE WITH YOUR, uh...MASK?
NO, MANDY.
I'VE ALREADY PUT IT ON.

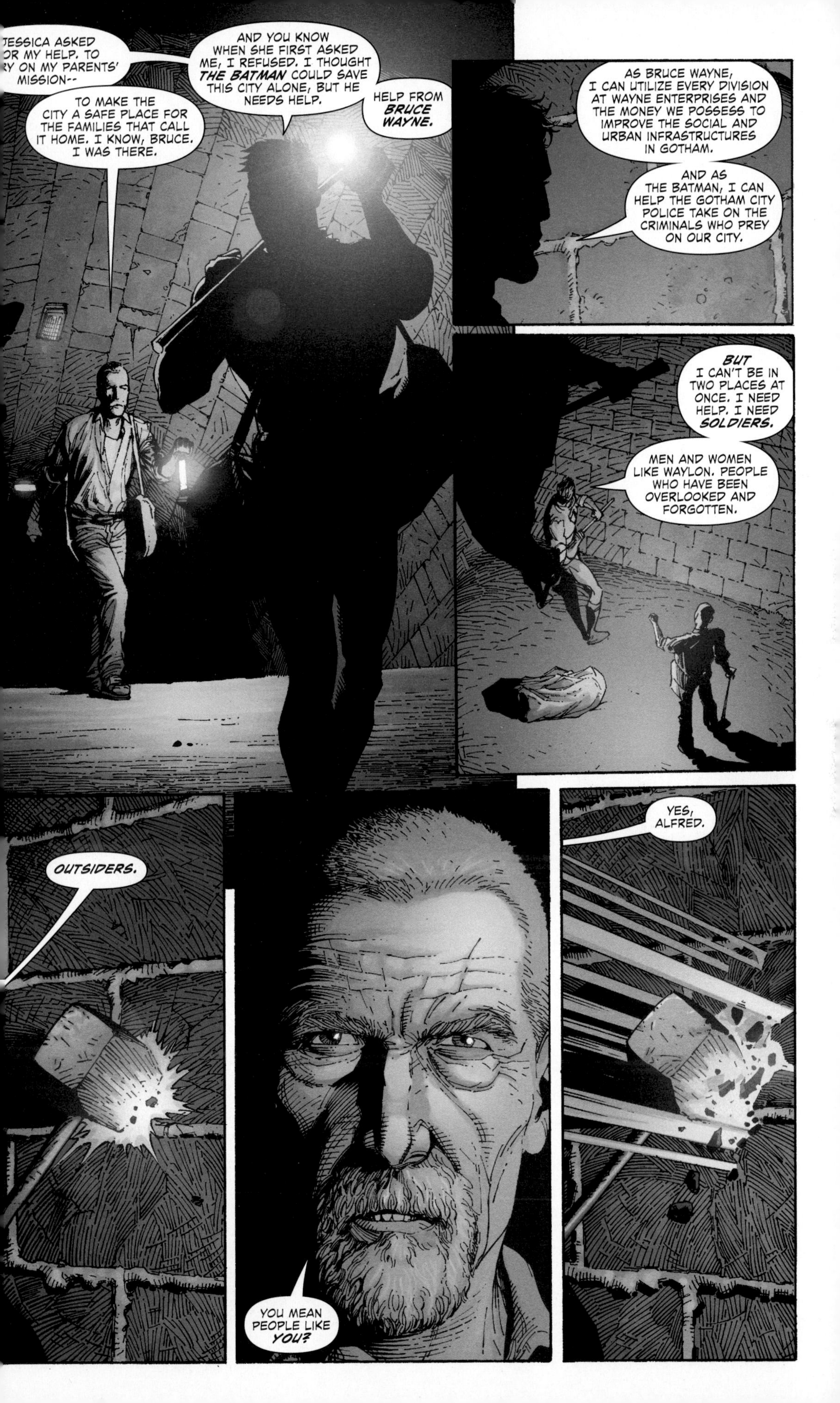
JESSICA ASKED
FOR MY HELP. TO
CARRY ON MY PARENTS' MISSION--
TO MAKE THE CITY A SAFE PLACE FOR THE FAMILIES THAT CALL IT HOME. I KNOW, BRUCE. I WAS THERE.
AND YOU KNOW WHEN SHE FIRST ASKED ME, I REFUSED. I THOUGHT THE BATMAN COULD SAVE THIS CITY ALONE, BUT HE NEEDS HELP.
HELP FROM BRUCE WAYNE.
AS BRUCE WAYNE, I CAN UTILIZE EVERY DIVISION AT WAYNE ENTERPRISES AND THE MONEY WE POSSESS TO IMPROVE THE SOCIAL AND URBAN INFRASTRUCTURES IN GOTHAM.
AND AS THE BATMAN, I CAN HELP THE GOTHAM CITY POLICE TAKE ON THE CRIMINALS WHO PREY ON OUR CITY.
BUT I CAN'T BE IN TWO PLACES AT ONCE. I NEED HELP. I NEED SOLDIERS.
MEN AND WOMEN LIKE WAYLON. PEOPLE WHO HAVE BEEN OVERLOOKED AND FORGOTTEN.
OUTSIDERS.
YOU MEAN PEOPLE LIKE YOU?
YES, ALFRED.

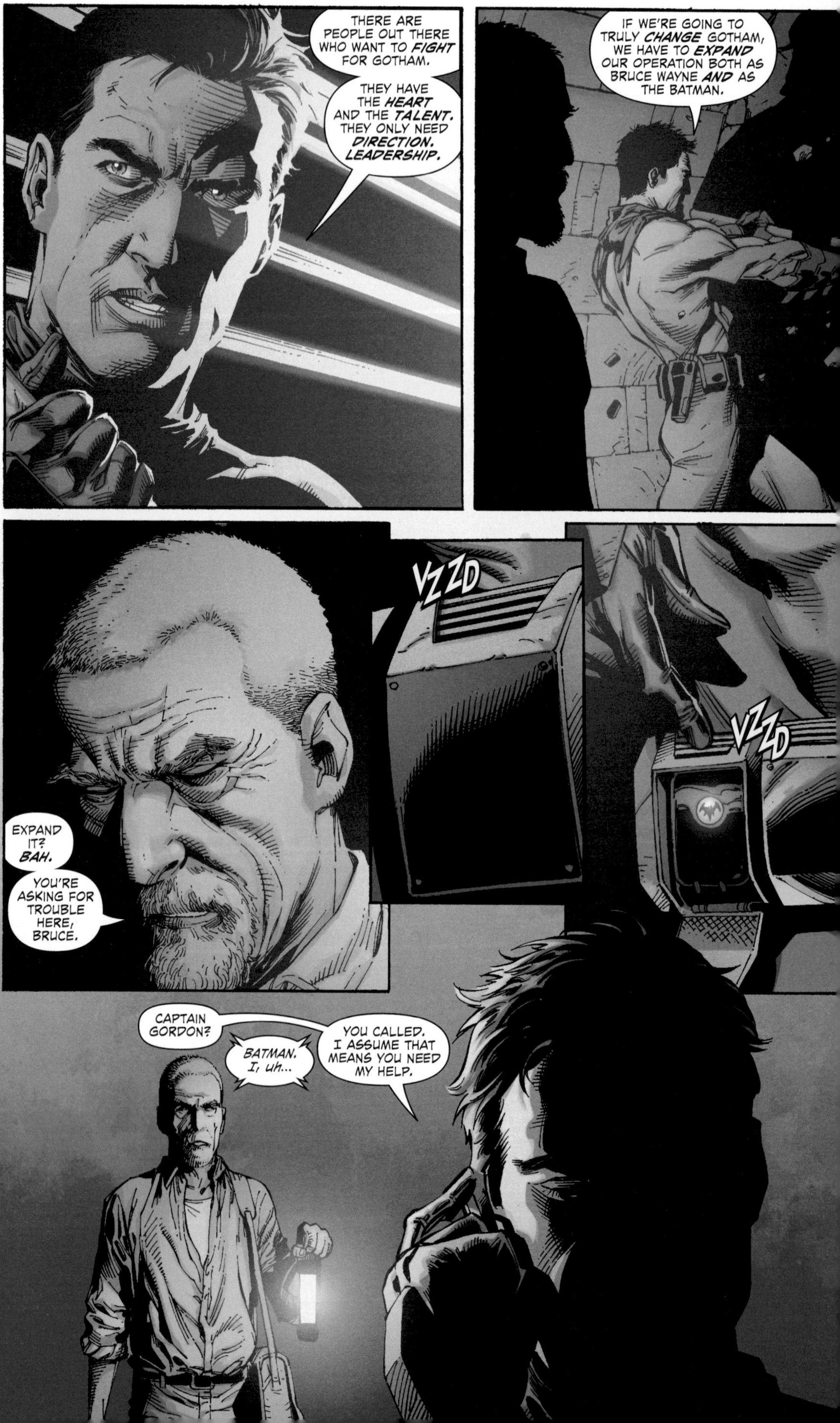

THERE ARE PEOPLE OUT THERE WHO WANT TO *FIGHT* FOR GOTHAM.
THEY HAVE THE *HEART* AND THE *TALENT.* THEY ONLY NEED *DIRECTION. LEADERSHIP.*
IF WE'RE GOING TO TRULY *CHANGE* GOTHAM, WE HAVE TO *EXPAND* OUR OPERATION BOTH AS BRUCE WAYNE *AND* AS THE BATMAN.
EXPAND IT? *BAH.*
YOU'RE ASKING FOR TROUBLE HERE, BRUCE.
VZZD
VZZD
CAPTAIN GORDON?
BATMAN. I, uh...
YOU CALLED. I ASSUME THAT MEANS YOU NEED MY HELP.

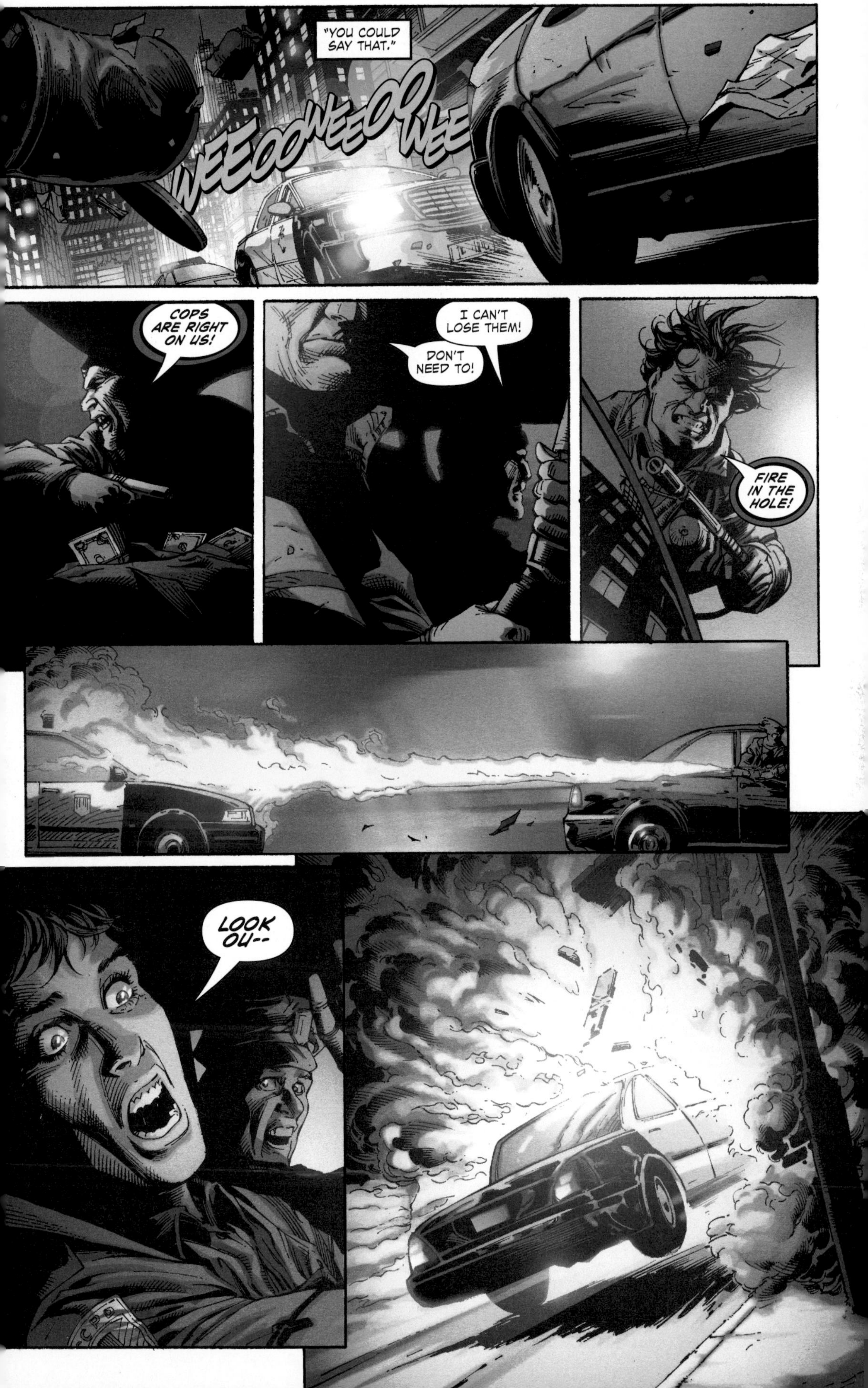
"YOU COULD SAY THAT."
WEEOOWEEOO WEE
COPS ARE RIGHT ON US!
I CAN'T LOSE THEM!
DON'T NEED TO!
FIRE IN THE HOLE!
LOOK OU--

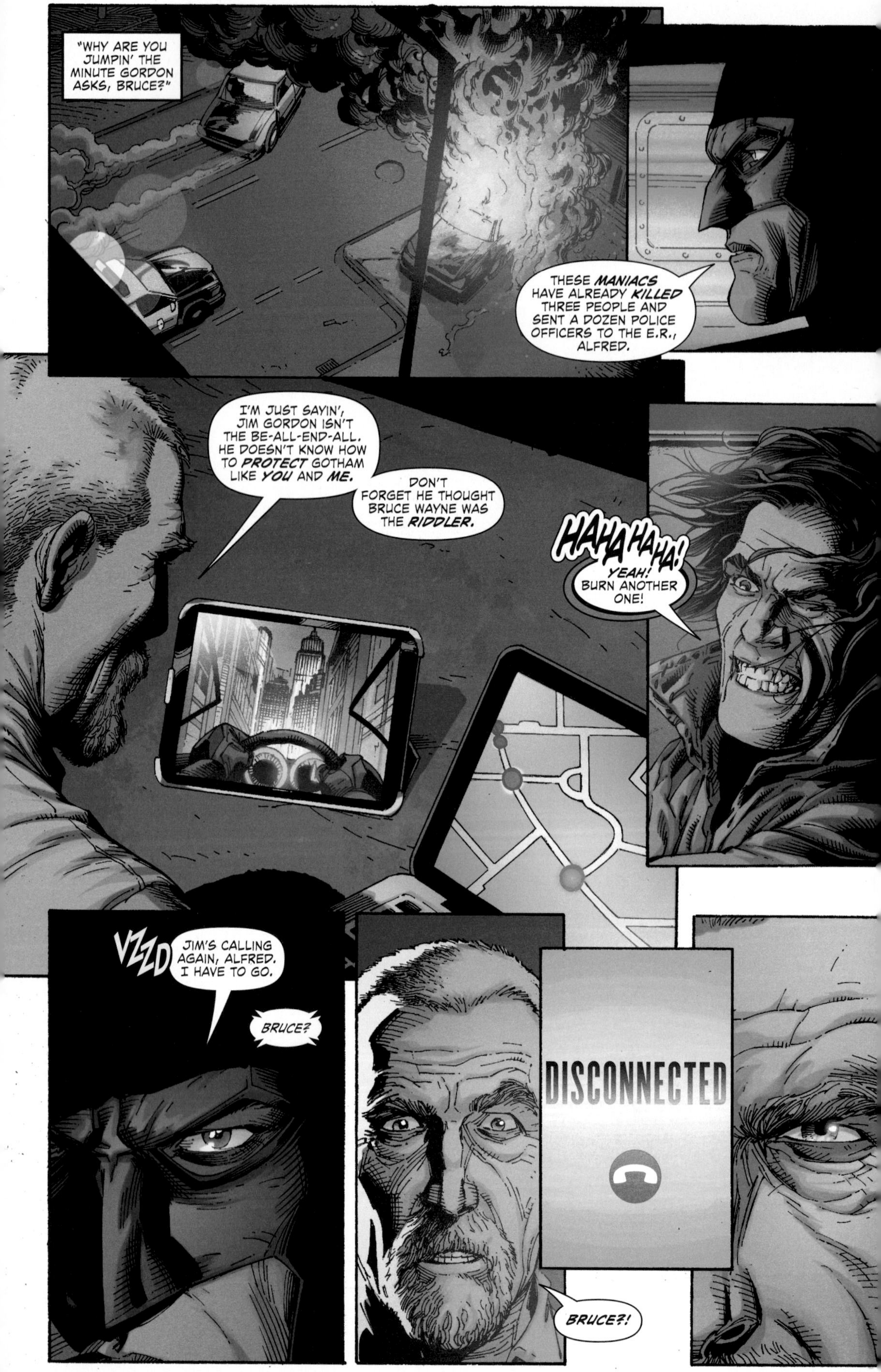
"WHY ARE YOU JUMPIN' THE MINUTE GORDON ASKS, BRUCE?"
THESE MANIACS HAVE ALREADY KILLED THREE PEOPLE AND SENT A DOZEN POLICE OFFICERS TO THE E.R., ALFRED.
I'M JUST SAYIN', JIM GORDON ISN'T THE BE-ALL-END-ALL. HE DOESN'T KNOW HOW TO PROTECT GOTHAM LIKE YOU AND ME.
DON'T FORGET HE THOUGHT BRUCE WAYNE WAS THE RIDDLER.
HAHAHAHA!
YEAH! BURN ANOTHER ONE!
VZZD
JIM'S CALLING AGAIN, ALFRED. I HAVE TO GO.
BRUCE?
DISCONNECTED
BRUCE?!

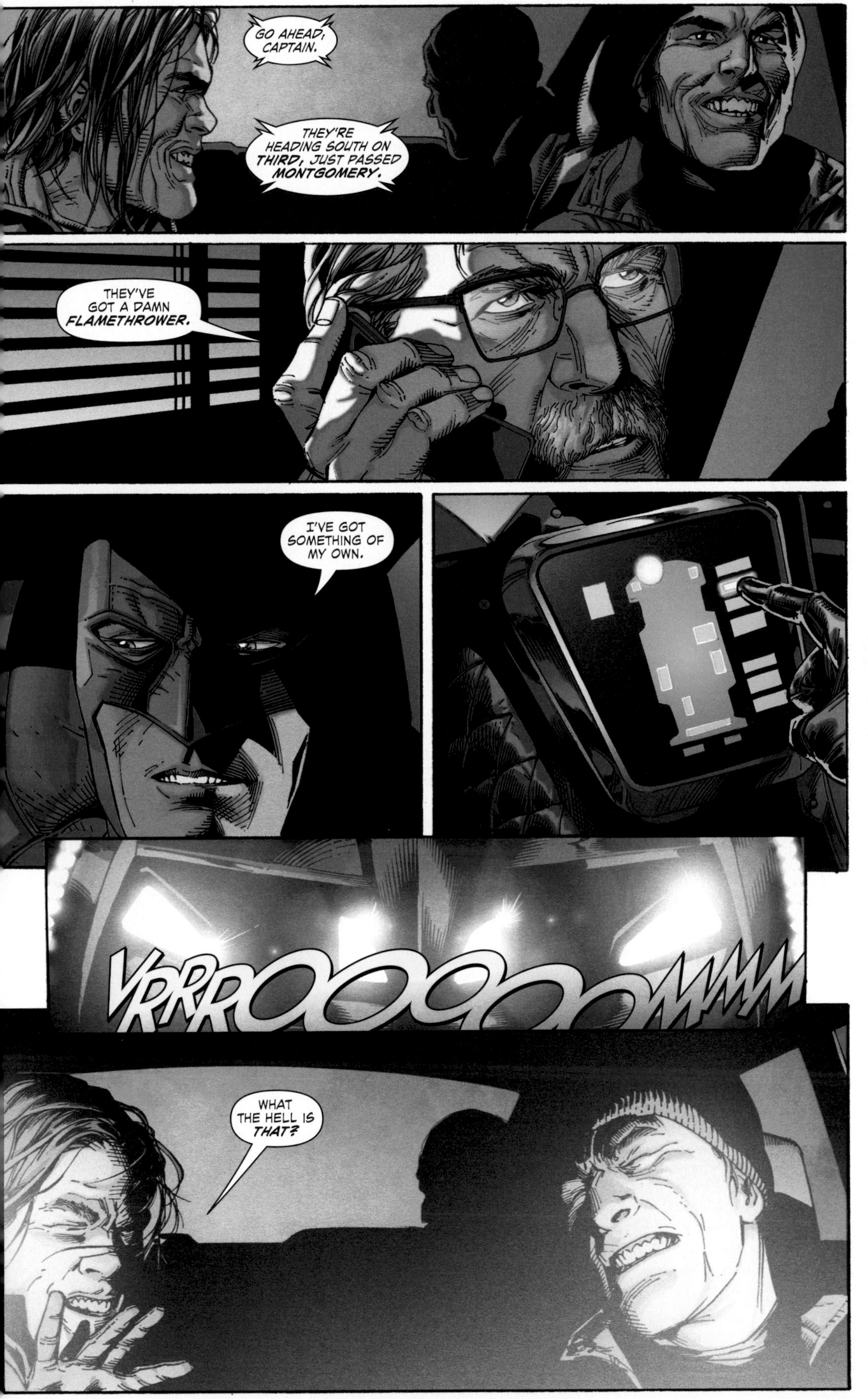
GO AHEAD, CAPTAIN.
THEY'RE HEADING SOUTH ON THIRD, JUST PASSED MONTGOMERY.
THEY'VE GOT A DAMN FLAMETHROWER.
I'VE GOT SOMETHING OF MY OWN.
VRRROOOOOMMM
WHAT THE HELL IS THAT?

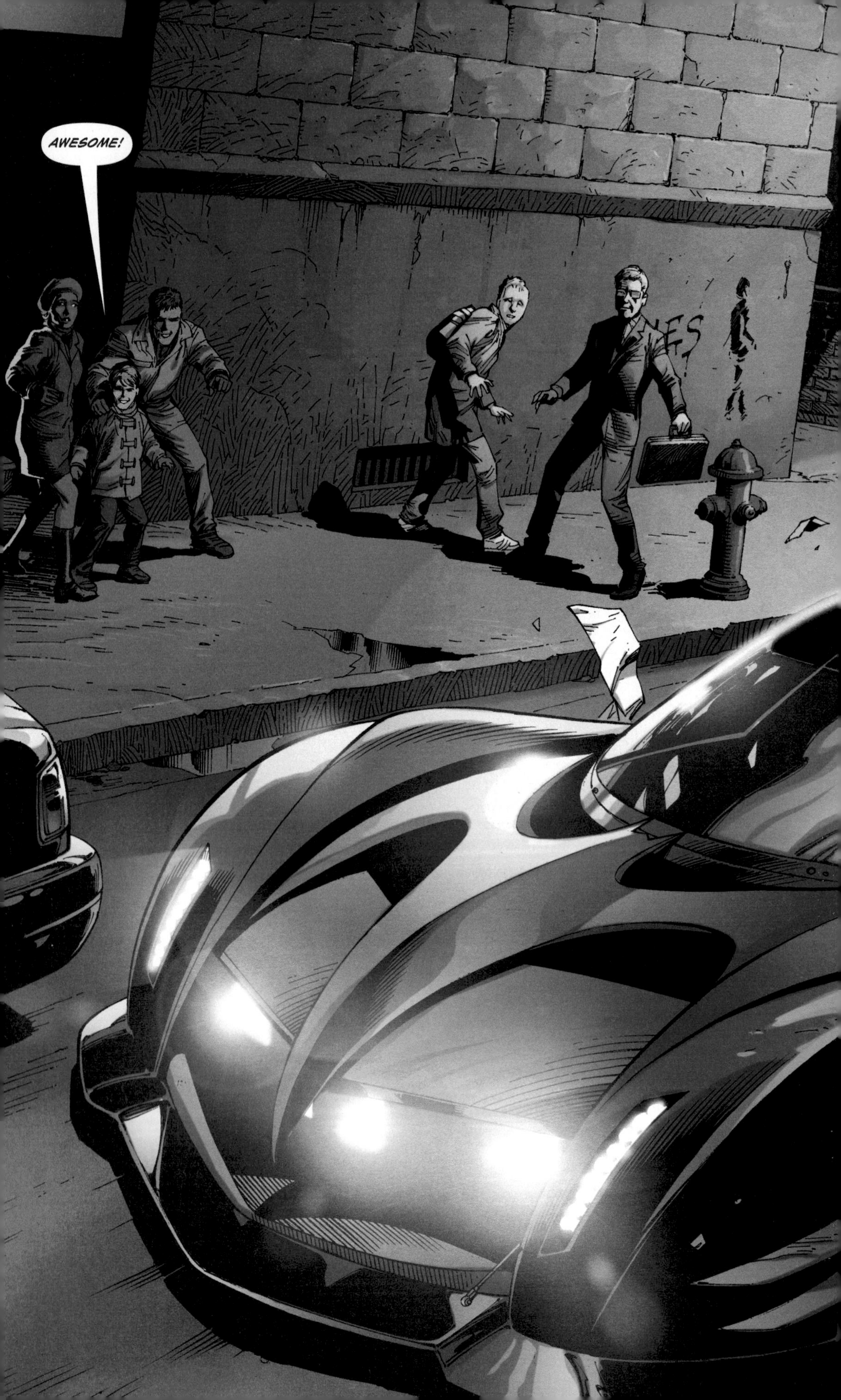
AWESOME!

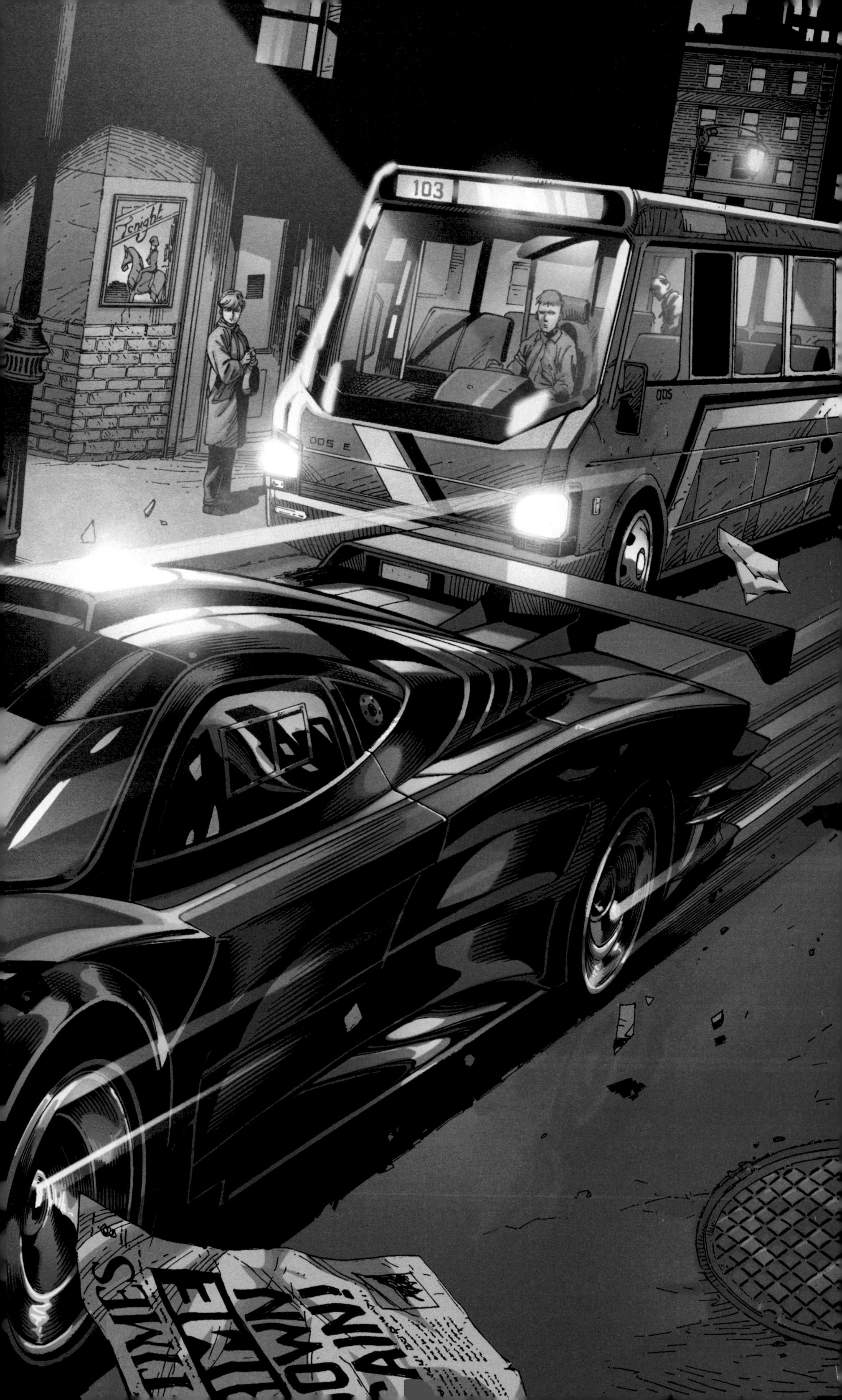
103
Tonight

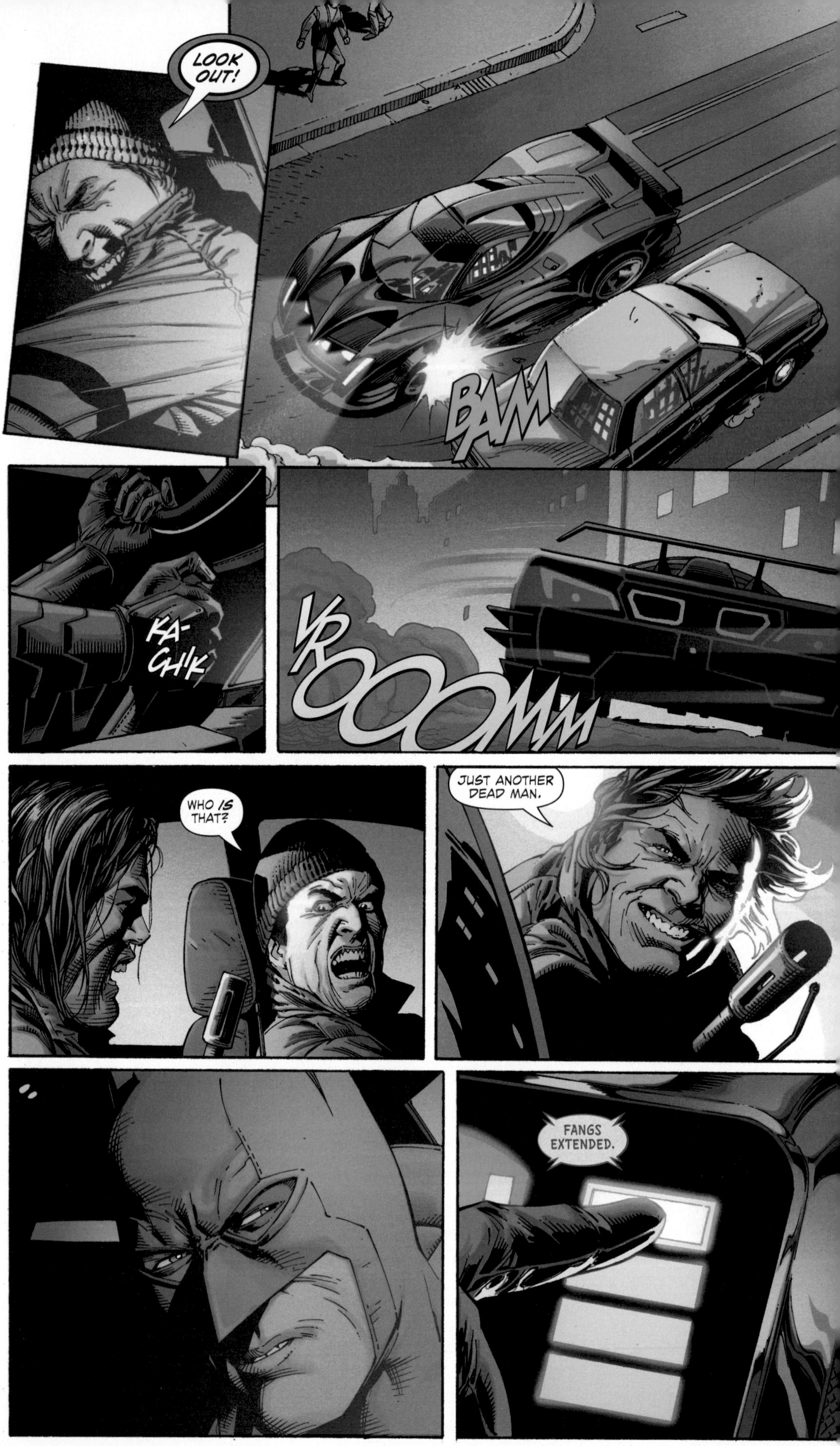
LOOK OUT!
BAM
KA-CHIK
VROOOMM
WHO IS THAT?
JUST ANOTHER DEAD MAN.
FANGS EXTENDED.

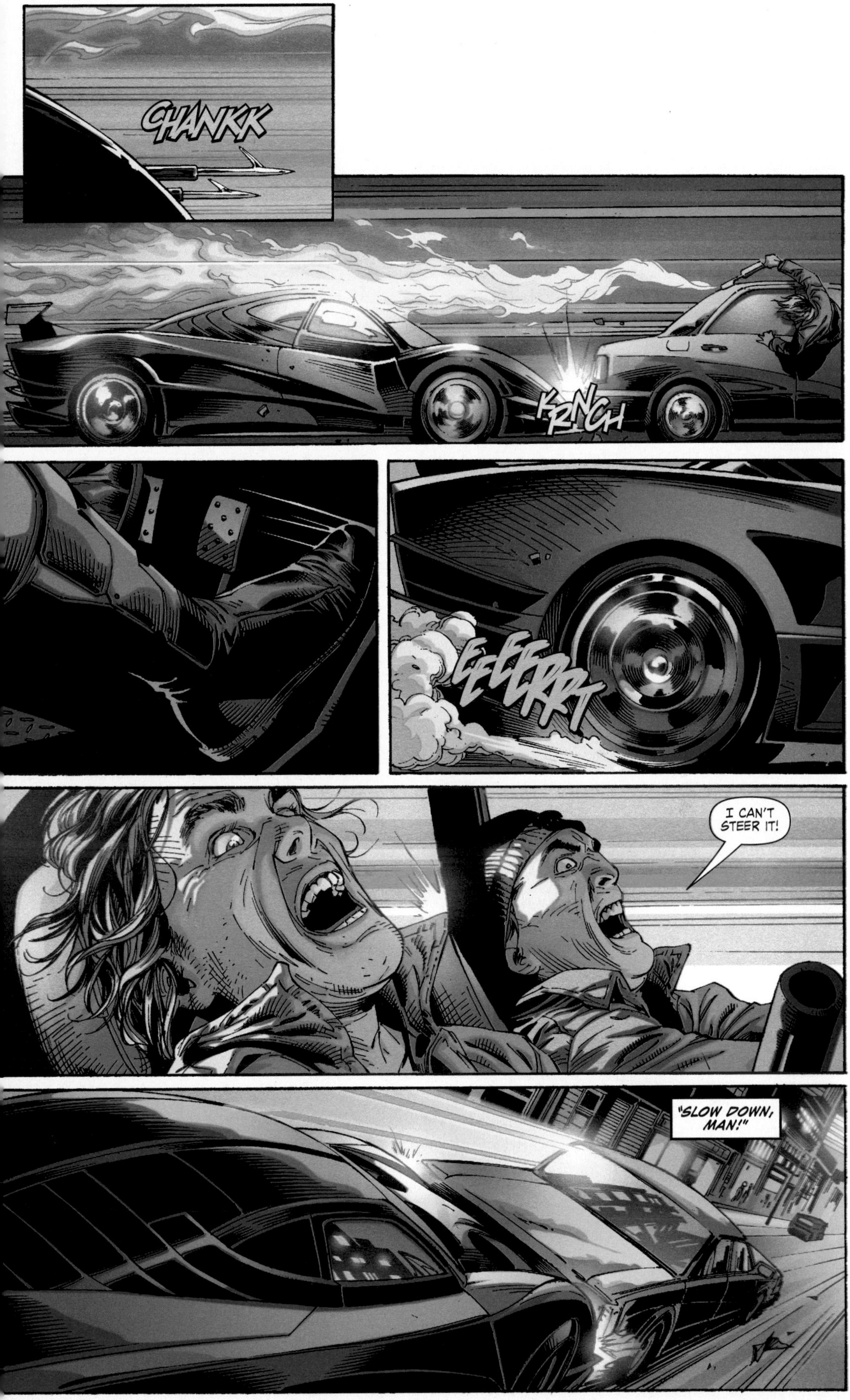
CHANKK
KRNCH
EEEERRRT
I CAN'T STEER IT!
"SLOW DOWN, MAN!"

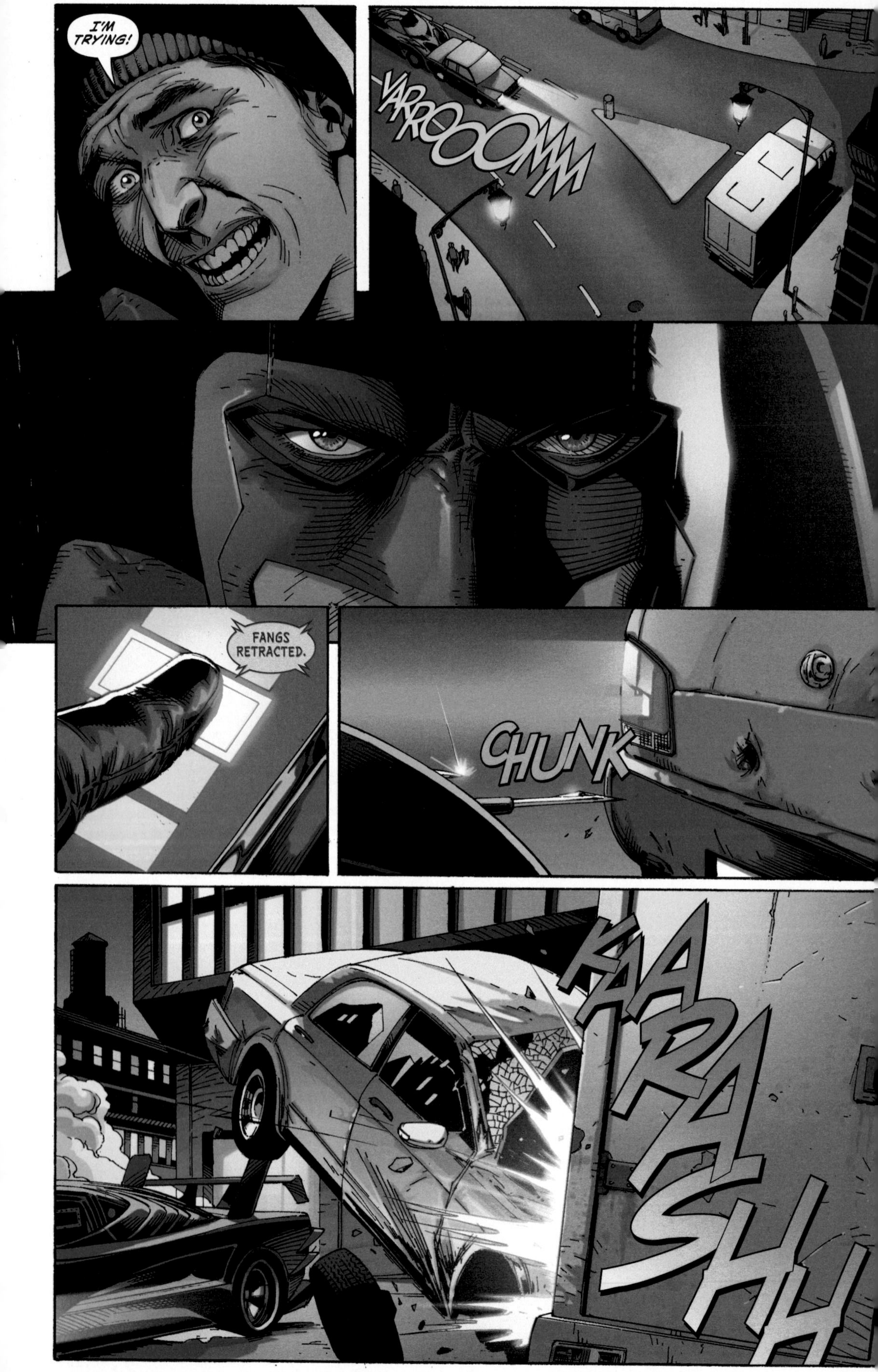

I'M TRYING!
VARROOOMM
FANGS RETRACTED.
CHUNK
KAARASHH

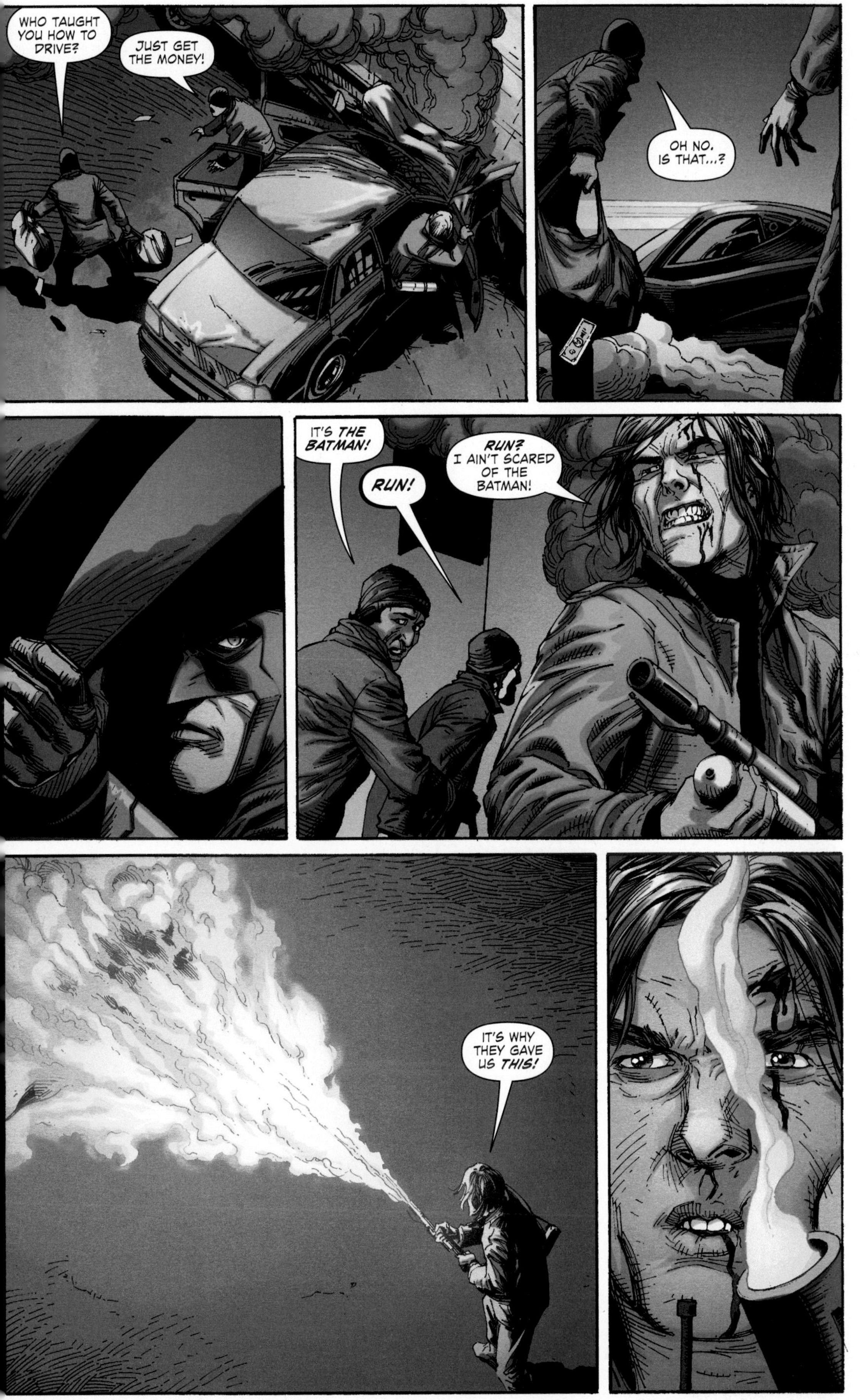
WHO TAUGHT YOU HOW TO DRIVE?
JUST GET THE MONEY!
OH NO. IS THAT...?
IT'S *THE BATMAN!*
RUN!
RUN? I AIN'T SCARED OF THE BATMAN!
IT'S WHY THEY GAVE US *THIS!*

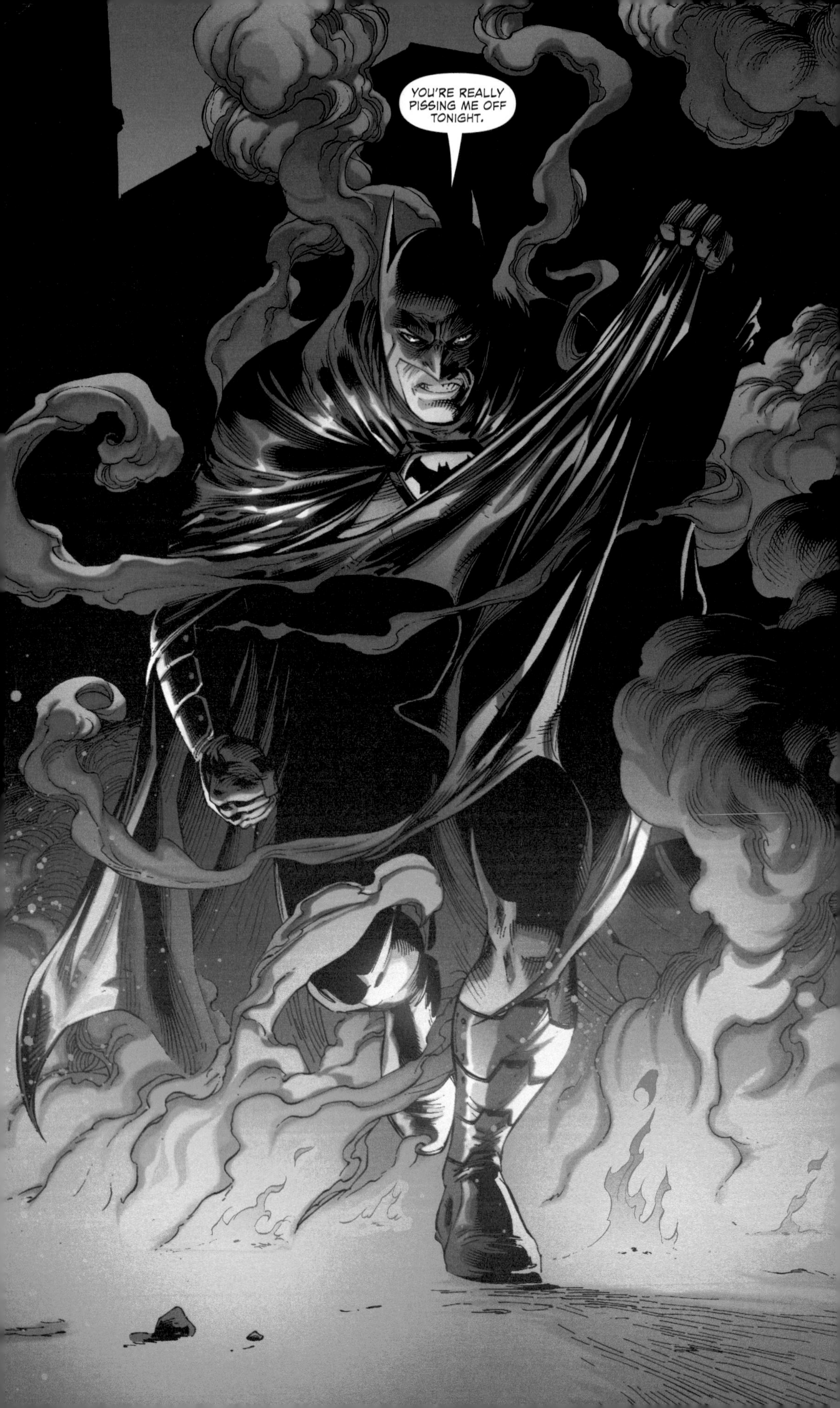
YOU'RE REALLY PISSING ME OFF TONIGHT.

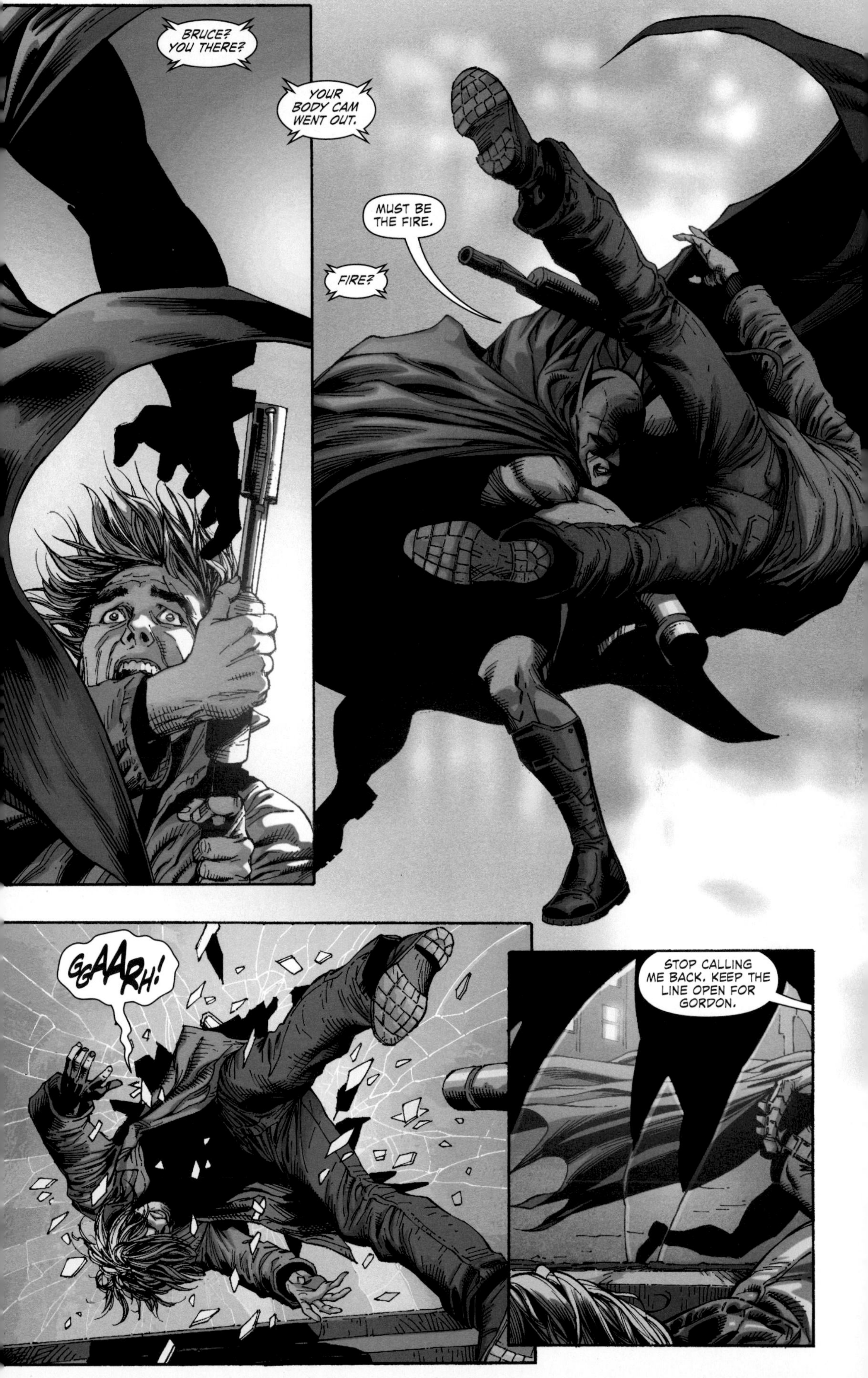

BRUCE? YOU THERE?
YOUR BODY CAM WENT OUT.
MUST BE THE FIRE.
FIRE?
GGAARH!
STOP CALLING ME BACK. KEEP THE LINE OPEN FOR GORDON.

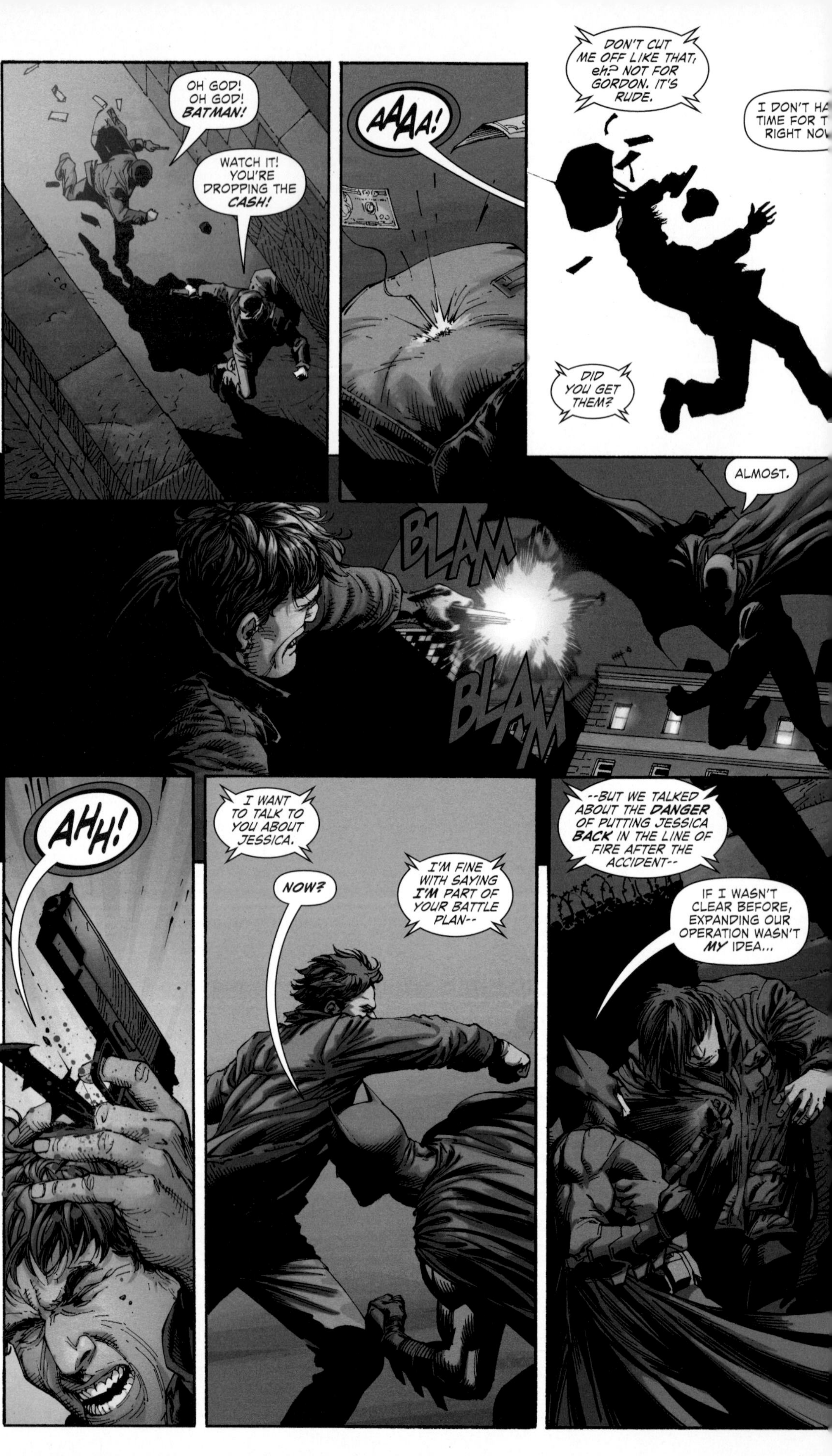
OH GOD! OH GOD! BATMAN!
WATCH IT! YOU'RE DROPPING THE CASH!
AAAA!
DON'T CUT ME OFF LIKE THAT, eh? NOT FOR GORDON. IT'S RUDE.
I DON'T HA TIME FOR T RIGHT NOW
DID YOU GET THEM?
ALMOST.
BLAM
BLAM
AHH!
I WANT TO TALK TO YOU ABOUT JESSICA.
NOW?
I'M FINE WITH SAYING I'M PART OF YOUR BATTLE PLAN--
--BUT WE TALKED ABOUT THE DANGER OF PUTTING JESSICA BACK IN THE LINE OF FIRE AFTER THE ACCIDENT--
IF I WASN'T CLEAR BEFORE, EXPANDING OUR OPERATION WASN'T MY IDEA...

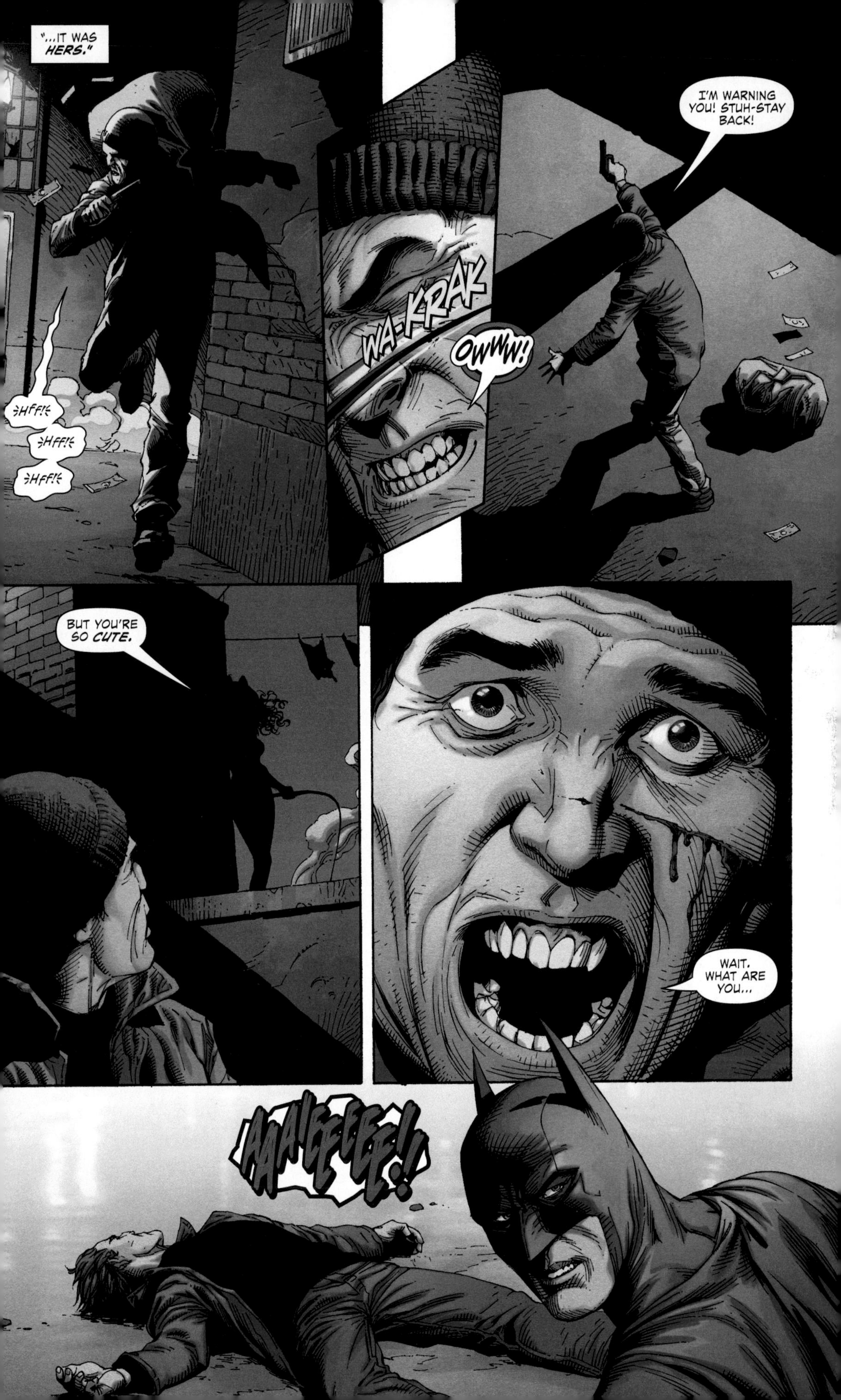
"...IT WAS HERS."
HFF!
HFF!
HFF!
WA-KRAK
OWWW!
I'M WARNING YOU! STUH-STAY BACK!
BUT YOU'RE SO CUTE.
WAIT. WHAT ARE YOU...
AAAIEEEEE!!

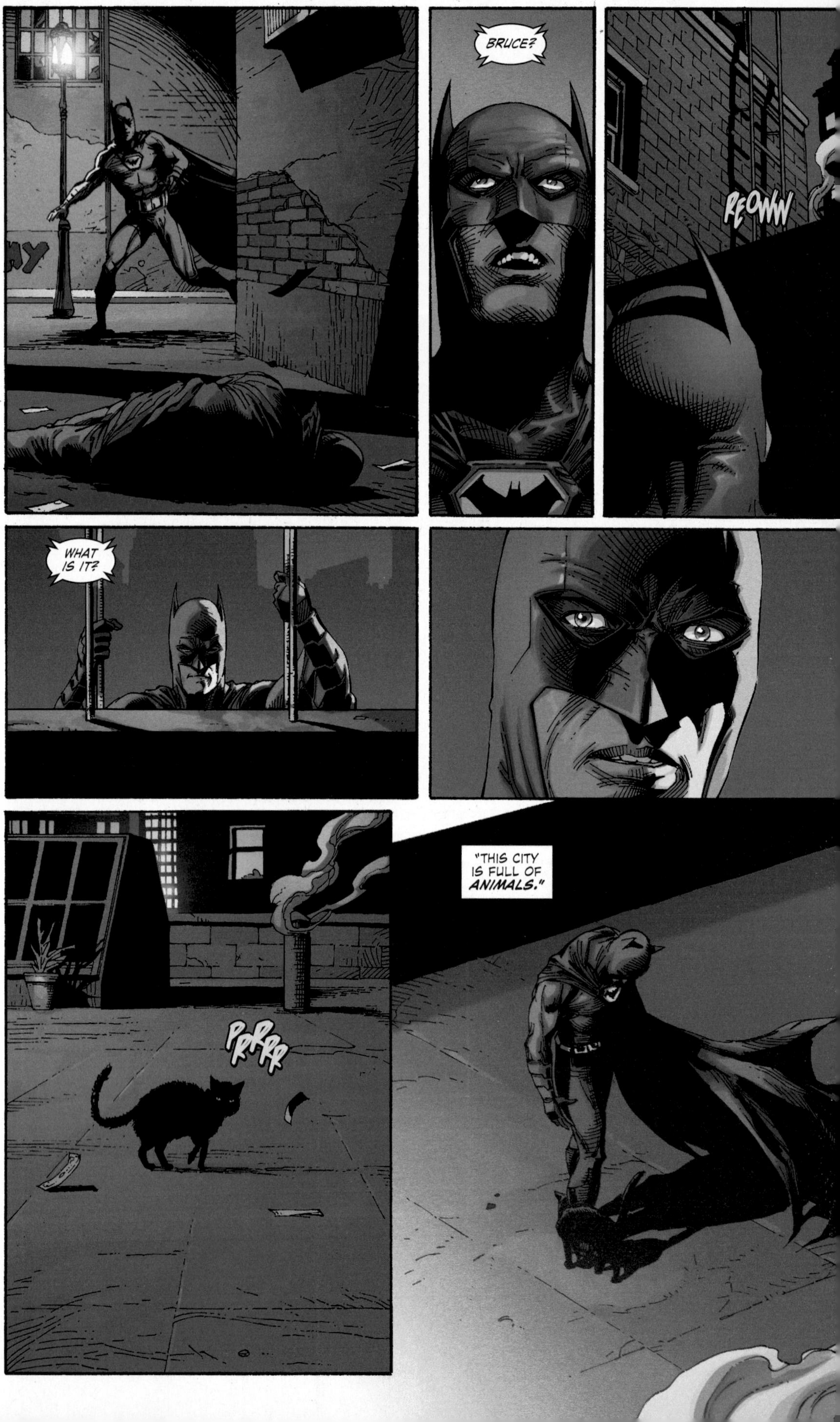
BRUCE?
PEOWW
WHAT IS IT?
"THIS CITY IS FULL OF ANIMALS."
PRRRR

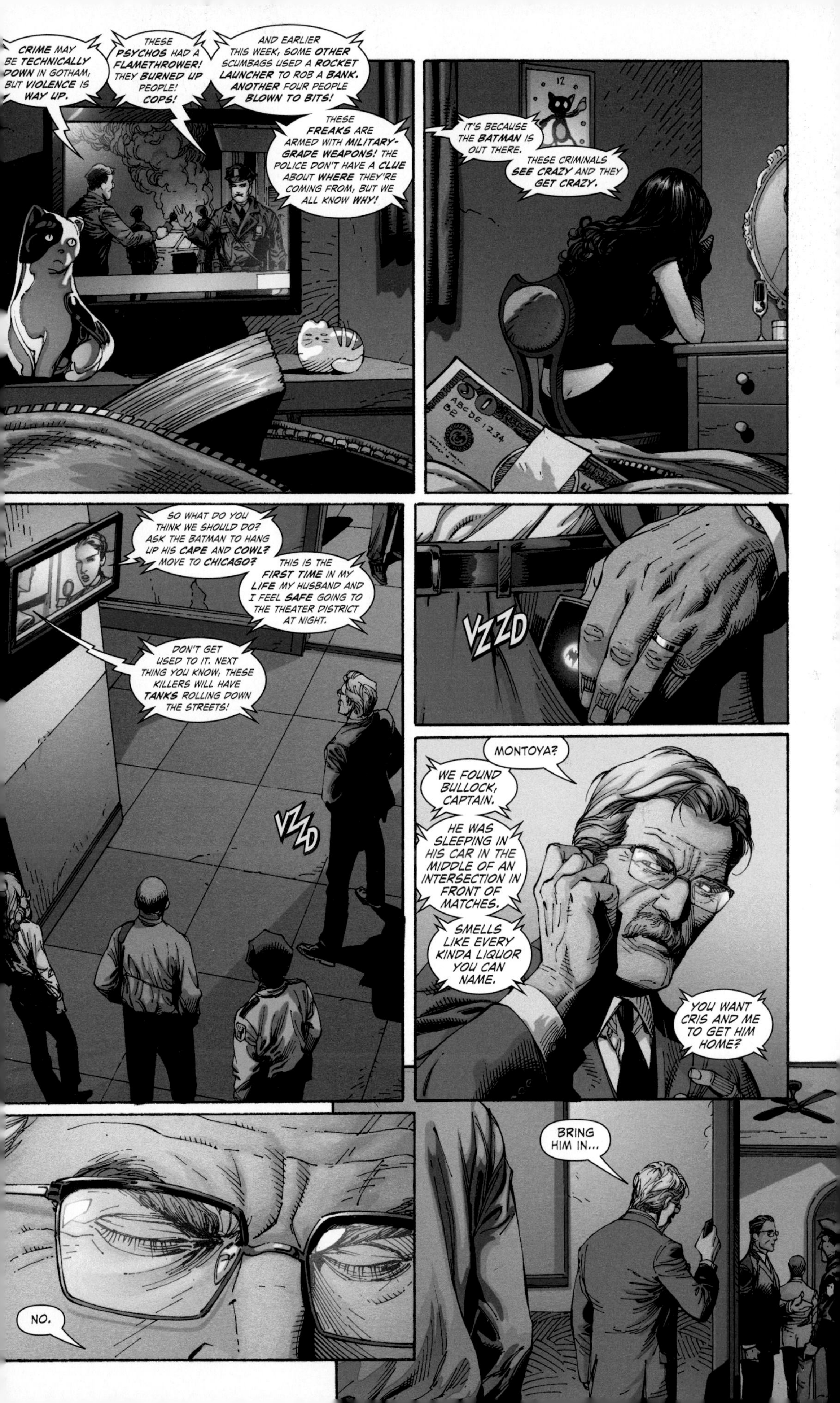
CRIME MAY BE TECHNICALLY DOWN IN GOTHAM, BUT VIOLENCE IS WAY UP.
THESE PSYCHOS HAD A FLAMETHROWER! THEY BURNED UP PEOPLE! COPS!
AND EARLIER THIS WEEK, SOME OTHER SCUMBAGS USED A ROCKET LAUNCHER TO ROB A BANK. ANOTHER FOUR PEOPLE BLOWN TO BITS!
THESE FREAKS ARE ARMED WITH MILITARY-GRADE WEAPONS! THE POLICE DON'T HAVE A CLUE ABOUT WHERE THEY'RE COMING FROM, BUT WE ALL KNOW WHY!
IT'S BECAUSE THE BATMAN IS OUT THERE.
THESE CRIMINALS SEE CRAZY AND THEY GET CRAZY.
SO WHAT DO YOU THINK WE SHOULD DO? ASK THE BATMAN TO HANG UP HIS CAPE AND COWL? MOVE TO CHICAGO?
THIS IS THE FIRST TIME IN MY LIFE MY HUSBAND AND I FEEL SAFE GOING TO THE THEATER DISTRICT AT NIGHT.
DON'T GET USED TO IT. NEXT THING YOU KNOW, THESE KILLERS WILL HAVE TANKS ROLLING DOWN THE STREETS!
VZZD
VZZD
MONTOYA?
WE FOUND BULLOCK, CAPTAIN.
HE WAS SLEEPING IN HIS CAR IN THE MIDDLE OF AN INTERSECTION IN FRONT OF MATCHES.
SMELLS LIKE EVERY KINDA LIQUOR YOU CAN NAME.
YOU WANT CRIS AND ME TO GET HIM HOME?
NO.
BRING HIM IN...

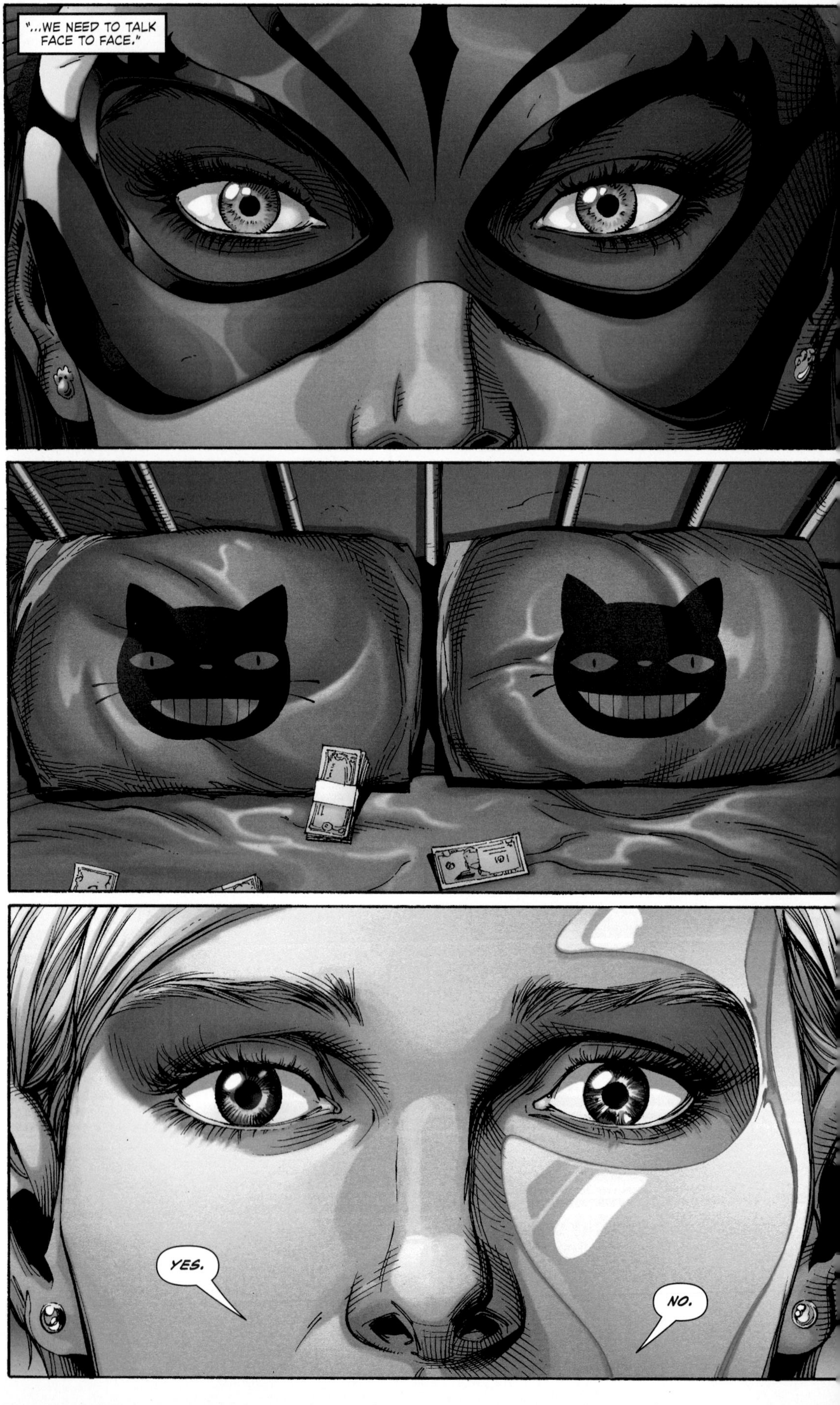
"...WE NEED TO TALK FACE TO FACE."
YES.
NO.

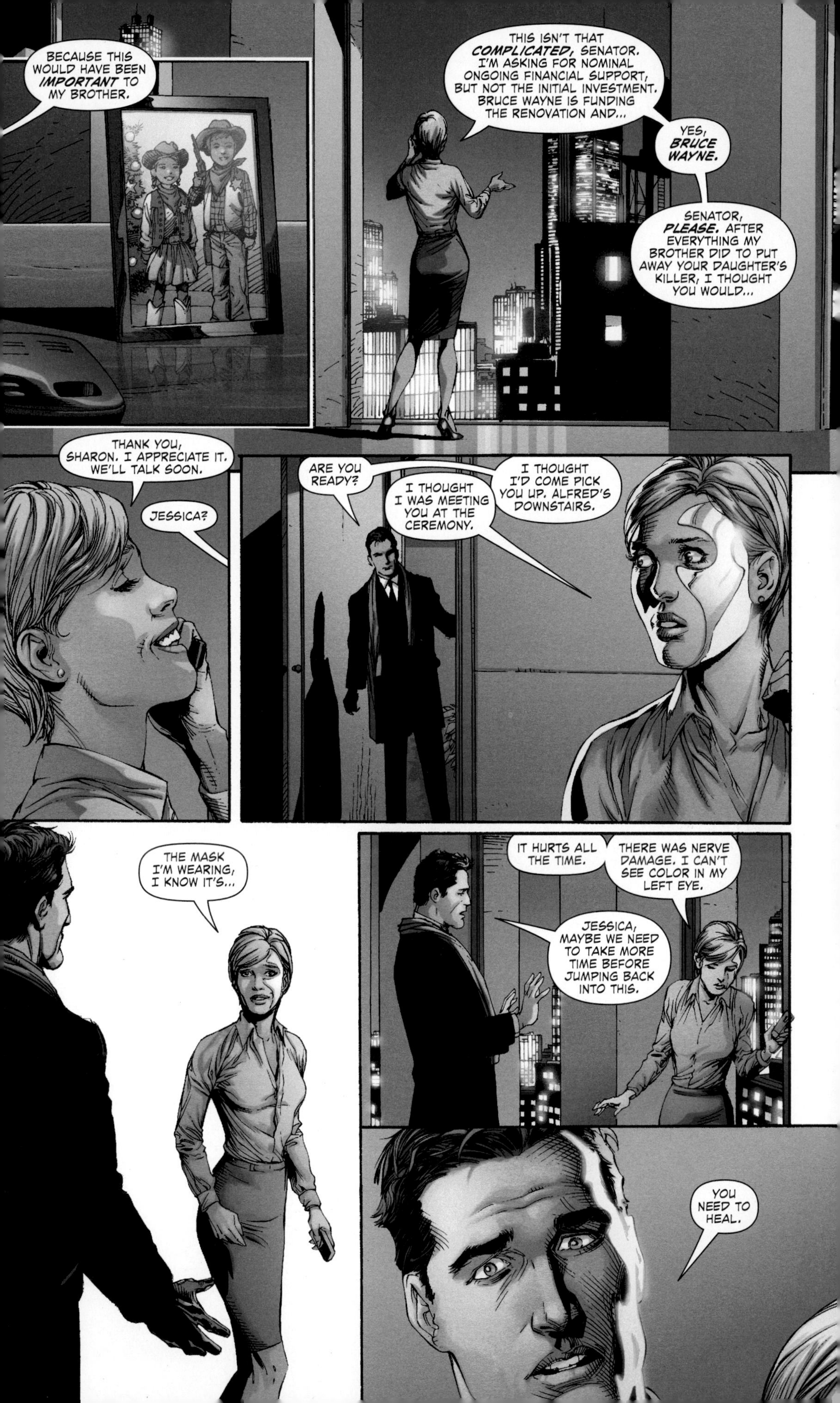
BECAUSE THIS WOULD HAVE BEEN IMPORTANT TO MY BROTHER.
THIS ISN'T THAT COMPLICATED, SENATOR. I'M ASKING FOR NOMINAL ONGOING FINANCIAL SUPPORT, BUT NOT THE INITIAL INVESTMENT. BRUCE WAYNE IS FUNDING THE RENOVATION AND...
YES, BRUCE WAYNE.
SENATOR, PLEASE. AFTER EVERYTHING MY BROTHER DID TO PUT AWAY YOUR DAUGHTER'S KILLER, I THOUGHT YOU WOULD...
THANK YOU, SHARON. I APPRECIATE IT. WE'LL TALK SOON.
JESSICA?
ARE YOU READY?
I THOUGHT I WAS MEETING YOU AT THE CEREMONY.
I THOUGHT I'D COME PICK YOU UP. ALFRED'S DOWNSTAIRS.
THE MASK I'M WEARING, I KNOW IT'S...
IT HURTS ALL THE TIME.
THERE WAS NERVE DAMAGE. I CAN'T SEE COLOR IN MY LEFT EYE.
JESSICA, MAYBE WE NEED TO TAKE MORE TIME BEFORE JUMPING BACK INTO THIS.
YOU NEED TO HEAL.

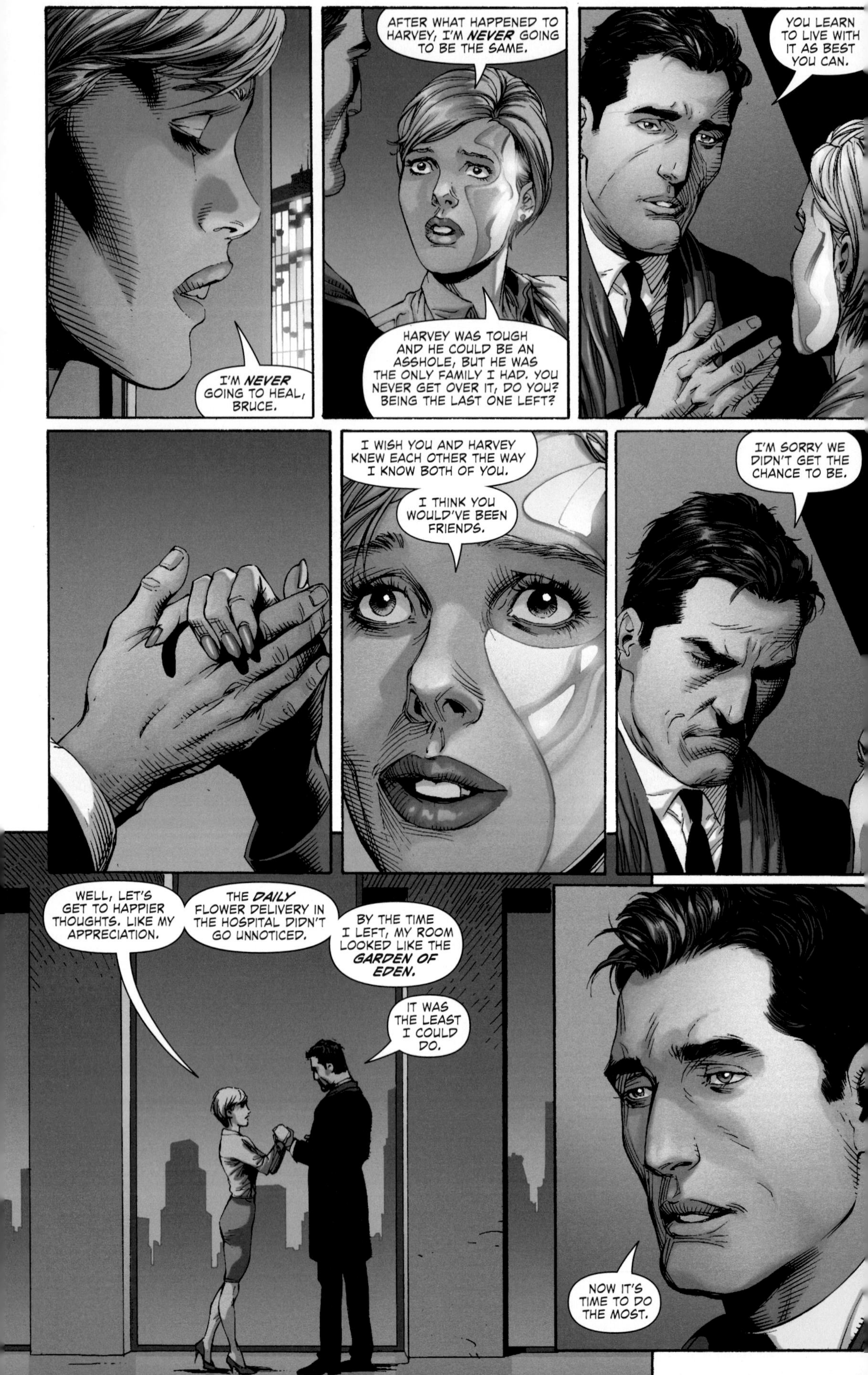

AFTER WHAT HAPPENED TO HARVEY, I'M *NEVER* GOING TO BE THE SAME.
I'M *NEVER* GOING TO HEAL, BRUCE.
HARVEY WAS TOUGH AND HE COULD BE AN ASSHOLE, BUT HE WAS THE ONLY FAMILY I HAD. YOU NEVER GET OVER IT, DO YOU? BEING THE LAST ONE LEFT?
YOU LEARN TO LIVE WITH IT AS BEST YOU CAN.
I WISH YOU AND HARVEY KNEW EACH OTHER THE WAY I KNOW BOTH OF YOU.
I THINK YOU WOULD'VE BEEN FRIENDS.
I'M SORRY WE DIDN'T GET THE CHANCE TO BE.
WELL, LET'S GET TO HAPPIER THOUGHTS. LIKE MY APPRECIATION.
THE *DAILY* FLOWER DELIVERY IN THE HOSPITAL DIDN'T GO UNNOTICED.
BY THE TIME I LEFT, MY ROOM LOOKED LIKE THE *GARDEN OF EDEN.*
IT WAS THE LEAST I COULD DO.
NOW IT'S TIME TO DO THE MOST.

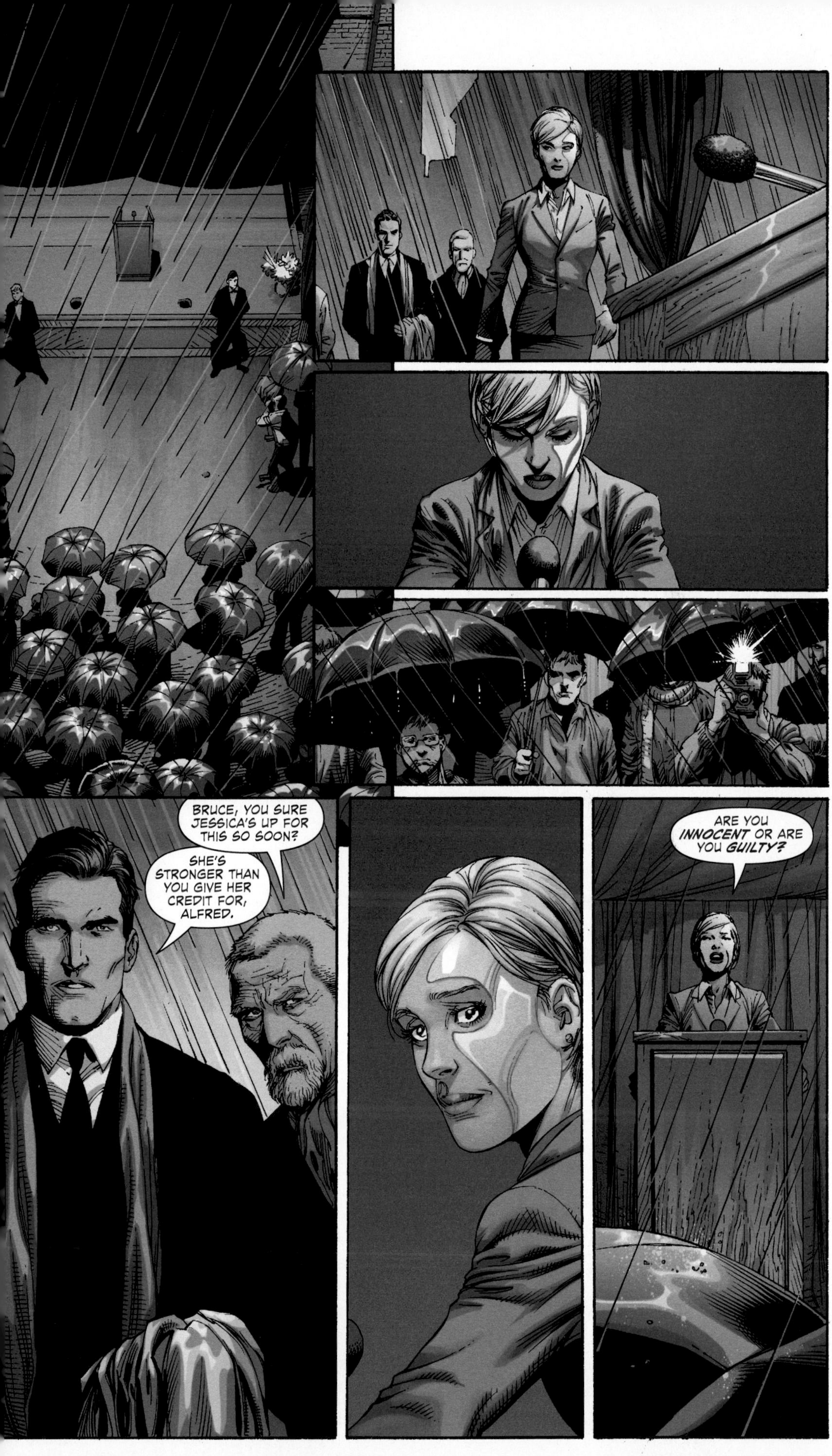
BRUCE, YOU SURE JESSICA'S UP FOR THIS SO SOON?
SHE'S STRONGER THAN YOU GIVE HER CREDIT FOR, ALFRED.
ARE YOU *INNOCENT* OR ARE YOU *GUILTY?*

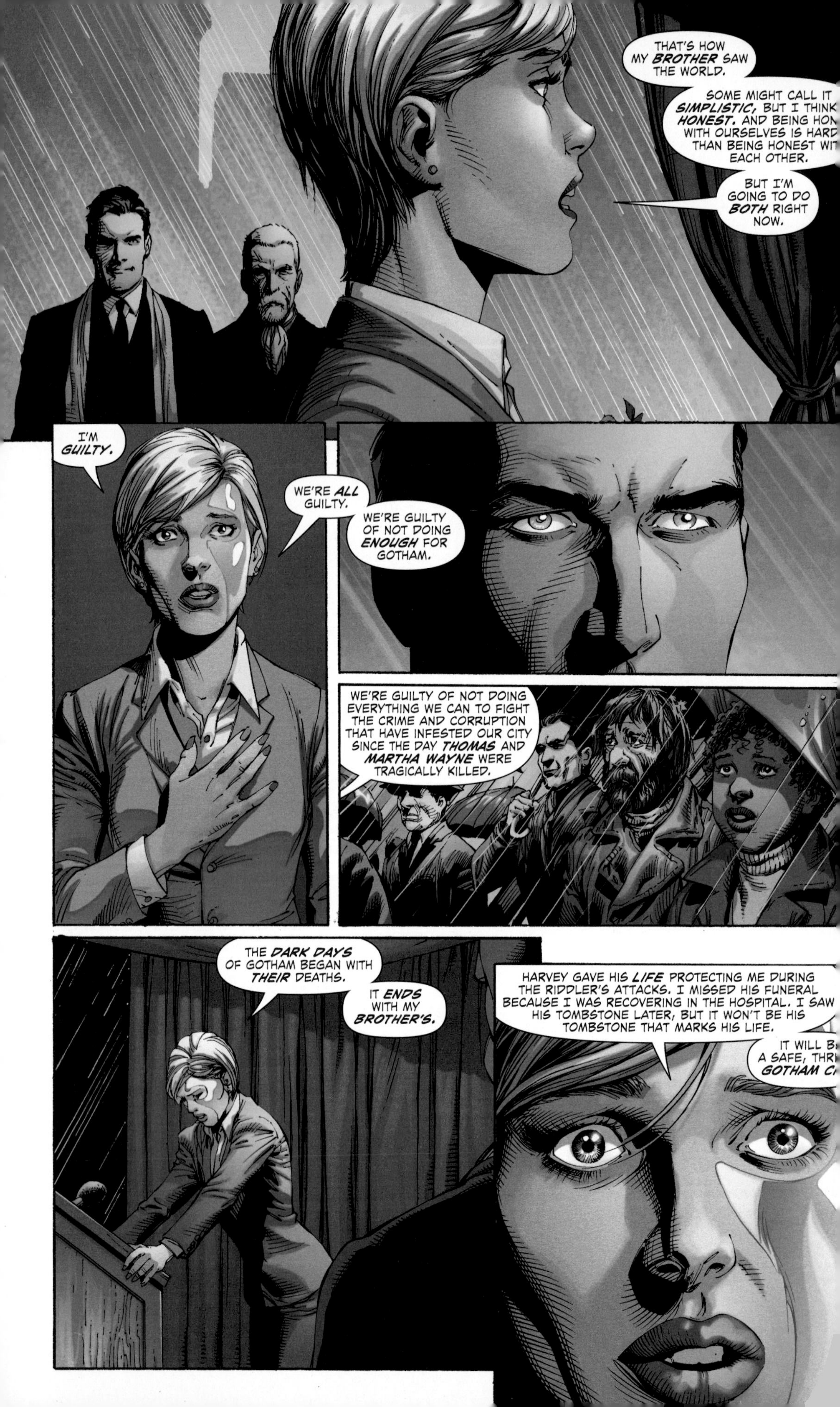
THAT'S HOW MY BROTHER SAW THE WORLD.
SOME MIGHT CALL IT SIMPLISTIC, BUT I THINK HONEST. AND BEING HON WITH OURSELVES IS HARD THAN BEING HONEST WIT EACH OTHER.
BUT I'M GOING TO DO BOTH RIGHT NOW.
I'M GUILTY.
WE'RE ALL GUILTY.
WE'RE GUILTY OF NOT DOING ENOUGH FOR GOTHAM.
WE'RE GUILTY OF NOT DOING EVERYTHING WE CAN TO FIGHT THE CRIME AND CORRUPTION THAT HAVE INFESTED OUR CITY SINCE THE DAY THOMAS AND MARTHA WAYNE WERE TRAGICALLY KILLED.
THE DARK DAYS OF GOTHAM BEGAN WITH THEIR DEATHS.
IT ENDS WITH MY BROTHER'S.
HARVEY GAVE HIS LIFE PROTECTING ME DURING THE RIDDLER'S ATTACKS. I MISSED HIS FUNERAL BECAUSE I WAS RECOVERING IN THE HOSPITAL. I SAW HIS TOMBSTONE LATER, BUT IT WON'T BE HIS TOMBSTONE THAT MARKS HIS LIFE.

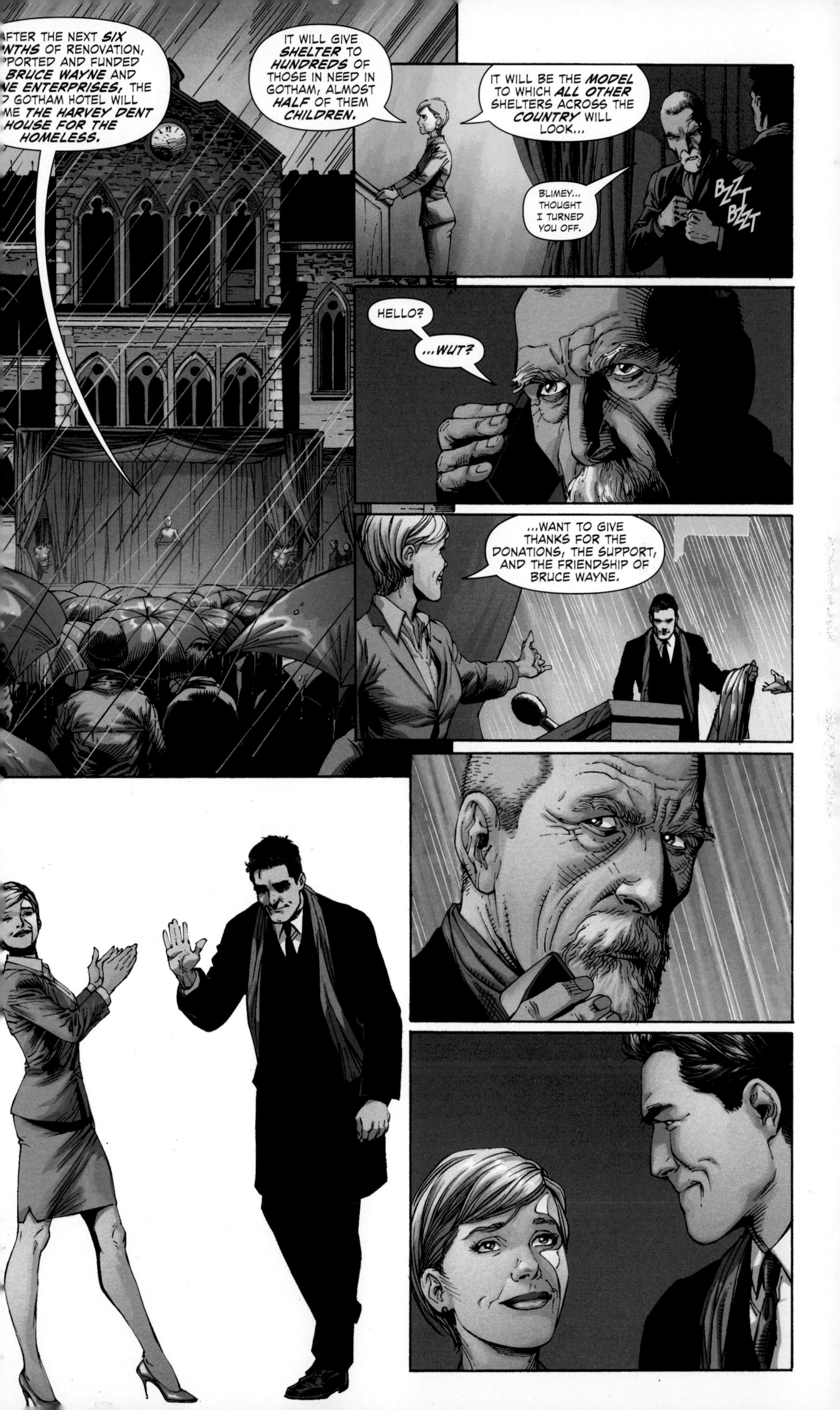

AFTER THE NEXT SIX
NTHS OF RENOVATION,
PORTED AND FUNDED
BRUCE WAYNE AND
NE ENTERPRISES, THE
D GOTHAM HOTEL WILL
ME THE HARVEY DENT
HOUSE FOR THE
HOMELESS.
IT WILL GIVE SHELTER TO HUNDREDS OF THOSE IN NEED IN GOTHAM, ALMOST HALF OF THEM CHILDREN.
IT WILL BE THE MODEL TO WHICH ALL OTHER SHELTERS ACROSS THE COUNTRY WILL LOOK...
BLIMEY... THOUGHT I TURNED YOU OFF.
BZZT BZZT
HELLO?
...WUT?
...WANT TO GIVE THANKS FOR THE DONATIONS, THE SUPPORT, AND THE FRIENDSHIP OF BRUCE WAYNE.

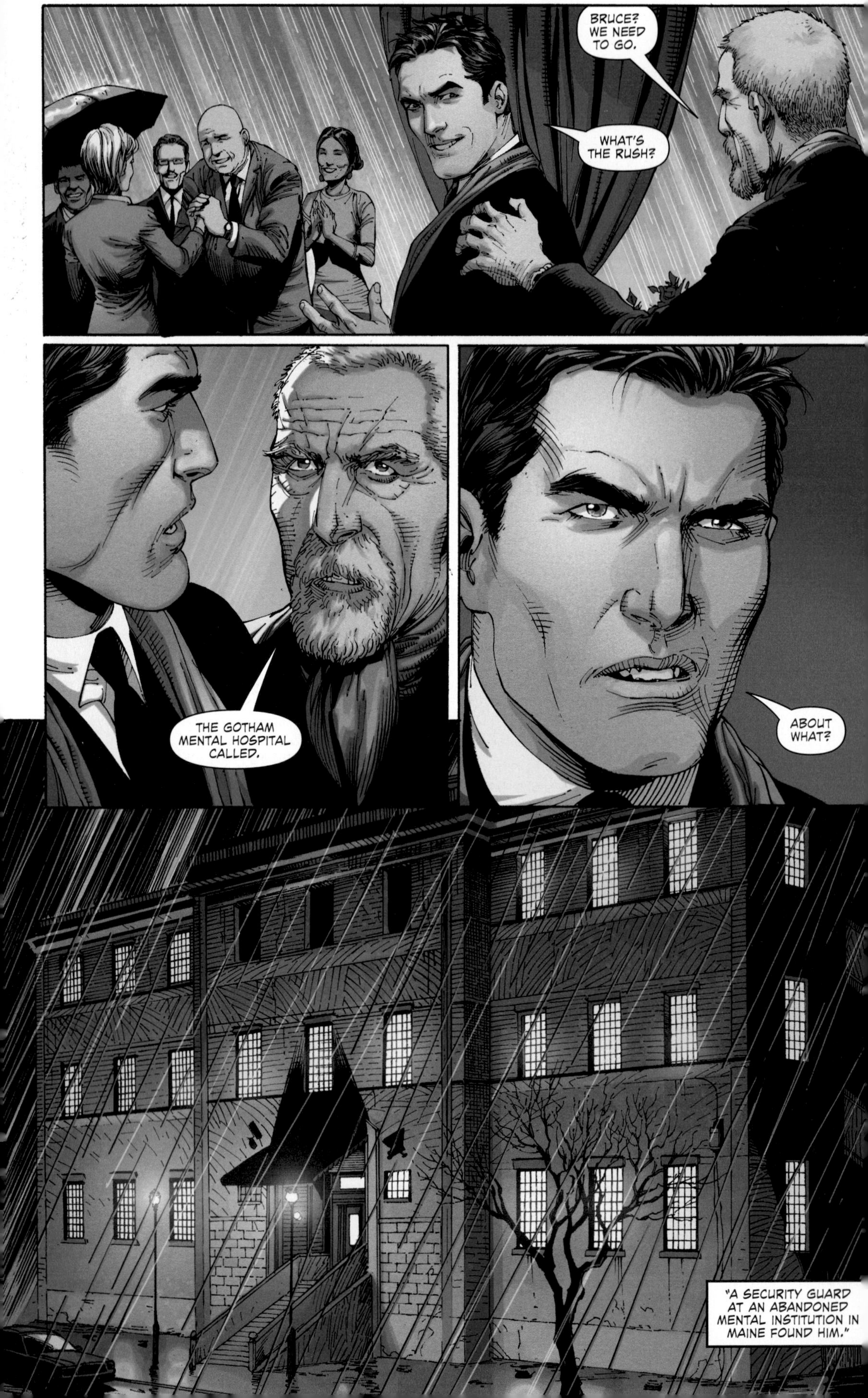
BRUCE? WE NEED TO GO.
WHAT'S THE RUSH?
THE GOTHAM MENTAL HOSPITAL CALLED.
ABOUT WHAT?
"A SECURITY GUARD AT AN ABANDONED MENTAL INSTITUTION IN MAINE FOUND HIM."

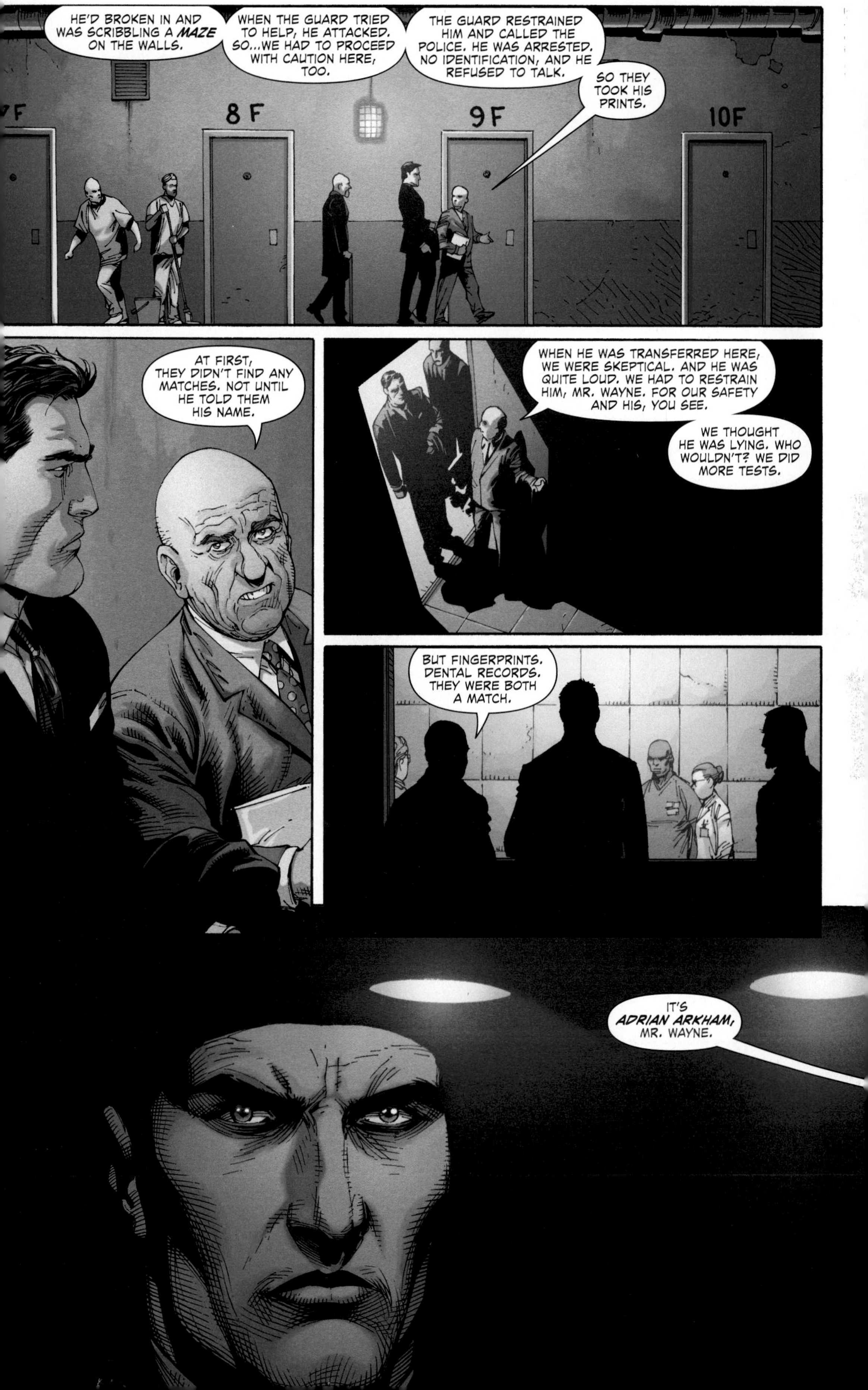
HE'D BROKEN IN AND WAS SCRIBBLING A *MAZE* ON THE WALLS.
WHEN THE GUARD TRIED TO HELP, HE ATTACKED. SO...WE HAD TO PROCEED WITH CAUTION HERE, TOO.
THE GUARD RESTRAINED HIM AND CALLED THE POLICE. HE WAS ARRESTED. NO IDENTIFICATION, AND HE REFUSED TO TALK.
SO THEY TOOK HIS PRINTS.
8 F
9F
10F
AT FIRST, THEY DIDN'T FIND ANY MATCHES. NOT UNTIL HE TOLD THEM HIS NAME.
WHEN HE WAS TRANSFERRED HERE, WE WERE SKEPTICAL. AND HE WAS QUITE LOUD. WE HAD TO RESTRAIN HIM, MR. WAYNE. FOR OUR SAFETY AND HIS, YOU SEE.
WE THOUGHT HE WAS LYING. WHO WOULDN'T? WE DID MORE TESTS.
BUT FINGERPRINTS. DENTAL RECORDS. THEY WERE BOTH A MATCH.
IT'S *ADRIAN ARKHAM,* MR. WAYNE.

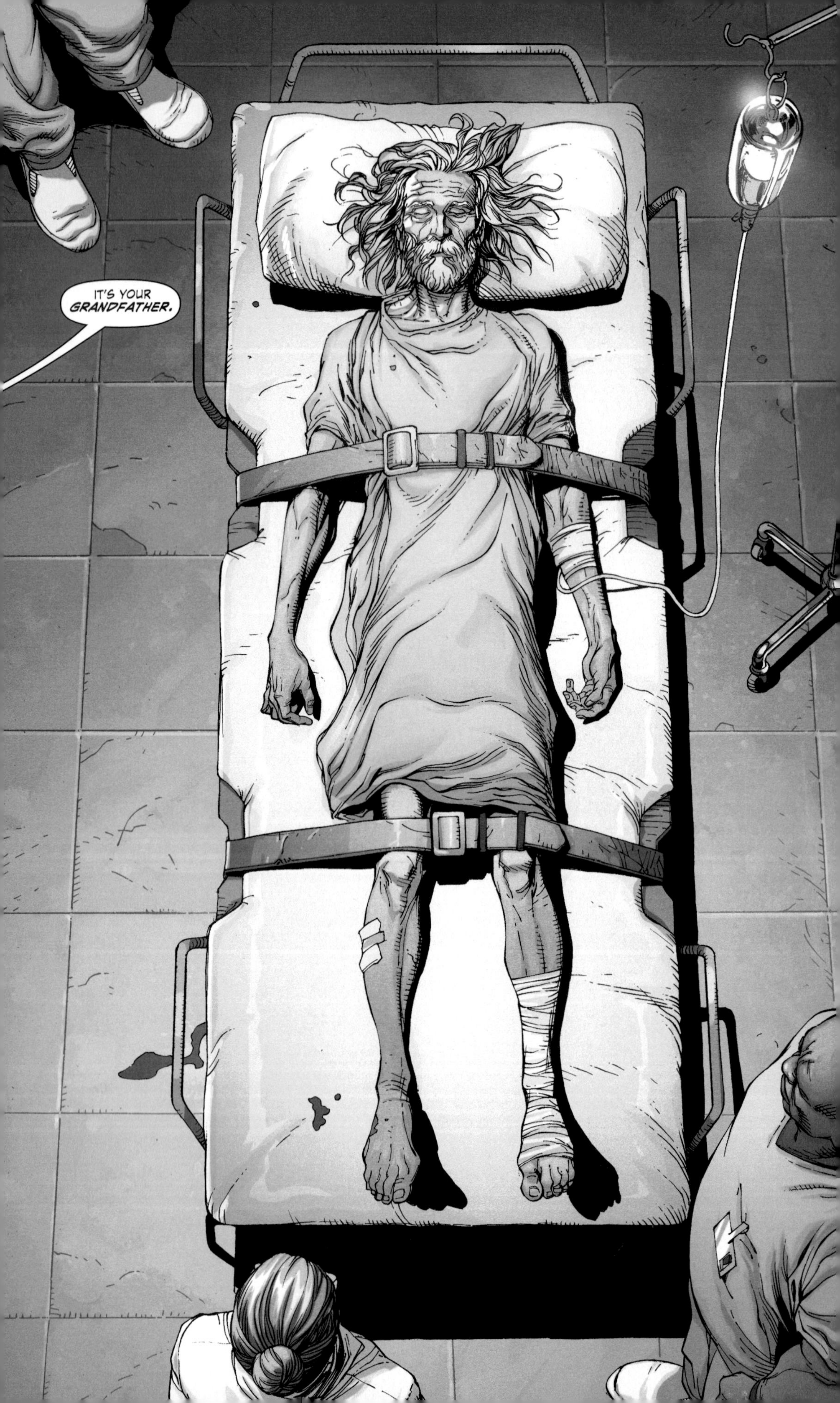
IT'S YOUR GRANDFATHER.

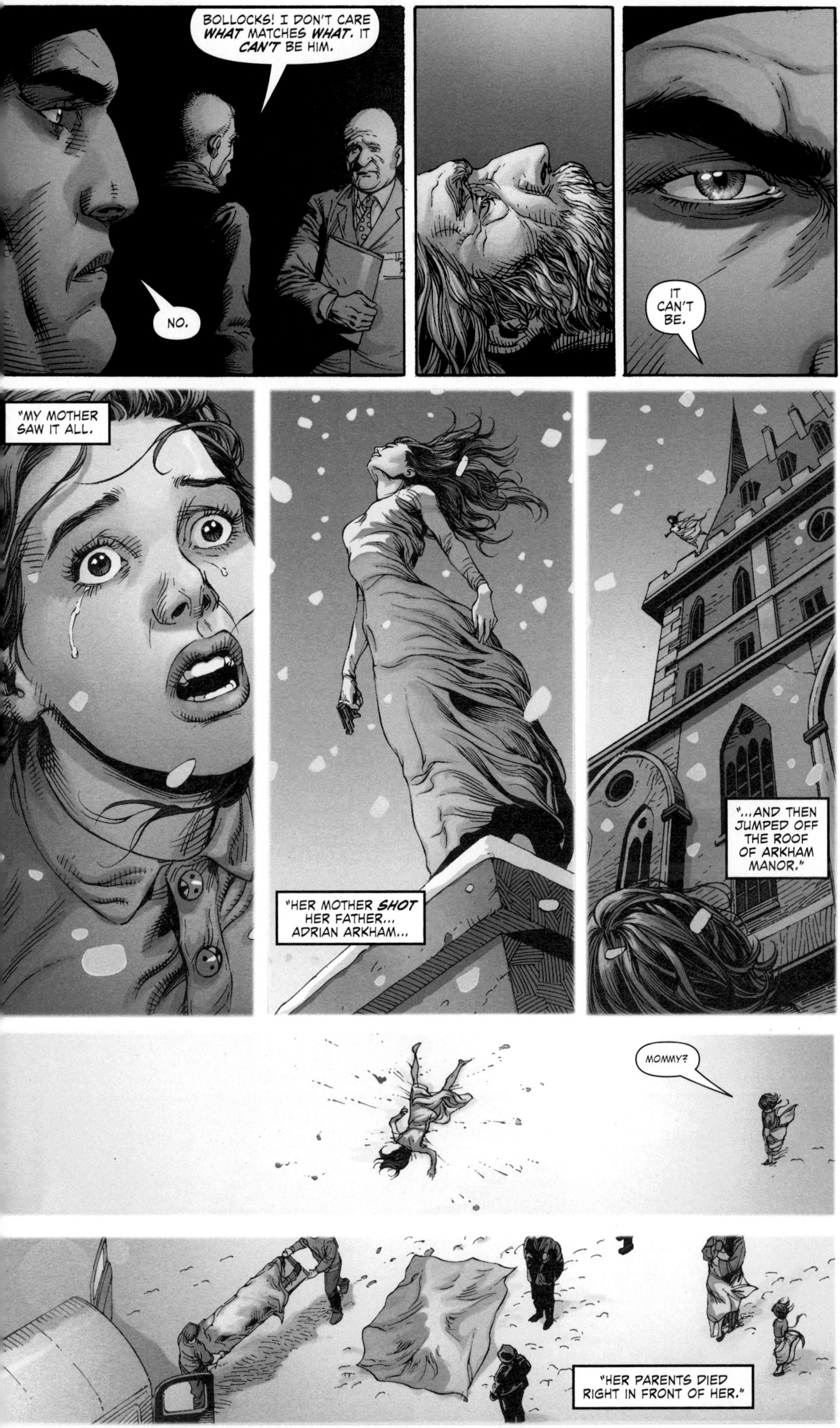
BOLLOCKS! I DON'T CARE WHAT MATCHES WHAT. IT CAN'T BE HIM.
NO.
IT CAN'T BE.
"MY MOTHER SAW IT ALL.
"HER MOTHER SHOT HER FATHER... ADRIAN ARKHAM...
"...AND THEN JUMPED OFF THE ROOF OF ARKHAM MANOR."
MOMMY?
"HER PARENTS DIED RIGHT IN FRONT OF HER."

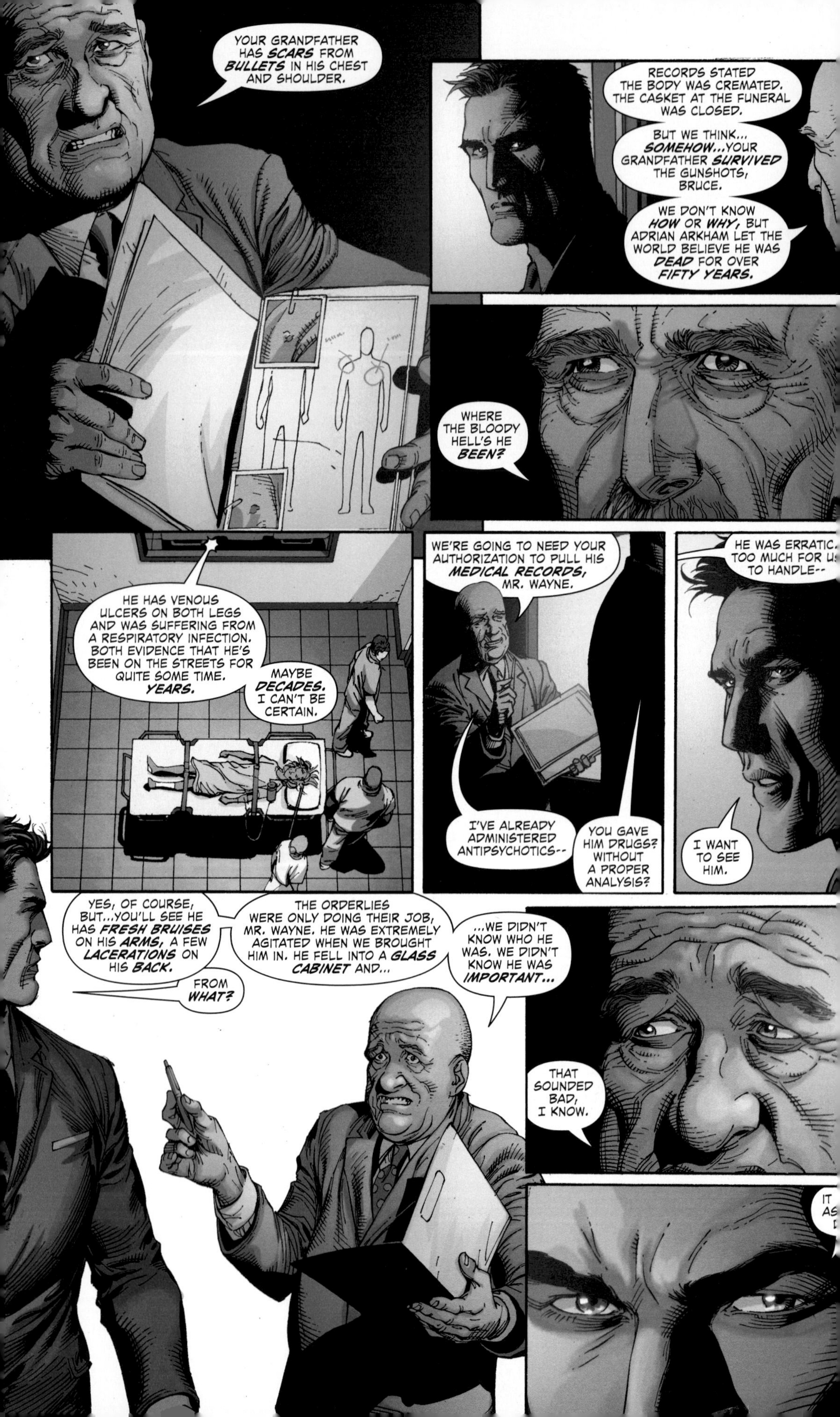
YOUR GRANDFATHER HAS SCARS FROM BULLETS IN HIS CHEST AND SHOULDER.
RECORDS STATED THE BODY WAS CREMATED. THE CASKET AT THE FUNERAL WAS CLOSED.
BUT WE THINK... SOMEHOW...YOUR GRANDFATHER SURVIVED THE GUNSHOTS, BRUCE.
WE DON'T KNOW HOW OR WHY, BUT ADRIAN ARKHAM LET THE WORLD BELIEVE HE WAS DEAD FOR OVER FIFTY YEARS.
WHERE THE BLOODY HELL'S HE BEEN?
HE HAS VENOUS ULCERS ON BOTH LEGS AND WAS SUFFERING FROM A RESPIRATORY INFECTION. BOTH EVIDENCE THAT HE'S BEEN ON THE STREETS FOR QUITE SOME TIME. YEARS.
MAYBE DECADES. I CAN'T BE CERTAIN.
WE'RE GOING TO NEED YOUR AUTHORIZATION TO PULL HIS MEDICAL RECORDS, MR. WAYNE.
I'VE ALREADY ADMINISTERED ANTIPSYCHOTICS--
YOU GAVE HIM DRUGS? WITHOUT A PROPER ANALYSIS?
HE WAS ERRATIC. TOO MUCH FOR US TO HANDLE--
I WANT TO SEE HIM.
YES, OF COURSE, BUT...YOU'LL SEE HE HAS FRESH BRUISES ON HIS ARMS, A FEW LACERATIONS ON HIS BACK.
FROM WHAT?
THE ORDERLIES WERE ONLY DOING THEIR JOB, MR. WAYNE. HE WAS EXTREMELY AGITATED WHEN WE BROUGHT HIM IN. HE FELL INTO A GLASS CABINET AND...
...WE DIDN'T KNOW WHO HE WAS. WE DIDN'T KNOW HE WAS IMPORTANT...
THAT SOUNDED BAD, I KNOW.

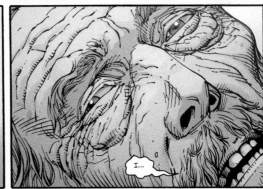

I....

I WANT TO
GO HOME.

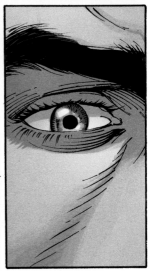

"DON'T YOU
WORRY..."

...I GOT THE GROCERIES.

LOTS OF *APPLES* AND *ORANGES.*

APPLES AND ORANGES?!

LEMME SEE.

Heh. THIS AIN'T FRUIT.

I WAS JOKIN', DUMBASS.

YOU WANT MORE? *GUNS. BOMBS.* EVEN GOT *BODY ARMOR,* I HEAR. THEY'RE HANDING IT OUT TOMORROW NIGHT.

WHERE AT?

THE HARVEY DENT HOUSE.

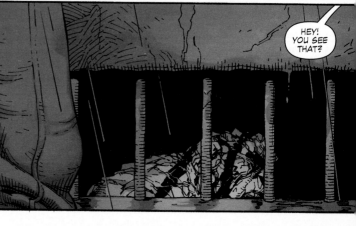

HEY! YOU SEE THAT?

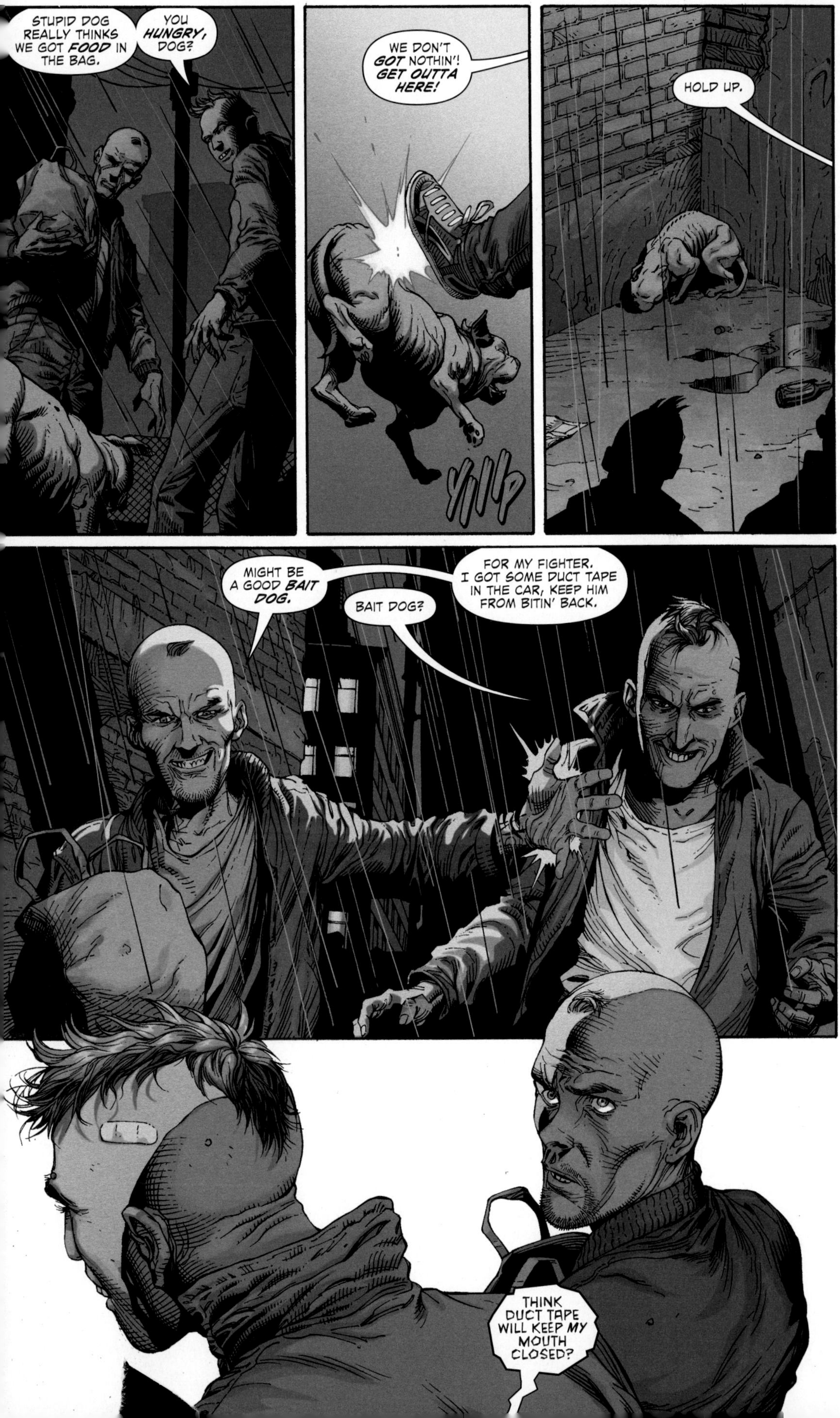
STUPID DOG REALLY THINKS WE GOT FOOD IN THE BAG.
YOU HUNGRY, DOG?
WE DON'T GOT NOTHIN'! GET OUTTA HERE!
YIIIP
HOLD UP.
MIGHT BE A GOOD BAIT DOG.
BAIT DOG?
FOR MY FIGHTER. I GOT SOME DUCT TAPE IN THE CAR, KEEP HIM FROM BITIN' BACK.
THINK DUCT TAPE WILL KEEP MY MOUTH CLOSED?

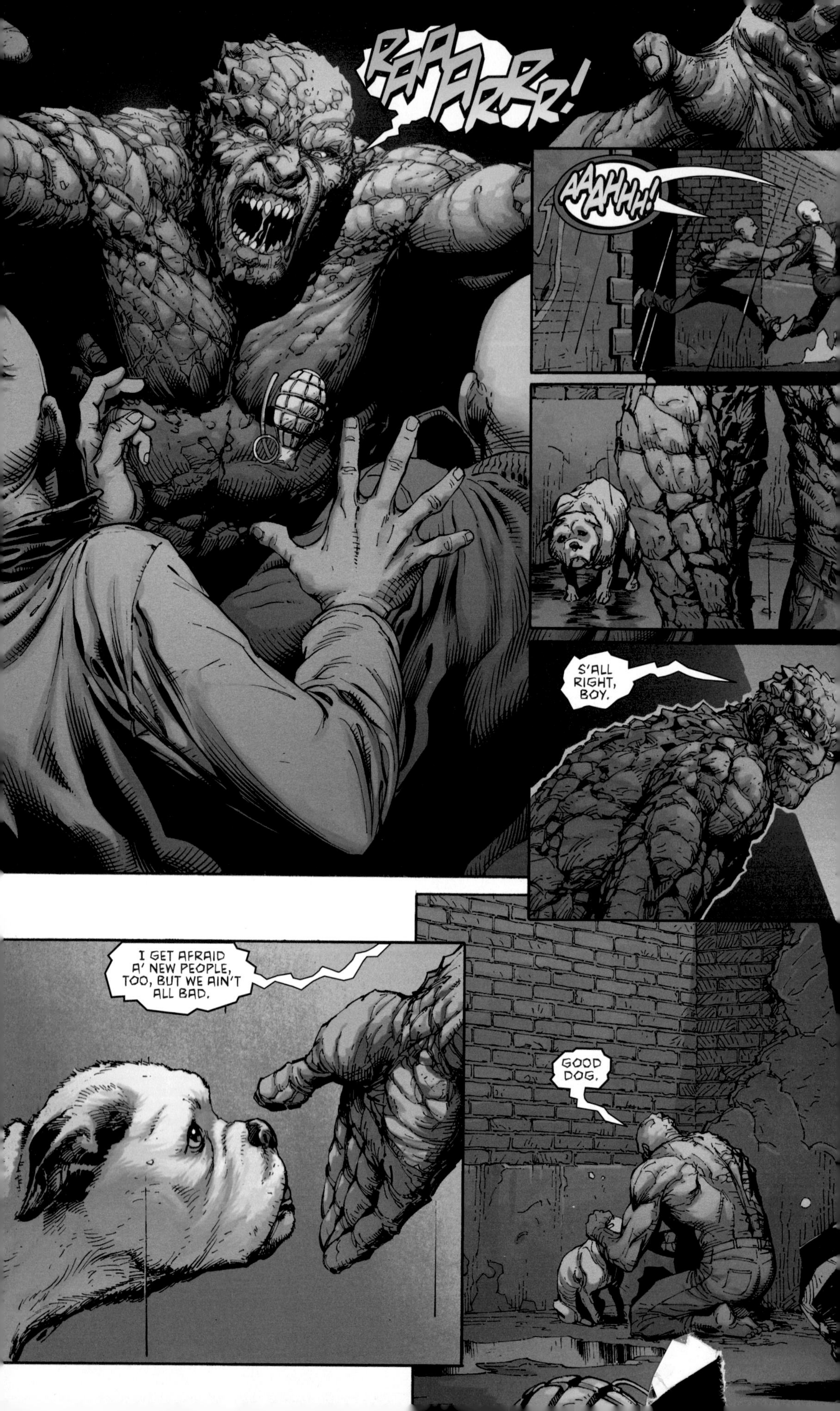

RAAARRRR!
AAAHHH!
S'ALL RIGHT, BOY.
I GET AFRAID A' NEW PEOPLE, TOO, BUT WE AIN'T ALL BAD.
GOOD DOG.

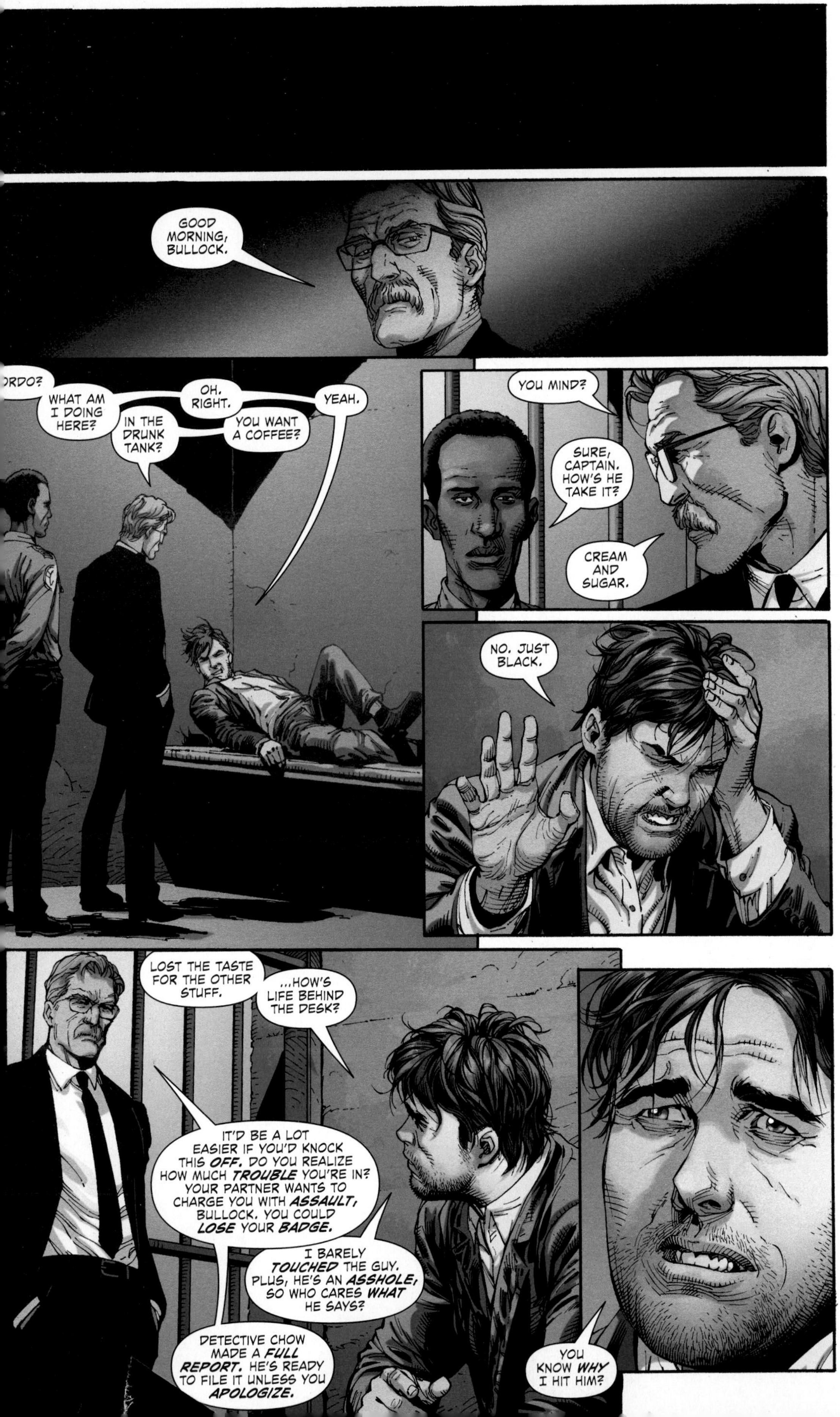

GOOD MORNING, BULLOCK.
ORDO?
WHAT AM I DOING HERE?
IN THE DRUNK TANK?
OH. RIGHT.
YOU WANT A COFFEE?
YEAH.
YOU MIND?
SURE, CAPTAIN. HOW'S HE TAKE IT?
CREAM AND SUGAR.
NO. JUST BLACK.
LOST THE TASTE FOR THE OTHER STUFF.
...HOW'S LIFE BEHIND THE DESK?
IT'D BE A LOT EASIER IF YOU'D KNOCK THIS OFF. DO YOU REALIZE HOW MUCH TROUBLE YOU'RE IN? YOUR PARTNER WANTS TO CHARGE YOU WITH ASSAULT, BULLOCK. YOU COULD LOSE YOUR BADGE.
I BARELY TOUCHED THE GUY. PLUS, HE'S AN ASSHOLE, SO WHO CARES WHAT HE SAYS?
DETECTIVE CHOW MADE A FULL REPORT. HE'S READY TO FILE IT UNLESS YOU APOLOGIZE.
YOU KNOW WHY I HIT HIM?

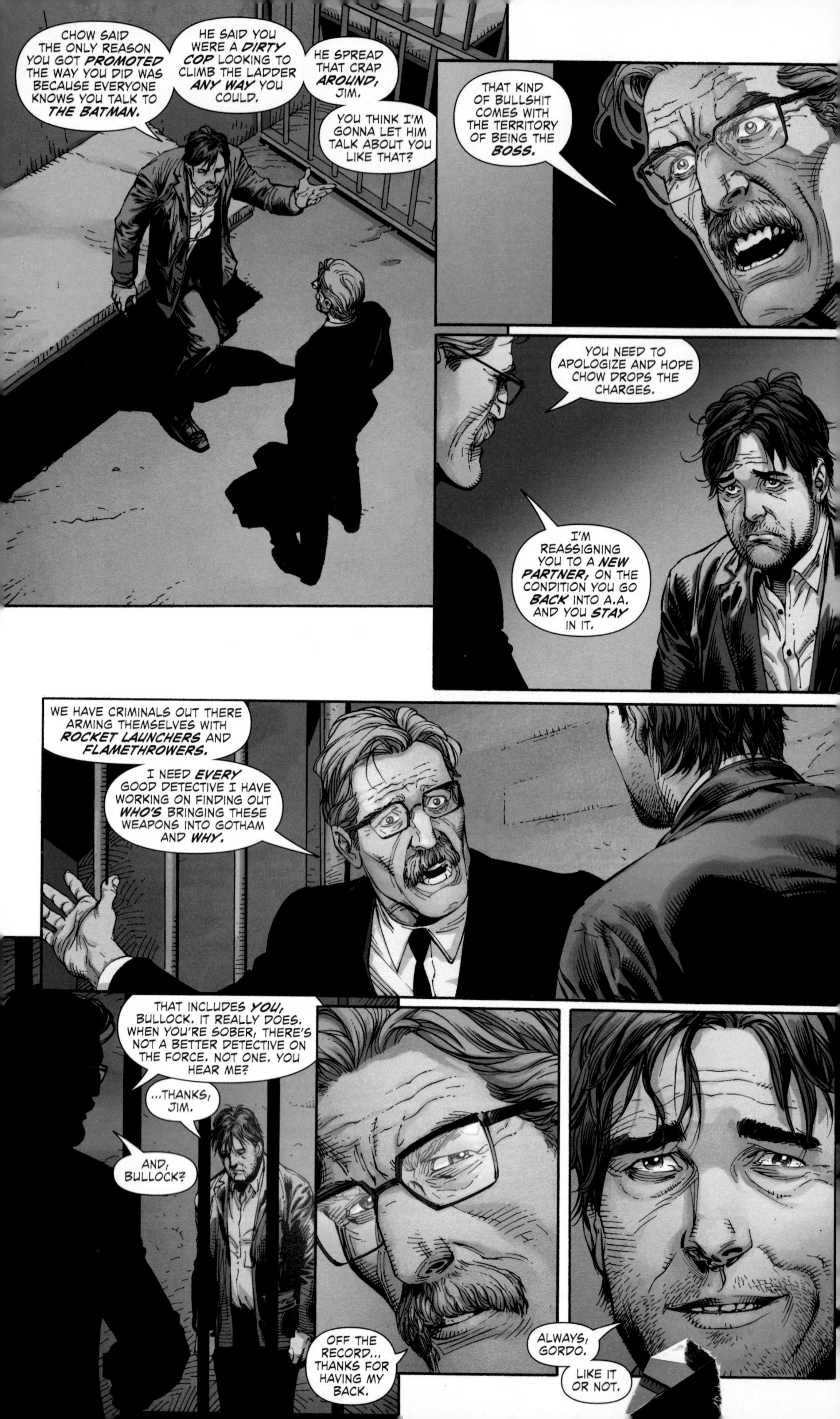
CHOW SAID THE ONLY REASON YOU GOT PROMOTED THE WAY YOU DID WAS BECAUSE EVERYONE KNOWS YOU TALK TO THE BATMAN.
HE SAID YOU WERE A DIRTY COP LOOKING TO CLIMB THE LADDER ANY WAY YOU COULD.
HE SPREAD THAT CRAP AROUND, JIM.
YOU THINK I'M GONNA LET HIM TALK ABOUT YOU LIKE THAT?
THAT KIND OF BULLSHIT COMES WITH THE TERRITORY OF BEING THE BOSS.
YOU NEED TO APOLOGIZE AND HOPE CHOW DROPS THE CHARGES.
I'M REASSIGNING YOU TO A NEW PARTNER, ON THE CONDITION YOU GO BACK INTO A.A. AND YOU STAY IN IT.
WE HAVE CRIMINALS OUT THERE ARMING THEMSELVES WITH ROCKET LAUNCHERS AND FLAMETHROWERS.
I NEED EVERY GOOD DETECTIVE I HAVE WORKING ON FINDING OUT WHO'S BRINGING THESE WEAPONS INTO GOTHAM AND WHY.
THAT INCLUDES YOU, BULLOCK. IT REALLY DOES. WHEN YOU'RE SOBER, THERE'S NOT A BETTER DETECTIVE ON THE FORCE. NOT ONE. YOU HEAR ME?
...THANKS, JIM.
AND, BULLOCK?
OFF THE RECORD... THANKS FOR HAVING MY BACK.
ALWAYS, GORDO.
LIKE IT OR NOT.

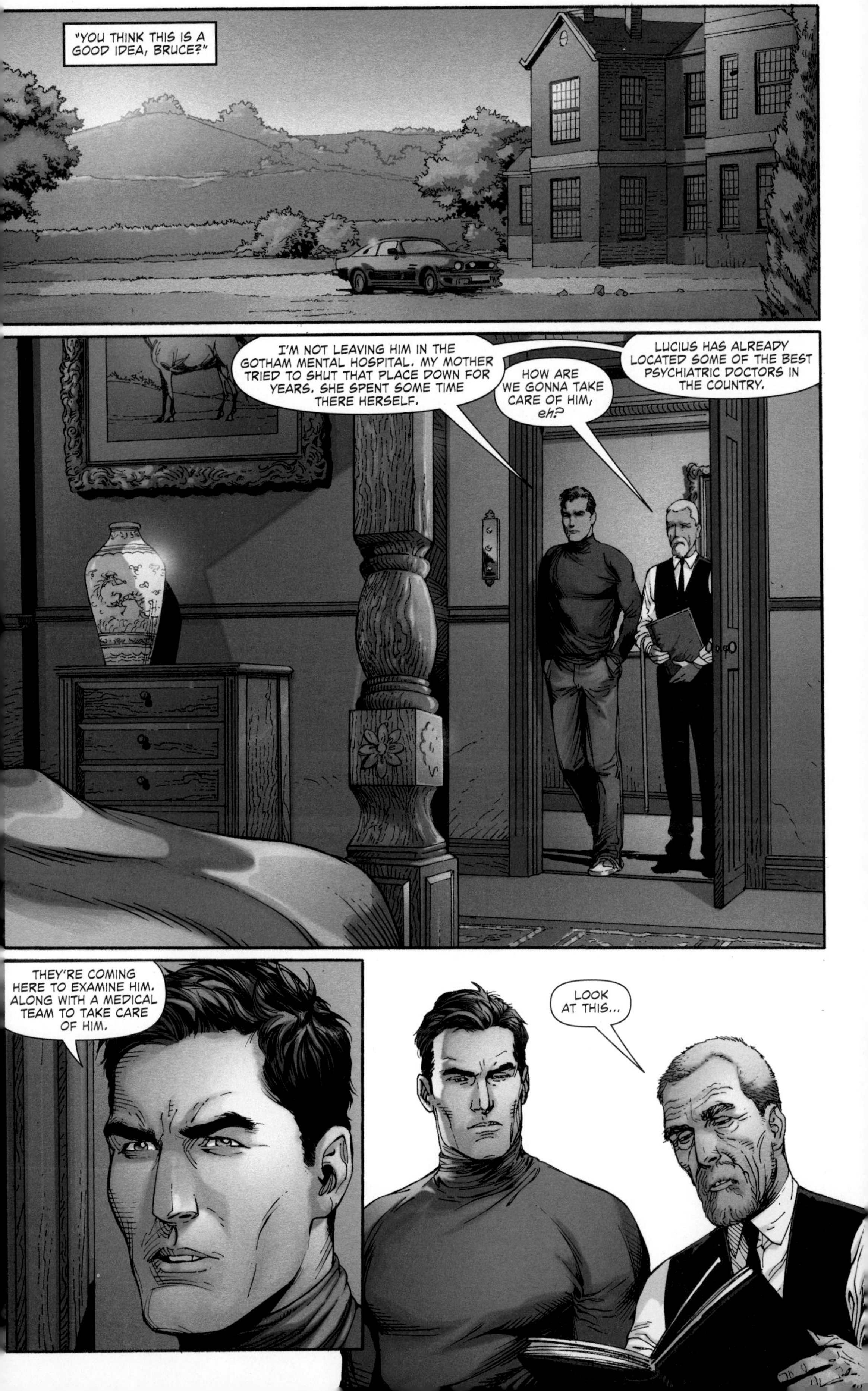
"YOU THINK THIS IS A GOOD IDEA, BRUCE?"
I'M NOT LEAVING HIM IN THE GOTHAM MENTAL HOSPITAL. MY MOTHER TRIED TO SHUT THAT PLACE DOWN FOR YEARS. SHE SPENT SOME TIME THERE HERSELF.
HOW ARE WE GONNA TAKE CARE OF HIM, *eh?*
LUCIUS HAS ALREADY LOCATED SOME OF THE BEST PSYCHIATRIC DOCTORS IN THE COUNTRY.
THEY'RE COMING HERE TO EXAMINE HIM. ALONG WITH A MEDICAL TEAM TO TAKE CARE OF HIM.
LOOK AT THIS...

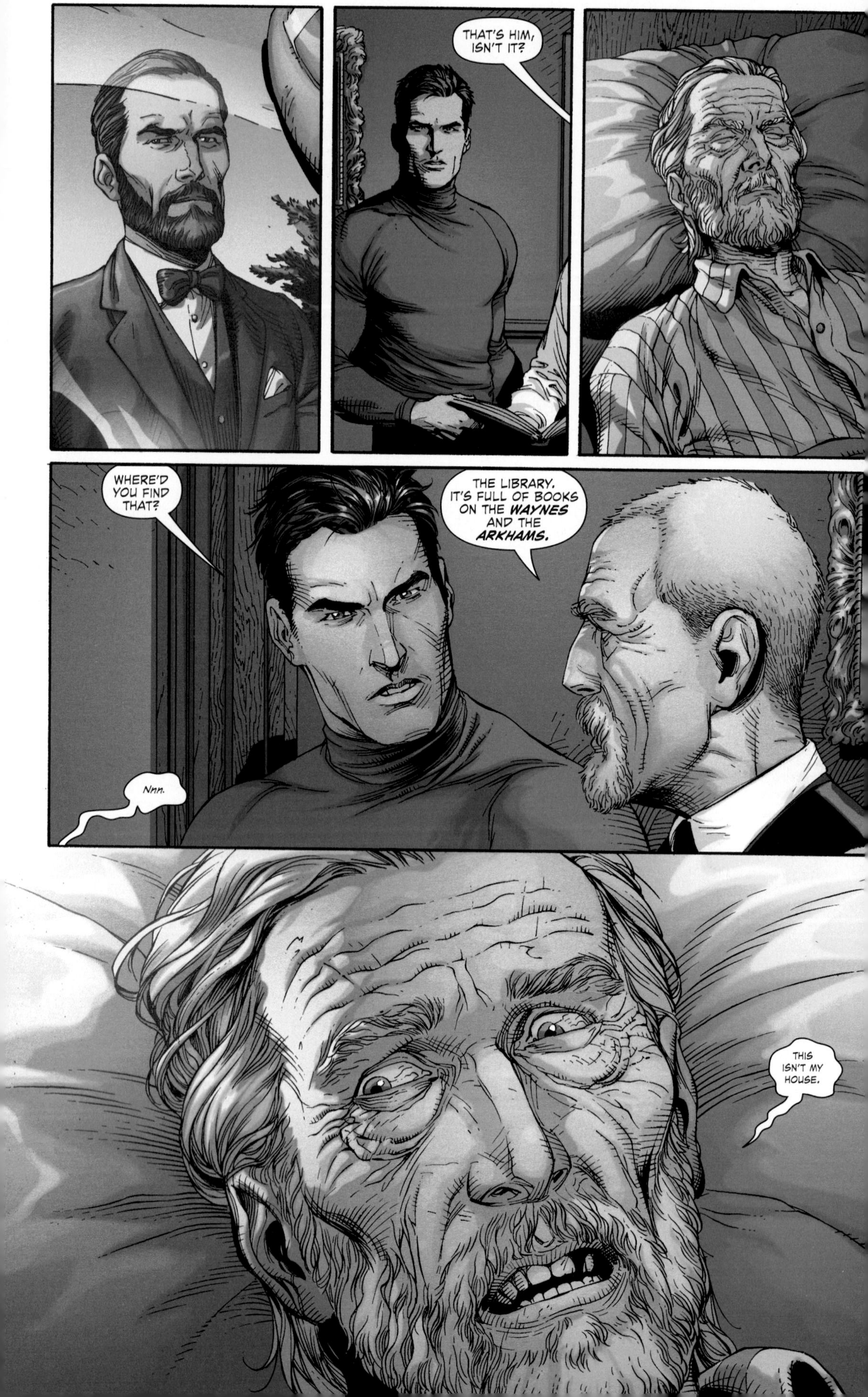

THAT'S HIM, ISN'T IT?
WHERE'D YOU FIND THAT?
THE LIBRARY. IT'S FULL OF BOOKS ON THE ***WAYNES*** AND THE ***ARKHAMS.***
Nnn.
THIS ISN'T MY HOUSE.

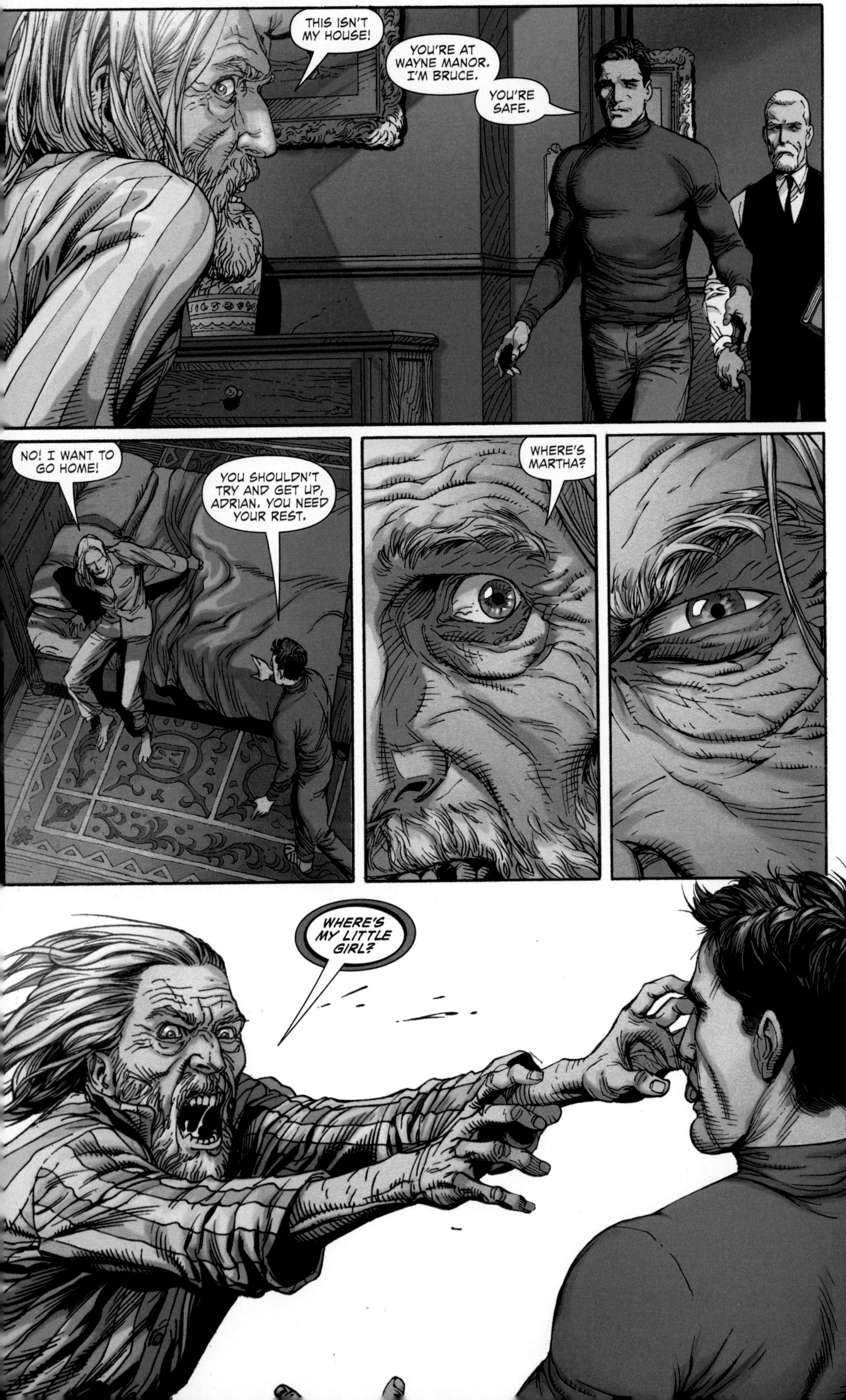
THIS ISN'T MY HOUSE!
YOU'RE AT WAYNE MANOR. I'M BRUCE.
YOU'RE SAFE.
NO! I WANT TO GO HOME!
YOU SHOULDN'T TRY AND GET UP, ADRIAN. YOU NEED YOUR REST.
WHERE'S MARTHA?
WHERE'S MY LITTLE GIRL?

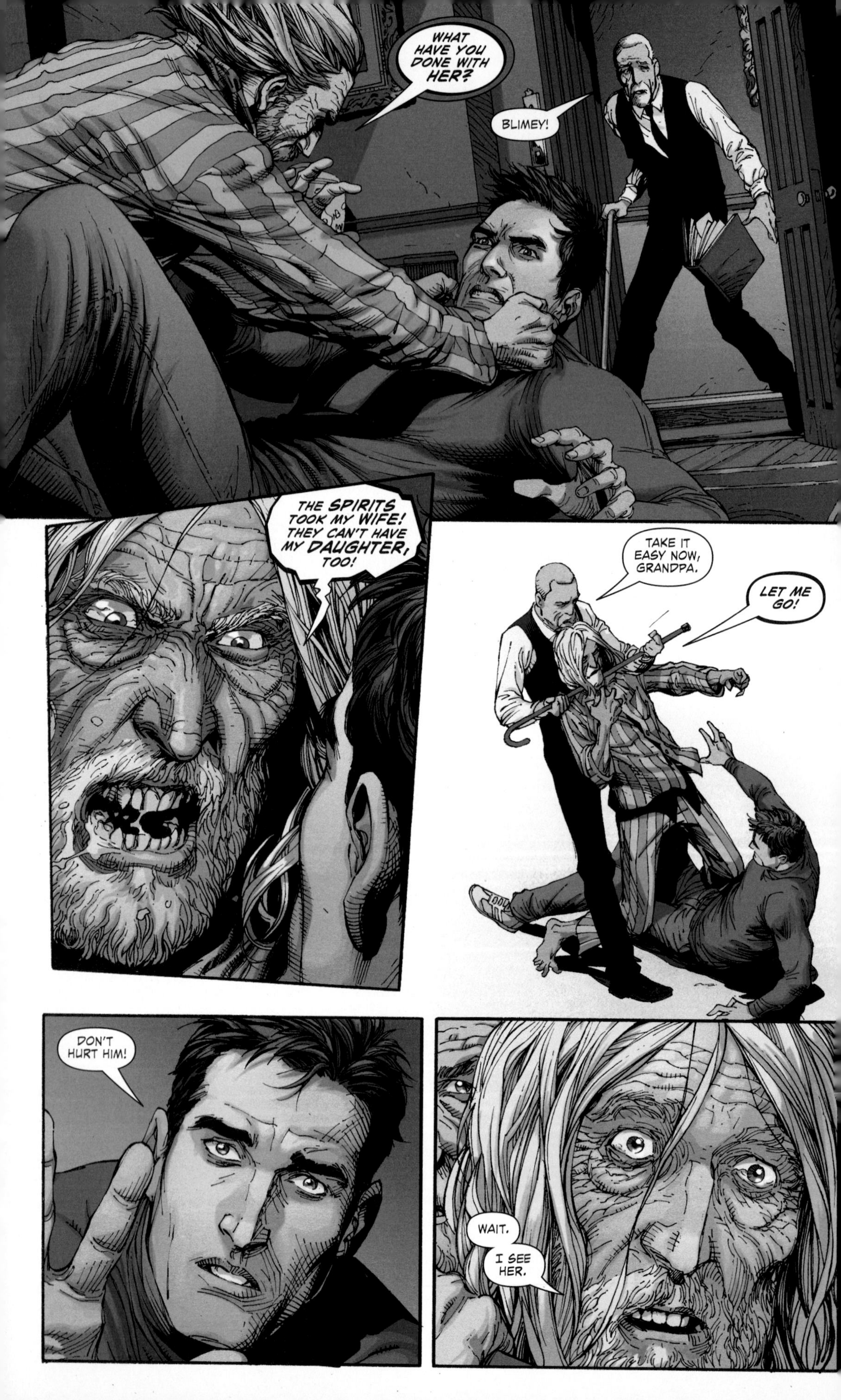
WHAT HAVE YOU DONE WITH HER?
BLIMEY!
THE SPIRITS TOOK MY WIFE! THEY CAN'T HAVE MY DAUGHTER, TOO!
TAKE IT EASY NOW, GRANDPA.
LET ME GO!
DON'T HURT HIM!
WAIT.
I SEE HER.

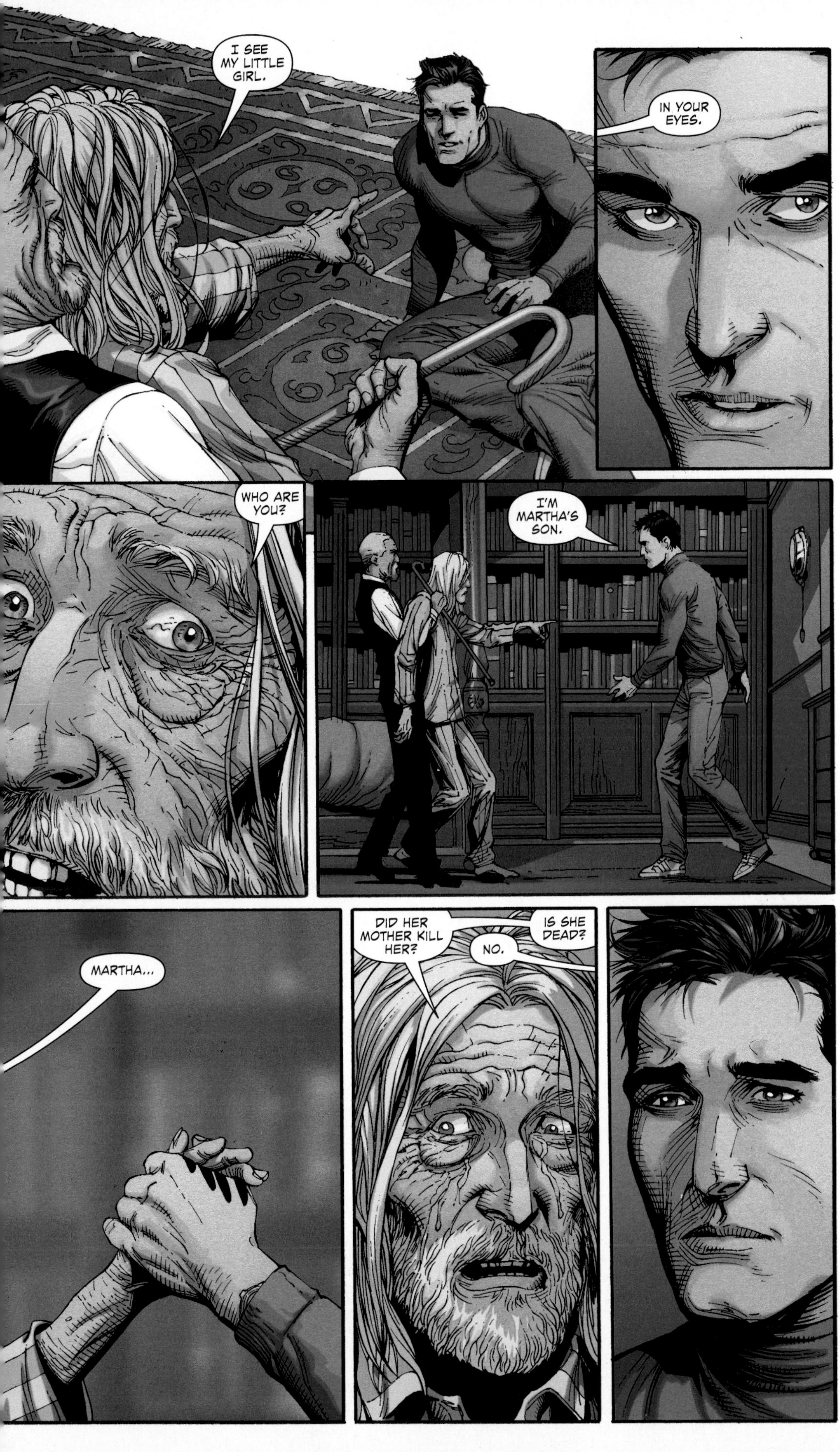
I SEE MY LITTLE GIRL.
IN YOUR EYES.
WHO ARE YOU?
I'M MARTHA'S SON.
MARTHA...
DID HER MOTHER KILL HER?
IS SHE DEAD?
NO.

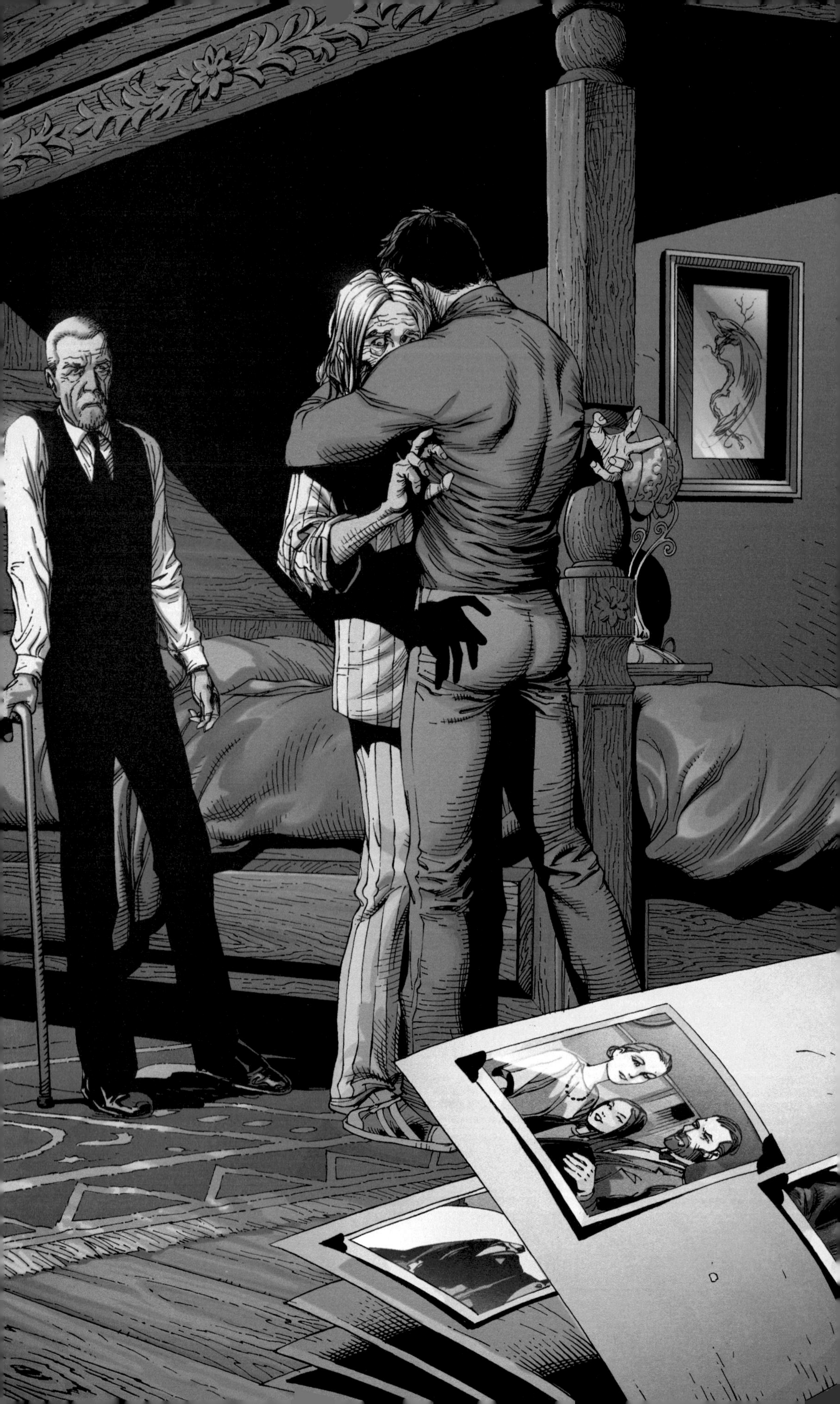

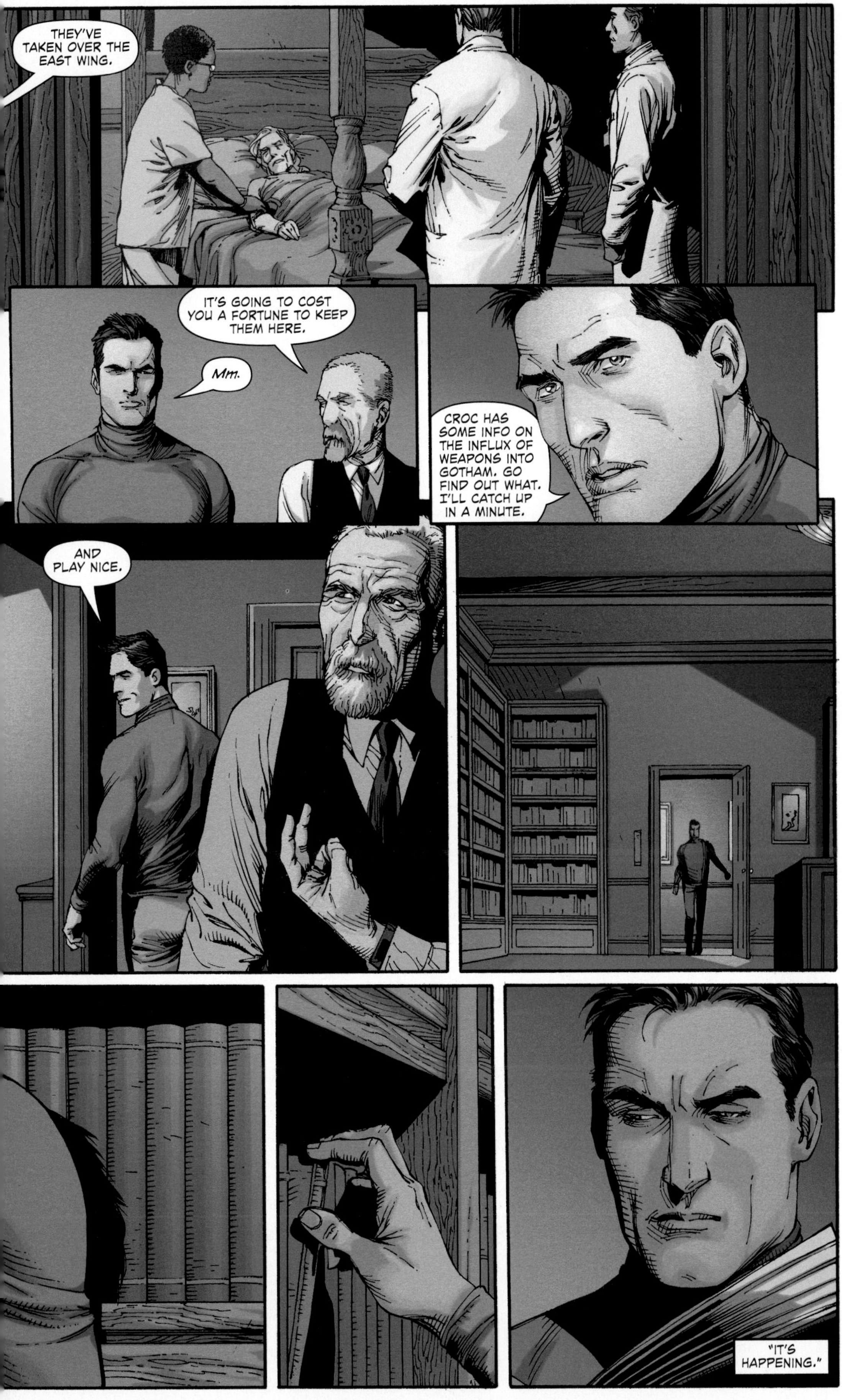
THEY'VE TAKEN OVER THE EAST WING.
IT'S GOING TO COST YOU A FORTUNE TO KEEP THEM HERE.
Mm.
CROC HAS SOME INFO ON THE INFLUX OF WEAPONS INTO GOTHAM. GO FIND OUT WHAT. I'LL CATCH UP IN A MINUTE.
AND PLAY NICE.
"IT'S HAPPENING."

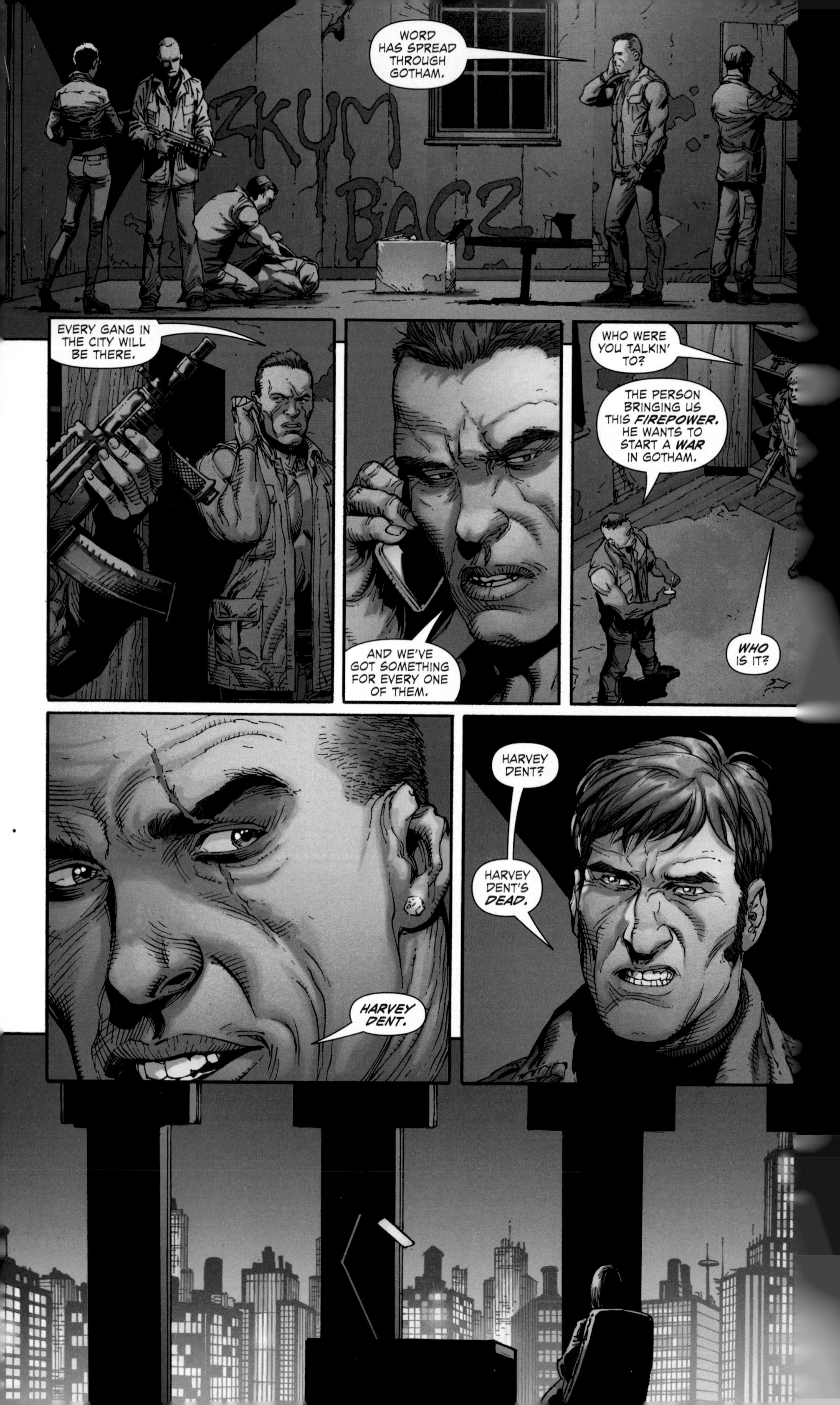
WORD HAS SPREAD THROUGH GOTHAM.
ZKUM BAGZ
EVERY GANG IN THE CITY WILL BE THERE.
AND WE'VE GOT SOMETHING FOR EVERY ONE OF THEM.
WHO WERE YOU TALKIN' TO?
THE PERSON BRINGING US THIS FIREPOWER. HE WANTS TO START A WAR IN GOTHAM.
WHO IS IT?
HARVEY DENT.
HARVEY DENT?
HARVEY DENT'S DEAD.

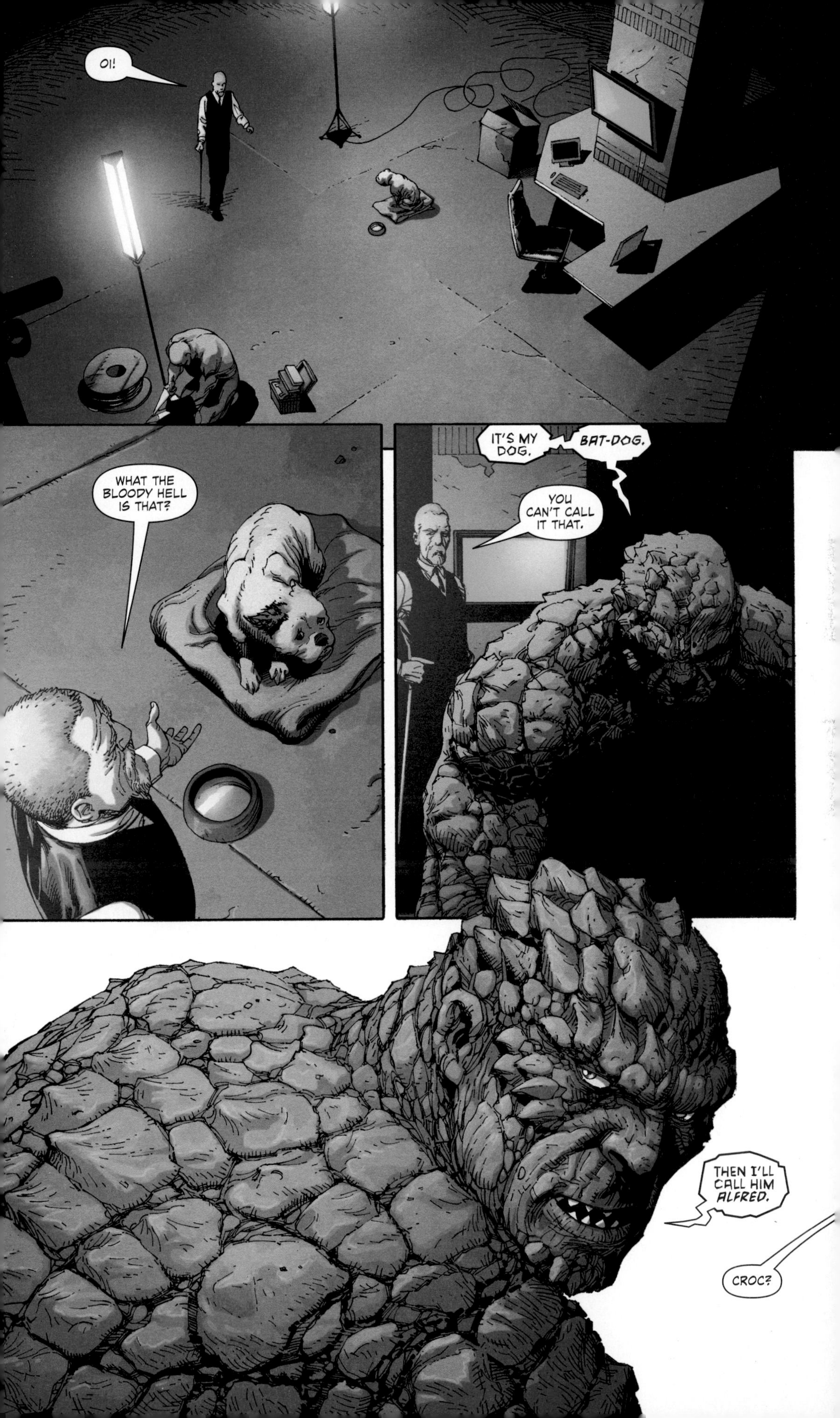
OI!
WHAT THE BLOODY HELL IS THAT?
IT'S MY DOG.
BAT-DOG.
YOU CAN'T CALL IT THAT.
THEN I'LL CALL HIM ALFRED.
CROC?

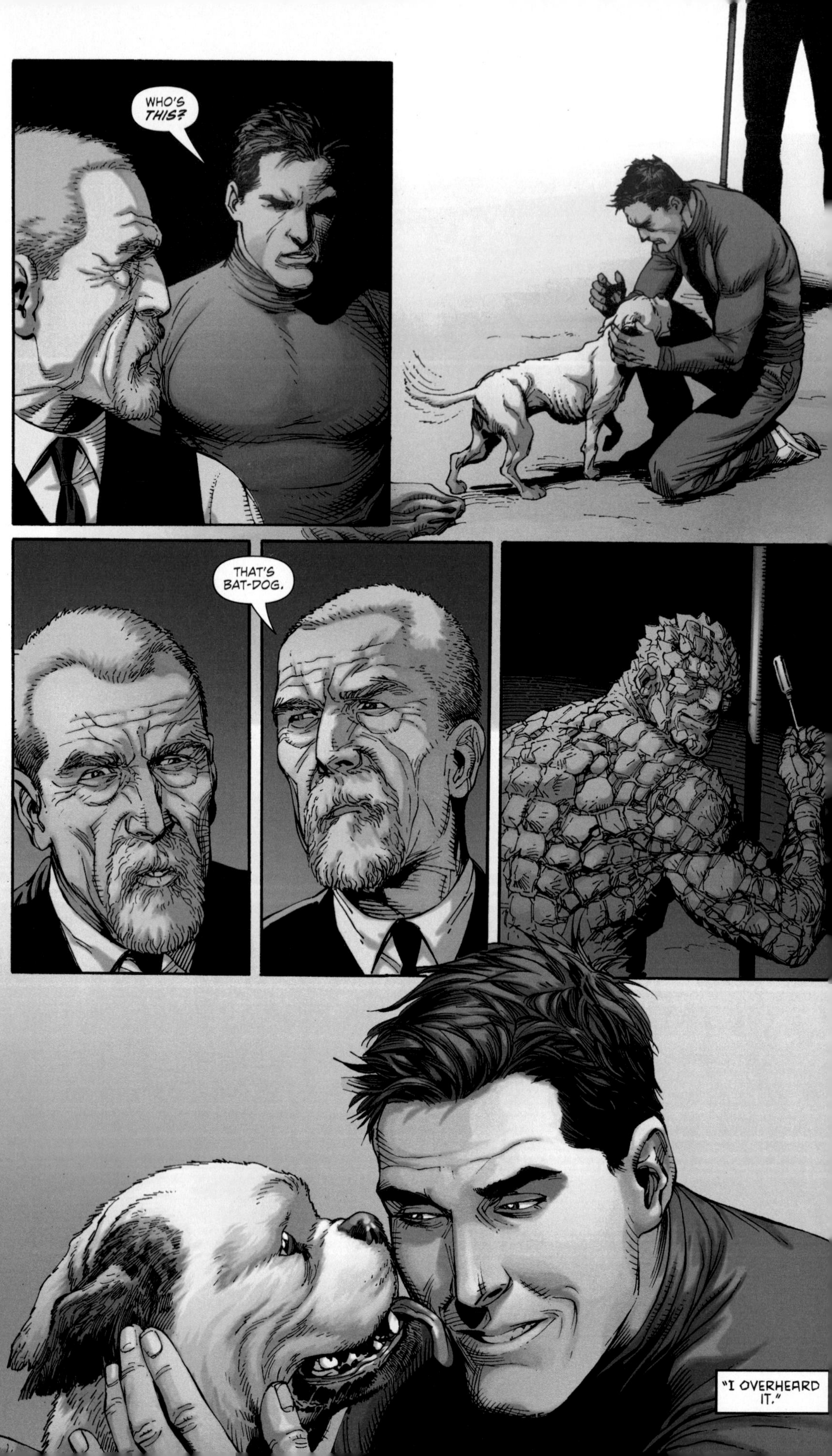

WHO'S *THIS?*
THAT'S BAT-DOG.
"I OVERHEARD IT."

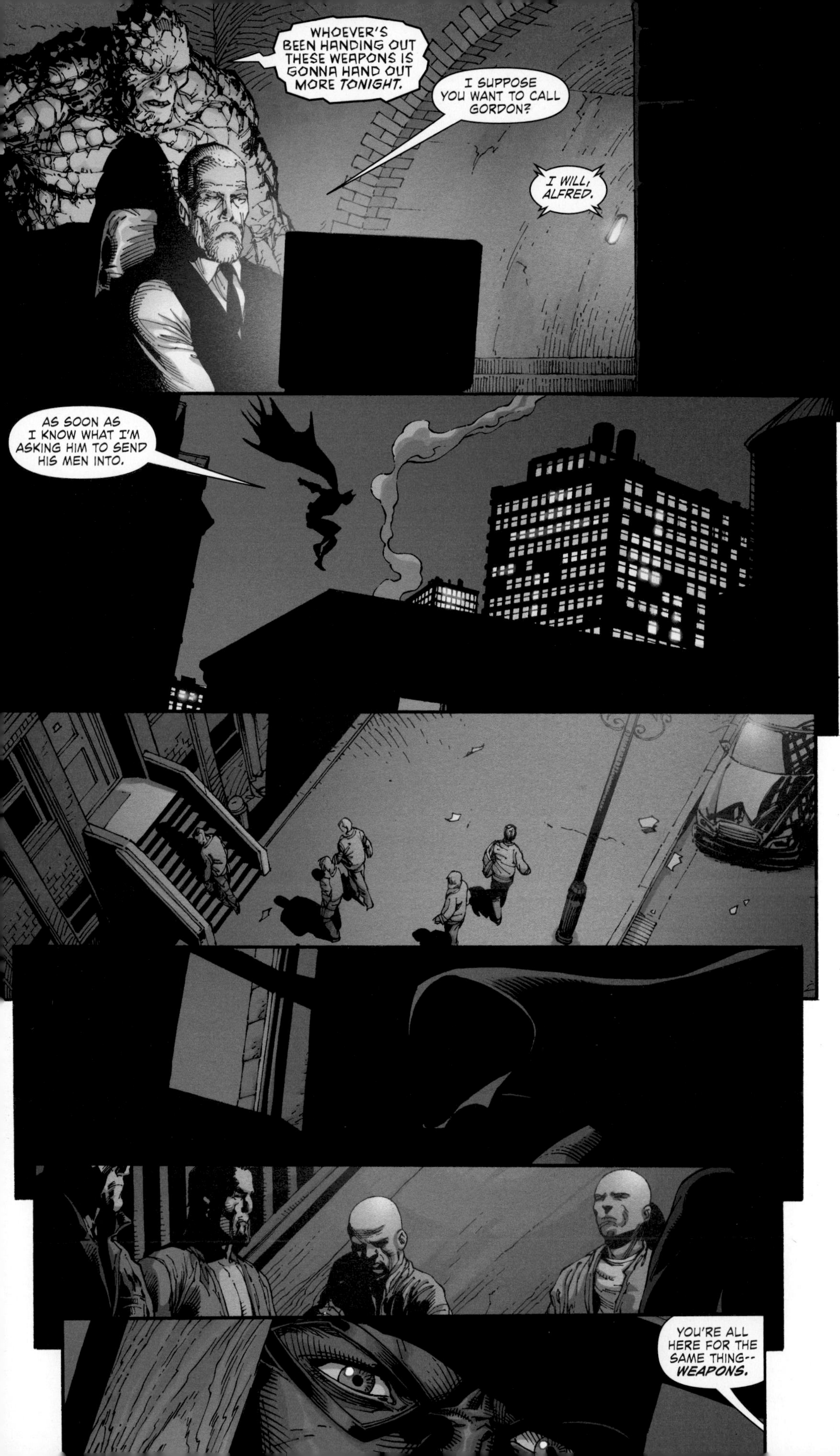
WHOEVER'S BEEN HANDING OUT THESE WEAPONS IS GONNA HAND OUT MORE *TONIGHT.*
I SUPPOSE YOU WANT TO CALL GORDON?
I WILL, ALFRED.
AS SOON AS I KNOW WHAT I'M ASKING HIM TO SEND HIS MEN INTO.
YOU'RE ALL HERE FOR THE SAME THING-- ***WEAPONS.***

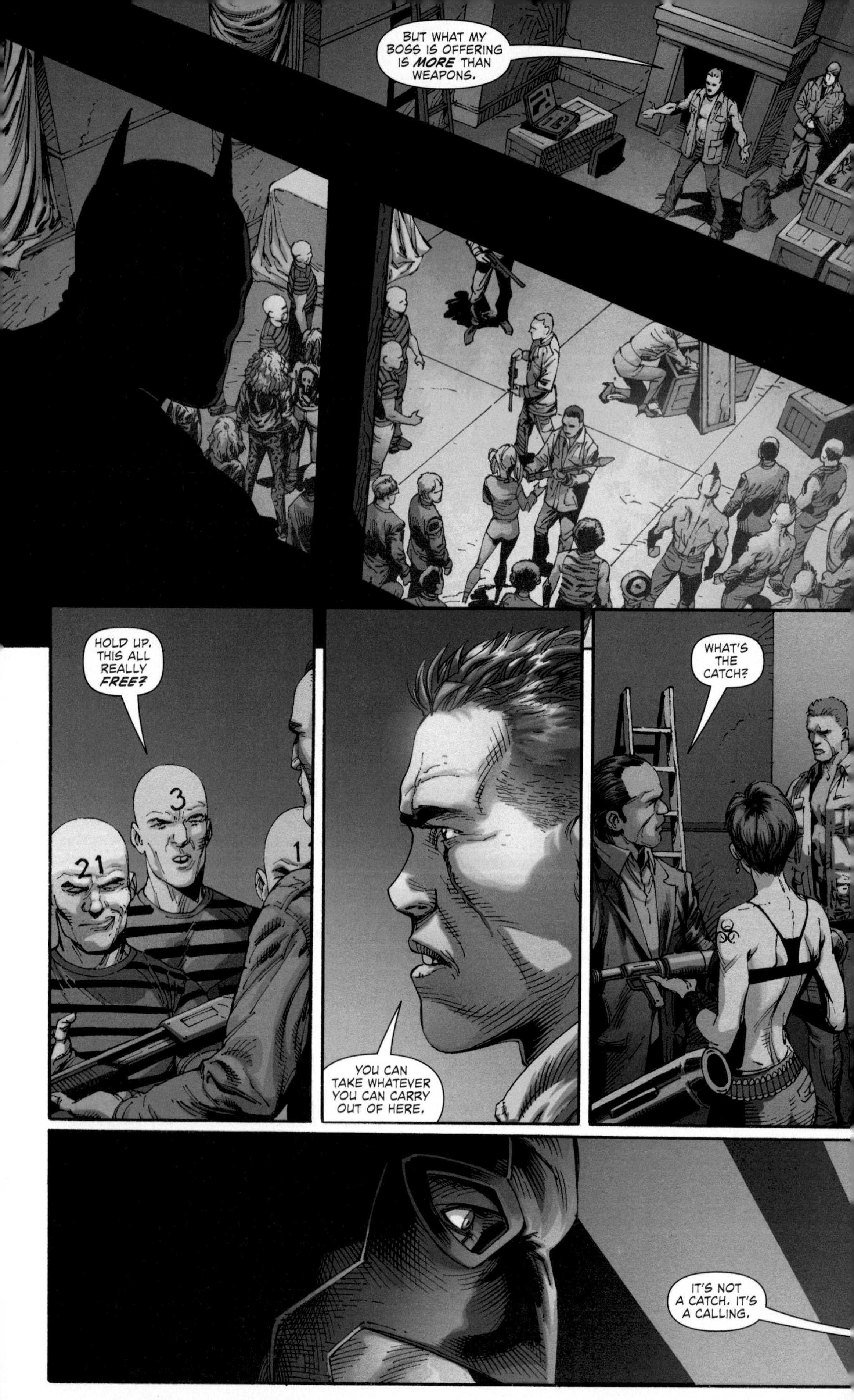
BUT WHAT MY BOSS IS OFFERING IS *MORE* THAN WEAPONS.
HOLD UP. THIS ALL REALLY *FREE?*
3
21
YOU CAN TAKE WHATEVER YOU CAN CARRY OUT OF HERE.
WHAT'S THE CATCH?
IT'S NOT A CATCH. IT'S A CALLING.

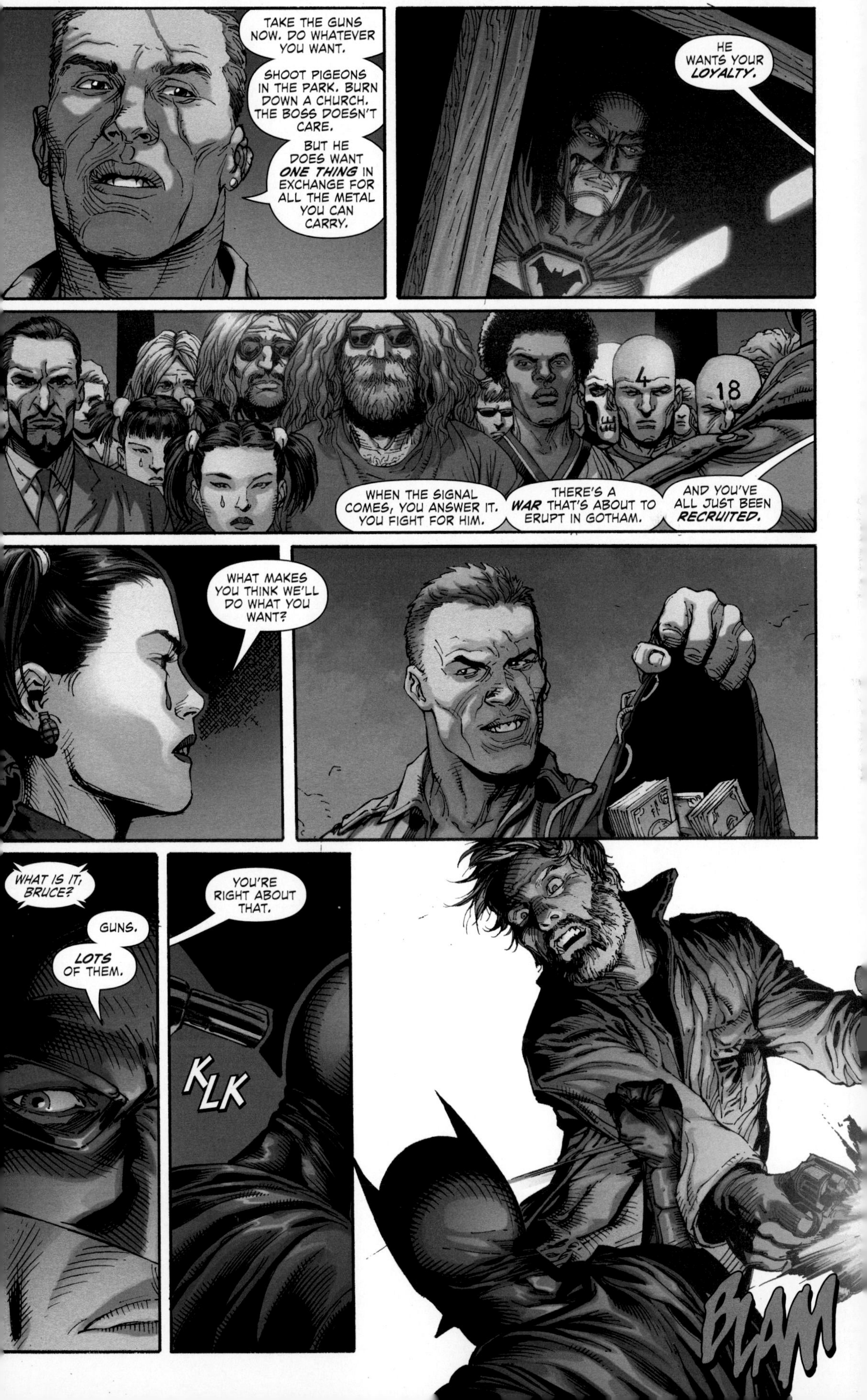
TAKE THE GUNS NOW. DO WHATEVER YOU WANT.
SHOOT PIGEONS IN THE PARK. BURN DOWN A CHURCH. THE BOSS DOESN'T CARE.
BUT HE DOES WANT ONE THING IN EXCHANGE FOR ALL THE METAL YOU CAN CARRY.
HE WANTS YOUR LOYALTY.
4
18
WHEN THE SIGNAL COMES, YOU ANSWER IT. YOU FIGHT FOR HIM.
THERE'S A WAR THAT'S ABOUT TO ERUPT IN GOTHAM.
AND YOU'VE ALL JUST BEEN RECRUITED.
WHAT MAKES YOU THINK WE'LL DO WHAT YOU WANT?
WHAT IS IT, BRUCE?
GUNS.
LOTS OF THEM.
YOU'RE RIGHT ABOUT THAT.
KLK
BLAM

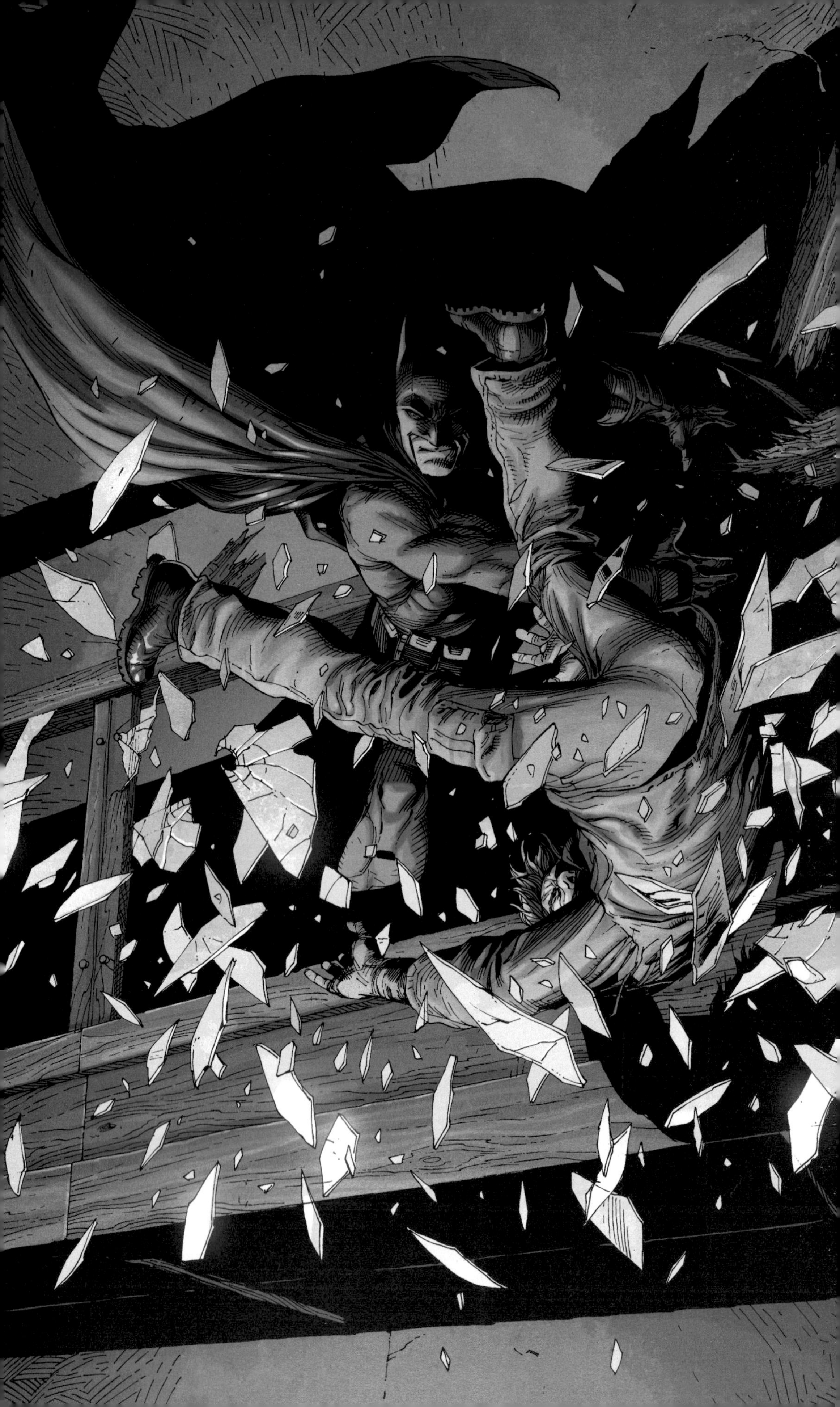

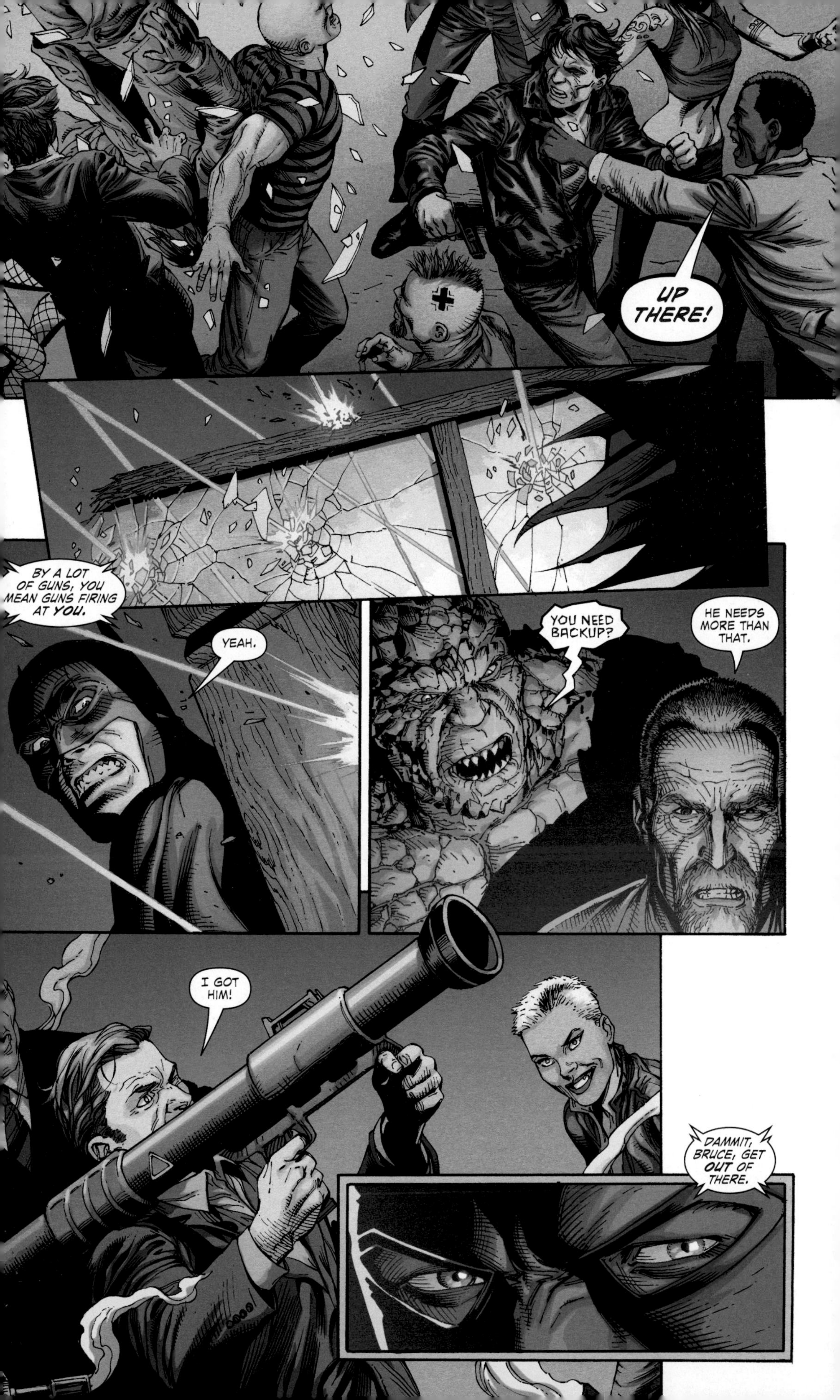
UP THERE!
BY A LOT OF GUNS, YOU MEAN GUNS FIRING AT YOU.
YEAH.
YOU NEED BACKUP?
HE NEEDS MORE THAN THAT.
I GOT HIM!
DAMMIT, BRUCE, GET OUT OF THERE.

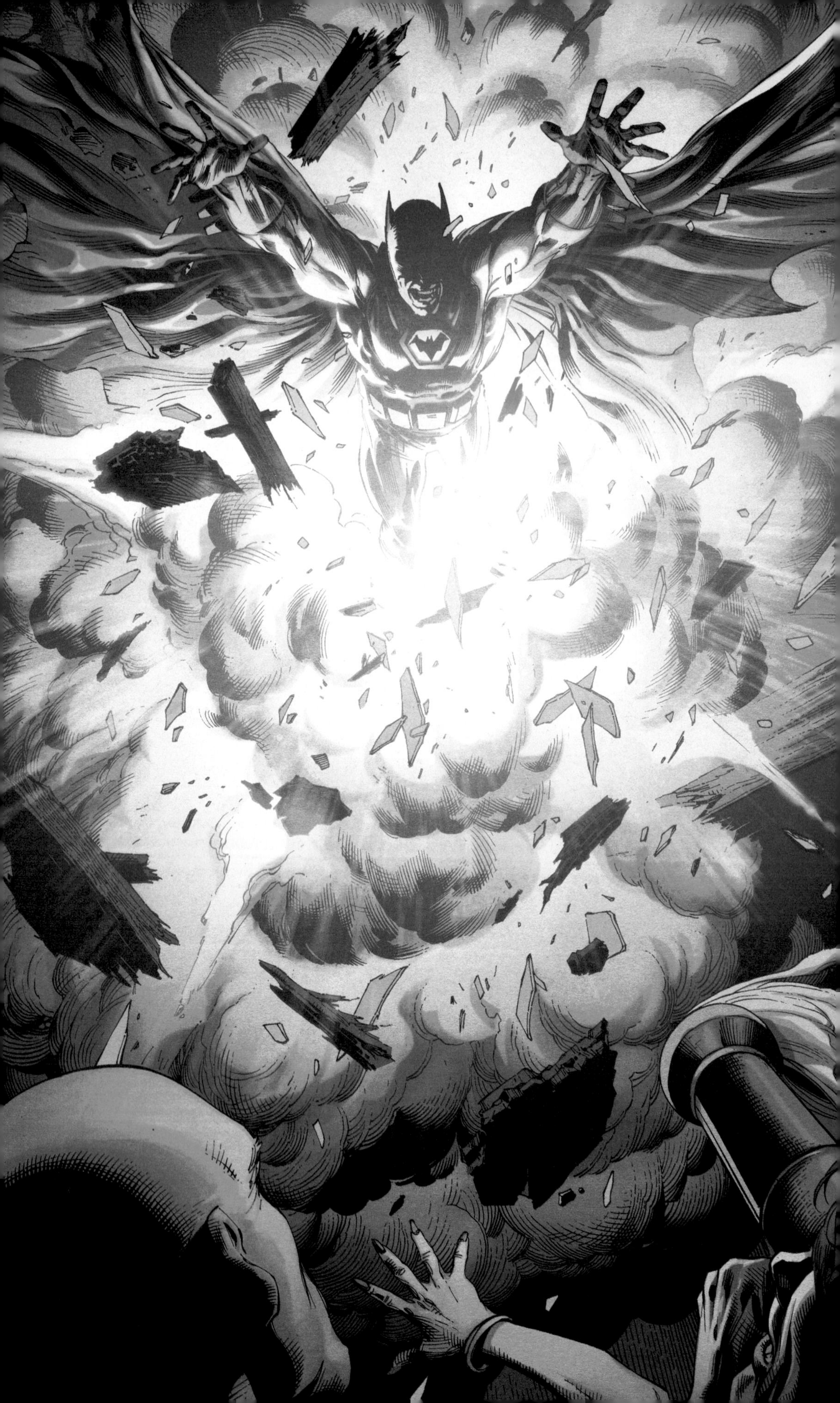

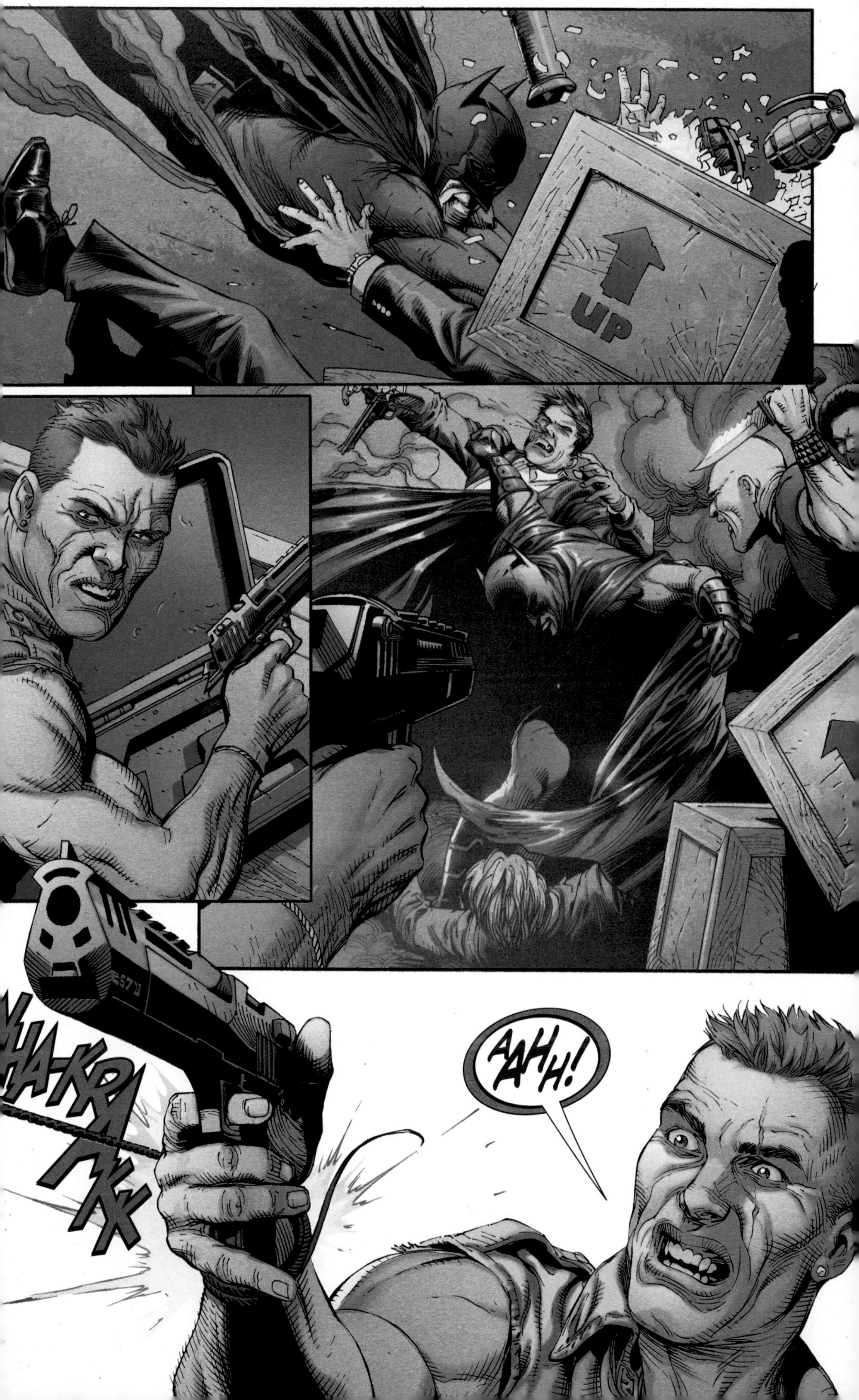
UP
AAHH!

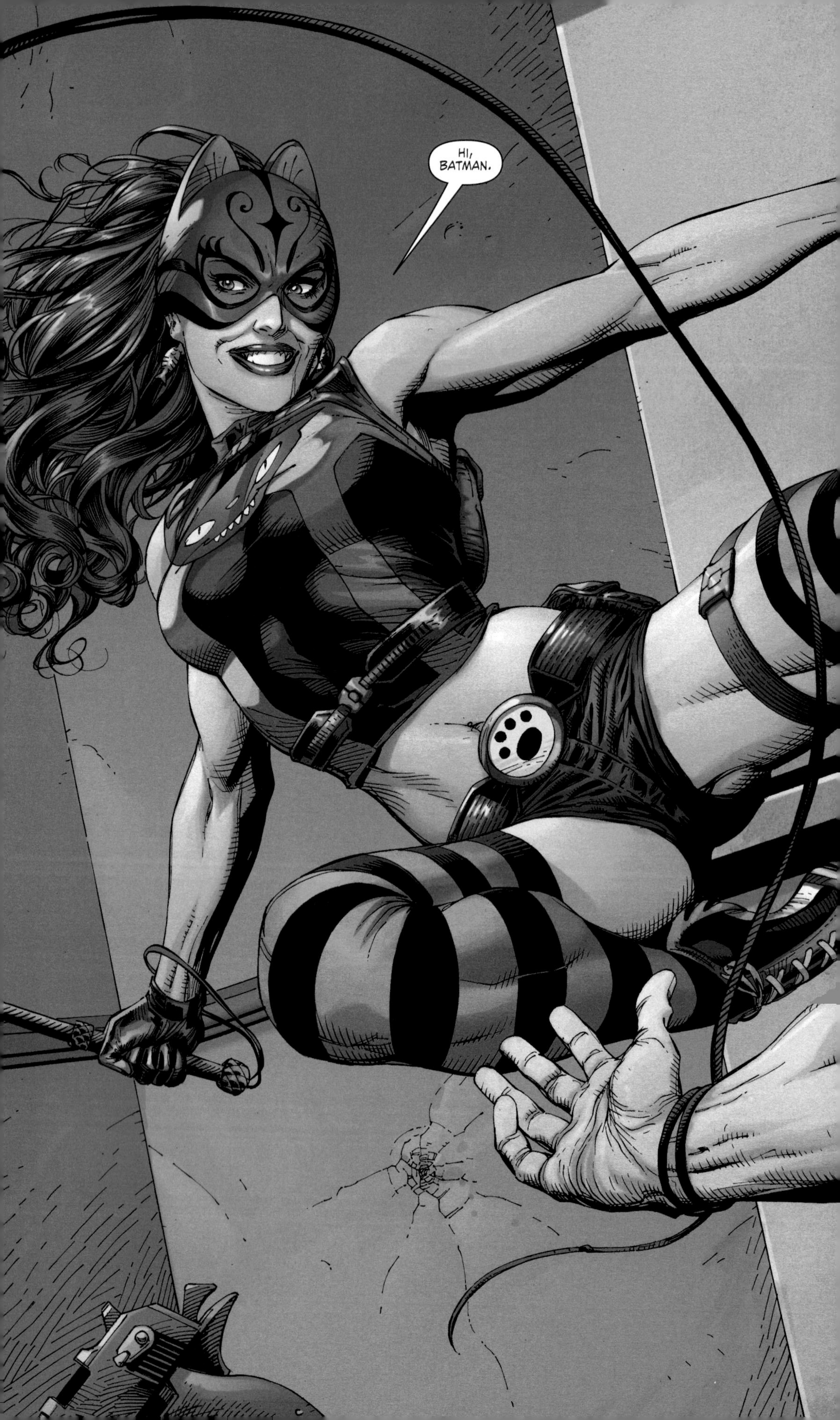
HI, BATMAN.

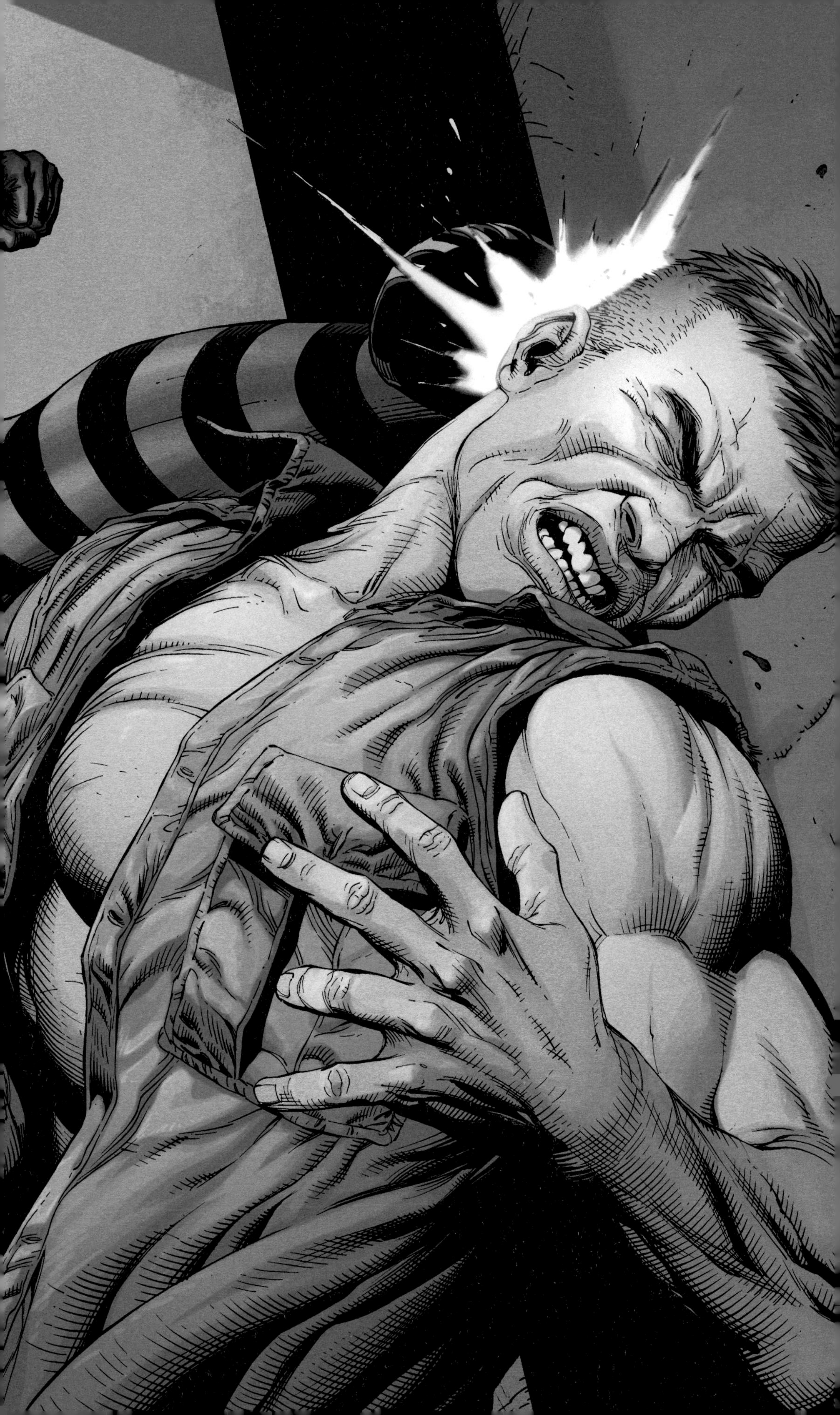

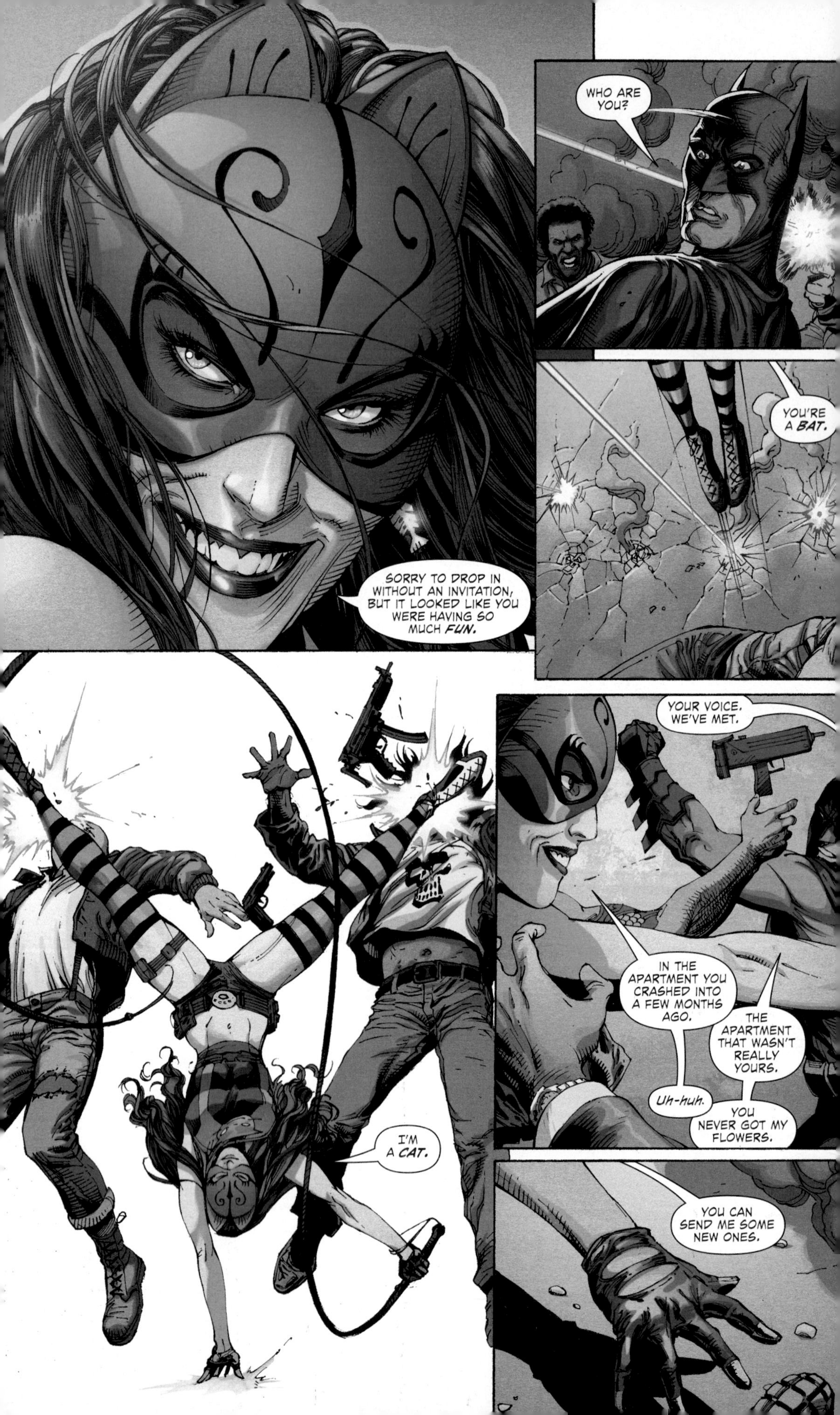
WHO ARE YOU?
YOU'RE A *BAT*.
SORRY TO DROP IN WITHOUT AN INVITATION, BUT IT LOOKED LIKE YOU WERE HAVING SO MUCH *FUN*.
I'M A *CAT*.
YOUR VOICE. WE'VE MET.
IN THE APARTMENT YOU CRASHED INTO A FEW MONTHS AGO.
THE APARTMENT THAT WASN'T REALLY YOURS.
Uh-huh.
YOU NEVER GOT MY FLOWERS.
YOU CAN SEND ME SOME NEW ONES.

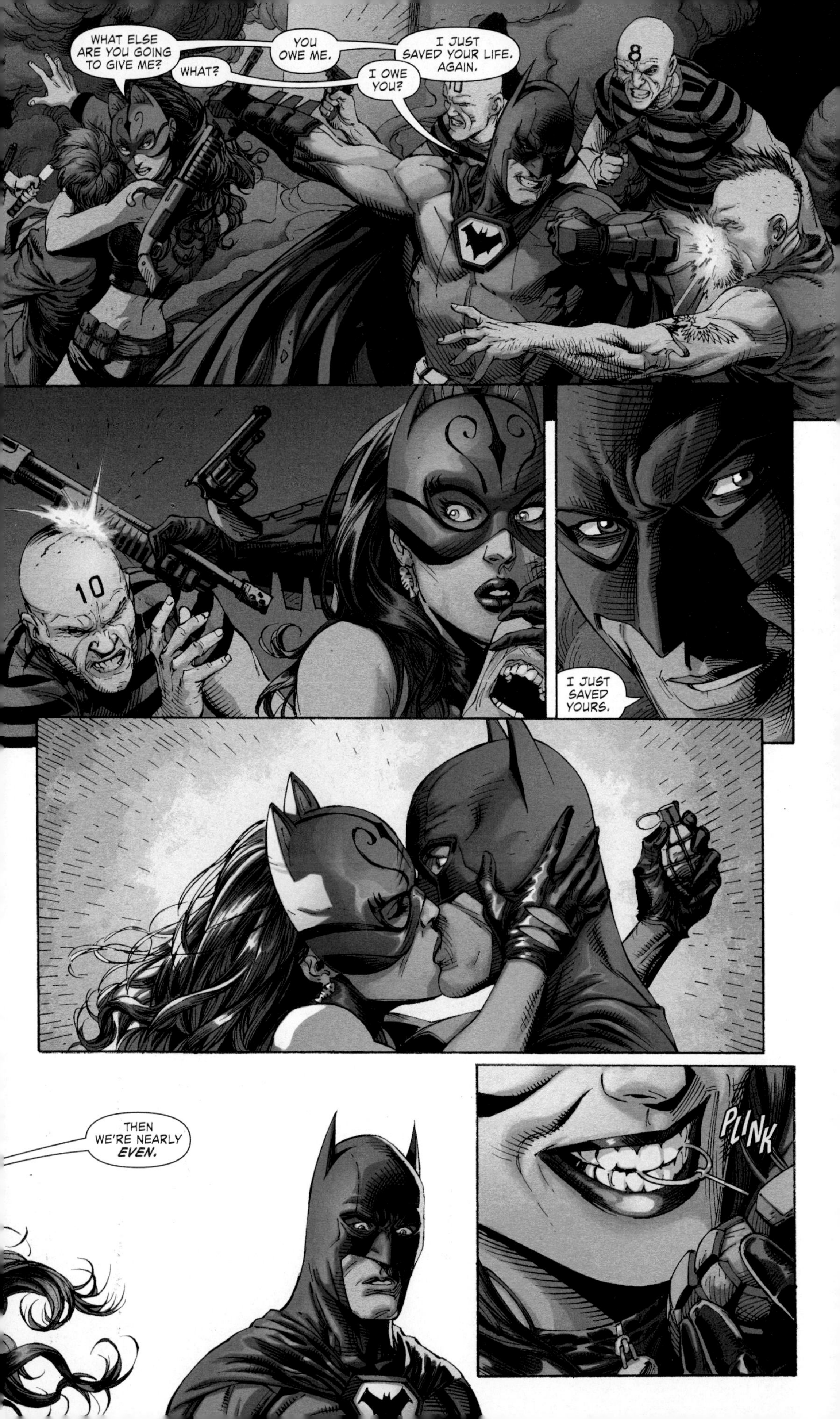

WHAT ELSE ARE YOU GOING TO GIVE ME?
WHAT?
YOU OWE ME.
I OWE YOU?
I JUST SAVED YOUR LIFE. AGAIN.
8
10
I JUST SAVED YOURS.
THEN WE'RE NEARLY *EVEN.*
PLINK

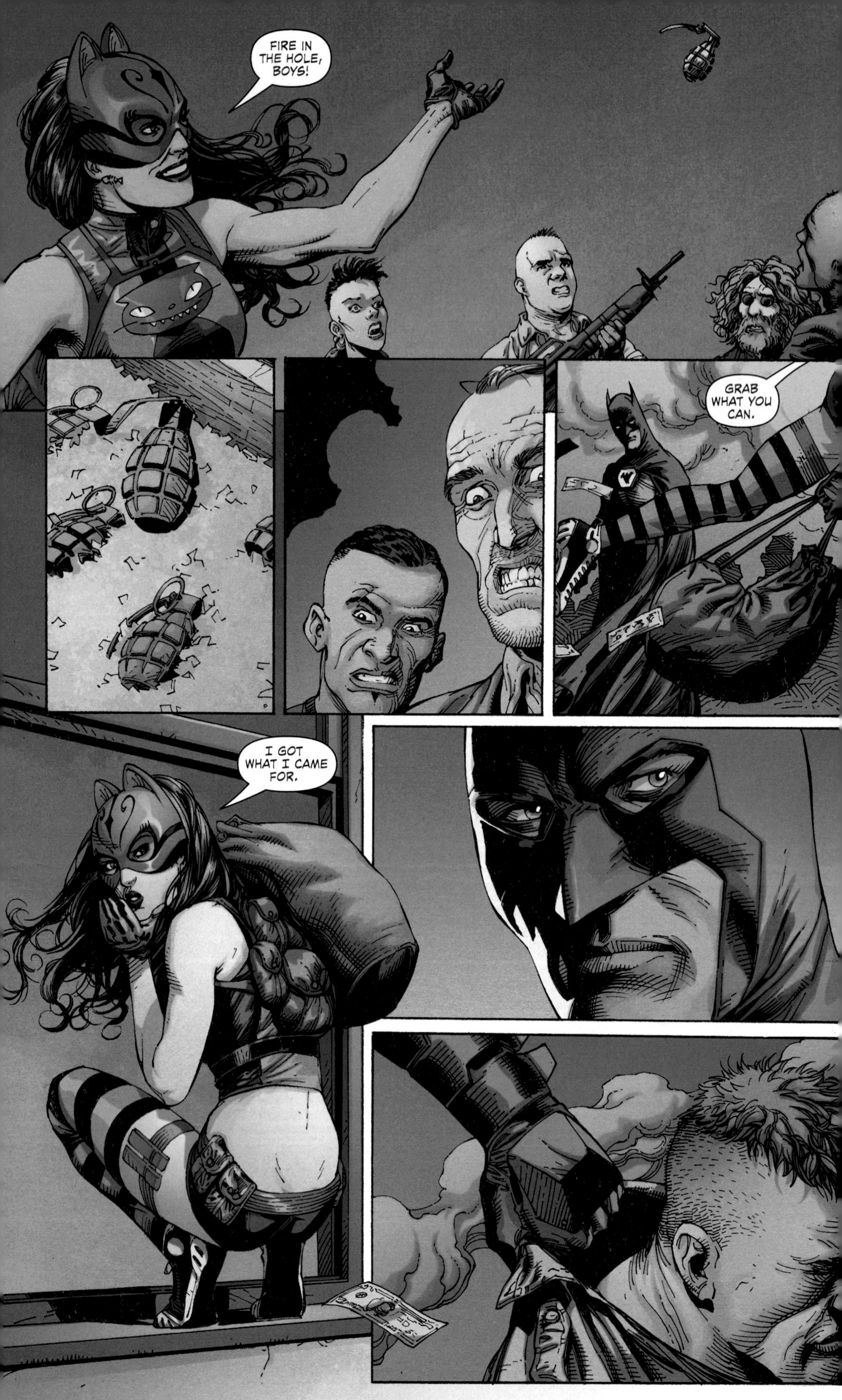
FIRE IN THE HOLE, BOYS!
GRAB WHAT YOU CAN.
I GOT WHAT I CAME FOR.

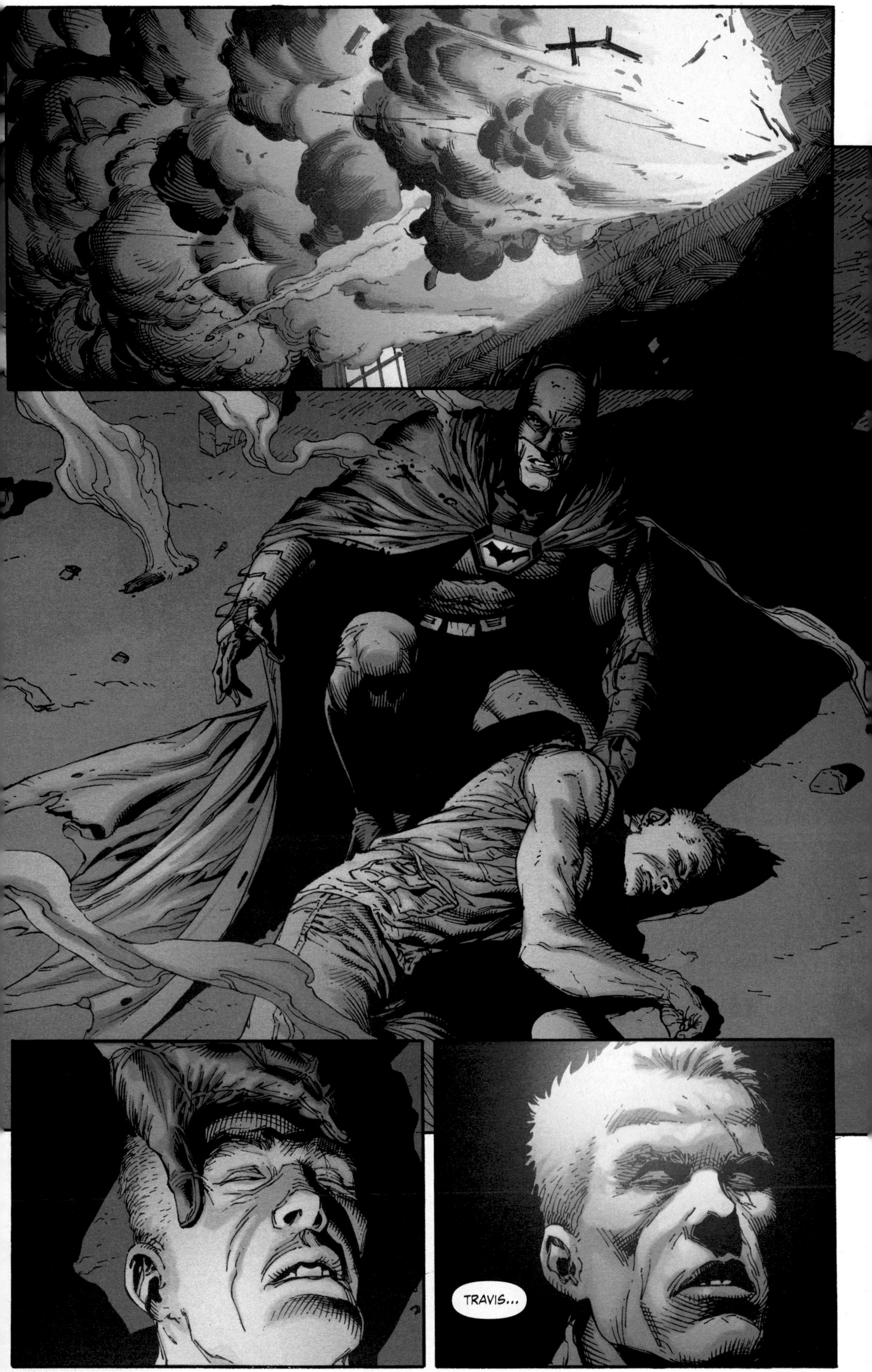
TRAVIS...

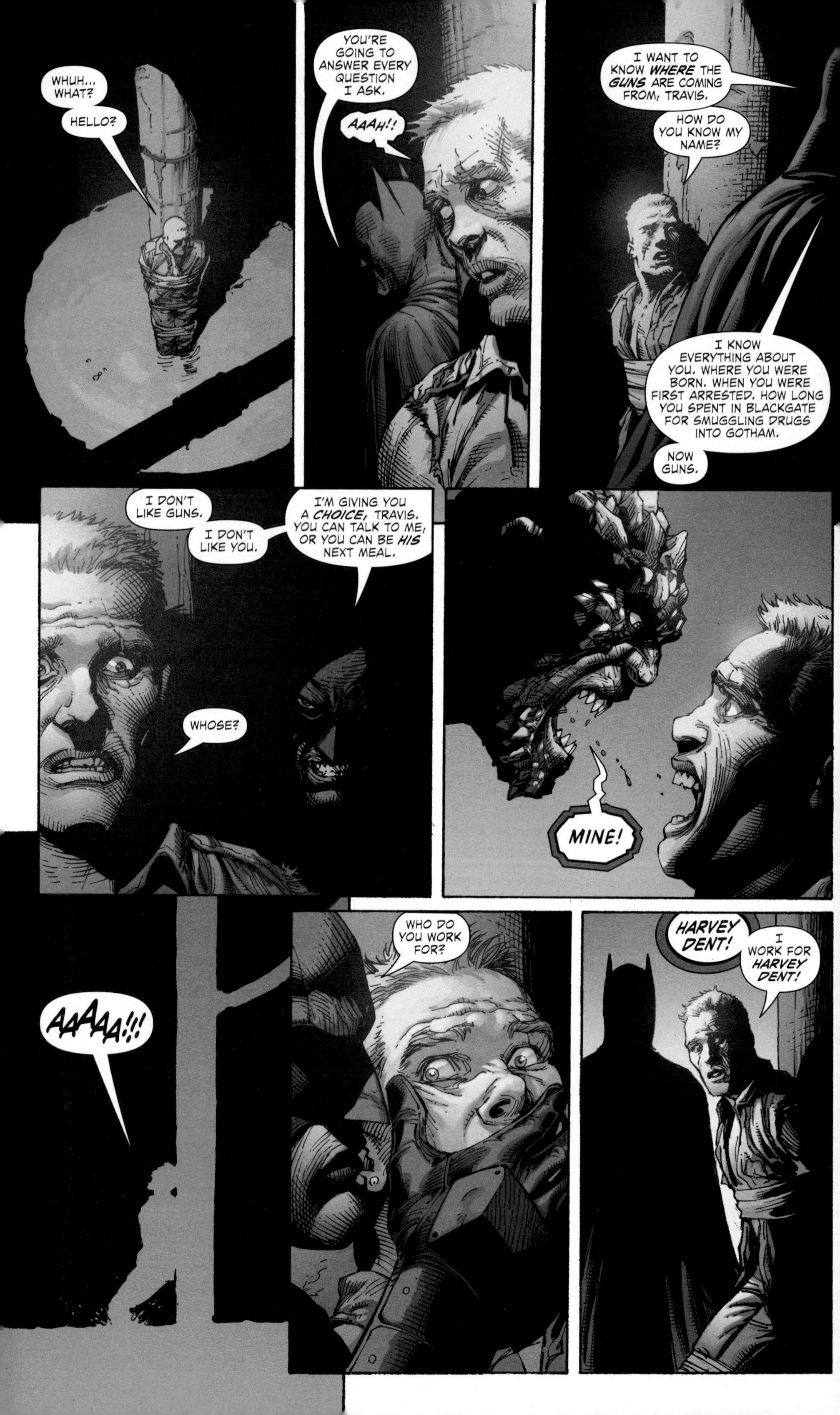
WHUH... WHAT?
HELLO?
YOU'RE GOING TO ANSWER EVERY QUESTION I ASK.
AAAH!!
I WANT TO KNOW WHERE THE GUNS ARE COMING FROM, TRAVIS.
HOW DO YOU KNOW MY NAME?
I KNOW EVERYTHING ABOUT YOU. WHERE YOU WERE BORN. WHEN YOU WERE FIRST ARRESTED. HOW LONG YOU SPENT IN BLACKGATE FOR SMUGGLING DRUGS INTO GOTHAM.
NOW GUNS.
I DON'T LIKE GUNS.
I DON'T LIKE YOU.
I'M GIVING YOU A CHOICE, TRAVIS. YOU CAN TALK TO ME, OR YOU CAN BE HIS NEXT MEAL.
WHOSE?
MINE!
AAAAA!!!
WHO DO YOU WORK FOR?
HARVEY DENT!
I WORK FOR HARVEY DENT!

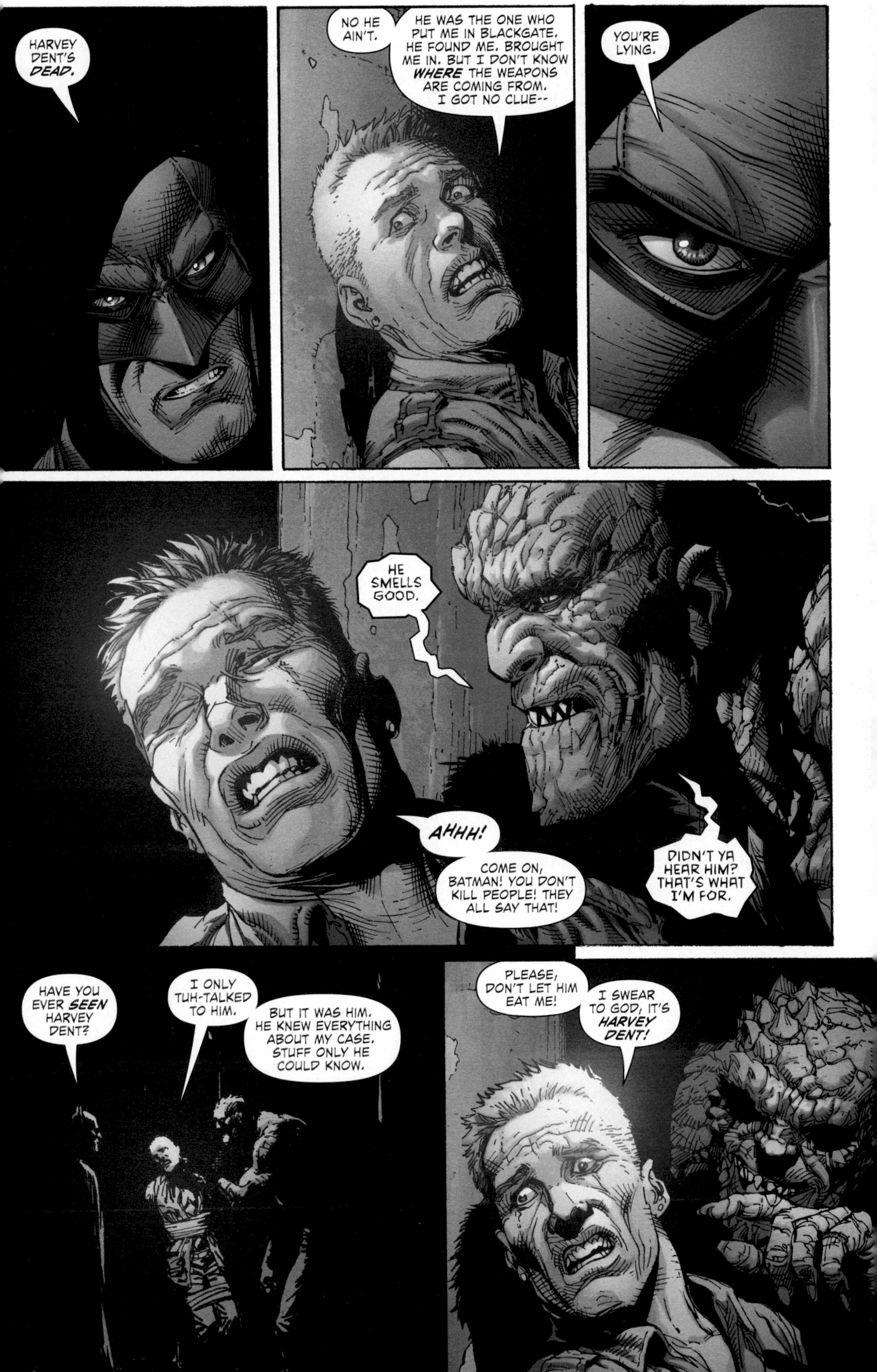
HARVEY DENT'S *DEAD.*
NO HE AIN'T.
HE WAS THE ONE WHO PUT ME IN BLACKGATE. HE FOUND ME. BROUGHT ME IN. BUT I DON'T KNOW *WHERE* THE WEAPONS ARE COMING FROM. I GOT NO CLUE--
YOU'RE LYING.
HE SMELLS GOOD.
AHHH!
COME ON, BATMAN! YOU DON'T KILL PEOPLE! THEY ALL SAY THAT!
DIDN'T YA HEAR HIM? THAT'S WHAT I'M FOR.
HAVE YOU EVER *SEEN* HARVEY DENT?
I ONLY TUH-TALKED TO HIM.
BUT IT WAS HIM. HE KNEW EVERYTHING ABOUT MY CASE. STUFF ONLY HE COULD KNOW.
PLEASE, DON'T LET HIM EAT ME!
I SWEAR TO GOD, IT'S *HARVEY DENT!*

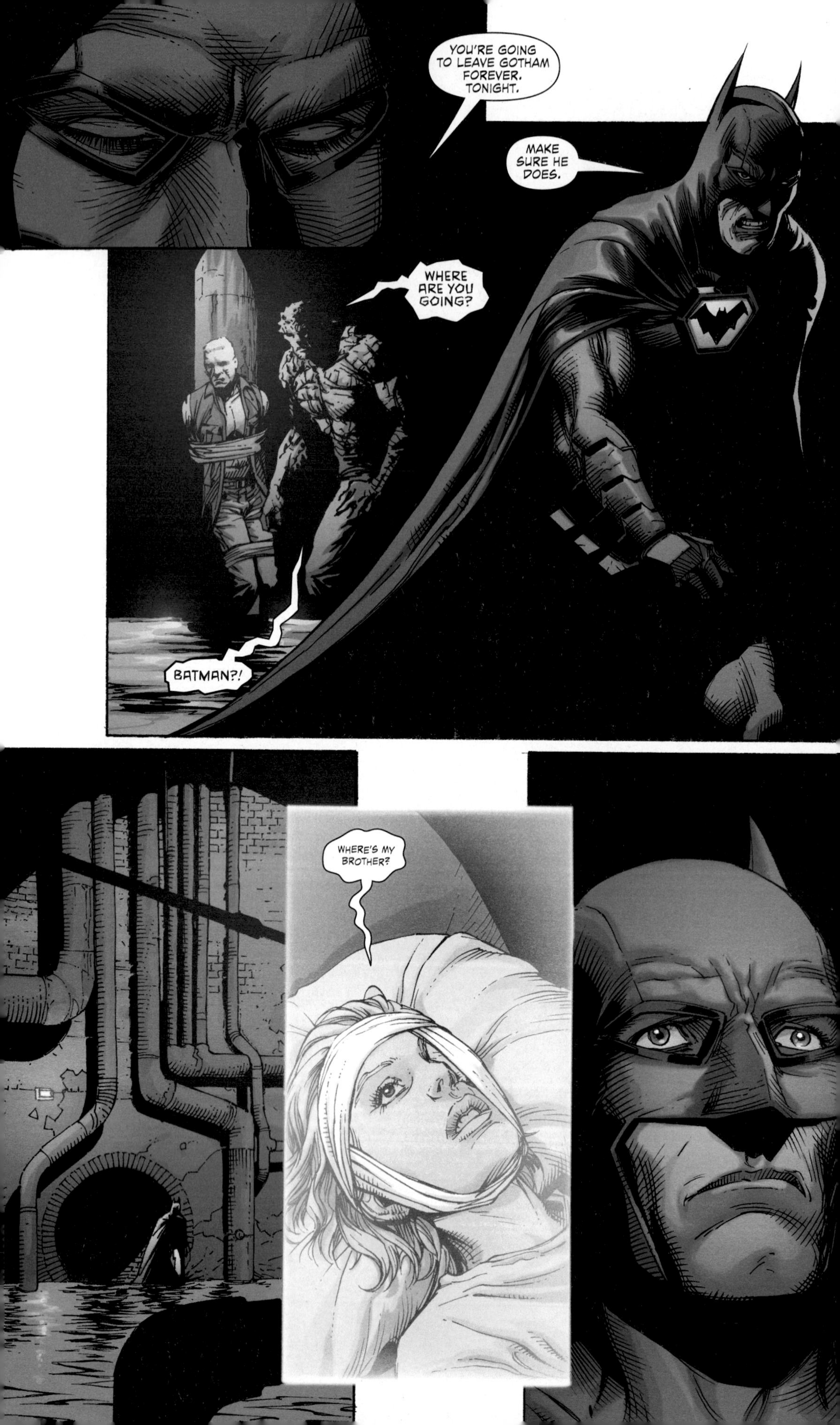
YOU'RE GOING TO LEAVE GOTHAM FOREVER. TONIGHT.
MAKE SURE HE DOES.
WHERE ARE YOU GOING?
BATMAN?!
WHERE'S MY BROTHER?

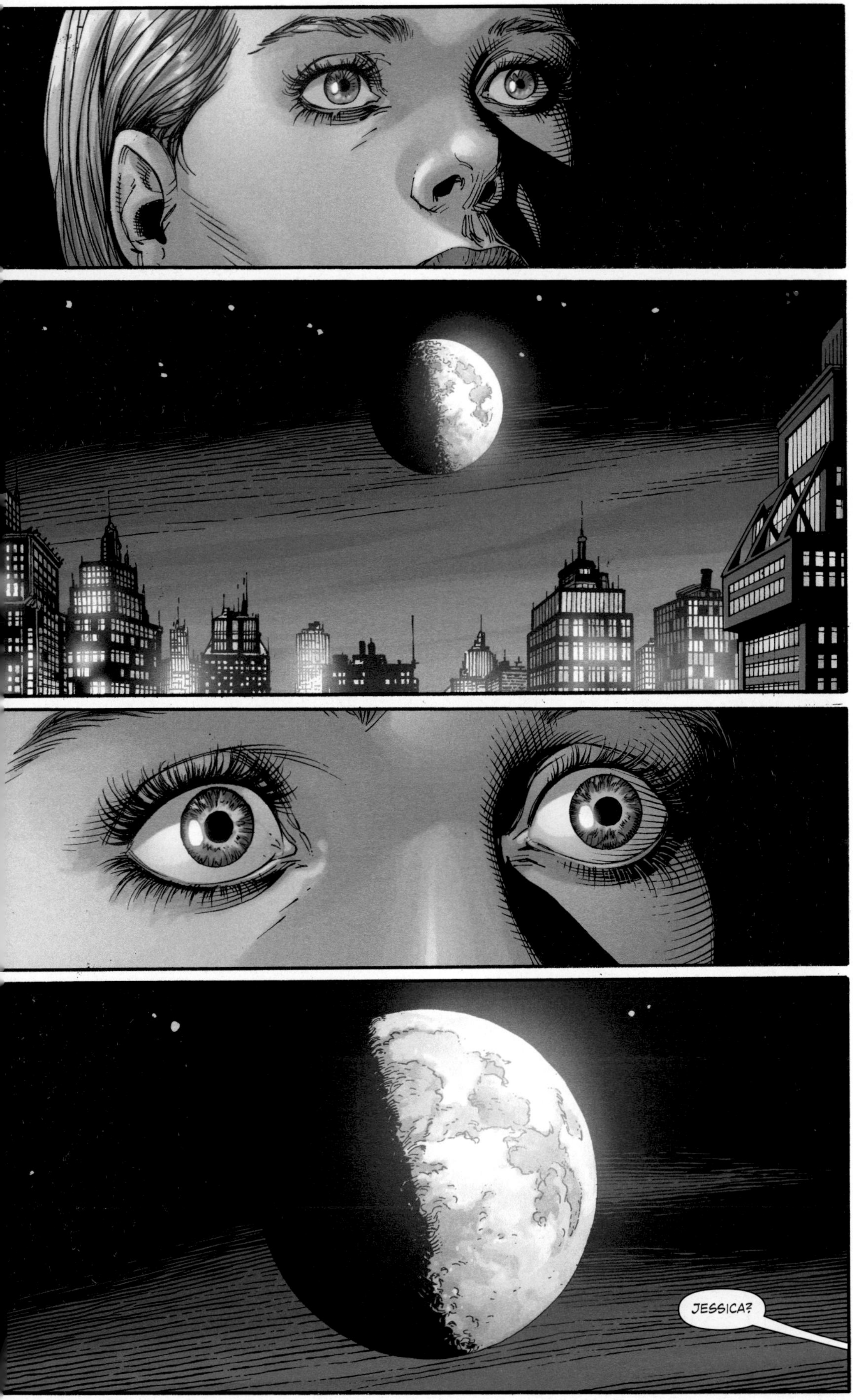
JESSICA?

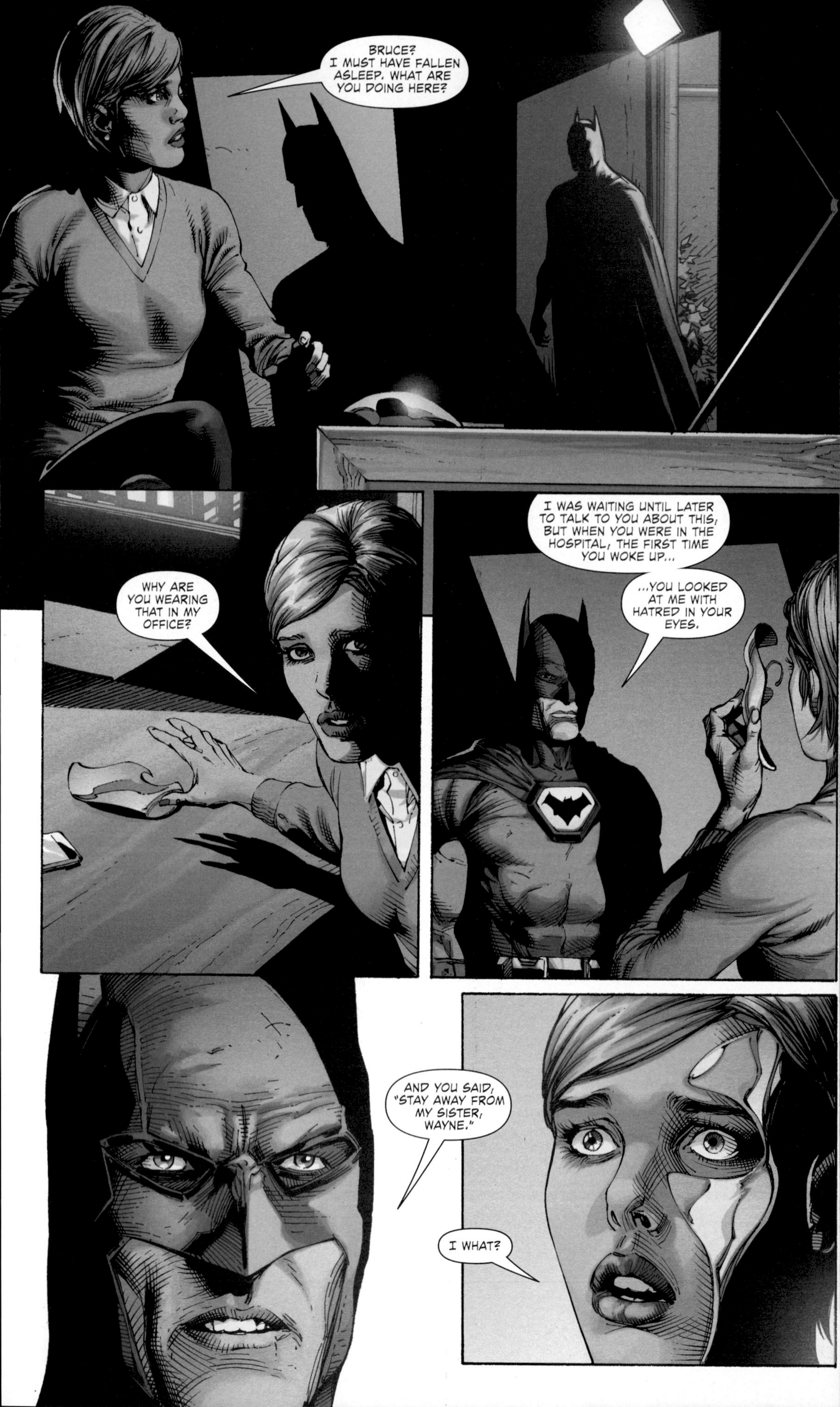

BRUCE? I MUST HAVE FALLEN ASLEEP. WHAT ARE YOU DOING HERE?
WHY ARE YOU WEARING THAT IN MY OFFICE?
I WAS WAITING UNTIL LATER TO TALK TO YOU ABOUT THIS, BUT WHEN YOU WERE IN THE HOSPITAL, THE FIRST TIME YOU WOKE UP...
...YOU LOOKED AT ME WITH HATRED IN YOUR EYES.
AND YOU SAID, "STAY AWAY FROM MY SISTER, WAYNE."
I WHAT?

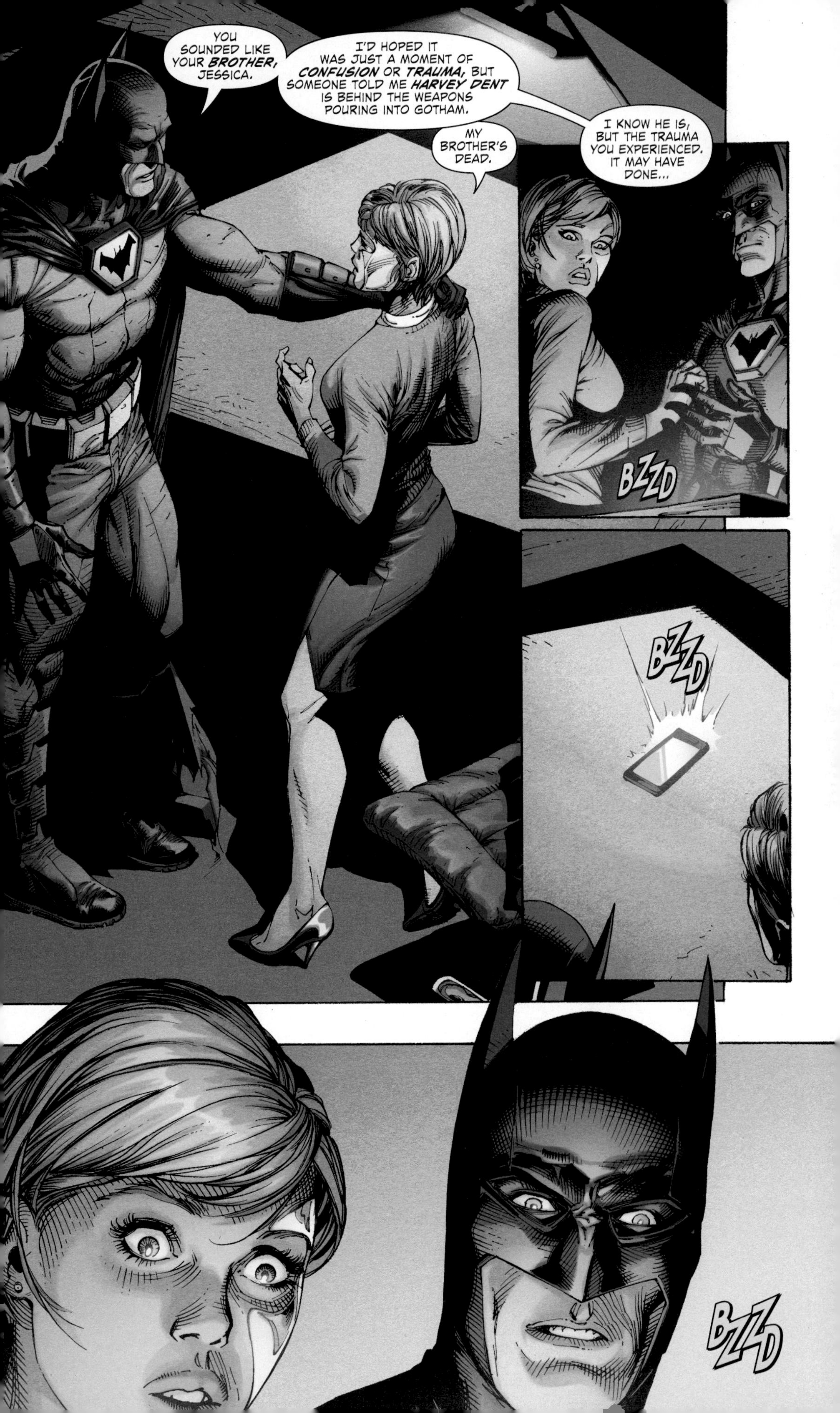
YOU SOUNDED LIKE YOUR BROTHER, JESSICA.
I'D HOPED IT WAS JUST A MOMENT OF CONFUSION OR TRAUMA, BUT SOMEONE TOLD ME HARVEY DENT IS BEHIND THE WEAPONS POURING INTO GOTHAM.
MY BROTHER'S DEAD.
I KNOW HE IS, BUT THE TRAUMA YOU EXPERIENCED. IT MAY HAVE DONE...
BZZD
BZZD
BZZD

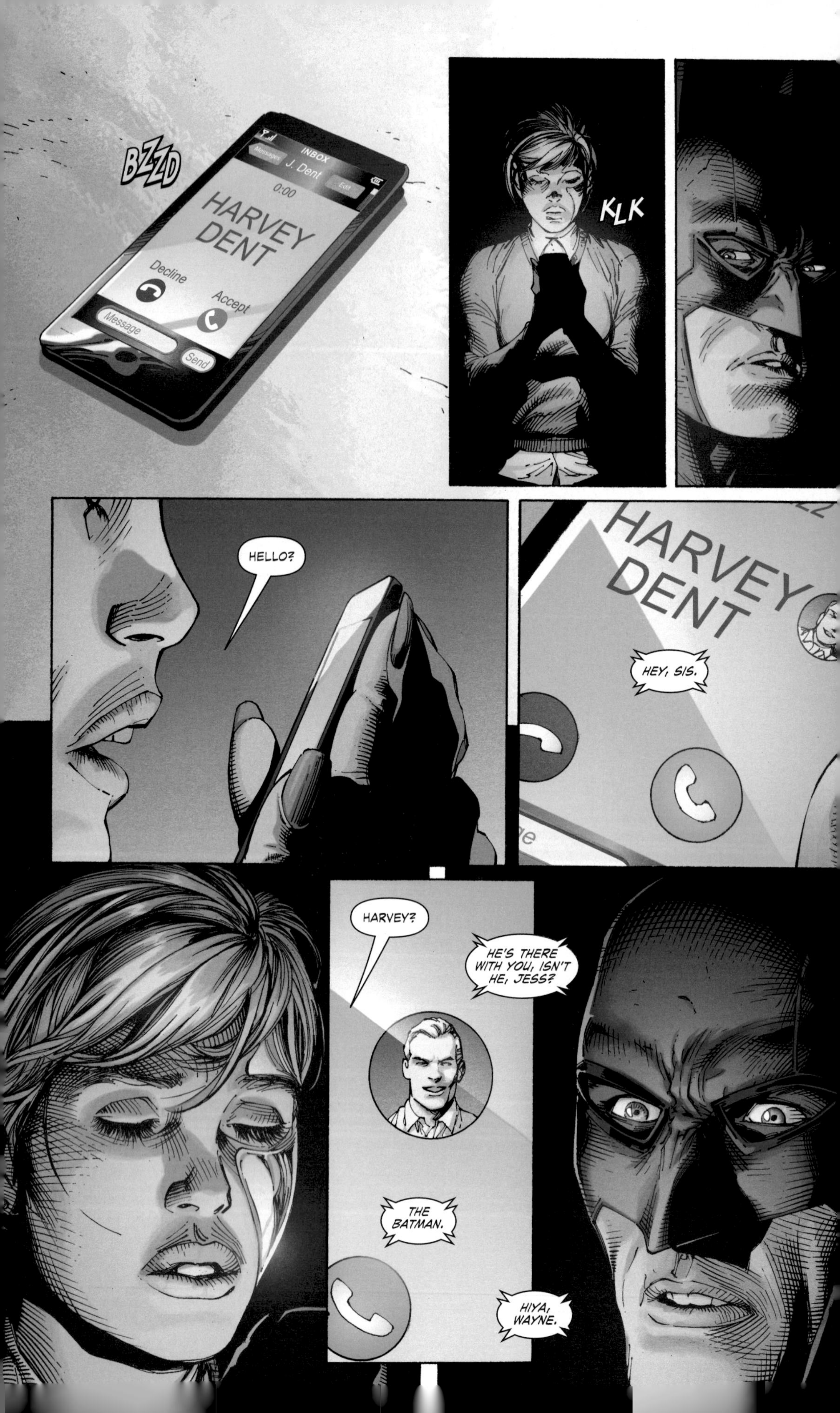
BZZD
INBOX
Messages
J. Dent
Edit
0:00
HARVEY DENT
Decline
Accept
Message
Send
KLK
HELLO?
HARVEY DENT
HEY, SIS.
HARVEY?
HE'S THERE WITH YOU, ISN'T HE, JESS?
THE BATMAN.
HIYA, WAYNE.

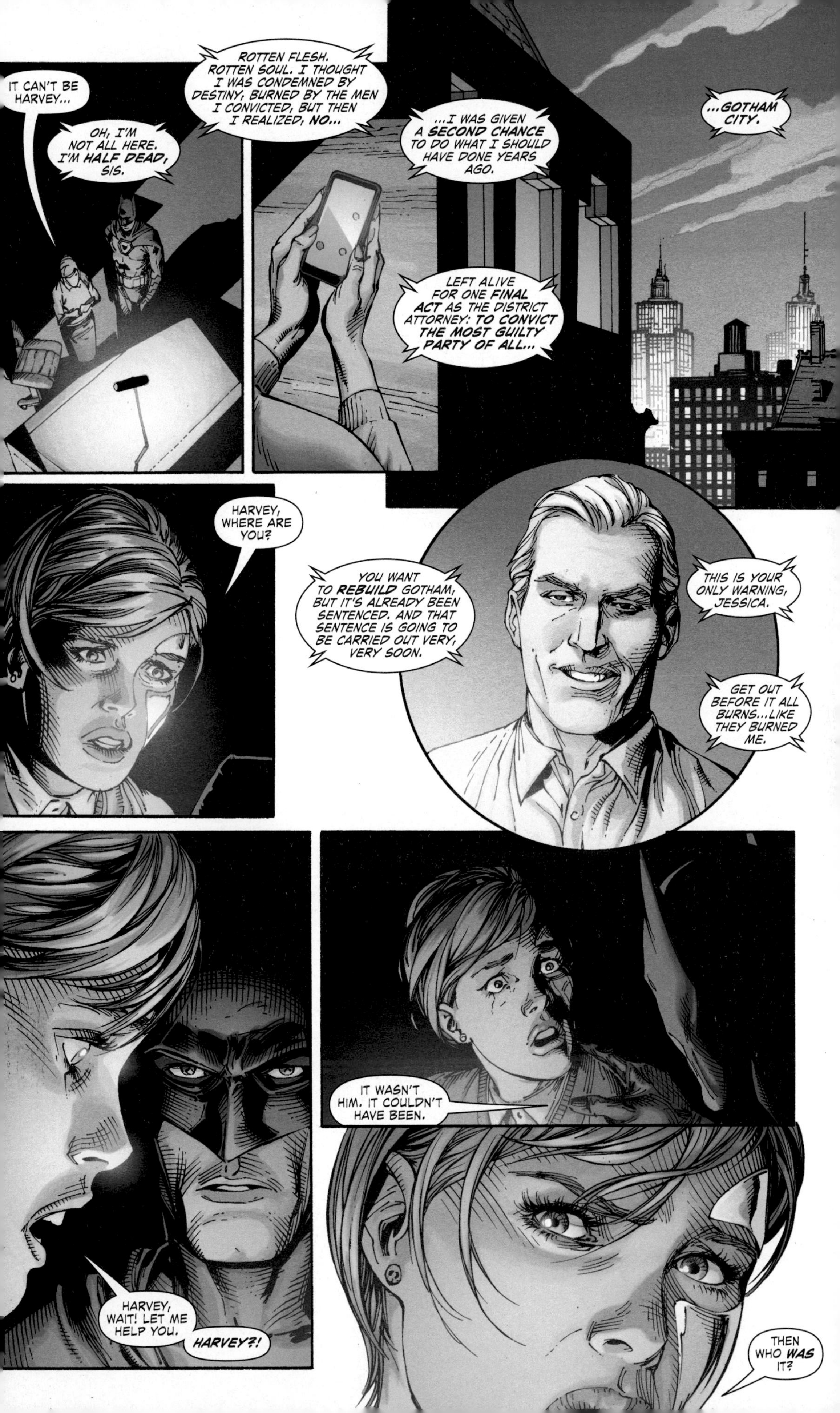

IT CAN'T BE HARVEY...
OH, I'M NOT ALL HERE. I'M **HALF DEAD,** SIS.
ROTTEN FLESH. ROTTEN SOUL. I THOUGHT I WAS CONDEMNED BY DESTINY, BURNED BY THE MEN I CONVICTED, BUT THEN I REALIZED, **NO...**
...I WAS GIVEN A **SECOND CHANCE** TO DO WHAT I SHOULD HAVE DONE YEARS AGO.
LEFT ALIVE FOR ONE **FINAL ACT** AS THE DISTRICT ATTORNEY: **TO CONVICT THE MOST GUILTY PARTY OF ALL...**
...GOTHAM CITY.
HARVEY, WHERE ARE YOU?
YOU WANT TO **REBUILD** GOTHAM, BUT IT'S ALREADY BEEN SENTENCED. AND THAT SENTENCE IS GOING TO BE CARRIED OUT VERY, VERY SOON.
THIS IS YOUR ONLY WARNING, JESSICA.
GET OUT BEFORE IT ALL BURNS...LIKE THEY BURNED ME.
HARVEY, WAIT! LET ME HELP YOU.
HARVEY?!
IT WASN'T HIM. IT COULDN'T HAVE BEEN.
THEN WHO **WAS** IT?

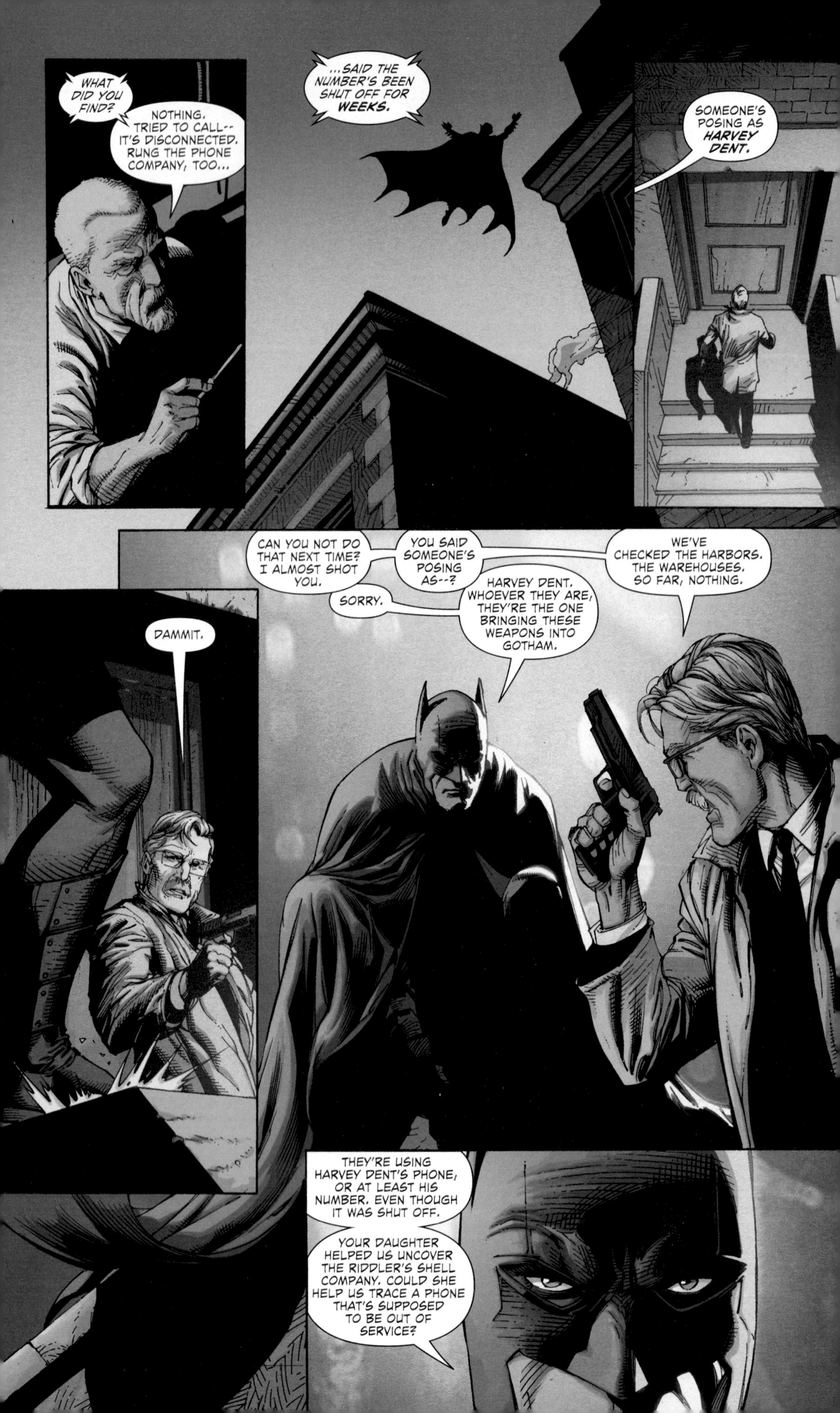
WHAT DID YOU FIND?
NOTHING. TRIED TO CALL-- IT'S DISCONNECTED. RUNG THE PHONE COMPANY, TOO...
...SAID THE NUMBER'S BEEN SHUT OFF FOR WEEKS.
SOMEONE'S POSING AS HARVEY DENT.
CAN YOU NOT DO THAT NEXT TIME? I ALMOST SHOT YOU.
SORRY.
YOU SAID SOMEONE'S POSING AS--?
HARVEY DENT. WHOEVER THEY ARE, THEY'RE THE ONE BRINGING THESE WEAPONS INTO GOTHAM.
WE'VE CHECKED THE HARBORS. THE WAREHOUSES. SO FAR, NOTHING.
DAMMIT.
THEY'RE USING HARVEY DENT'S PHONE, OR AT LEAST HIS NUMBER. EVEN THOUGH IT WAS SHUT OFF.
YOUR DAUGHTER HELPED US UNCOVER THE RIDDLER'S SHELL COMPANY. COULD SHE HELP US TRACE A PHONE THAT'S SUPPOSED TO BE OUT OF SERVICE?

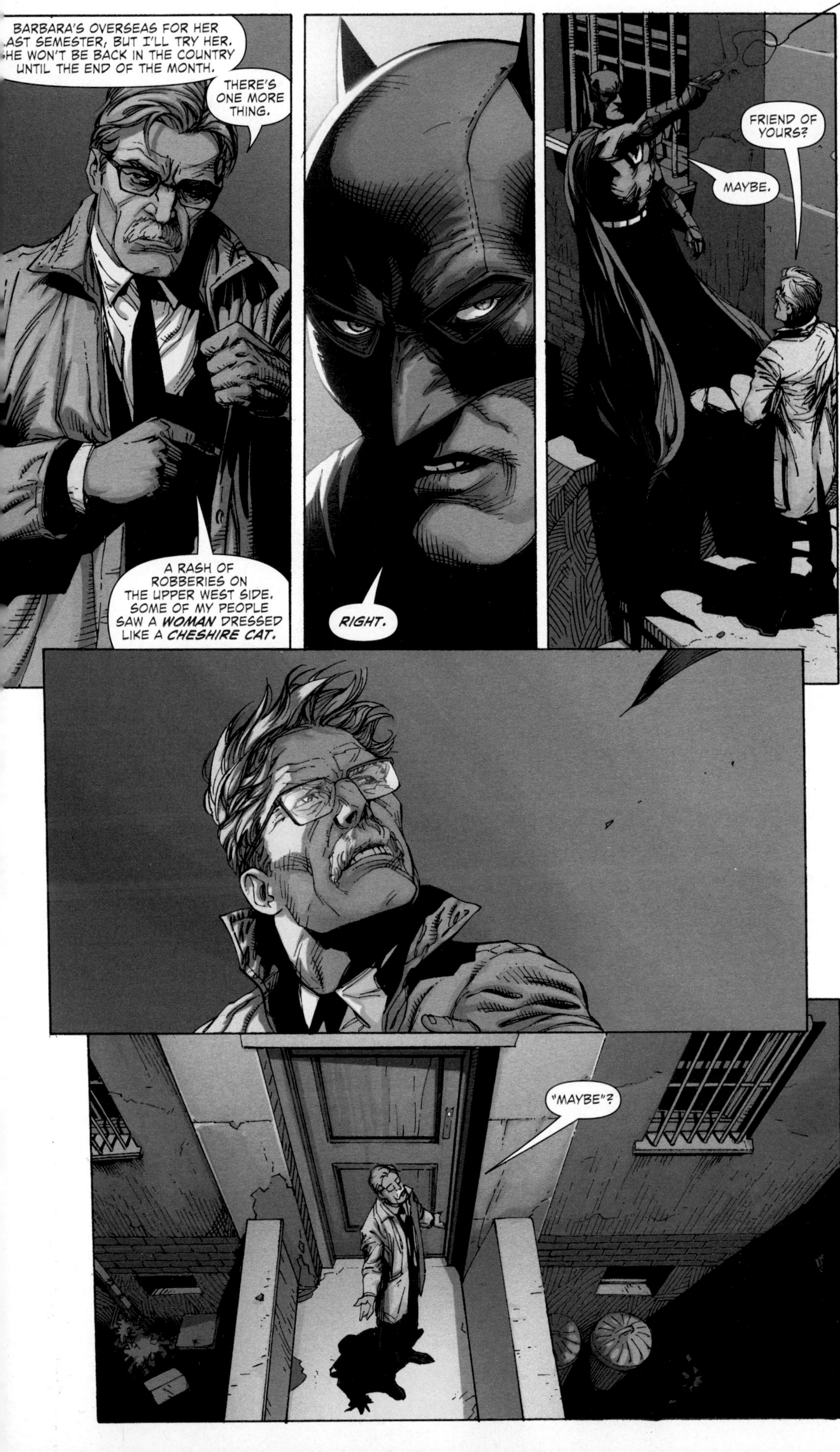

BARBARA'S OVERSEAS FOR HER AST SEMESTER, BUT I'LL TRY HER. HE WON'T BE BACK IN THE COUNTRY UNTIL THE END OF THE MONTH.
THERE'S ONE MORE THING.
A RASH OF ROBBERIES ON THE UPPER WEST SIDE. SOME OF MY PEOPLE SAW A *WOMAN* DRESSED LIKE A *CHESHIRE CAT.*
RIGHT.
FRIEND OF YOURS?
MAYBE.
"MAYBE"?

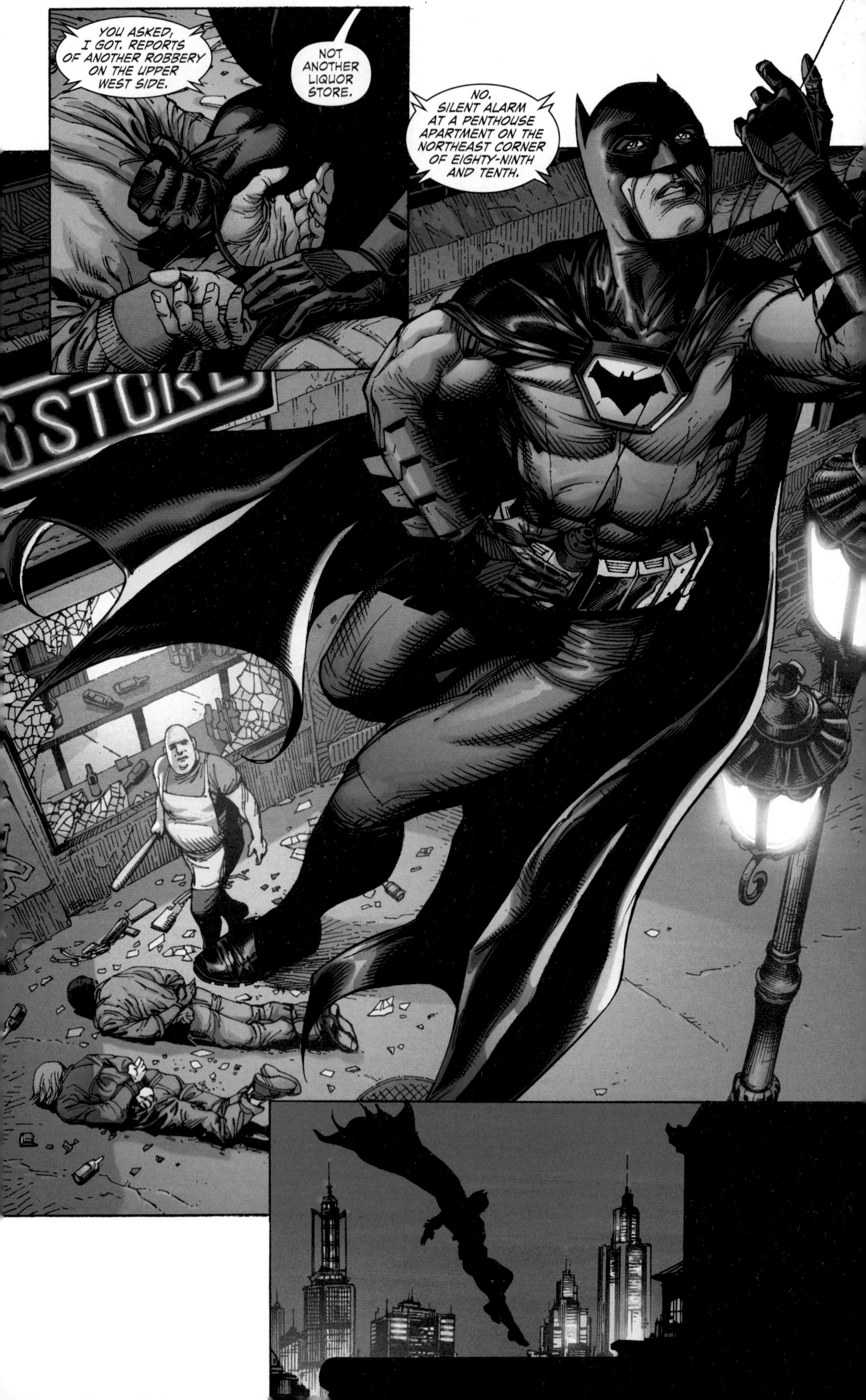
YOU ASKED, I GOT. REPORTS OF ANOTHER ROBBERY ON THE UPPER WEST SIDE.
NOT ANOTHER LIQUOR STORE.
NO. SILENT ALARM AT A PENTHOUSE APARTMENT ON THE NORTHEAST CORNER OF EIGHTY-NINTH AND TENTH.
STORE

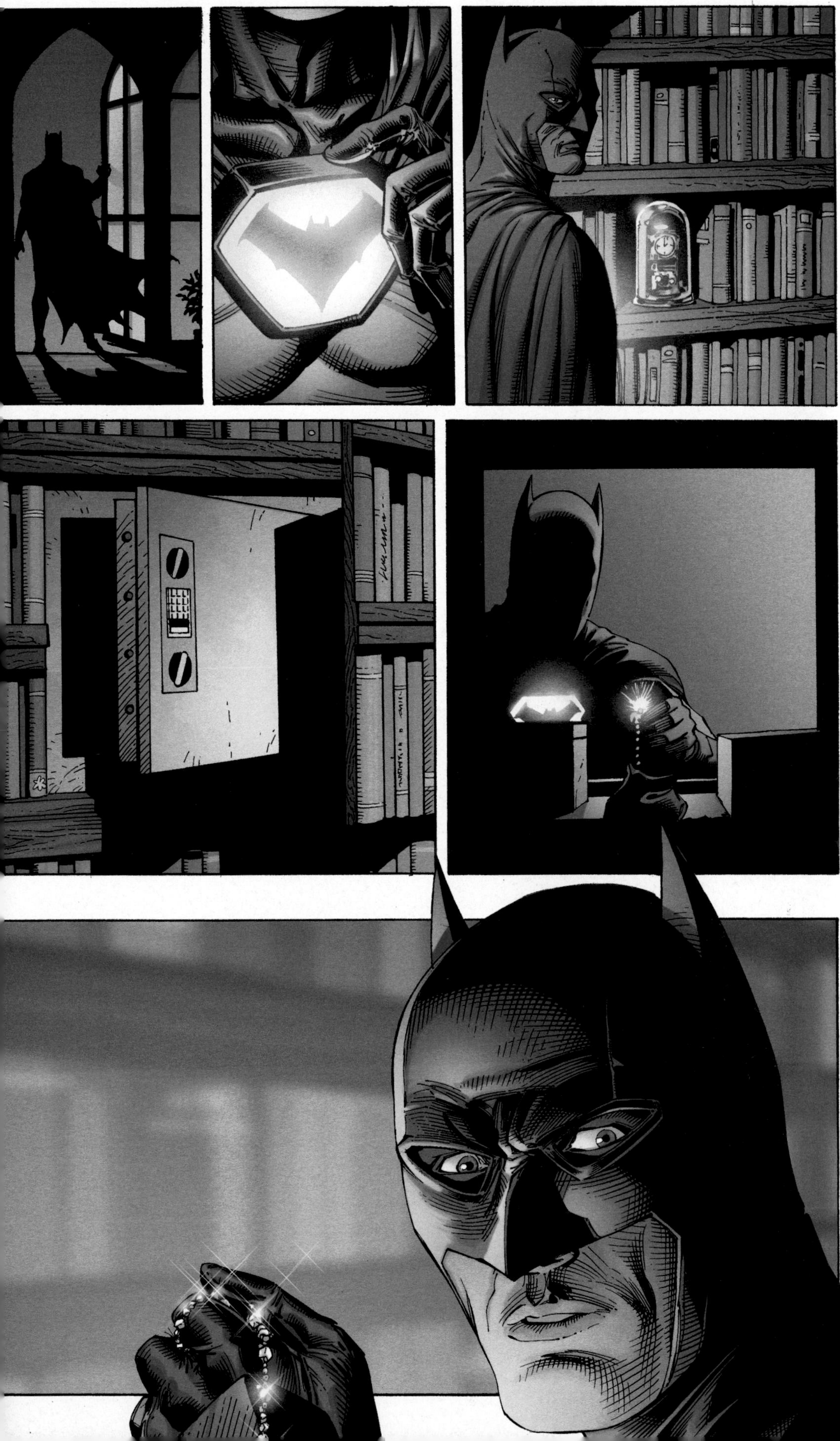

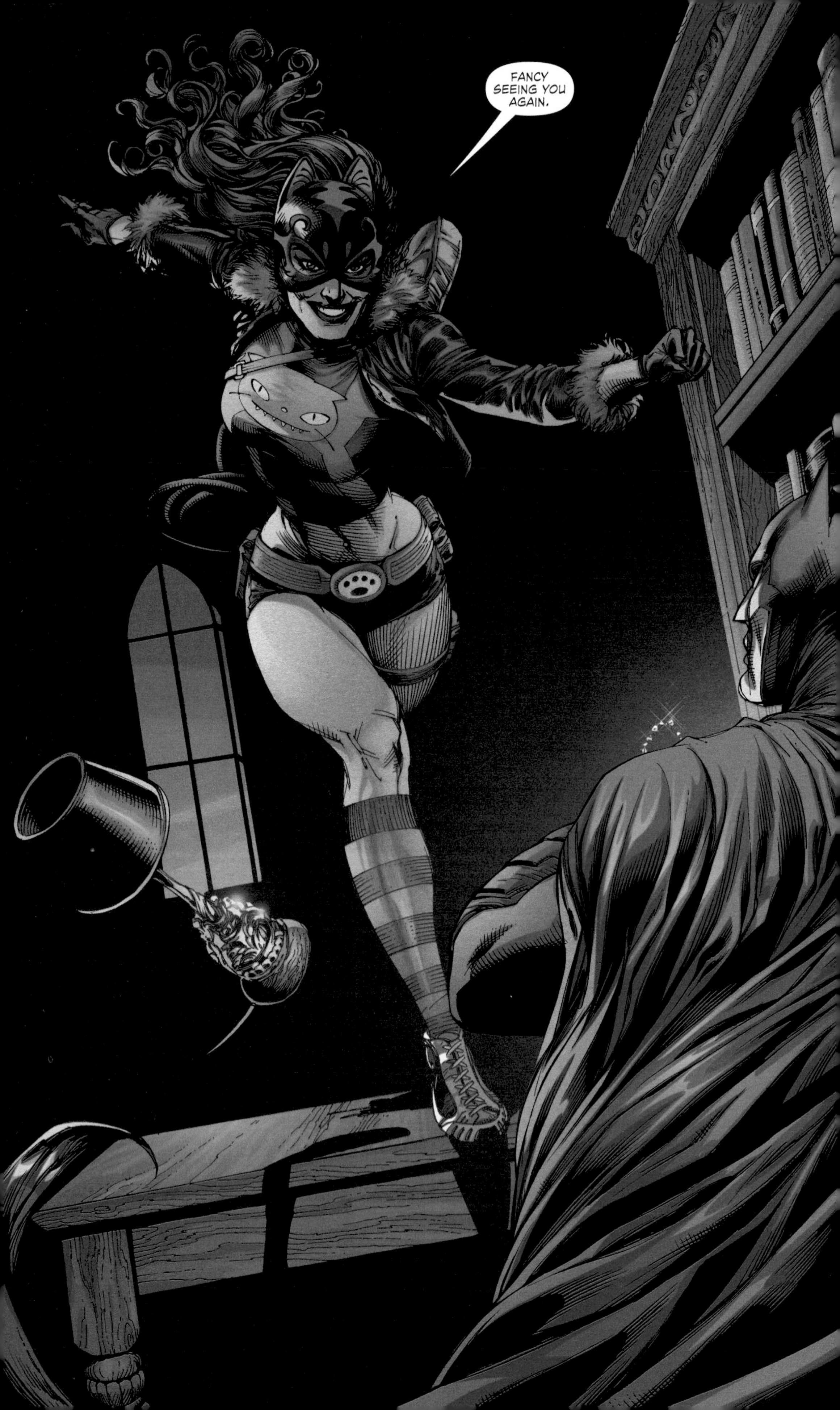
FANCY SEEING YOU AGAIN.

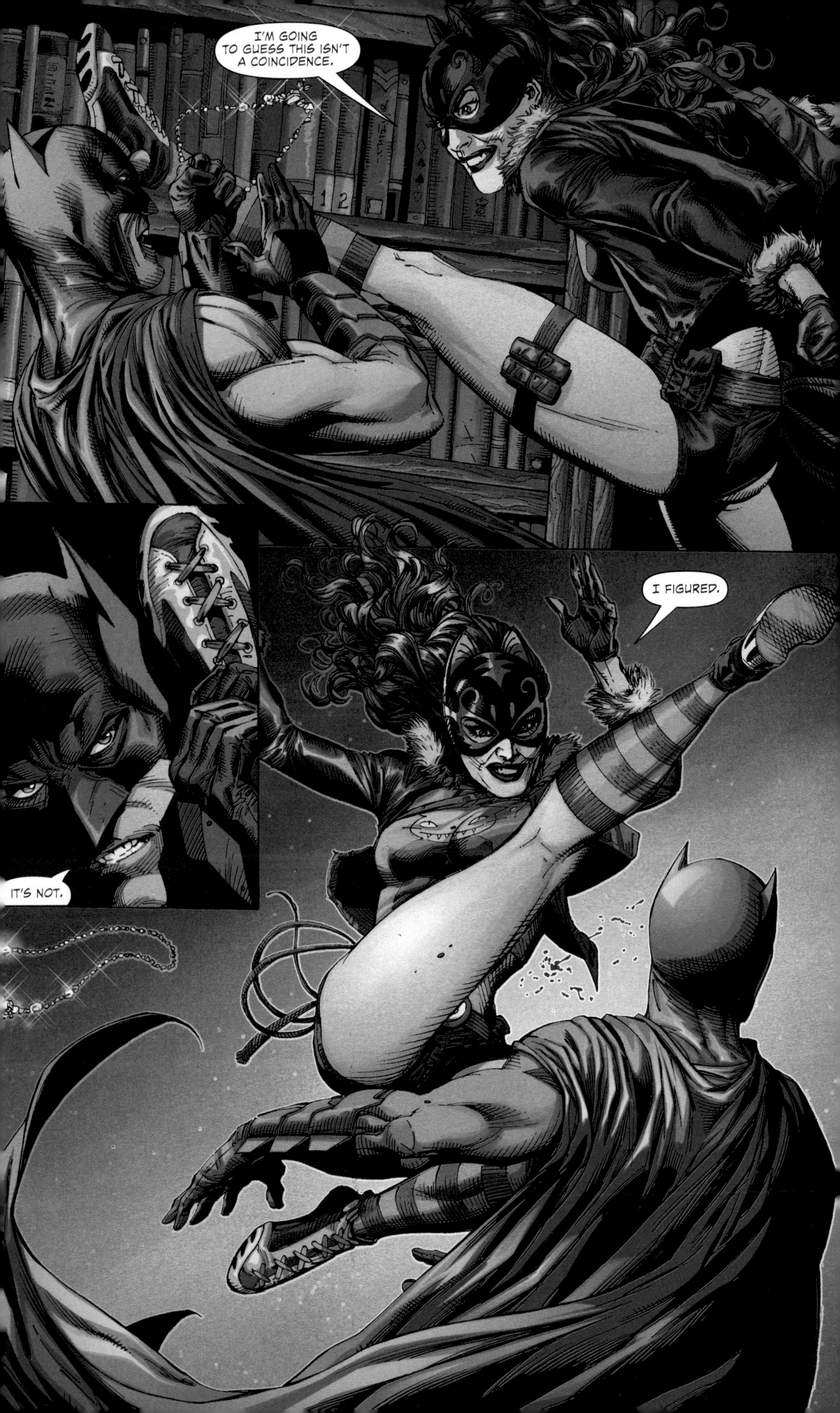
I'M GOING TO GUESS THIS ISN'T A COINCIDENCE.
I FIGURED.
IT'S NOT.

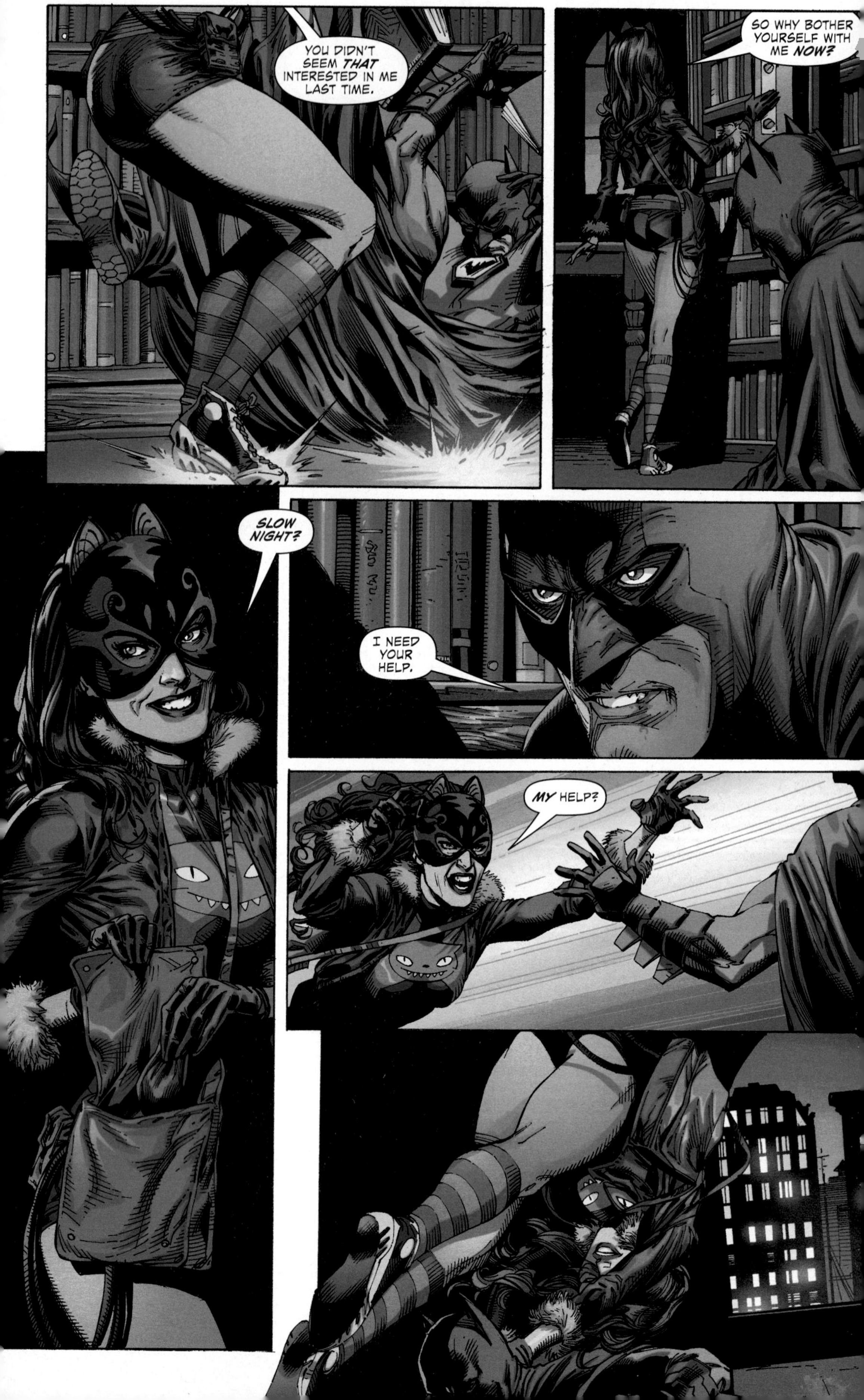
YOU DIDN'T SEEM THAT INTERESTED IN ME LAST TIME.
SO WHY BOTHER YOURSELF WITH ME NOW?
SLOW NIGHT?
I NEED YOUR HELP.
MY HELP?

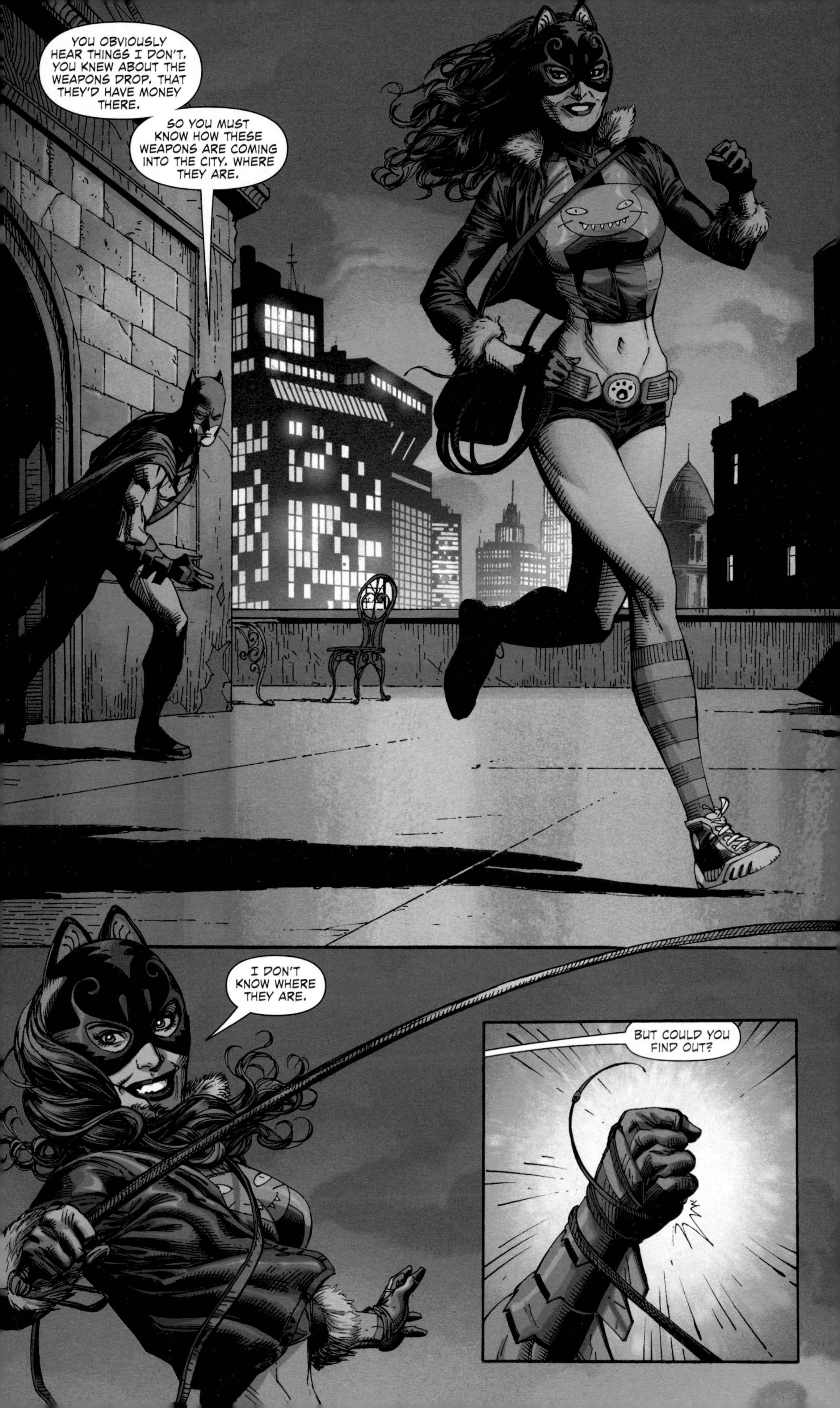
YOU OBVIOUSLY HEAR THINGS I DON'T. YOU KNEW ABOUT THE WEAPONS DROP. THAT THEY'D HAVE MONEY THERE.
SO YOU MUST KNOW HOW THESE WEAPONS ARE COMING INTO THE CITY. WHERE THEY ARE.
I DON'T KNOW WHERE THEY ARE.
BUT COULD YOU FIND OUT?

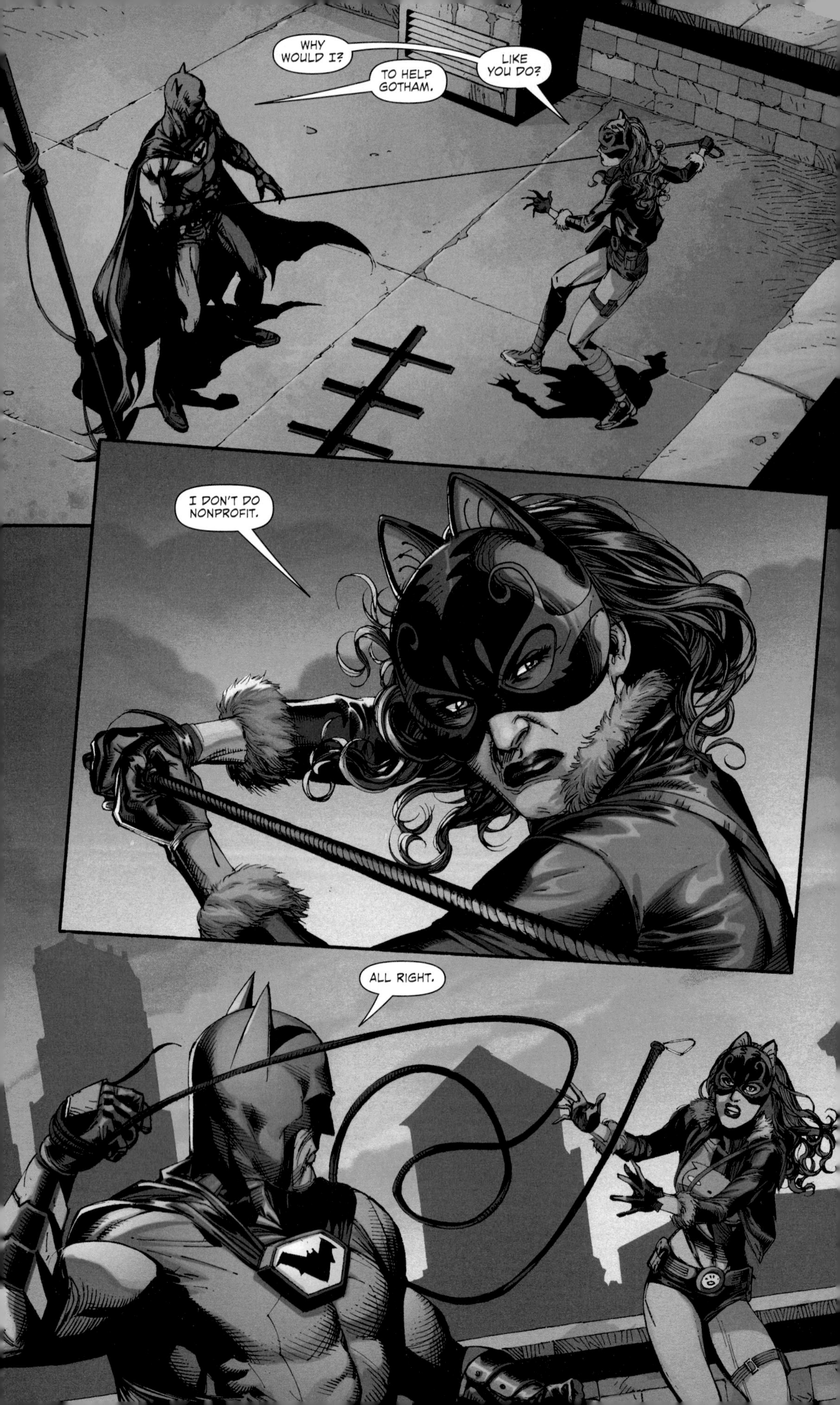
WHY WOULD I?
TO HELP GOTHAM.
LIKE YOU DO?
I DON'T DO NONPROFIT.
ALL RIGHT.

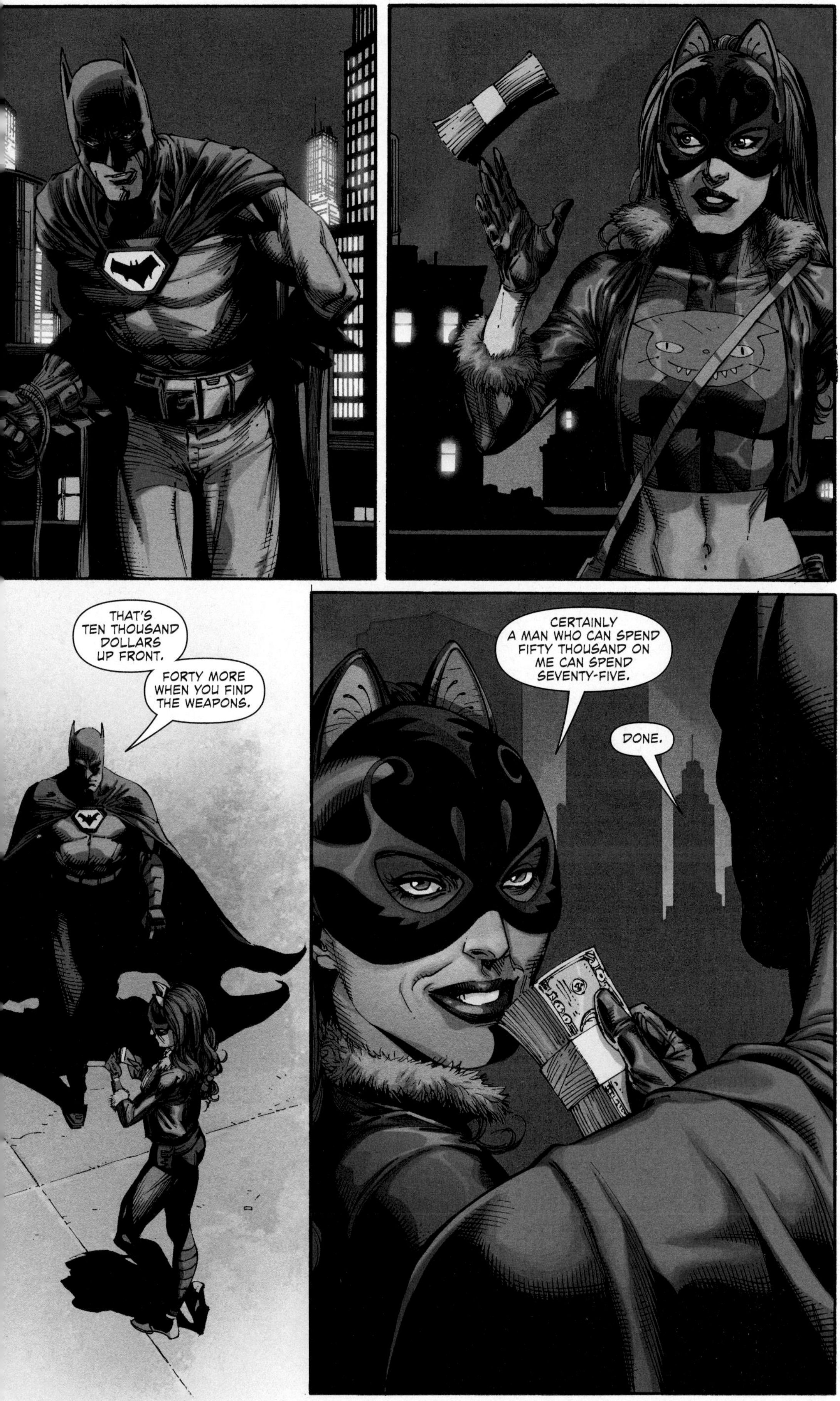
THAT'S TEN THOUSAND DOLLARS UP FRONT.
FORTY MORE WHEN YOU FIND THE WEAPONS.
CERTAINLY A MAN WHO CAN SPEND FIFTY THOUSAND ON ME CAN SPEND SEVENTY-FIVE.
DONE.

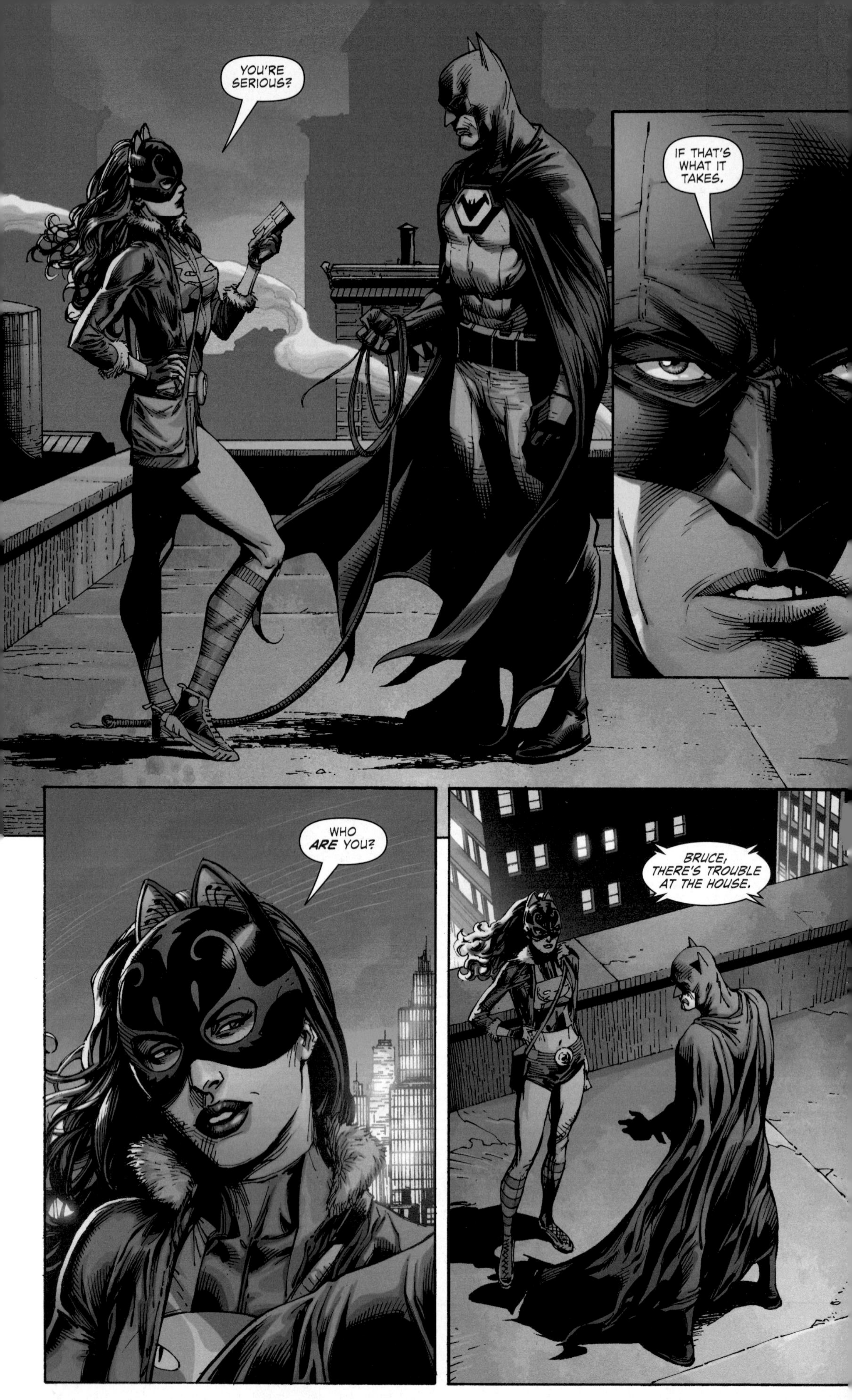

YOU'RE SERIOUS?
IF THAT'S WHAT IT TAKES.
WHO ARE YOU?
BRUCE, THERE'S TROUBLE AT THE HOUSE.

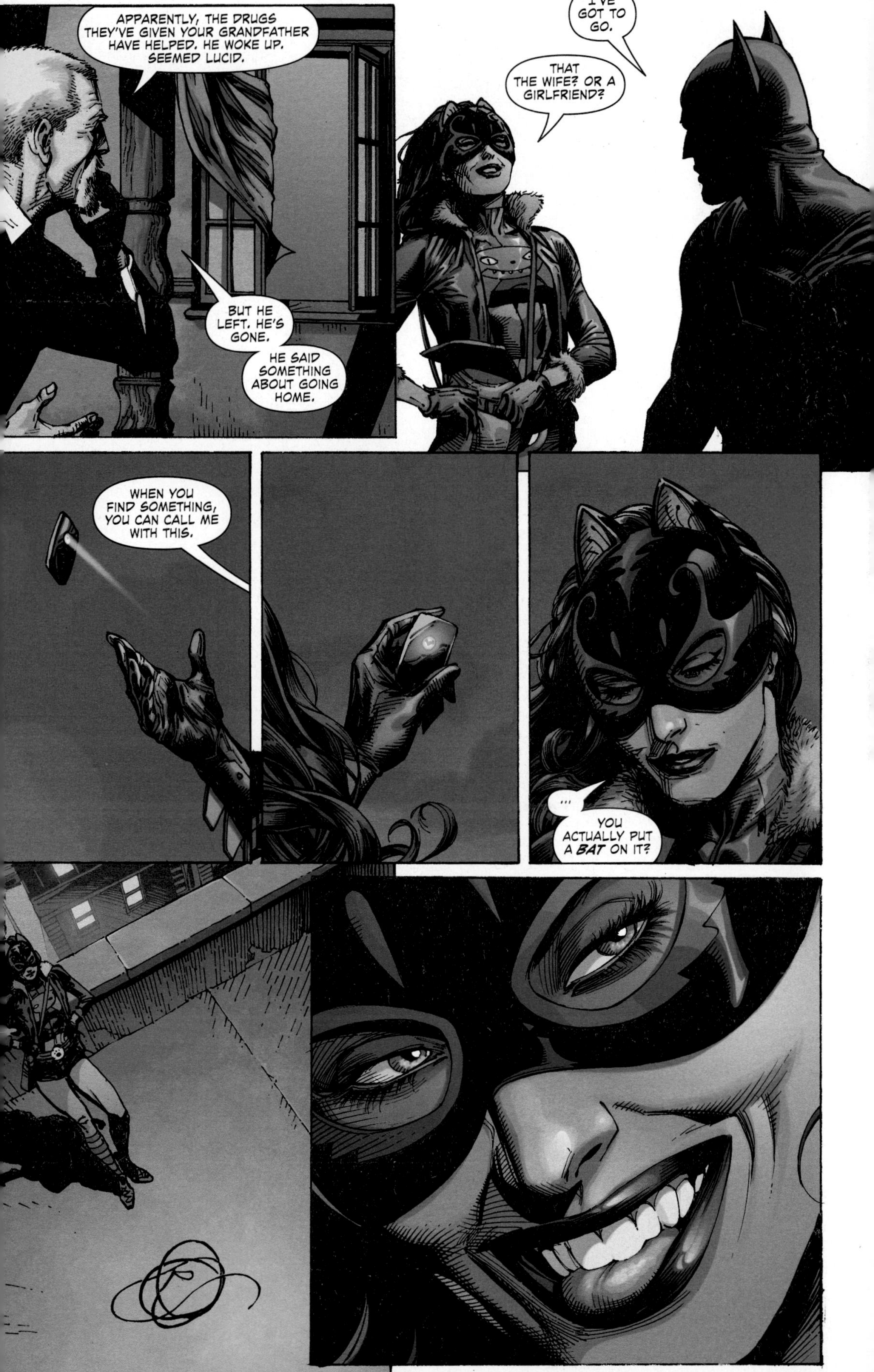
APPARENTLY, THE DRUGS THEY'VE GIVEN YOUR GRANDFATHER HAVE HELPED. HE WOKE UP. SEEMED LUCID.
BUT HE LEFT. HE'S GONE.
HE SAID SOMETHING ABOUT GOING HOME.
I'VE GOT TO GO.
THAT THE WIFE? OR A GIRLFRIEND?
WHEN YOU FIND SOMETHING, YOU CAN CALL ME WITH THIS.
...
YOU ACTUALLY PUT A *BAT* ON IT?

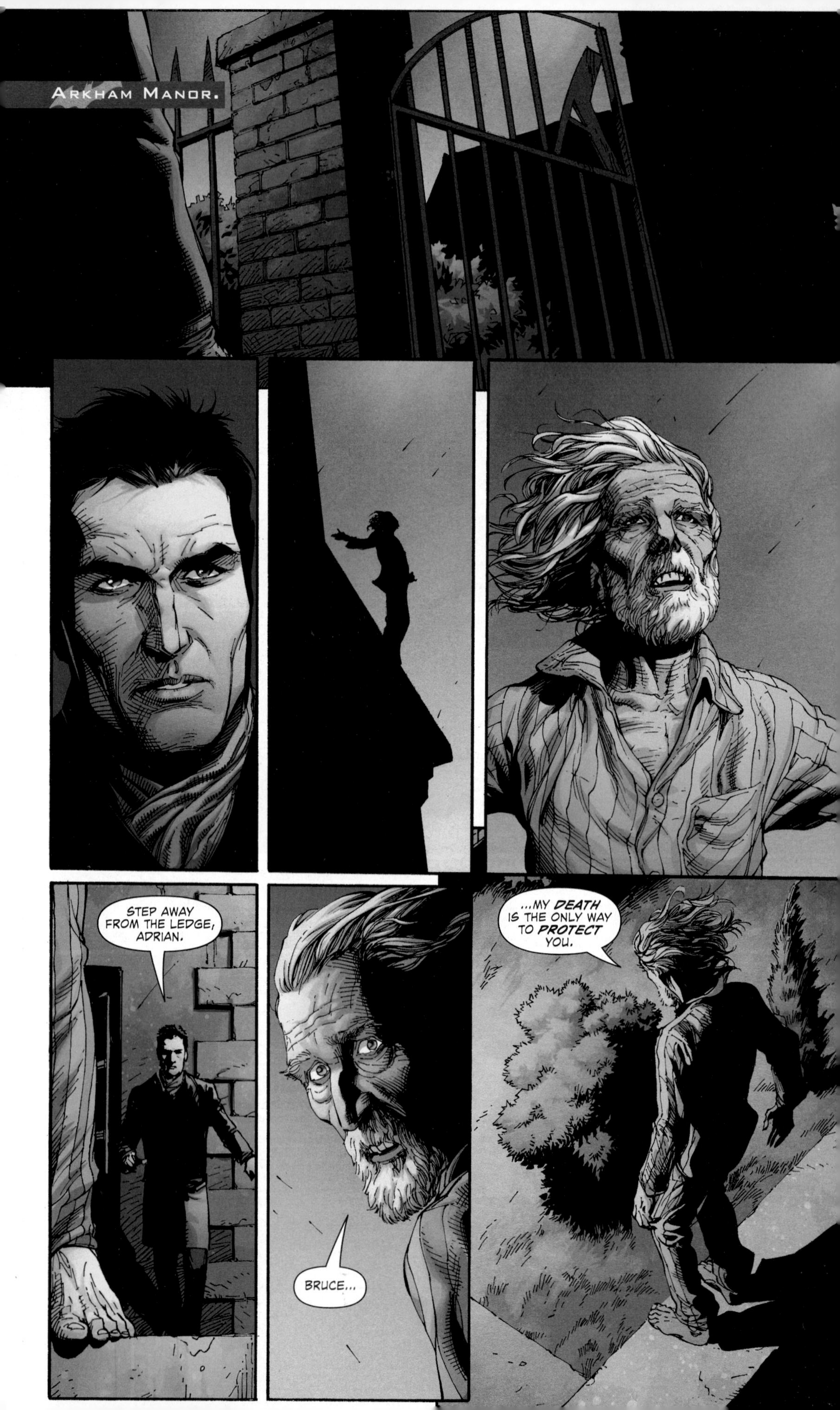
ARKHAM MANOR.
STEP AWAY FROM THE LEDGE, ADRIAN.
BRUCE...
...MY DEATH IS THE ONLY WAY TO PROTECT YOU.

"THE ONLY WAY TO SAVE YOU FROM THEIR RAGE."

HELLO?

HARVEY? IS THIS REALLY YOU?

WHERE ARE YOU?

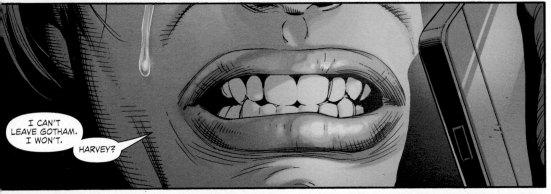

PLEASE, TELL ME.

I CAN'T LEAVE GOTHAM. I WON'T.

HARVEY?

...I LOVE YOU TOO.

"THEY WANT YOU DEAD, BRUCE."

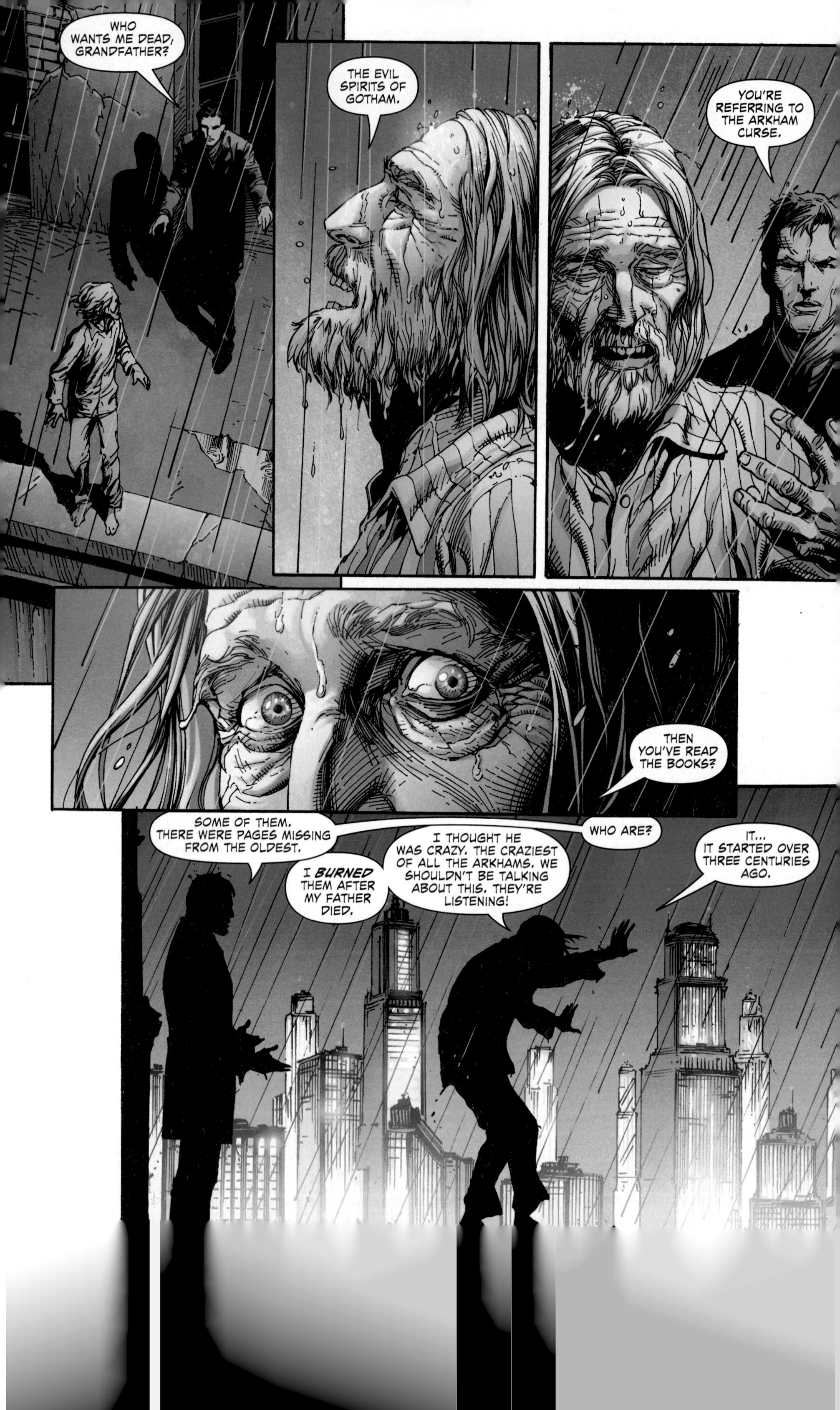

WHO WANTS ME DEAD, GRANDFATHER?
THE EVIL SPIRITS OF GOTHAM.
YOU'RE REFERRING TO THE ARKHAM CURSE.
THEN YOU'VE READ THE BOOKS?
SOME OF THEM. THERE WERE PAGES MISSING FROM THE OLDEST.
I BURNED THEM AFTER MY FATHER DIED.
I THOUGHT HE WAS CRAZY. THE CRAZIEST OF ALL THE ARKHAMS. WE SHOULDN'T BE TALKING ABOUT THIS. THEY'RE LISTENING!
WHO ARE?
IT... IT STARTED OVER THREE CENTURIES AGO.

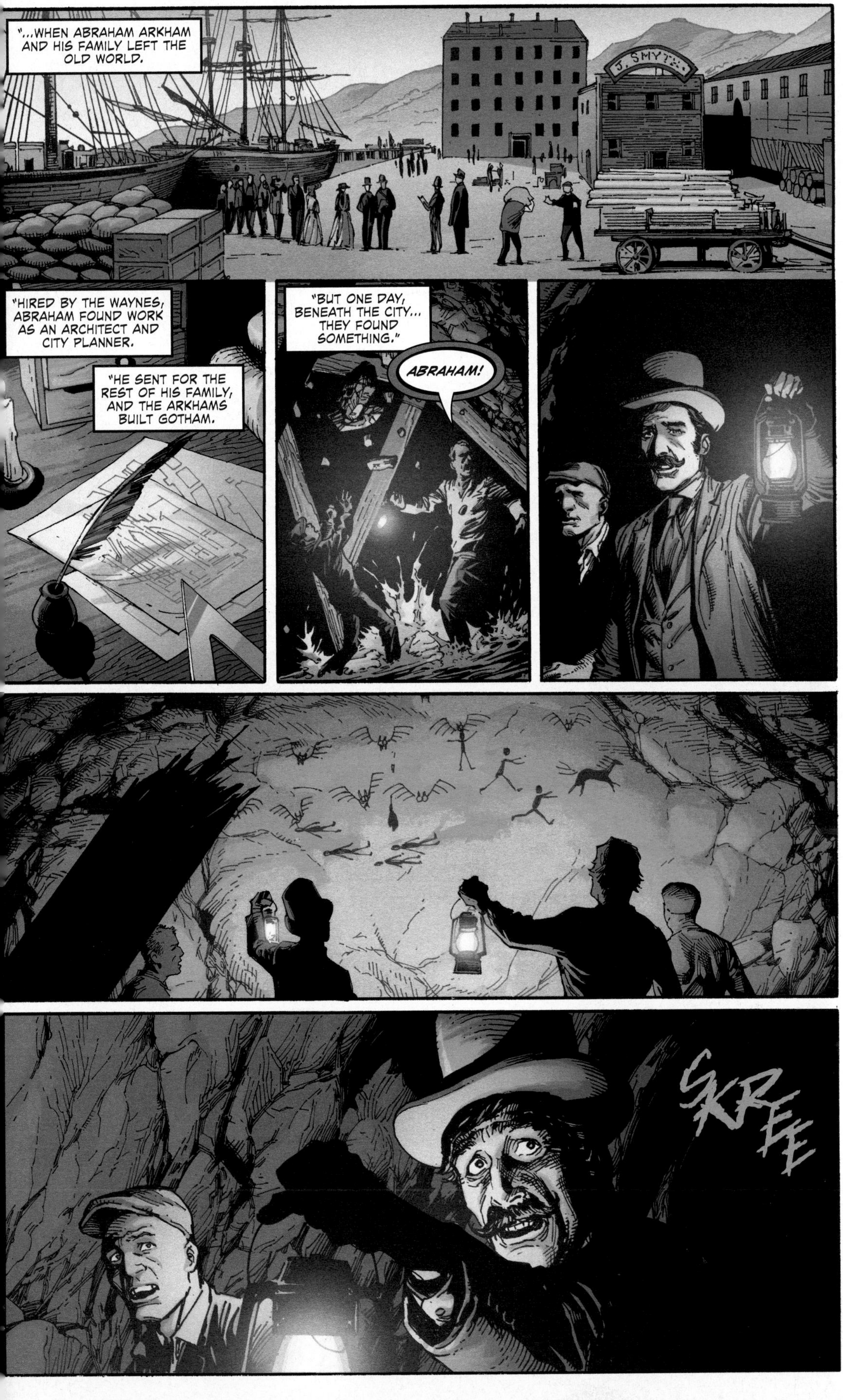
"...WHEN ABRAHAM ARKHAM AND HIS FAMILY LEFT THE OLD WORLD.
J. SMYT
"HIRED BY THE WAYNES, ABRAHAM FOUND WORK AS AN ARCHITECT AND CITY PLANNER.
"HE SENT FOR THE REST OF HIS FAMILY, AND THE ARKHAMS BUILT GOTHAM.
"BUT ONE DAY, BENEATH THE CITY... THEY FOUND SOMETHING."
ABRAHAM!
SKREE

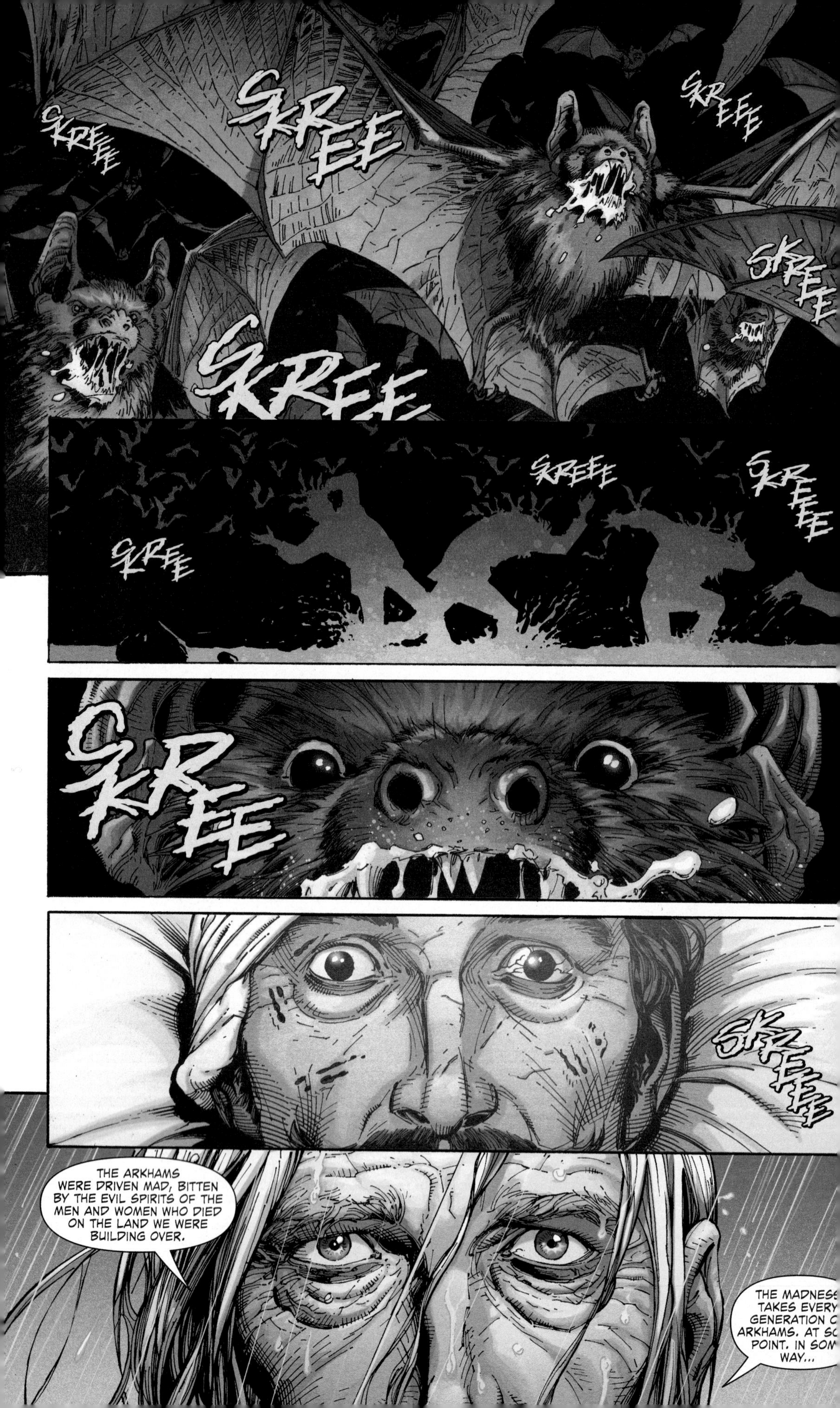
SKREEE
SKREE
SKREEE
SKREEE
SKREE
SKREEE
SKREEE
SKREE
SKREE
SKREEE
THE ARKHAMS WERE DRIVEN MAD, BITTEN BY THE EVIL SPIRITS OF THE MEN AND WOMEN WHO DIED ON THE LAND WE WERE BUILDING OVER.
THE MADNESS TAKES EVERY GENERATION OF ARKHAMS. AT SO POINT. IN SOM WAY...

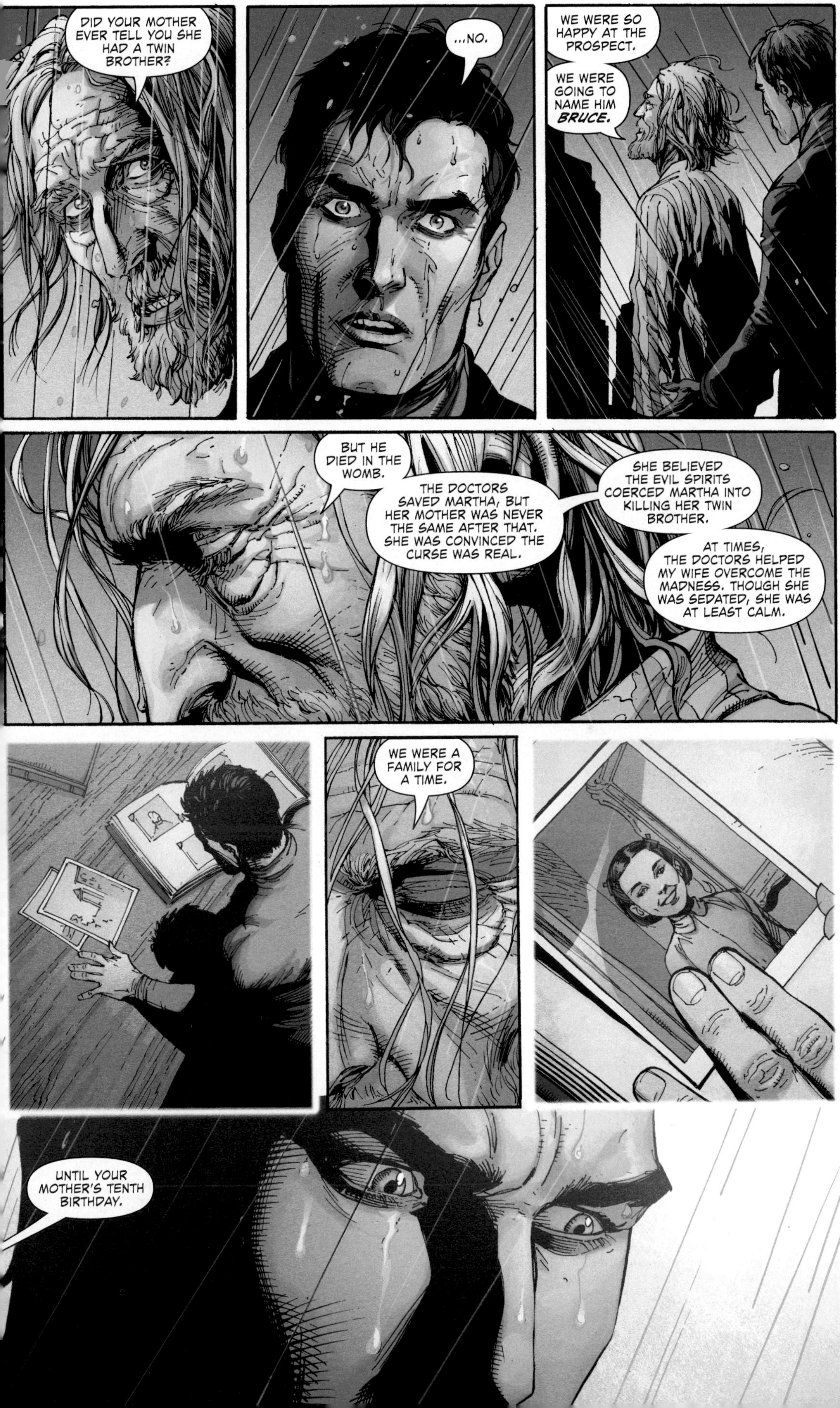
DID YOUR MOTHER EVER TELL YOU SHE HAD A TWIN BROTHER?
...NO.
WE WERE SO HAPPY AT THE PROSPECT.
WE WERE GOING TO NAME HIM BRUCE.
BUT HE DIED IN THE WOMB.
THE DOCTORS SAVED MARTHA, BUT HER MOTHER WAS NEVER THE SAME AFTER THAT. SHE WAS CONVINCED THE CURSE WAS REAL.
SHE BELIEVED THE EVIL SPIRITS COERCED MARTHA INTO KILLING HER TWIN BROTHER.
AT TIMES, THE DOCTORS HELPED MY WIFE OVERCOME THE MADNESS. THOUGH SHE WAS SEDATED, SHE WAS AT LEAST CALM.
WE WERE A FAMILY FOR A TIME.
UNTIL YOUR MOTHER'S TENTH BIRTHDAY.

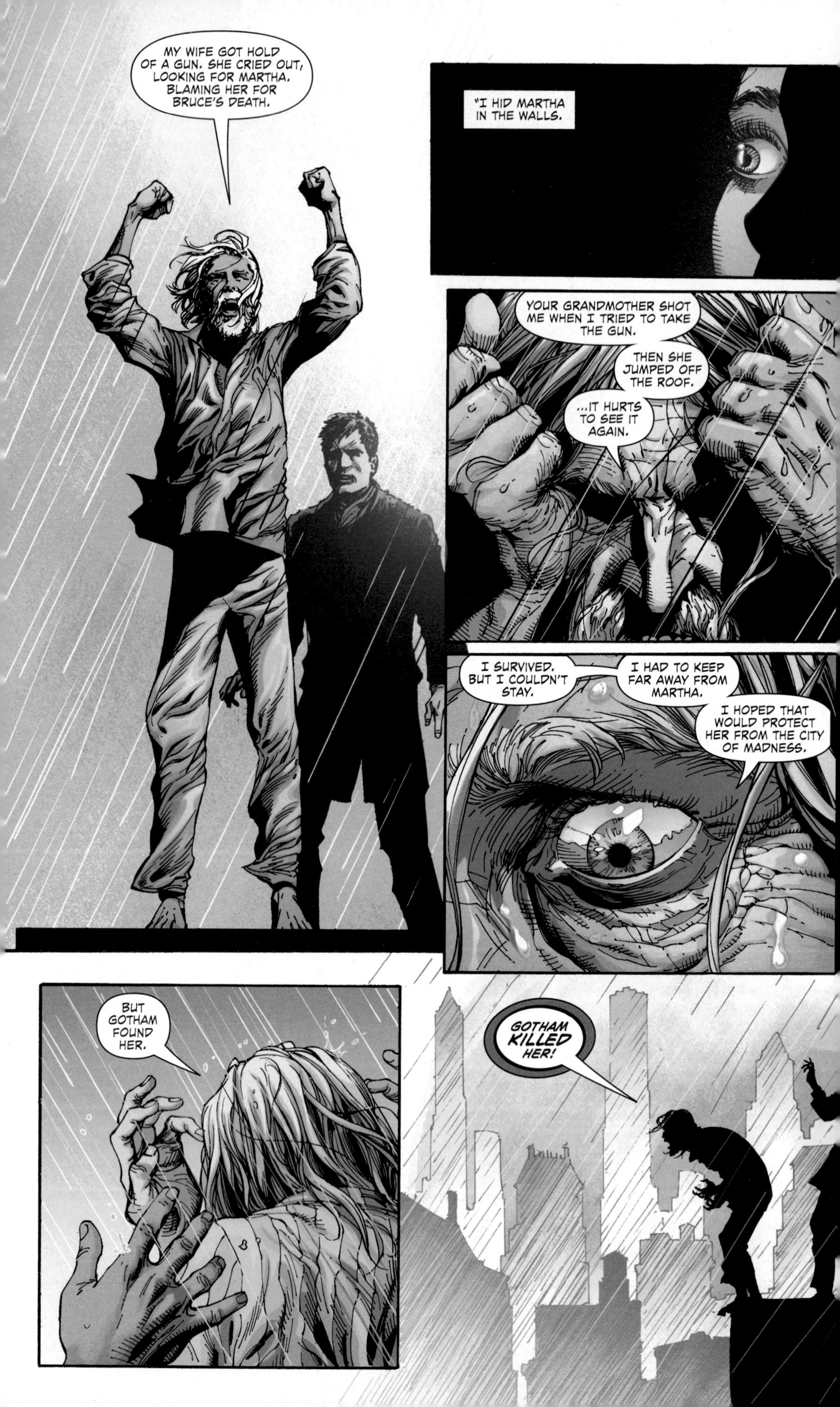

MY WIFE GOT HOLD OF A GUN. SHE CRIED OUT, LOOKING FOR MARTHA. BLAMING HER FOR BRUCE'S DEATH.
"I HID MARTHA IN THE WALLS.
YOUR GRANDMOTHER SHOT ME WHEN I TRIED TO TAKE THE GUN.
THEN SHE JUMPED OFF THE ROOF.
...IT HURTS TO SEE IT AGAIN.
I SURVIVED. BUT I COULDN'T STAY.
I HAD TO KEEP FAR AWAY FROM MARTHA.
I HOPED THAT WOULD PROTECT HER FROM THE CITY OF MADNESS.
BUT GOTHAM FOUND HER.
GOTHAM KILLED HER!

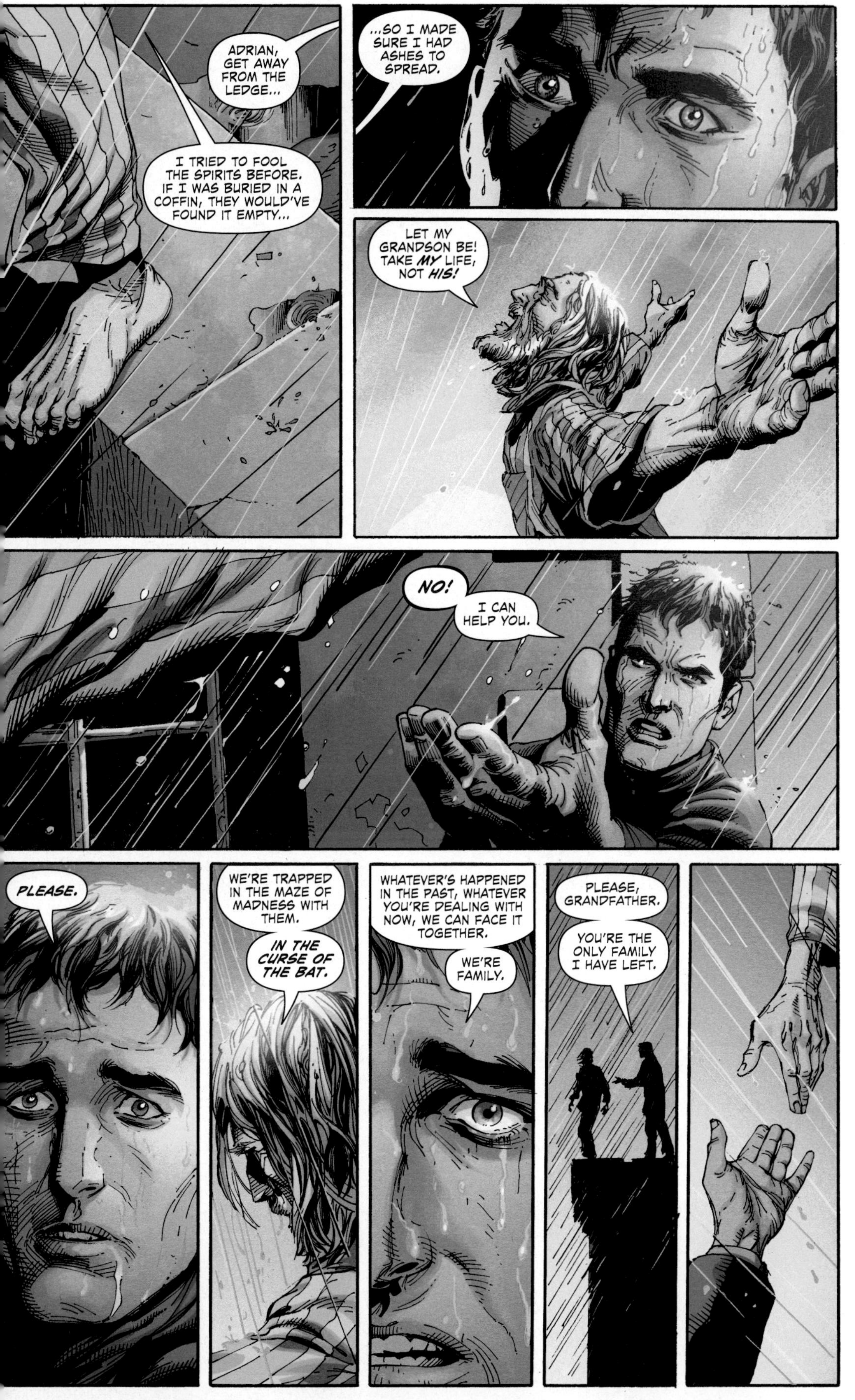
ADRIAN, GET AWAY FROM THE LEDGE...
I TRIED TO FOOL THE SPIRITS BEFORE. IF I WAS BURIED IN A COFFIN, THEY WOULD'VE FOUND IT EMPTY...
...SO I MADE SURE I HAD ASHES TO SPREAD.
LET MY GRANDSON BE! TAKE *MY* LIFE, NOT *HIS!*
NO!
I CAN HELP YOU.
PLEASE.
WE'RE TRAPPED IN THE MAZE OF MADNESS WITH THEM.
IN THE CURSE OF THE BAT.
WHATEVER'S HAPPENED IN THE PAST, WHATEVER YOU'RE DEALING WITH NOW, WE CAN FACE IT TOGETHER.
WE'RE FAMILY.
PLEASE, GRANDFATHER.
YOU'RE THE ONLY FAMILY I HAVE LEFT.

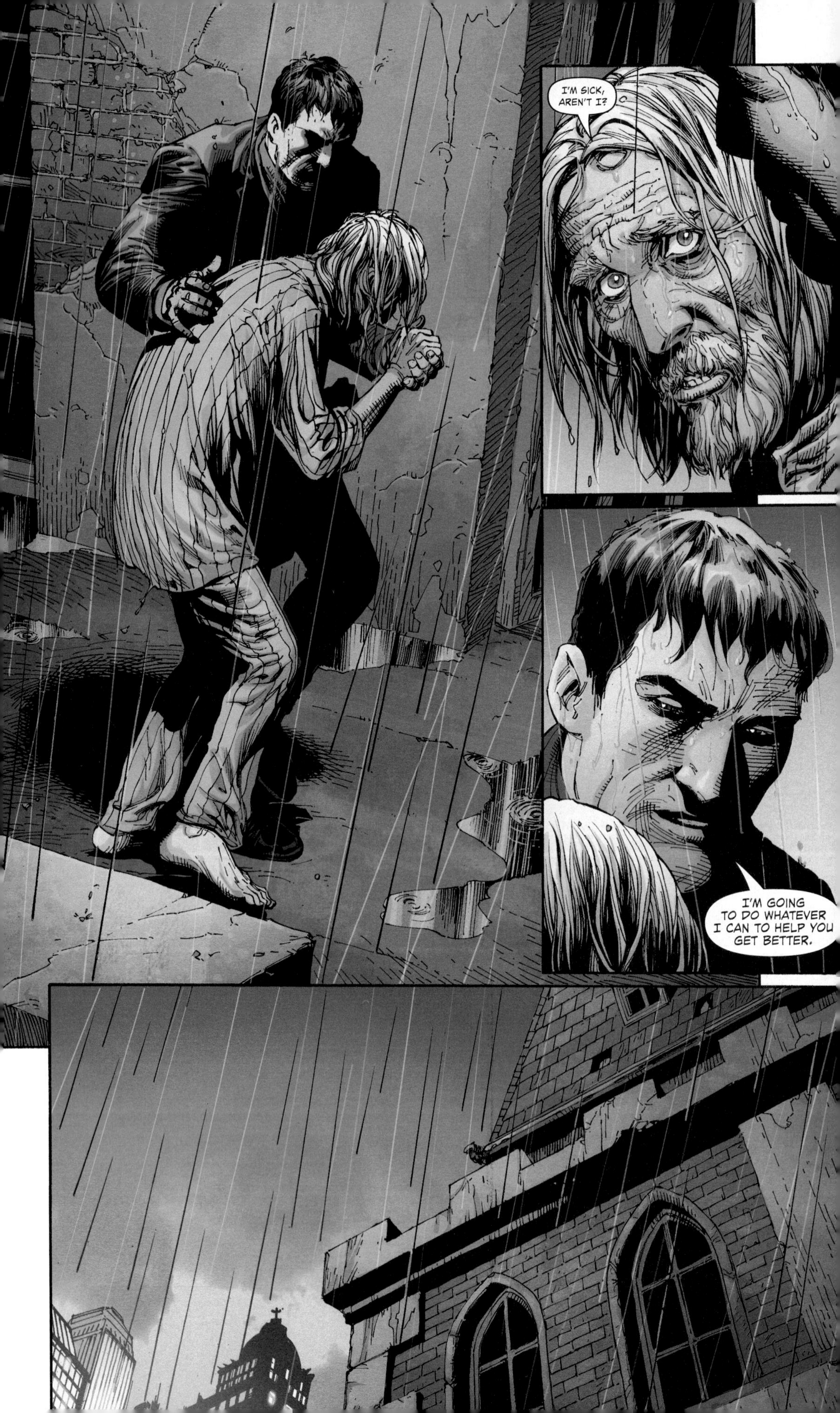
I'M SICK, AREN'T I?
I'M GOING TO DO WHATEVER I CAN TO HELP YOU GET BETTER.

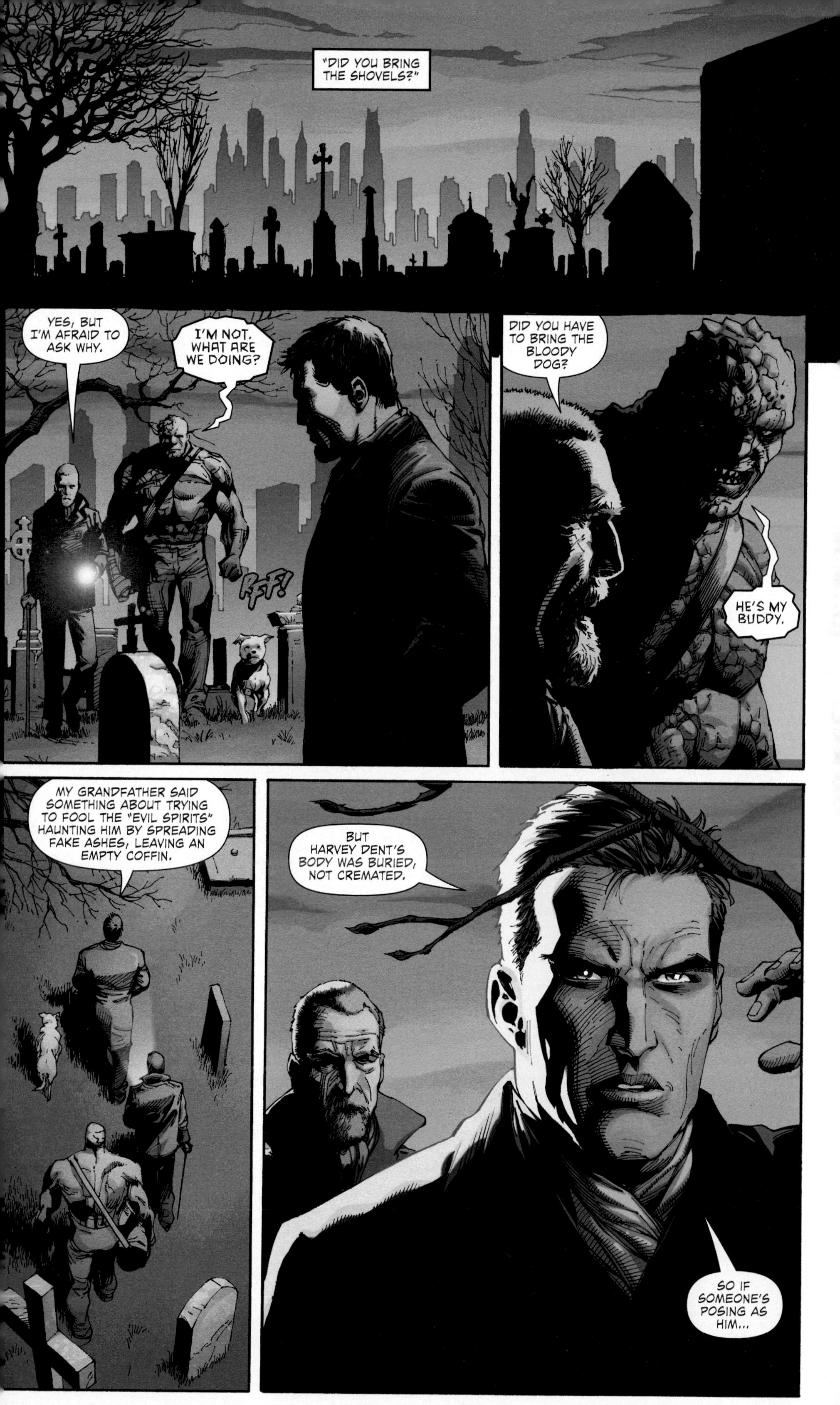
"DID YOU BRING THE SHOVELS?"
YES, BUT I'M AFRAID TO ASK WHY.
I'M NOT. WHAT ARE WE DOING?
RFF!
DID YOU HAVE TO BRING THE BLOODY DOG?
HE'S MY BUDDY.
MY GRANDFATHER SAID SOMETHING ABOUT TRYING TO FOOL THE "EVIL SPIRITS" HAUNTING HIM BY SPREADING FAKE ASHES, LEAVING AN EMPTY COFFIN.
BUT HARVEY DENT'S BODY WAS BURIED, NOT CREMATED.
SO IF SOMEONE'S POSING AS HIM...

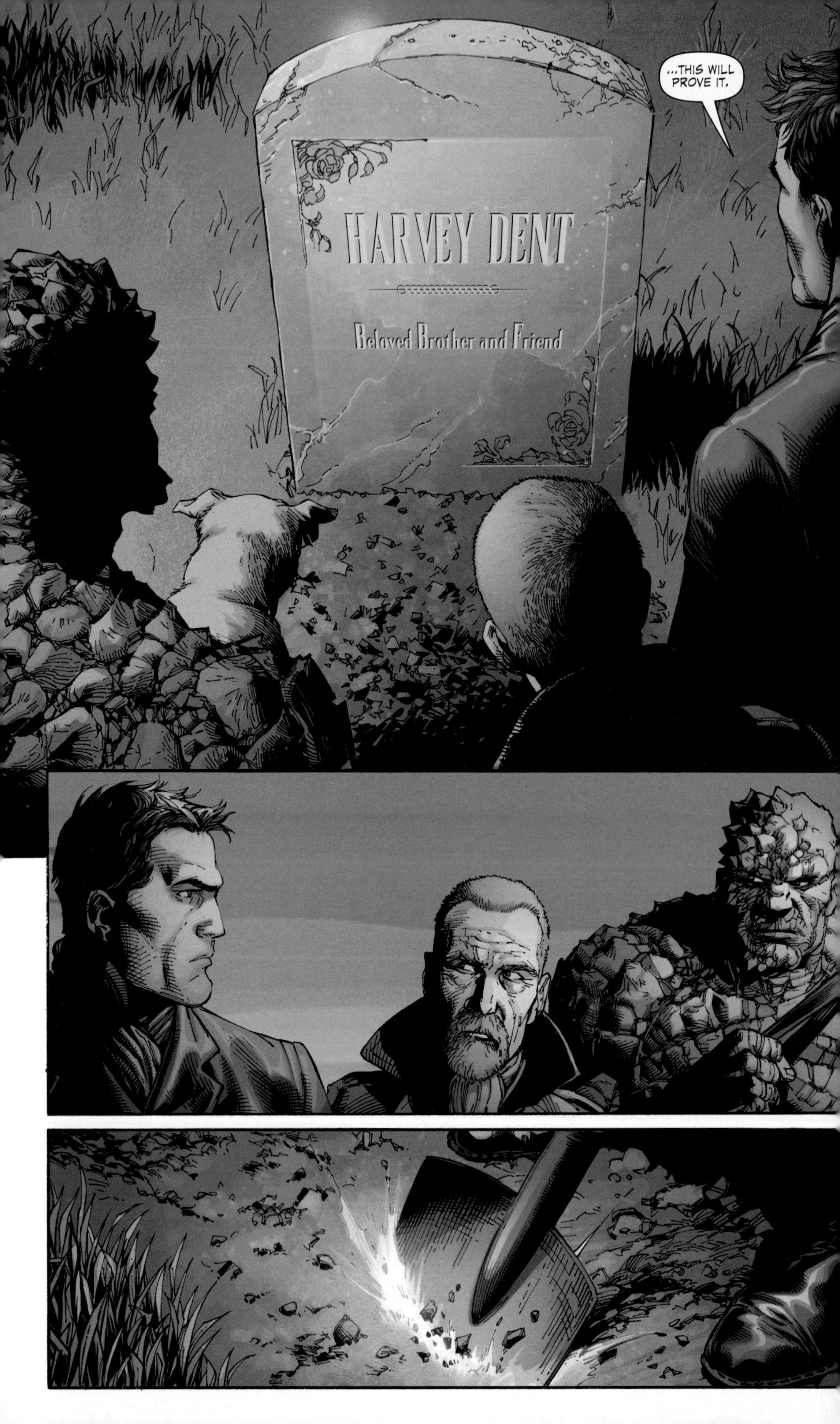
...THIS WILL PROVE IT.
HARVEY DENT
Beloved Brother and Friend

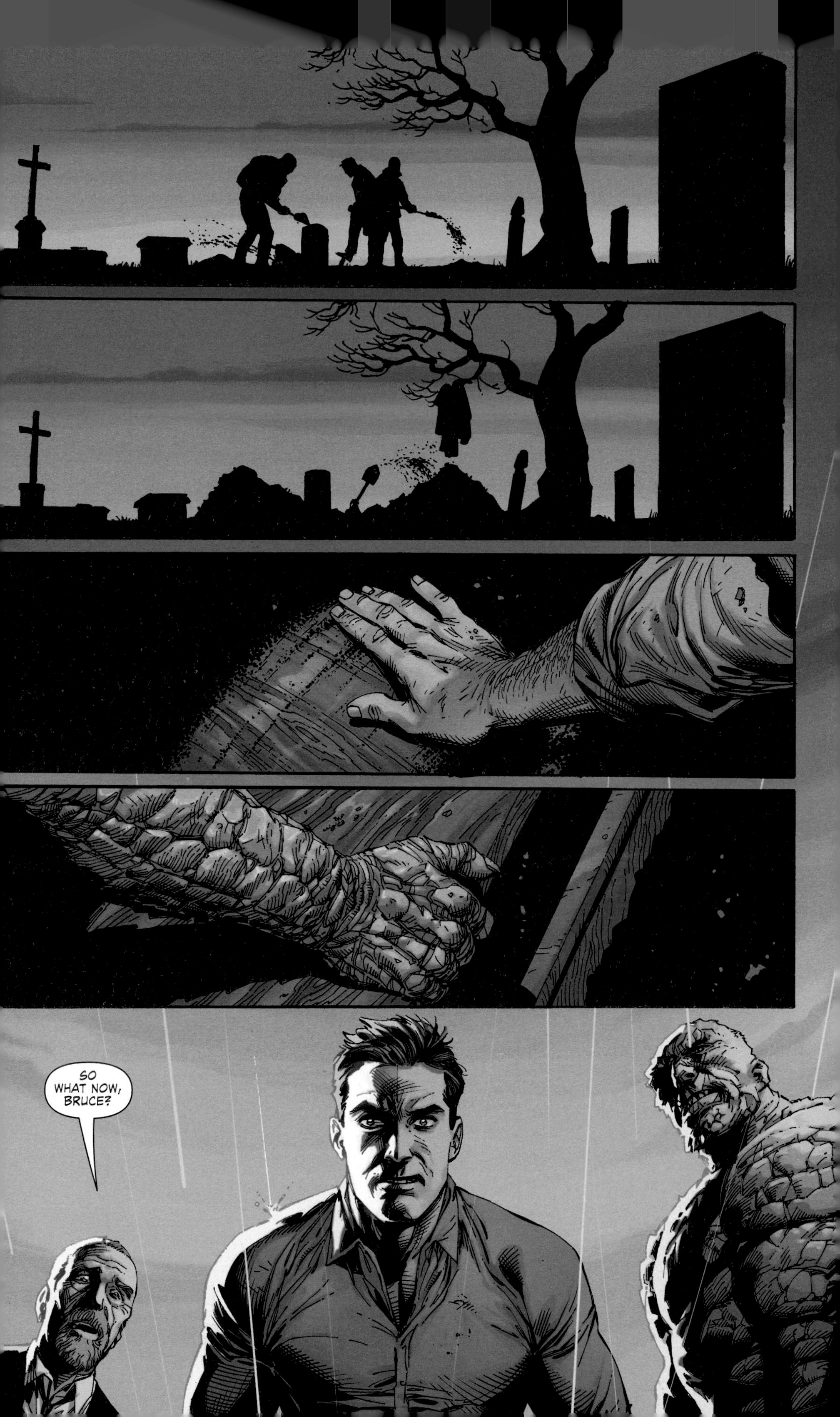
SO WHAT NOW, BRUCE?

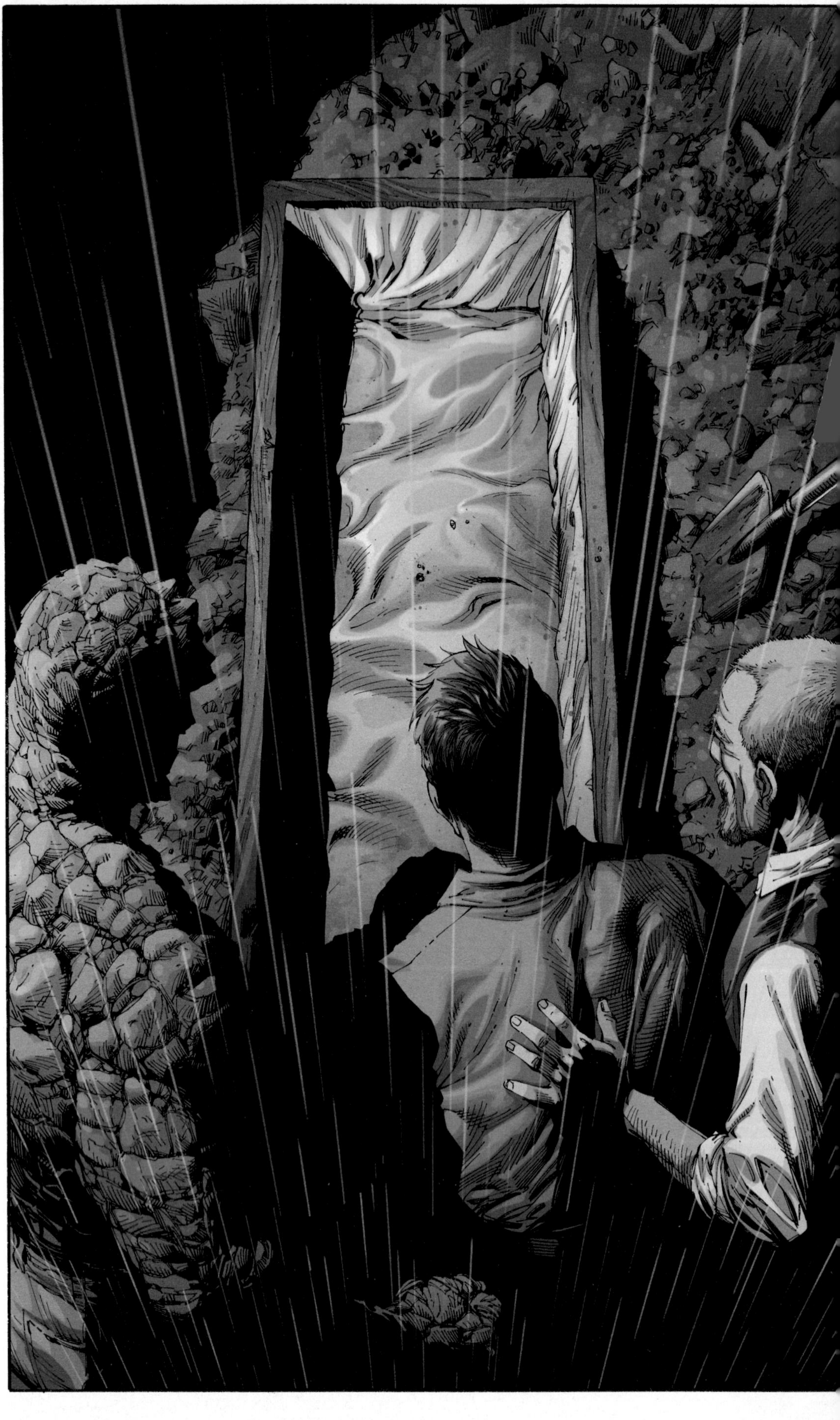

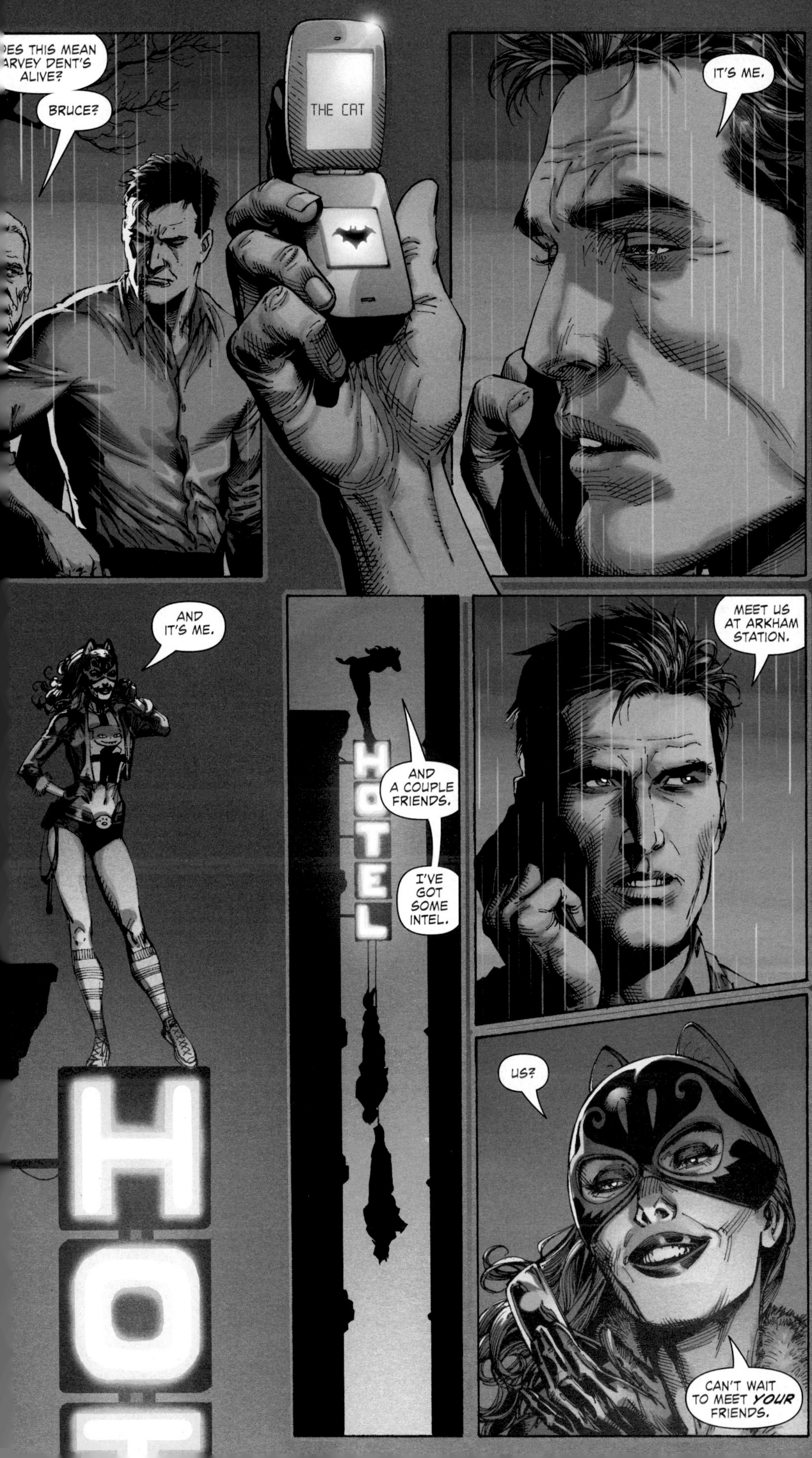
ES THIS MEAN ARVEY DENT'S ALIVE?
BRUCE?
THE CAT
IT'S ME.
AND IT'S ME.
HOTEL
AND A COUPLE FRIENDS.
I'VE GOT SOME INTEL.
MEET US AT ARKHAM STATION.
US?
CAN'T WAIT TO MEET *YOUR* FRIENDS.

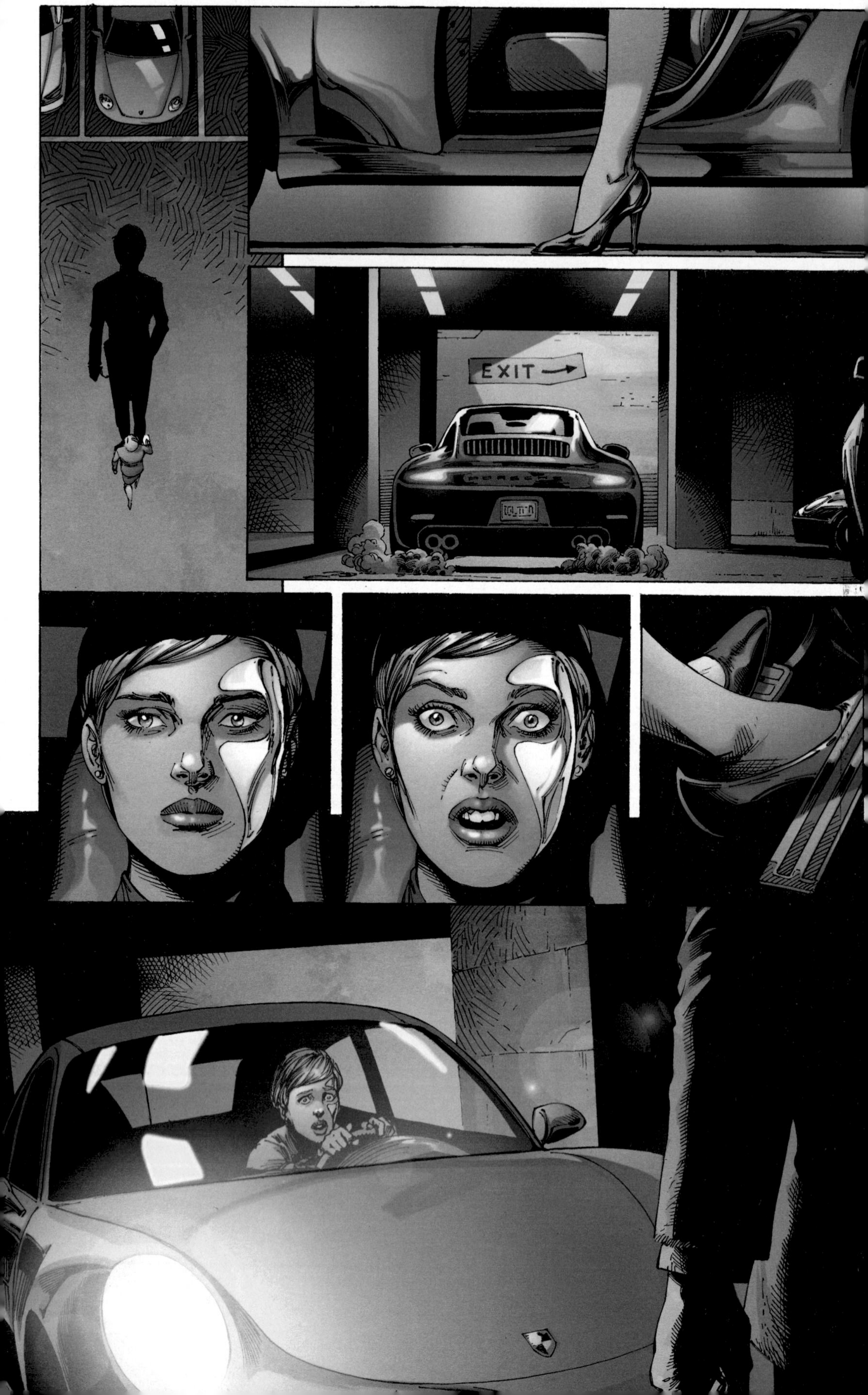
EXIT

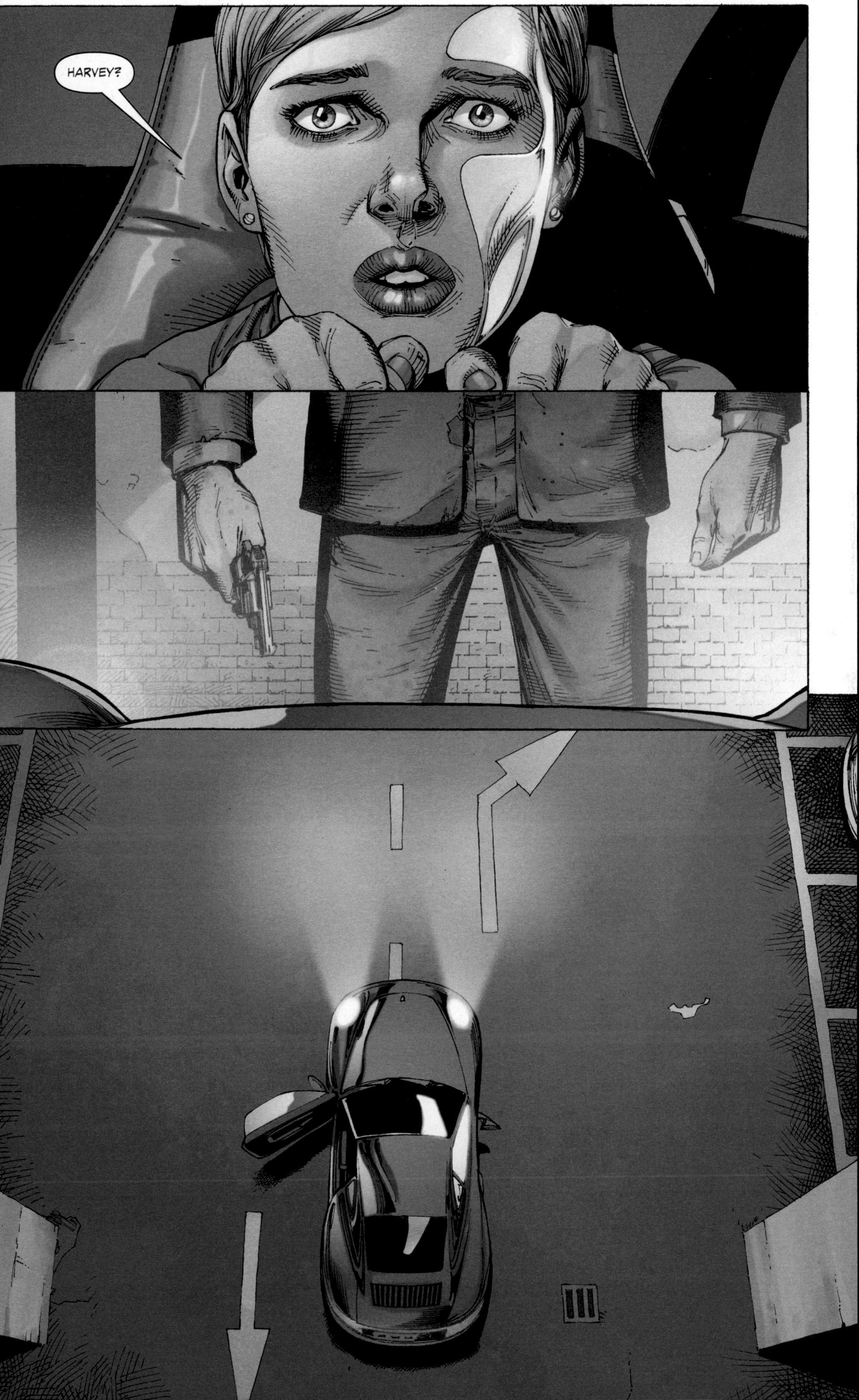
HARVEY?

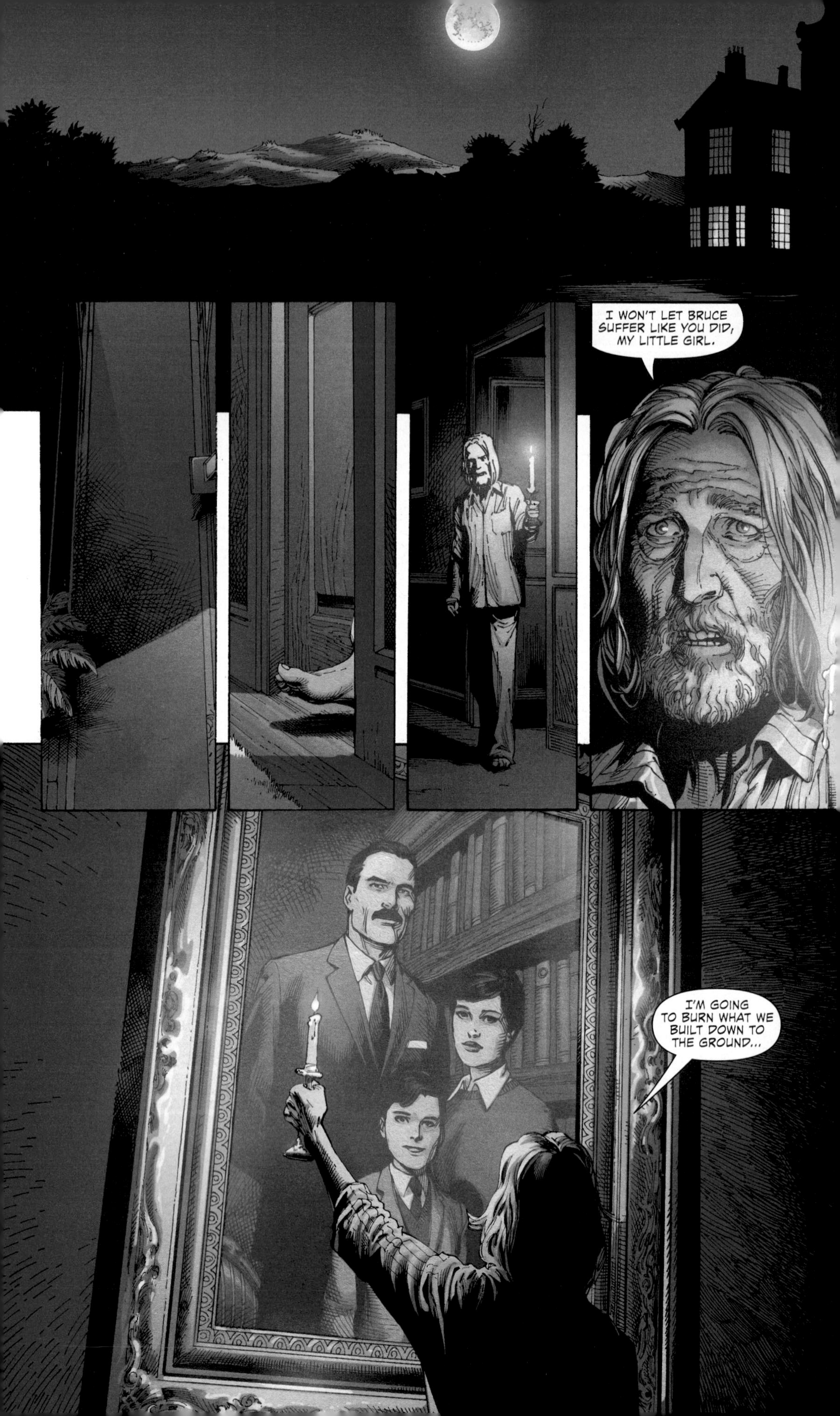
I WON'T LET BRUCE SUFFER LIKE YOU DID, MY LITTLE GIRL.
I'M GOING TO BURN WHAT WE BUILT DOWN TO THE GROUND...

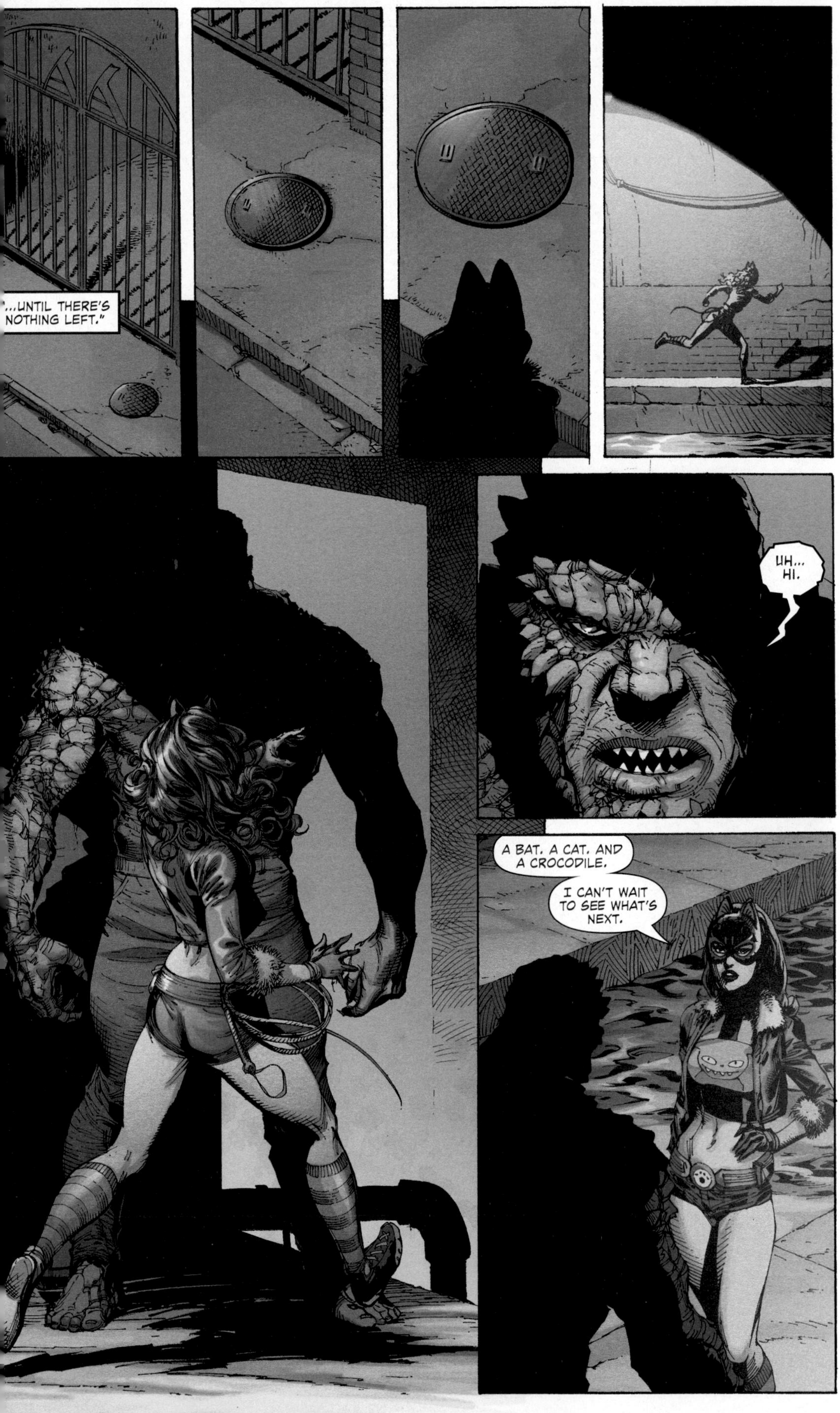
"...UNTIL THERE'S NOTHING LEFT."
UH... HI.
A BAT. A CAT. AND A CROCODILE.
I CAN'T WAIT TO SEE WHAT'S NEXT.

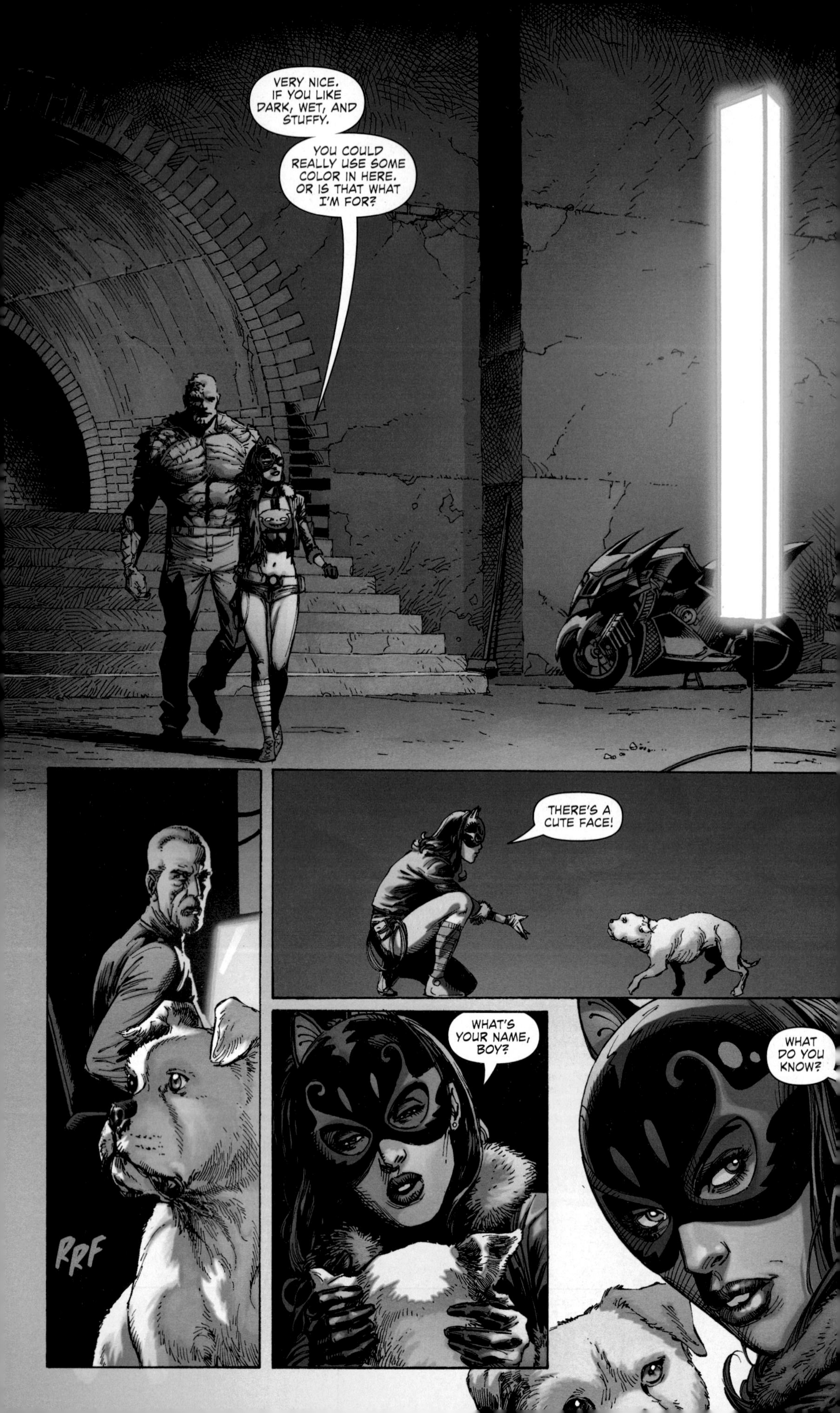
VERY NICE. IF YOU LIKE DARK, WET, AND STUFFY.
YOU COULD REALLY USE SOME COLOR IN HERE. OR IS THAT WHAT I'M FOR?
THERE'S A CUTE FACE!
WHAT'S YOUR NAME, BOY?
WHAT DO YOU KNOW?
RRF

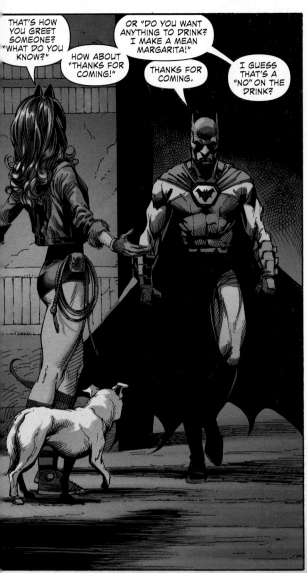

THAT'S HOW YOU GREET SOMEONE? "WHAT DO YOU KNOW?"

HOW ABOUT "THANKS FOR COMING!"

OR "DO YOU WANT ANYTHING TO DRINK? I MAKE A MEAN MARGARITA!"

THANKS FOR COMING.

I GUESS THAT'S A "NO" ON THE DRINK?

YOU'VE MET WAYLON. AND THE DOG.

THIS IS ALFRED.

NOW THAT WE'VE GOT THAT OUT OF THE WAY, WHAT DID YOU FIND OUT?

MY TURN TO GET TO THE *POINT:* WHERE'S THE REST OF MY MONEY?

OKAY.

SHE'S GETTIN' *PAID* FOR THIS?

THE *WEAPONS* WILL BE CROSSING INTO GOTHAM TONIGHT.

AND AS SOON AS THEY GET *DISTRIBUTED,* HARVEY DENT IS GOING TO LIGHT THE SIGNAL.

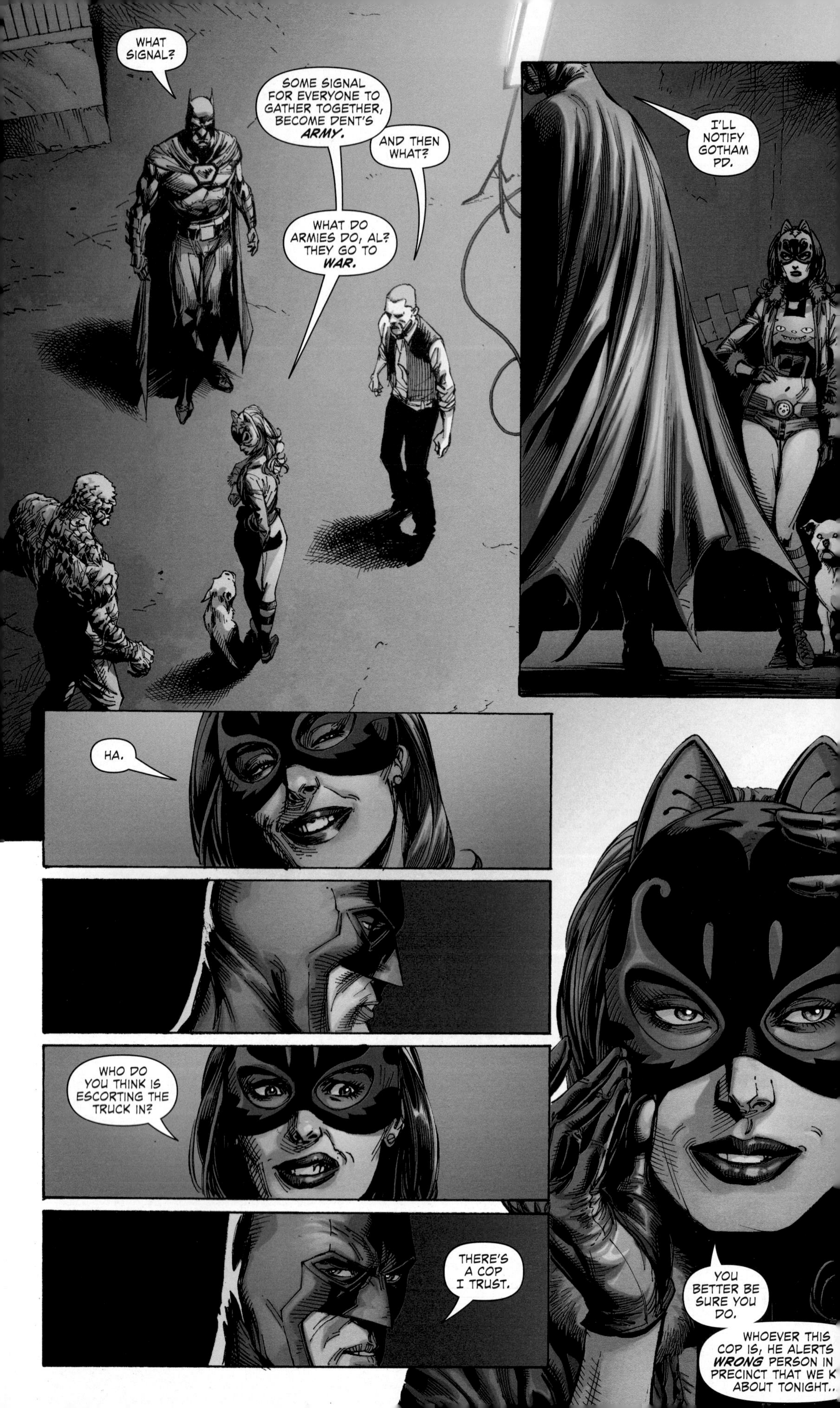
WHAT SIGNAL?
SOME SIGNAL FOR EVERYONE TO GATHER TOGETHER, BECOME DENT'S **ARMY.**
AND THEN WHAT?
WHAT DO ARMIES DO, AL? THEY GO TO **WAR.**
I'LL NOTIFY GOTHAM PD.
HA.
WHO DO YOU THINK IS ESCORTING THE TRUCK IN?
THERE'S A COP I TRUST.
YOU BETTER BE SURE YOU DO.
WHOEVER THIS COP IS, HE ALERTS **WRONG** PERSON IN PRECINCT THAT WE K ABOUT TONIGHT..

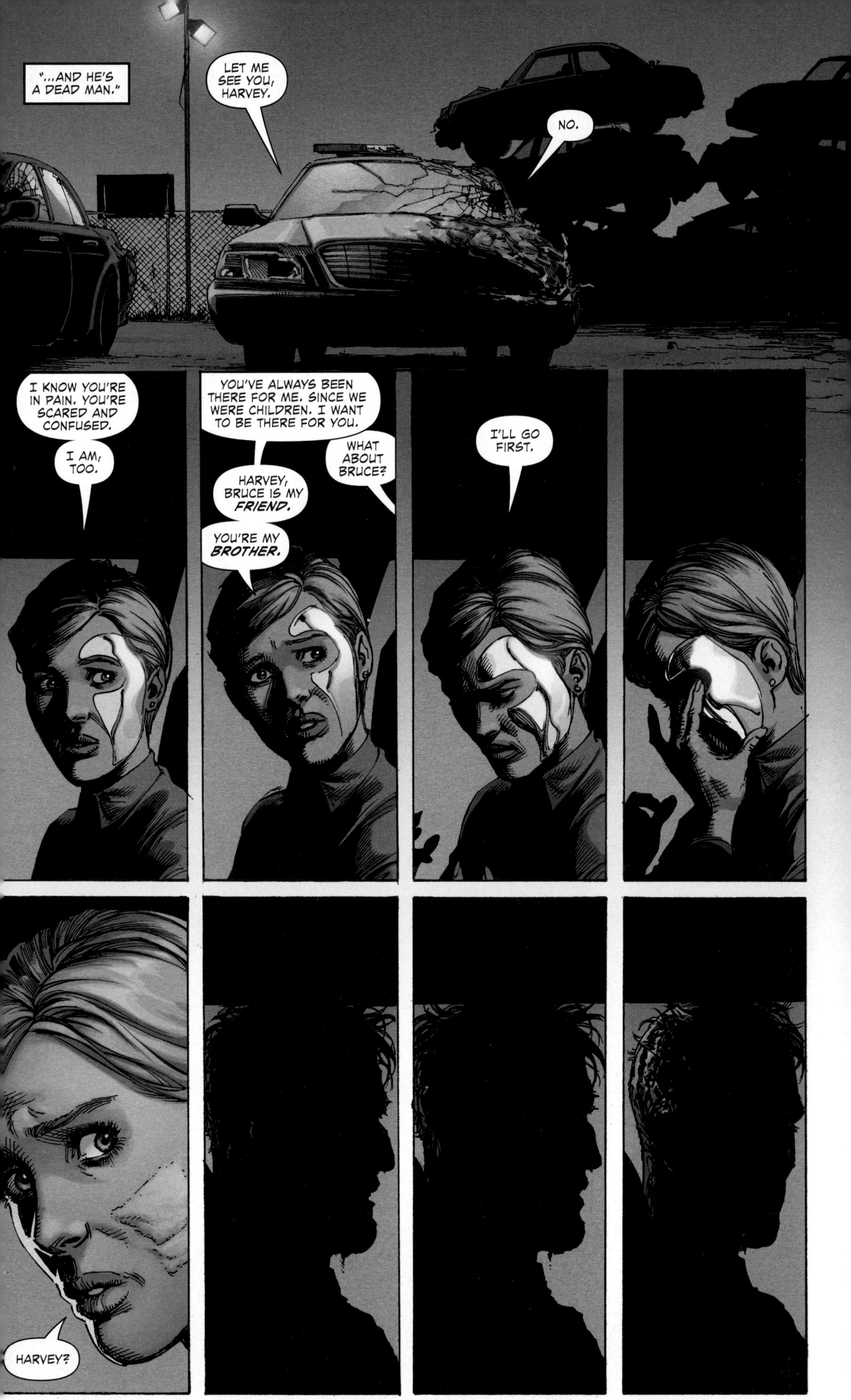
"...AND HE'S A DEAD MAN."
LET ME SEE YOU, HARVEY.
NO.
I KNOW YOU'RE IN PAIN. YOU'RE SCARED AND CONFUSED.
I AM, TOO.
YOU'VE ALWAYS BEEN THERE FOR ME. SINCE WE WERE CHILDREN. I WANT TO BE THERE FOR YOU.
WHAT ABOUT BRUCE?
HARVEY, BRUCE IS MY FRIEND.
YOU'RE MY BROTHER.
I'LL GO FIRST.
HARVEY?

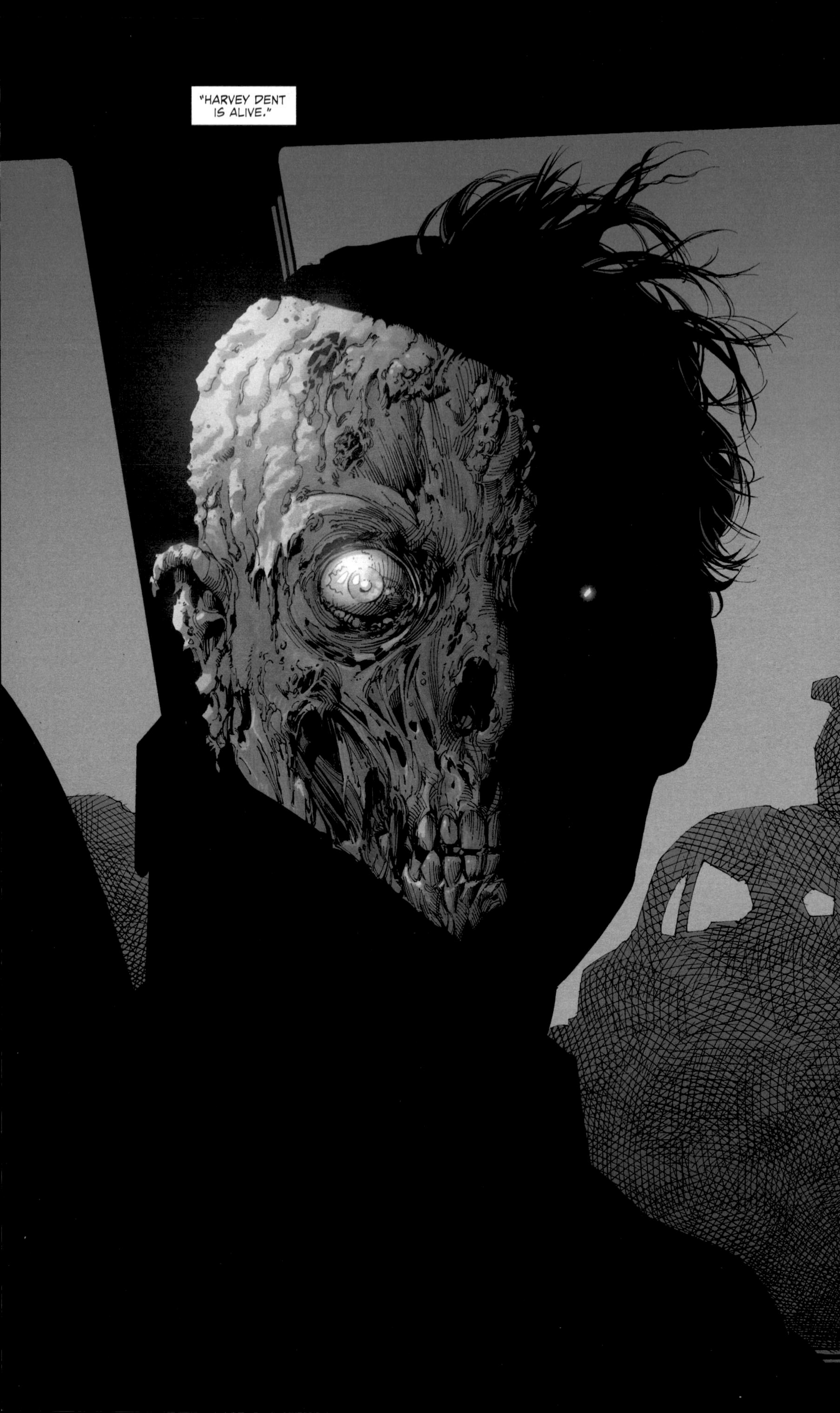
"HARVEY DENT IS ALIVE."

"I DON'T KNOW WHERE HE IS, JIM, BUT HE'S GOING TO *LIGHT* SOME KIND OF SIGNAL TO DEPLOY THE CRIMINALS HE'S ARMED."
"WHEN?"
POLICE
"THE LAST SHIPMENT IS COMING INTO GOTHAM TONIGHT...
SCHOTT'S TOYS
"...FROM AN ARMS DEALER IN METROPOLIS.
"WITH ENOUGH WEAPONS TO TURN GOTHAM CITY INTO A *WAR ZONE.*"
AR-30
ANGER
RPG-7
EXPL
Gotham City
13 miles

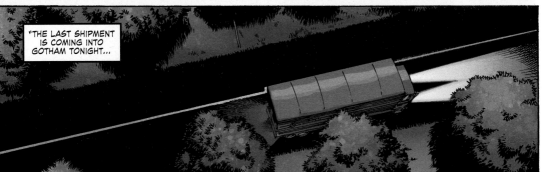

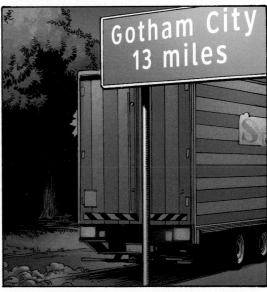

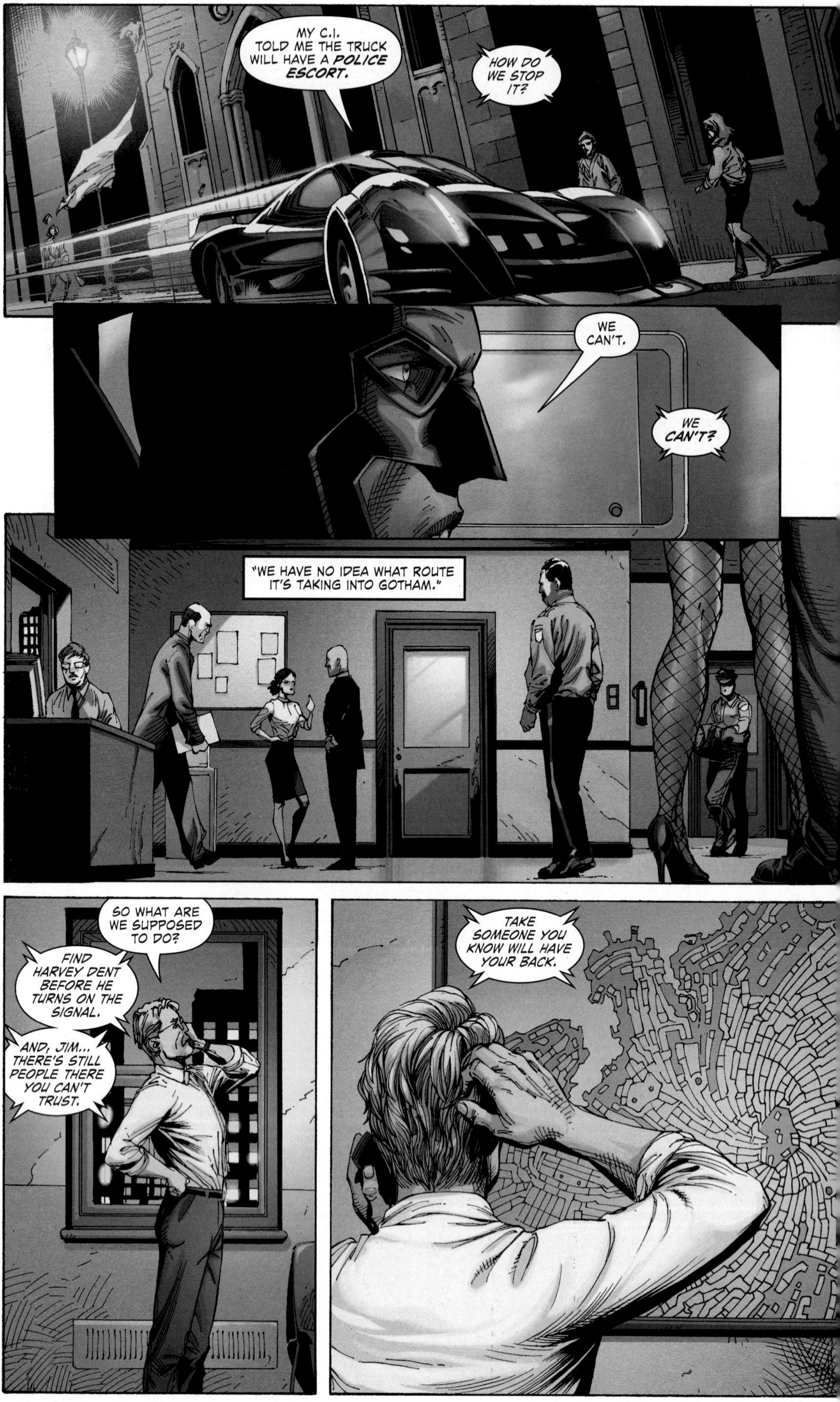
MY C.I. TOLD ME THE TRUCK WILL HAVE A POLICE ESCORT.
HOW DO WE STOP IT?
WE CAN'T.
WE CAN'T?
"WE HAVE NO IDEA WHAT ROUTE IT'S TAKING INTO GOTHAM."
SO WHAT ARE WE SUPPOSED TO DO?
FIND HARVEY DENT BEFORE HE TURNS ON THE SIGNAL.
AND, JIM... THERE'S STILL PEOPLE THERE YOU CAN'T TRUST.
TAKE SOMEONE YOU KNOW WILL HAVE YOUR BACK.

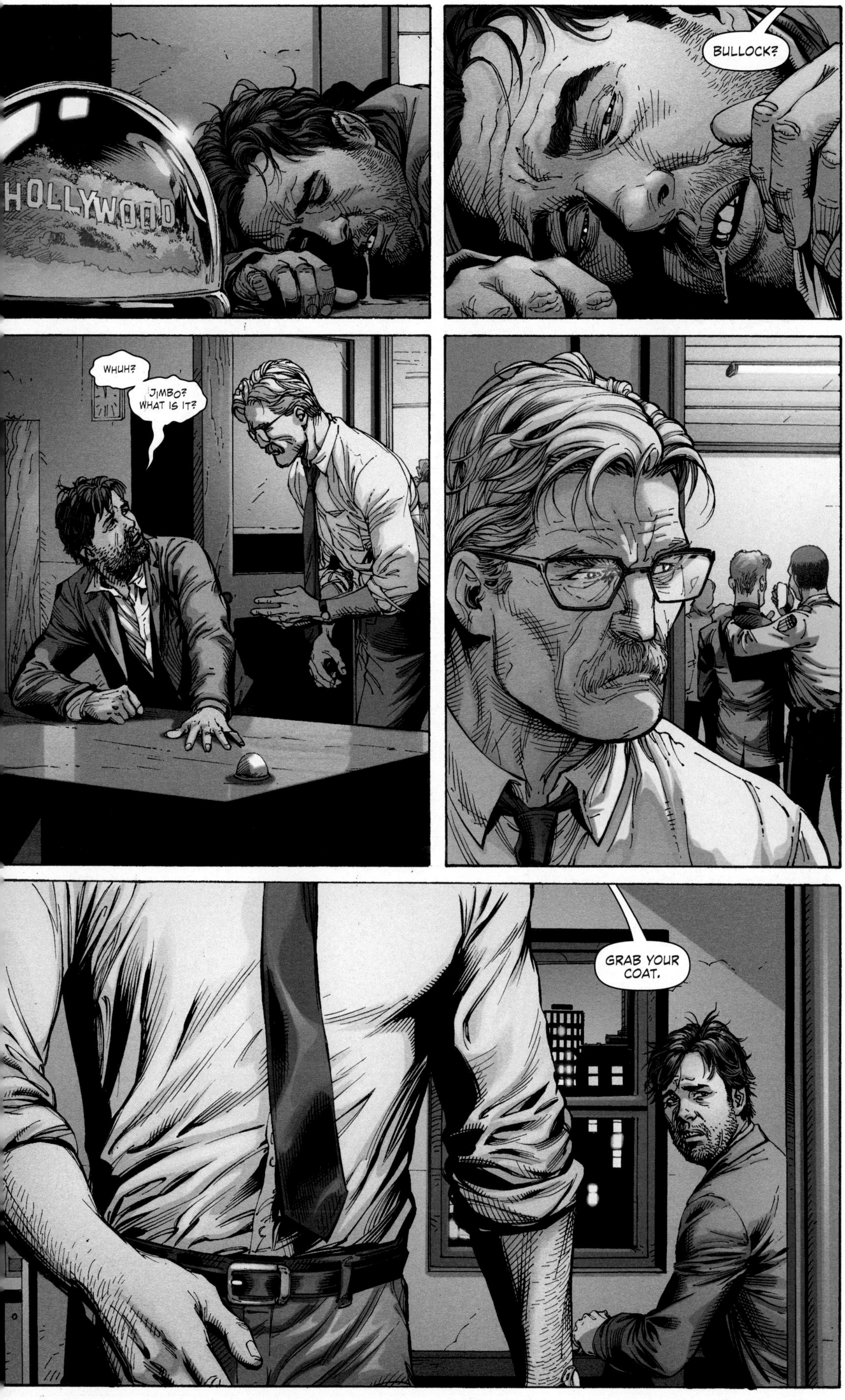
HOLLYWOOD
BULLOCK?
WHUH?
JIMBO? WHAT IS IT?
GRAB YOUR COAT.

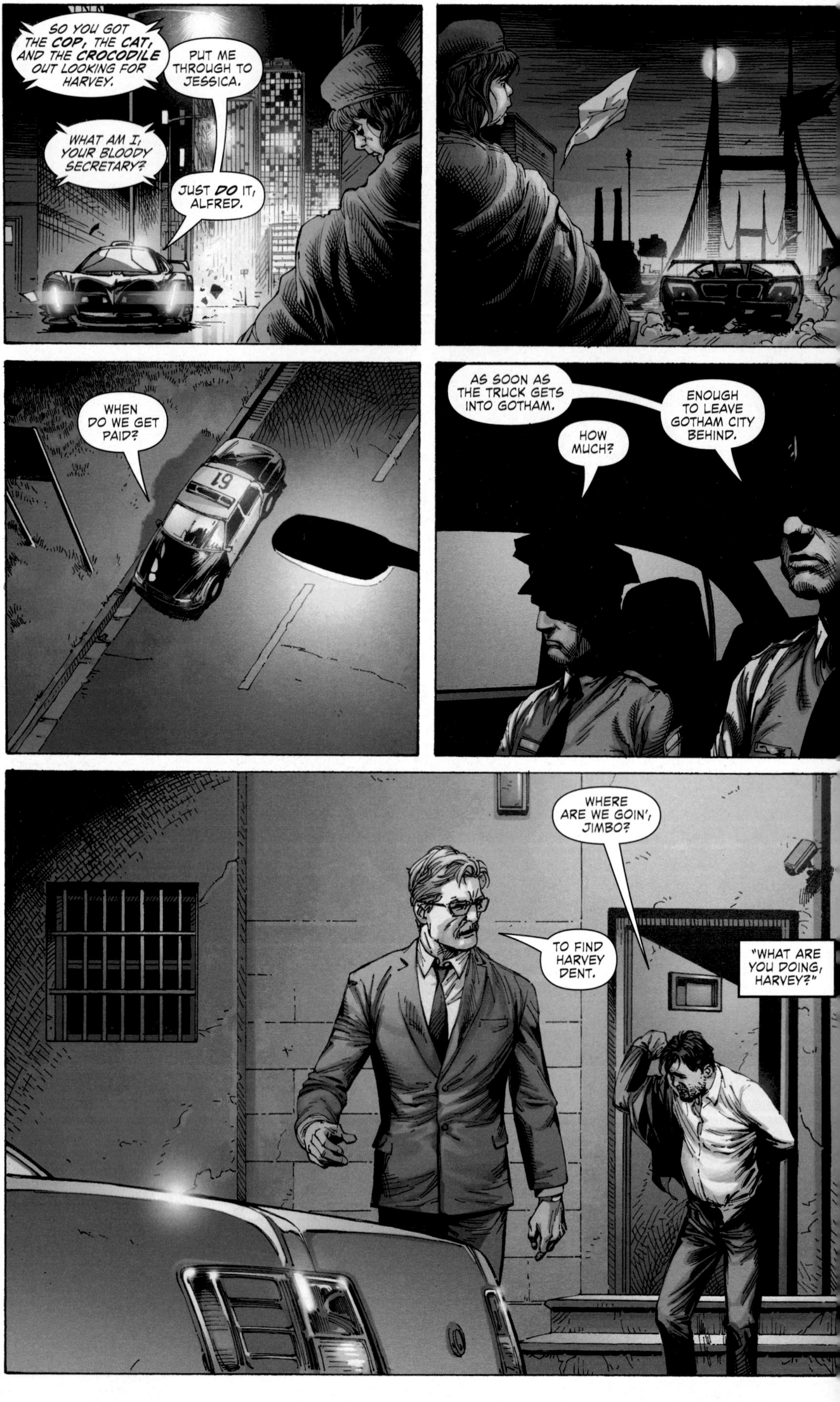
SO YOU GOT THE COP, THE CAT, AND THE CROCODILE OUT LOOKING FOR HARVEY.
PUT ME THROUGH TO JESSICA.
WHAT AM I, YOUR BLOODY SECRETARY?
JUST DO IT, ALFRED.
WHEN DO WE GET PAID?
AS SOON AS THE TRUCK GETS INTO GOTHAM.
HOW MUCH?
ENOUGH TO LEAVE GOTHAM CITY BEHIND.
WHERE ARE WE GOIN', JIMBO?
TO FIND HARVEY DENT.
"WHAT ARE YOU DOING, HARVEY?"

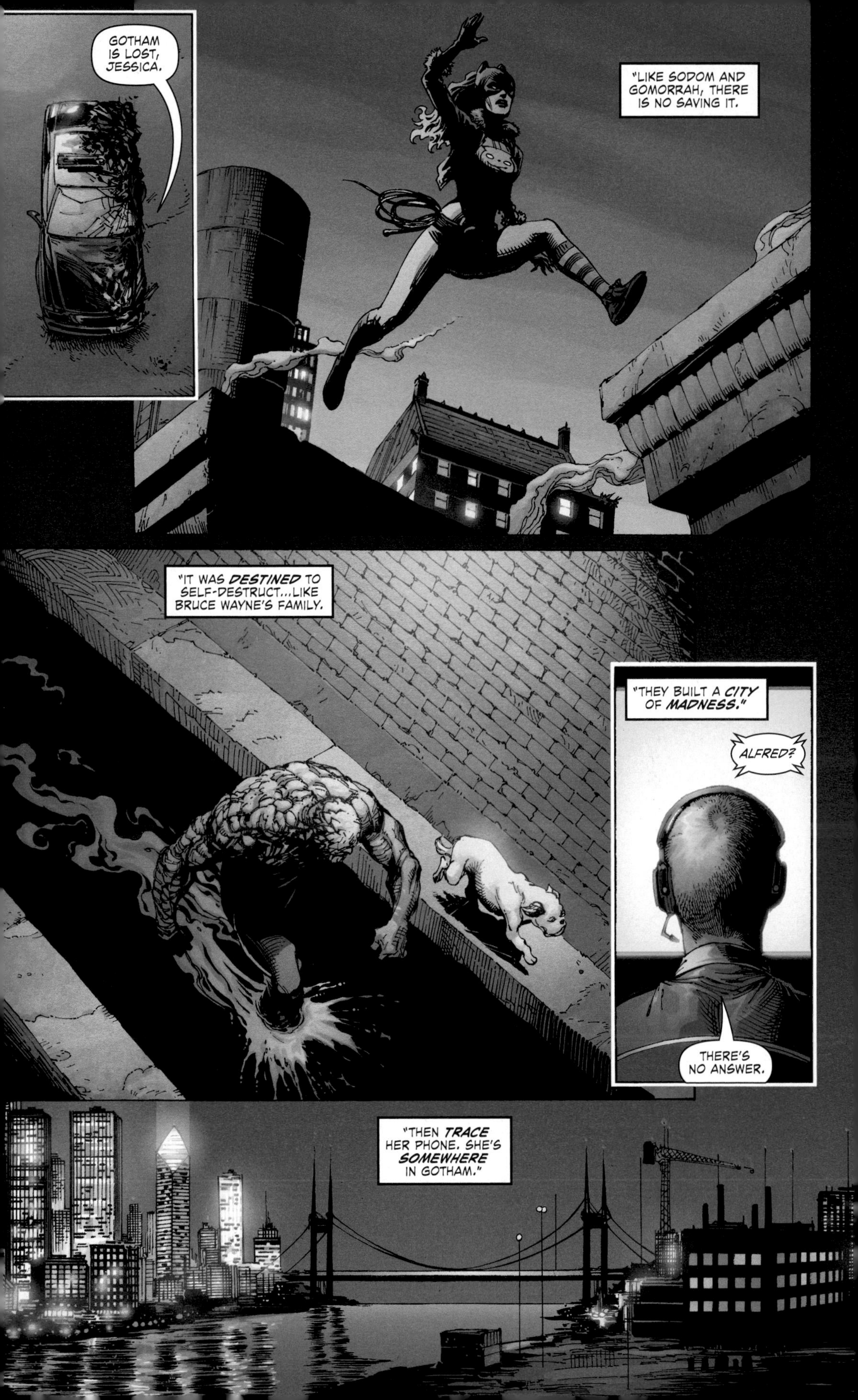
GOTHAM IS LOST, JESSICA.
"LIKE SODOM AND GOMORRAH, THERE IS NO SAVING IT.
"IT WAS DESTINED TO SELF-DESTRUCT...LIKE BRUCE WAYNE'S FAMILY.
"THEY BUILT A CITY OF MADNESS."
ALFRED?
THERE'S NO ANSWER.
"THEN TRACE HER PHONE. SHE'S SOMEWHERE IN GOTHAM."

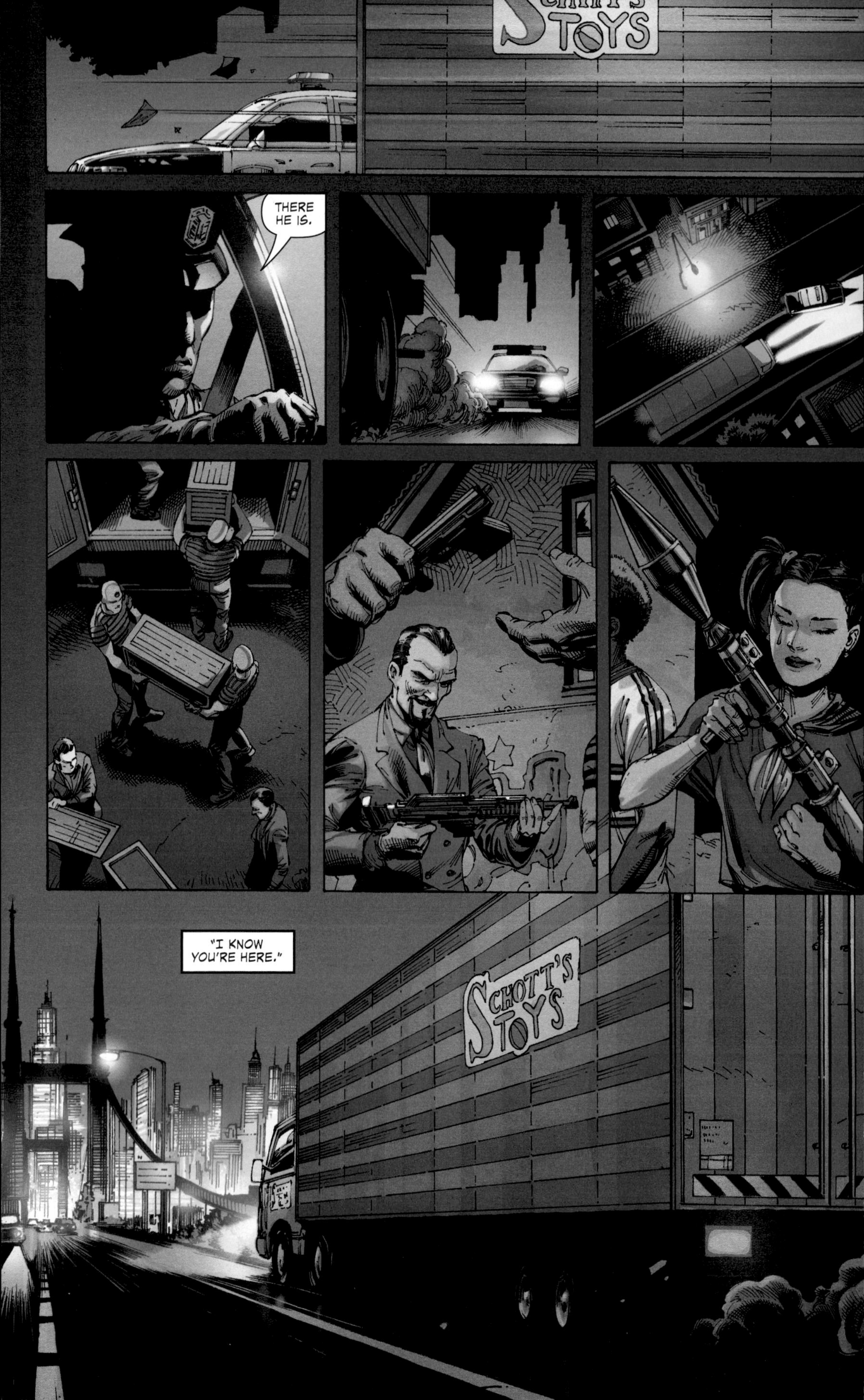
SCHOTT'S TOYS
THERE HE IS.
"I KNOW YOU'RE HERE."
SCHOTT'S TOYS

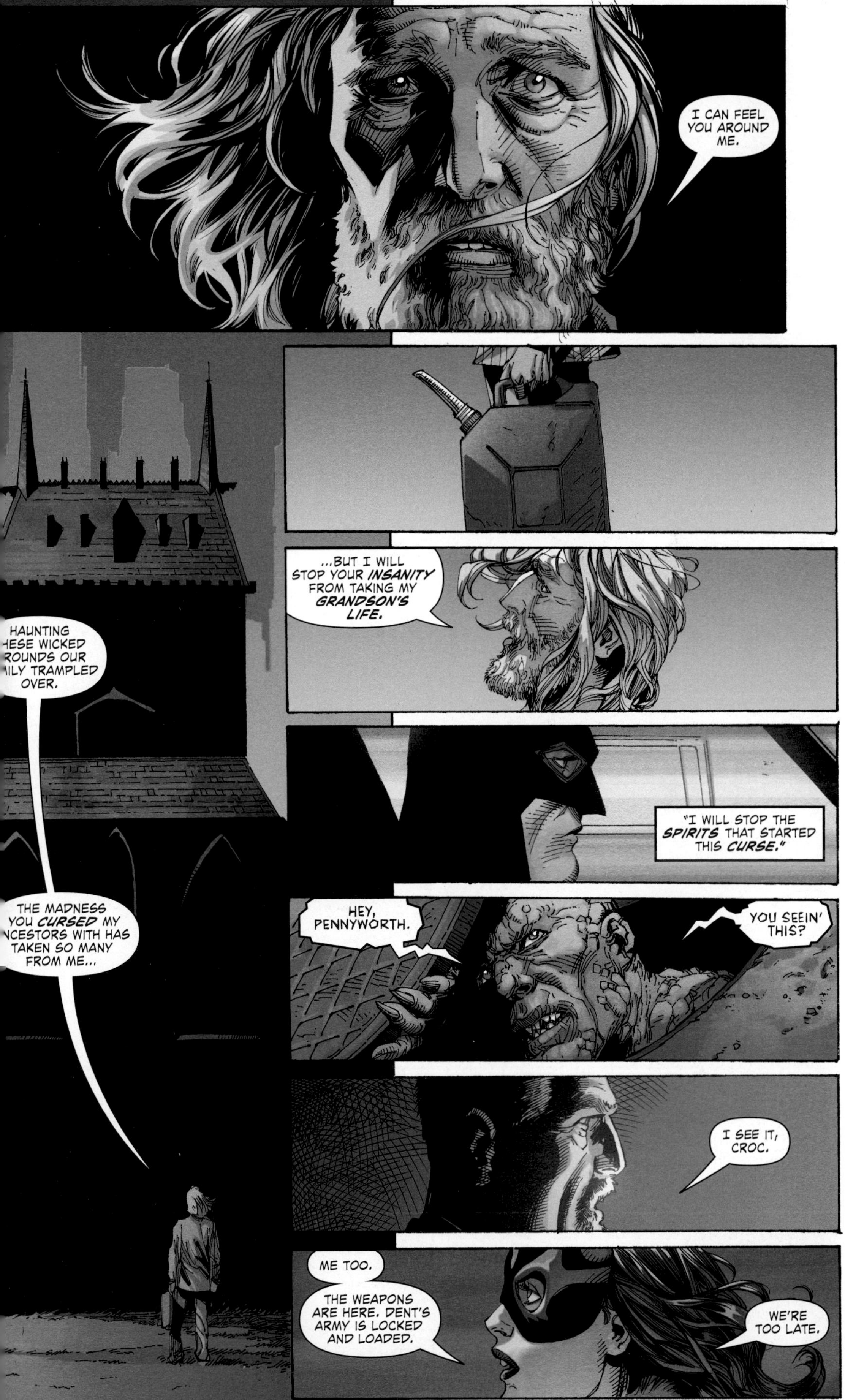
I CAN FEEL YOU AROUND ME.
...BUT I WILL STOP YOUR INSANITY FROM TAKING MY GRANDSON'S LIFE.
HAUNTING HESE WICKED ROUNDS OUR ILY TRAMPLED OVER.
"I WILL STOP THE SPIRITS THAT STARTED THIS CURSE."
THE MADNESS YOU CURSED MY NCESTORS WITH HAS TAKEN SO MANY FROM ME...
HEY, PENNYWORTH.
YOU SEEIN' THIS?
I SEE IT, CROC.
ME TOO.
THE WEAPONS ARE HERE. DENT'S ARMY IS LOCKED AND LOADED.
WE'RE TOO LATE.

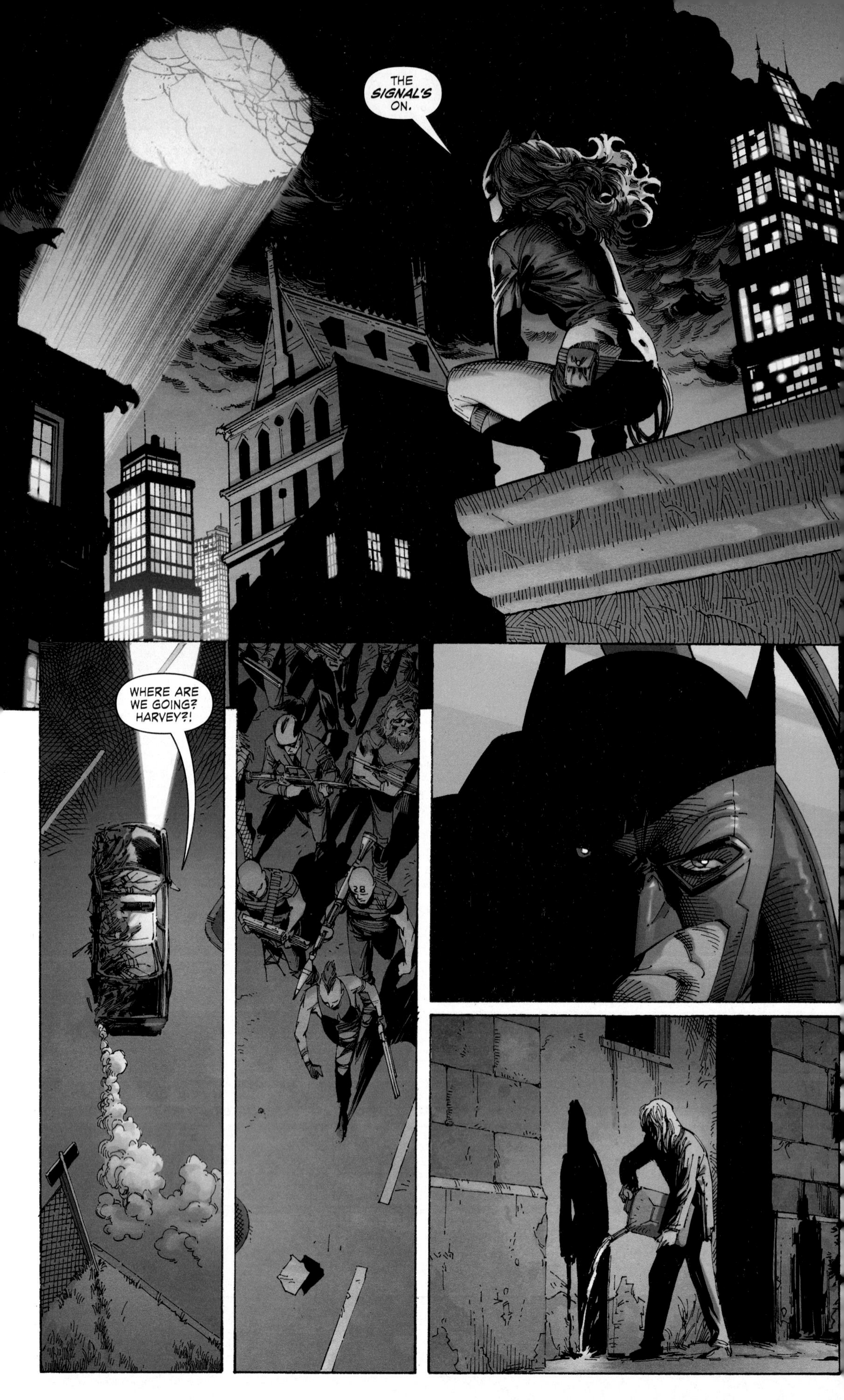
THE *SIGNAL'S* ON.
WHERE ARE WE GOING? HARVEY?!

"THEY'RE FILLING THE *STREETS.*

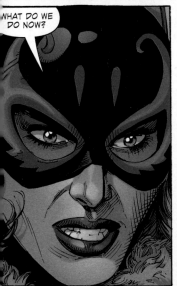

WHAT DO WE DO NOW?

BRUCE, IT'S JUST YOU AND ME ON THE LINE.

WHAT IS IT, ALFRED?

I TRACED JESSICA'S PHONE.

EEEEET

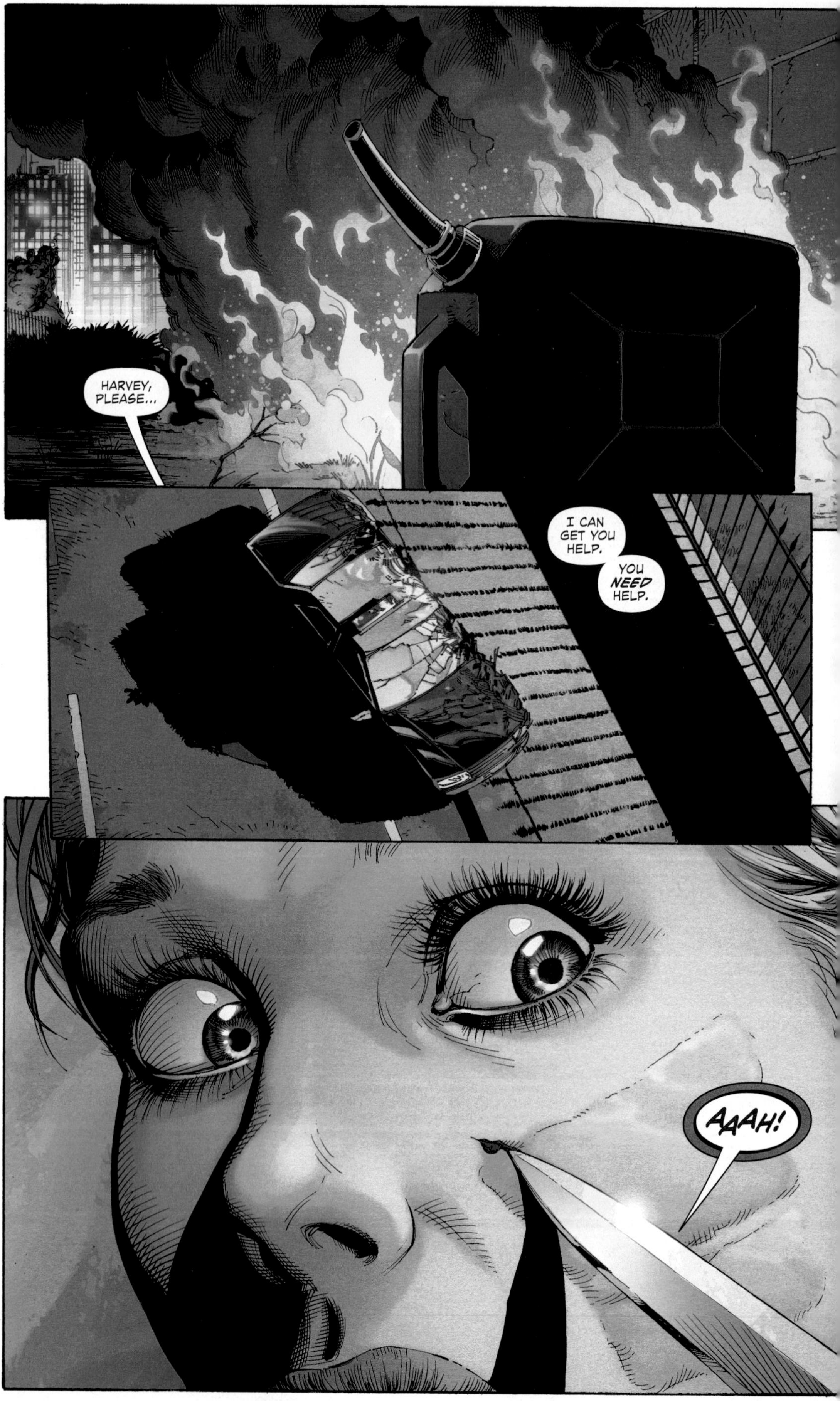
HARVEY, PLEASE...
I CAN GET YOU HELP.
YOU NEED HELP.
AAAH!

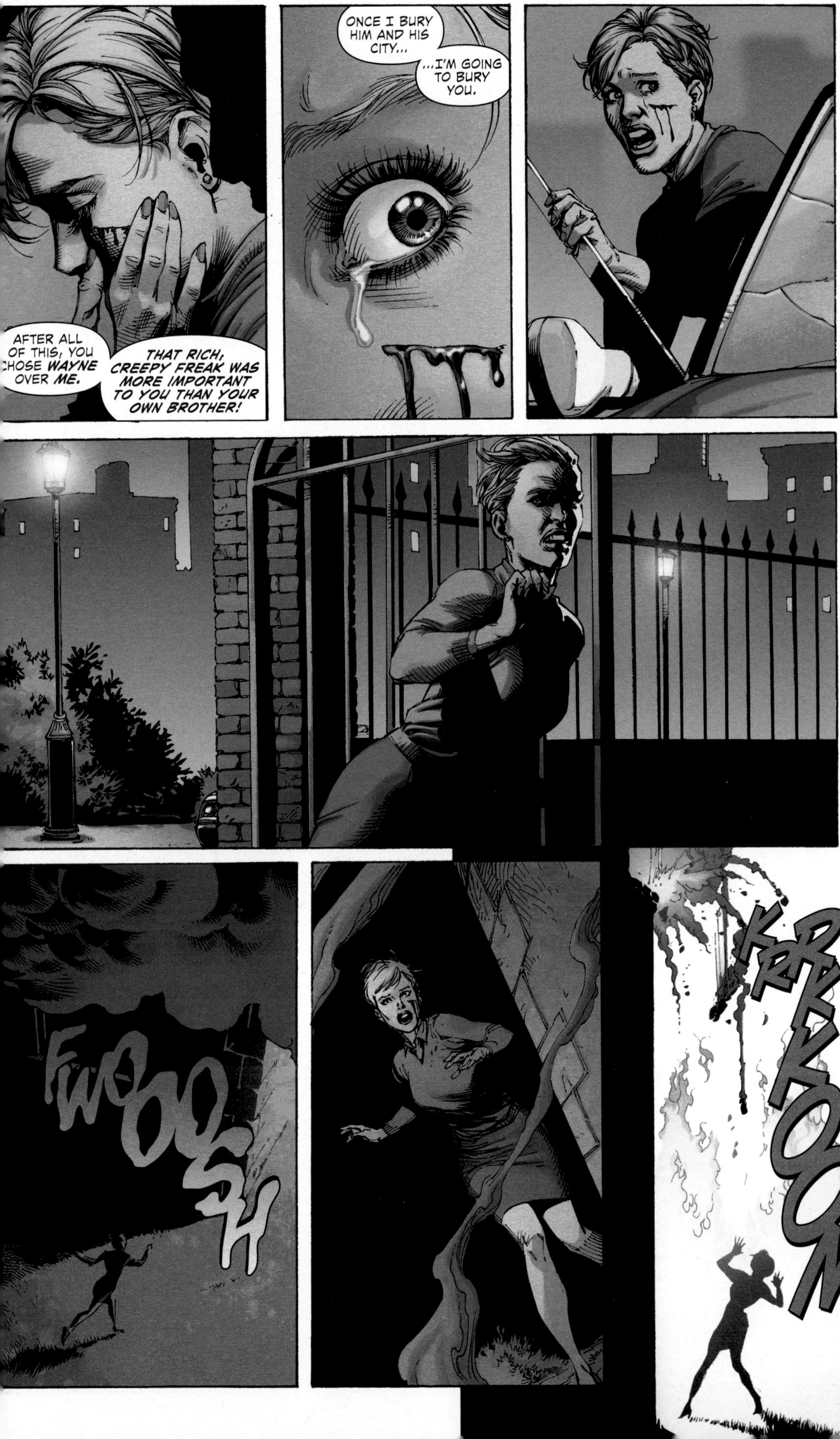
AFTER ALL OF THIS, YOU CHOSE WAYNE OVER ME.
THAT RICH, CREEPY FREAK WAS MORE IMPORTANT TO YOU THAN YOUR OWN BROTHER!
ONCE I BURY HIM AND HIS CITY...
...I'M GOING TO BURY YOU.
FWOOOSH
KRRKOOOM

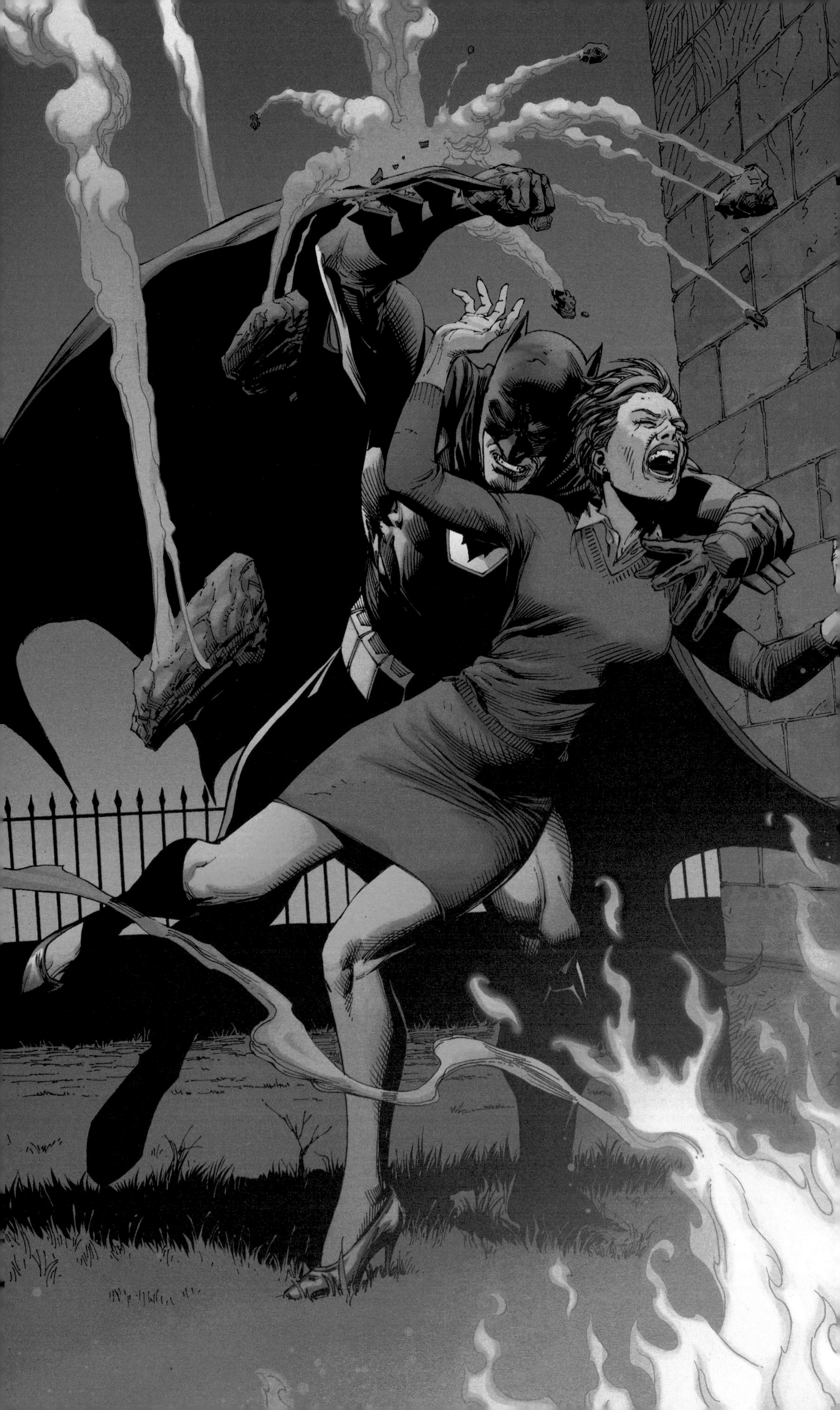

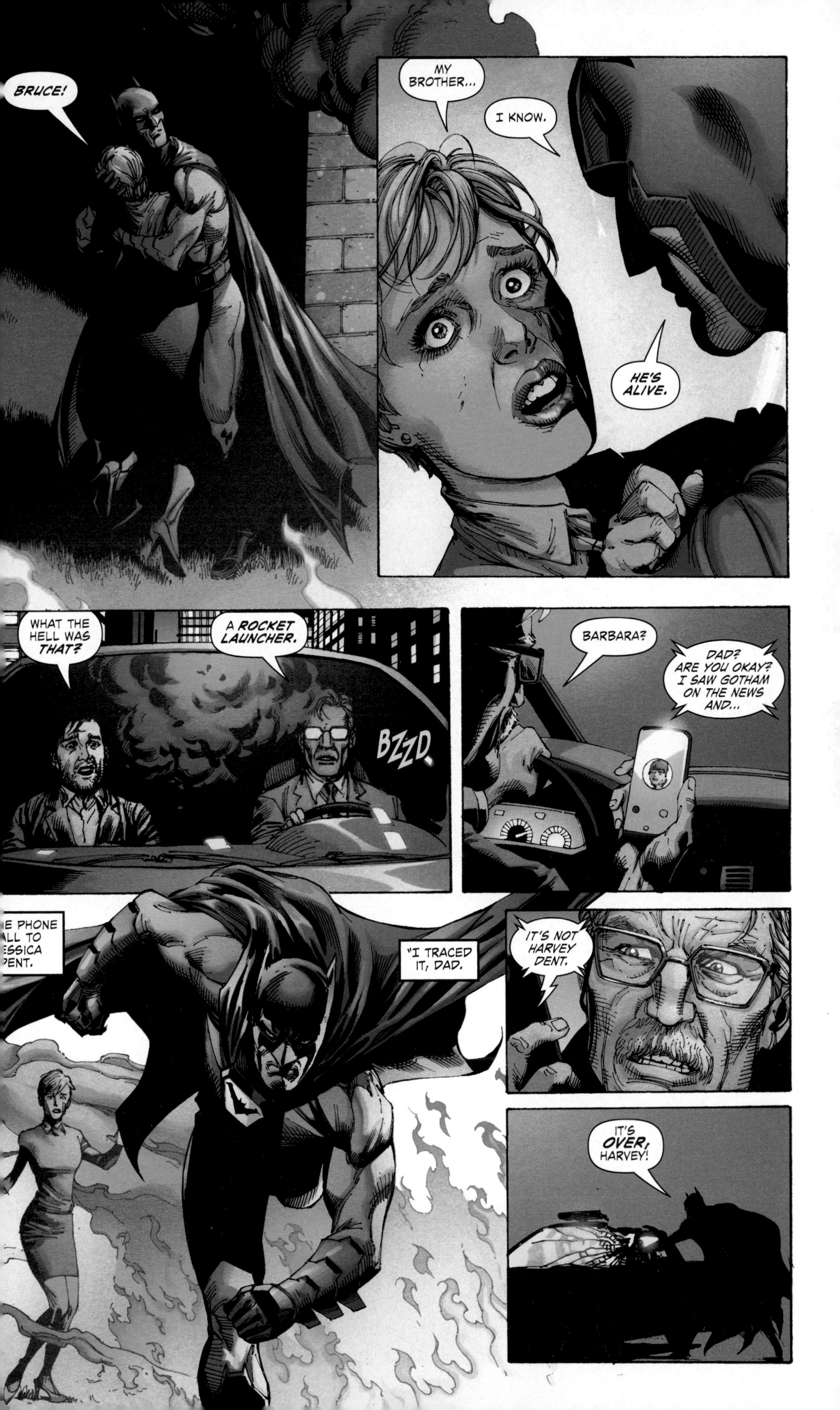

BRUCE!
MY BROTHER...
I KNOW.
HE'S ALIVE.
WHAT THE HELL WAS THAT?
A ROCKET LAUNCHER.
BZZD.
BARBARA?
DAD? ARE YOU OKAY? I SAW GOTHAM ON THE NEWS AND...
E PHONE
ALL TO
ESSICA
DENT.
"I TRACED IT, DAD.
IT'S NOT HARVEY DENT.
IT'S OVER, HARVEY!

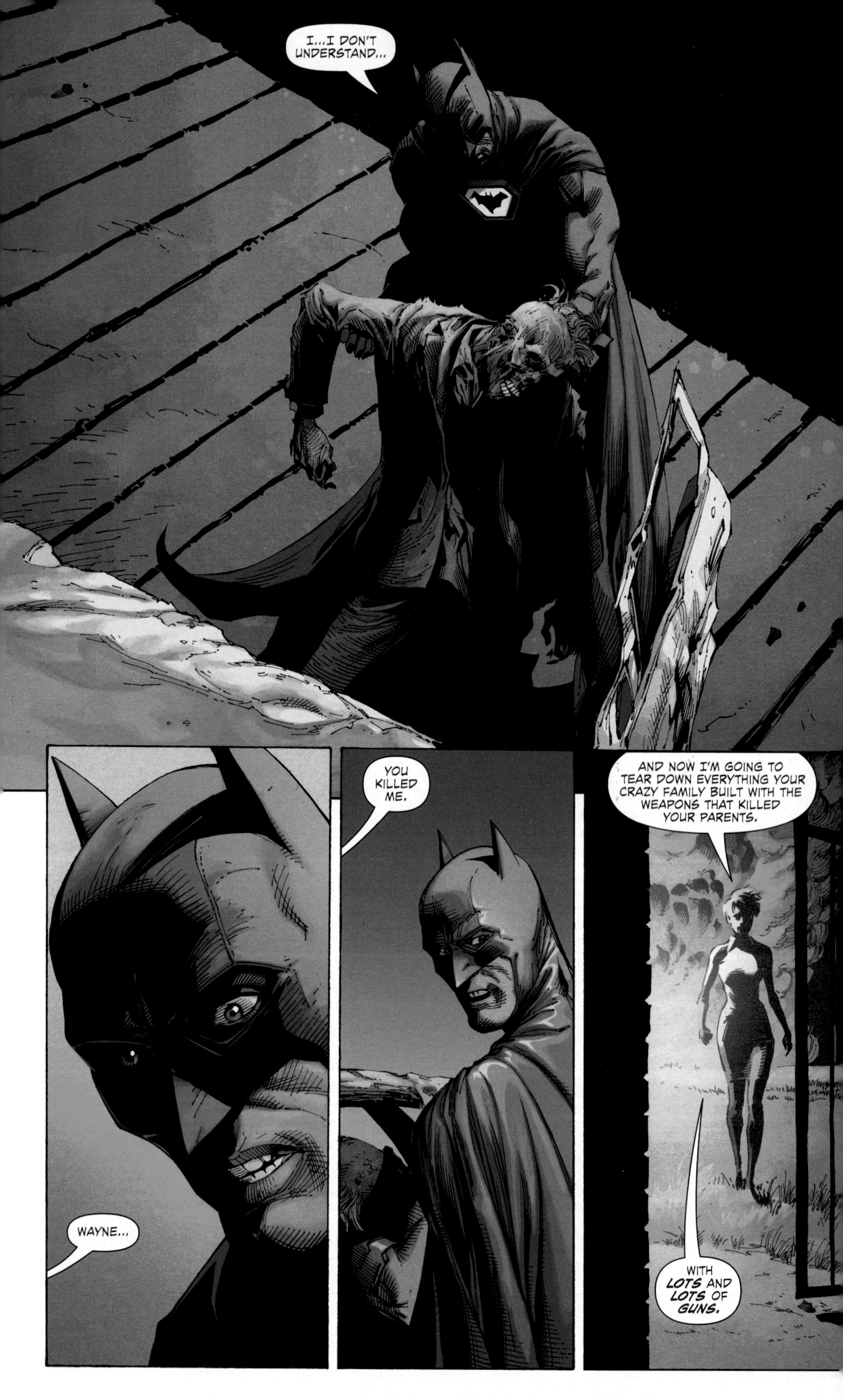
I...I DON'T UNDERSTAND...
WAYNE...
YOU KILLED ME.
AND NOW I'M GOING TO TEAR DOWN EVERYTHING YOUR CRAZY FAMILY BUILT WITH THE WEAPONS THAT KILLED YOUR PARENTS.
WITH *LOTS* AND *LOTS* OF *GUNS.*

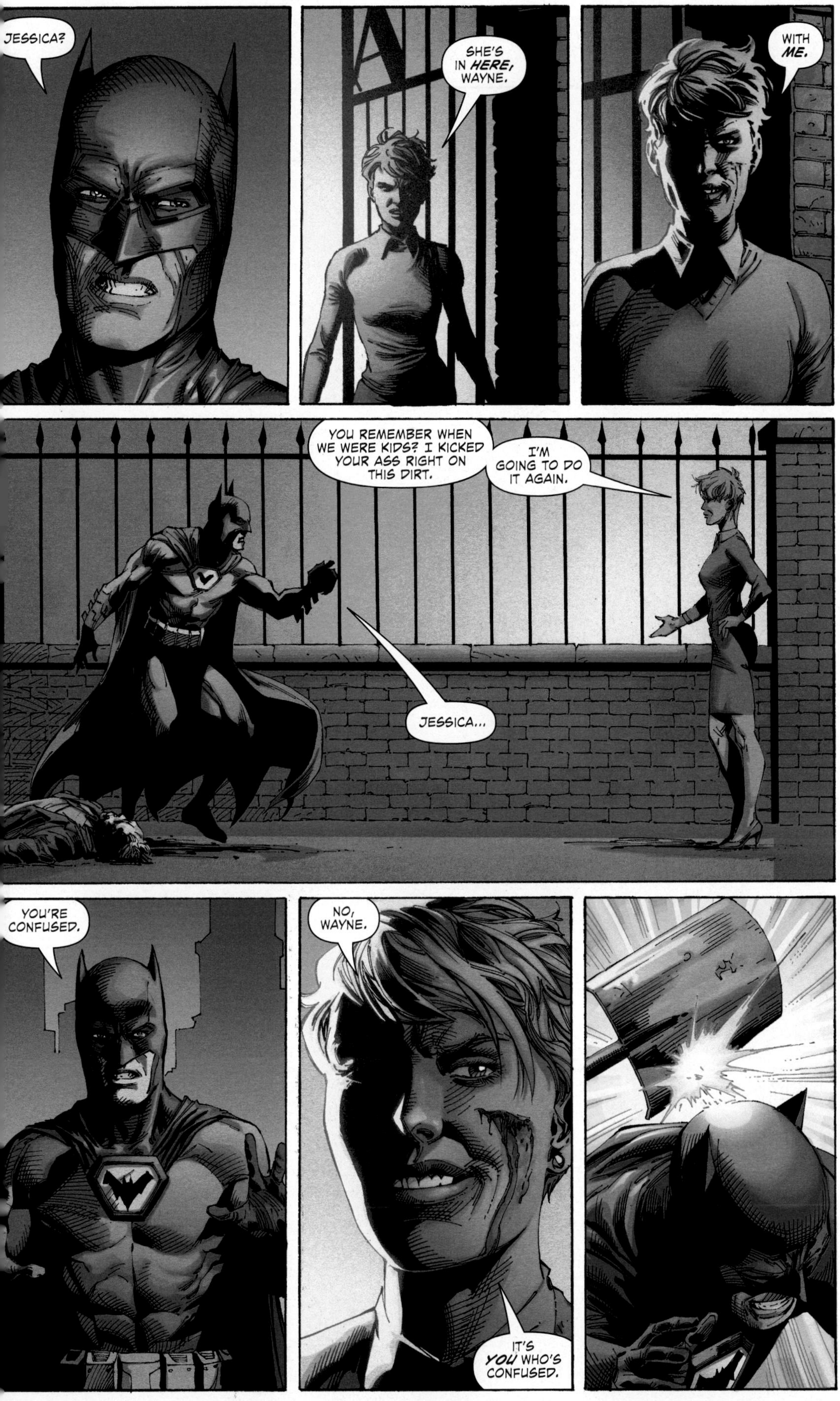
JESSICA?
SHE'S IN *HERE,* WAYNE.
WITH *ME.*
YOU REMEMBER WHEN WE WERE KIDS? I KICKED YOUR ASS RIGHT ON THIS DIRT.
I'M GOING TO DO IT AGAIN.
JESSICA...
YOU'RE CONFUSED.
NO, WAYNE.
IT'S *YOU* WHO'S CONFUSED.

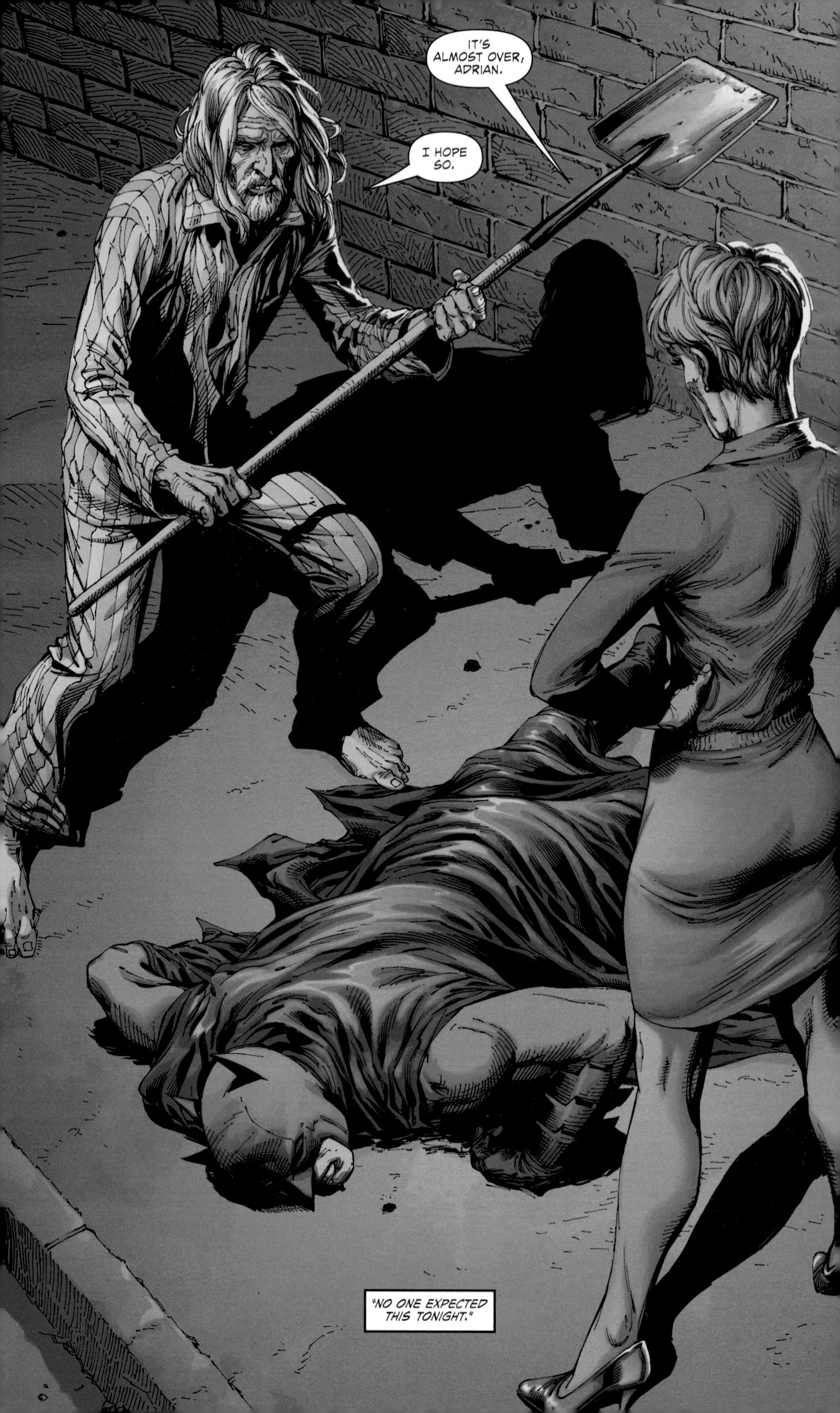
IT'S ALMOST OVER, ADRIAN.
I HOPE SO.
"NO ONE EXPECTED THIS TONIGHT."

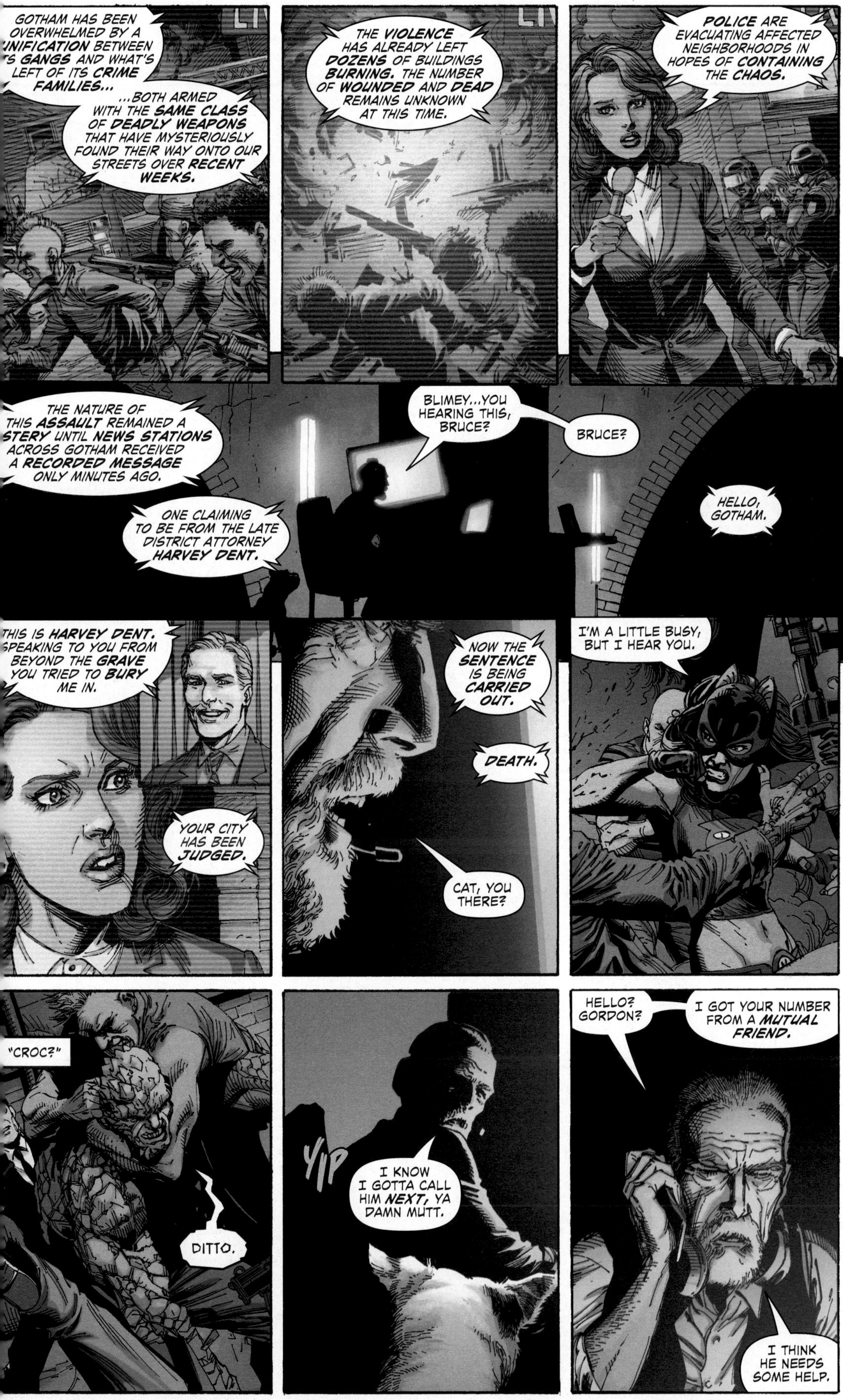

GOTHAM HAS BEEN OVERWHELMED BY A UNIFICATION BETWEEN ITS GANGS AND WHAT'S LEFT OF ITS CRIME FAMILIES...
...BOTH ARMED WITH THE SAME CLASS OF DEADLY WEAPONS THAT HAVE MYSTERIOUSLY FOUND THEIR WAY ONTO OUR STREETS OVER RECENT WEEKS.
THE VIOLENCE HAS ALREADY LEFT DOZENS OF BUILDINGS BURNING. THE NUMBER OF WOUNDED AND DEAD REMAINS UNKNOWN AT THIS TIME.
POLICE ARE EVACUATING AFFECTED NEIGHBORHOODS IN HOPES OF CONTAINING THE CHAOS.
THE NATURE OF THIS ASSAULT REMAINED A MYSTERY UNTIL NEWS STATIONS ACROSS GOTHAM RECEIVED A RECORDED MESSAGE ONLY MINUTES AGO.
ONE CLAIMING TO BE FROM THE LATE DISTRICT ATTORNEY HARVEY DENT.
BLIMEY...YOU HEARING THIS, BRUCE?
BRUCE?
HELLO, GOTHAM.
THIS IS HARVEY DENT. SPEAKING TO YOU FROM BEYOND THE GRAVE YOU TRIED TO BURY ME IN.
YOUR CITY HAS BEEN JUDGED.
NOW THE SENTENCE IS BEING CARRIED OUT.
DEATH.
CAT, YOU THERE?
I'M A LITTLE BUSY, BUT I HEAR YOU.
"CROC?"
DITTO.
YIP
I KNOW I GOTTA CALL HIM NEXT, YA DAMN MUTT.
HELLO? GORDON?
I GOT YOUR NUMBER FROM A MUTUAL FRIEND.
I THINK HE NEEDS SOME HELP.

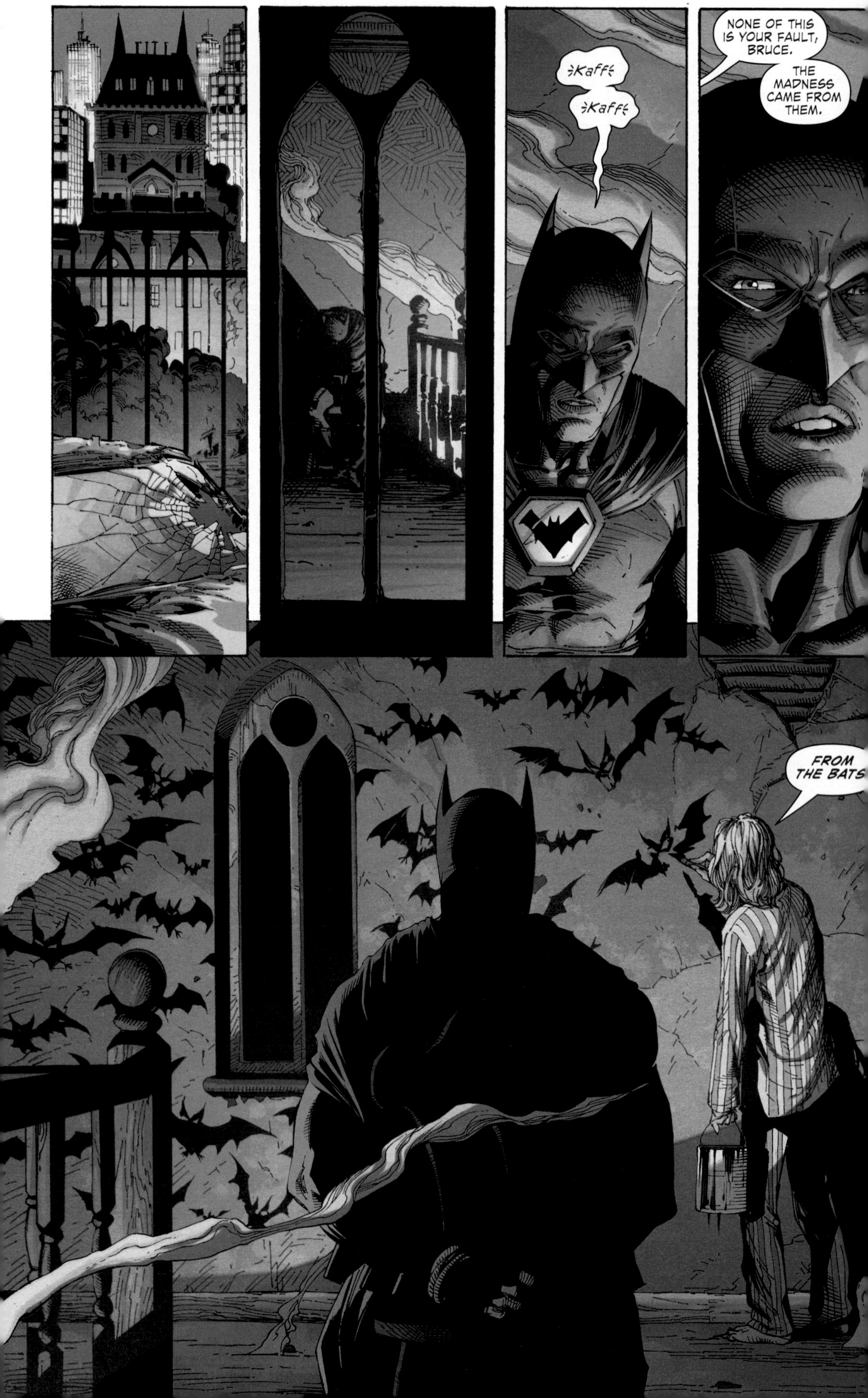

Kaff
Kaff
NONE OF THIS IS YOUR FAULT, BRUCE.
THE MADNESS CAME FROM THEM.
FROM THE BATS

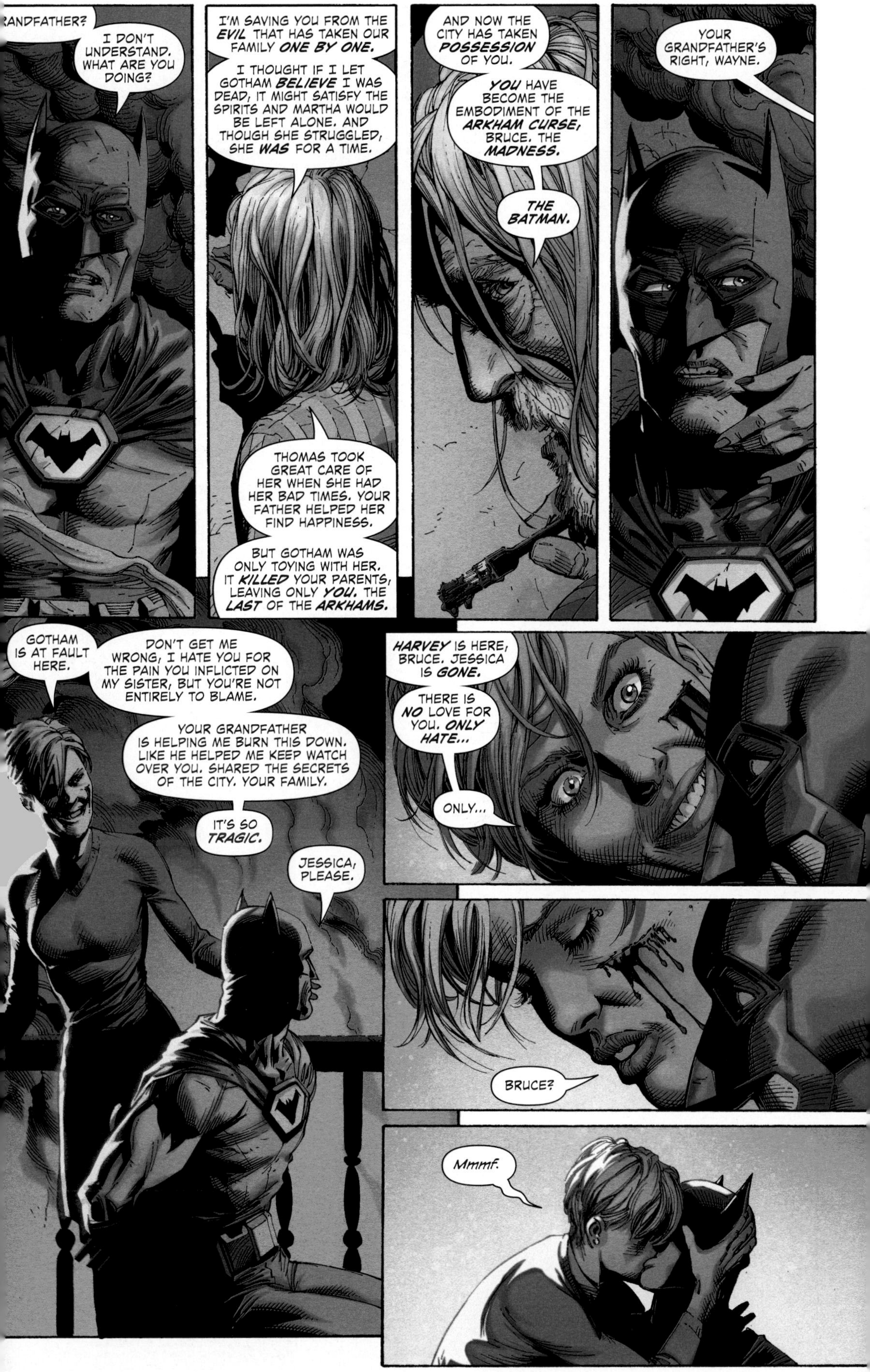

RANDFATHER?
I DON'T UNDERSTAND. WHAT ARE YOU DOING?
I'M SAVING YOU FROM THE EVIL THAT HAS TAKEN OUR FAMILY ONE BY ONE.
I THOUGHT IF I LET GOTHAM BELIEVE I WAS DEAD, IT MIGHT SATISFY THE SPIRITS AND MARTHA WOULD BE LEFT ALONE. AND THOUGH SHE STRUGGLED, SHE WAS FOR A TIME.
THOMAS TOOK GREAT CARE OF HER WHEN SHE HAD HER BAD TIMES. YOUR FATHER HELPED HER FIND HAPPINESS.
BUT GOTHAM WAS ONLY TOYING WITH HER. IT KILLED YOUR PARENTS, LEAVING ONLY YOU. THE LAST OF THE ARKHAMS.
AND NOW THE CITY HAS TAKEN POSSESSION OF YOU.
YOU HAVE BECOME THE EMBODIMENT OF THE ARKHAM CURSE, BRUCE. THE MADNESS.
THE BATMAN.
YOUR GRANDFATHER'S RIGHT, WAYNE.
GOTHAM IS AT FAULT HERE.
DON'T GET ME WRONG, I HATE YOU FOR THE PAIN YOU INFLICTED ON MY SISTER, BUT YOU'RE NOT ENTIRELY TO BLAME.
YOUR GRANDFATHER IS HELPING ME BURN THIS DOWN. LIKE HE HELPED ME KEEP WATCH OVER YOU. SHARED THE SECRETS OF THE CITY. YOUR FAMILY.
IT'S SO TRAGIC.
JESSICA, PLEASE.
HARVEY IS HERE, BRUCE. JESSICA IS GONE.
THERE IS NO LOVE FOR YOU. ONLY HATE...
ONLY...
BRUCE?
Mmmf.

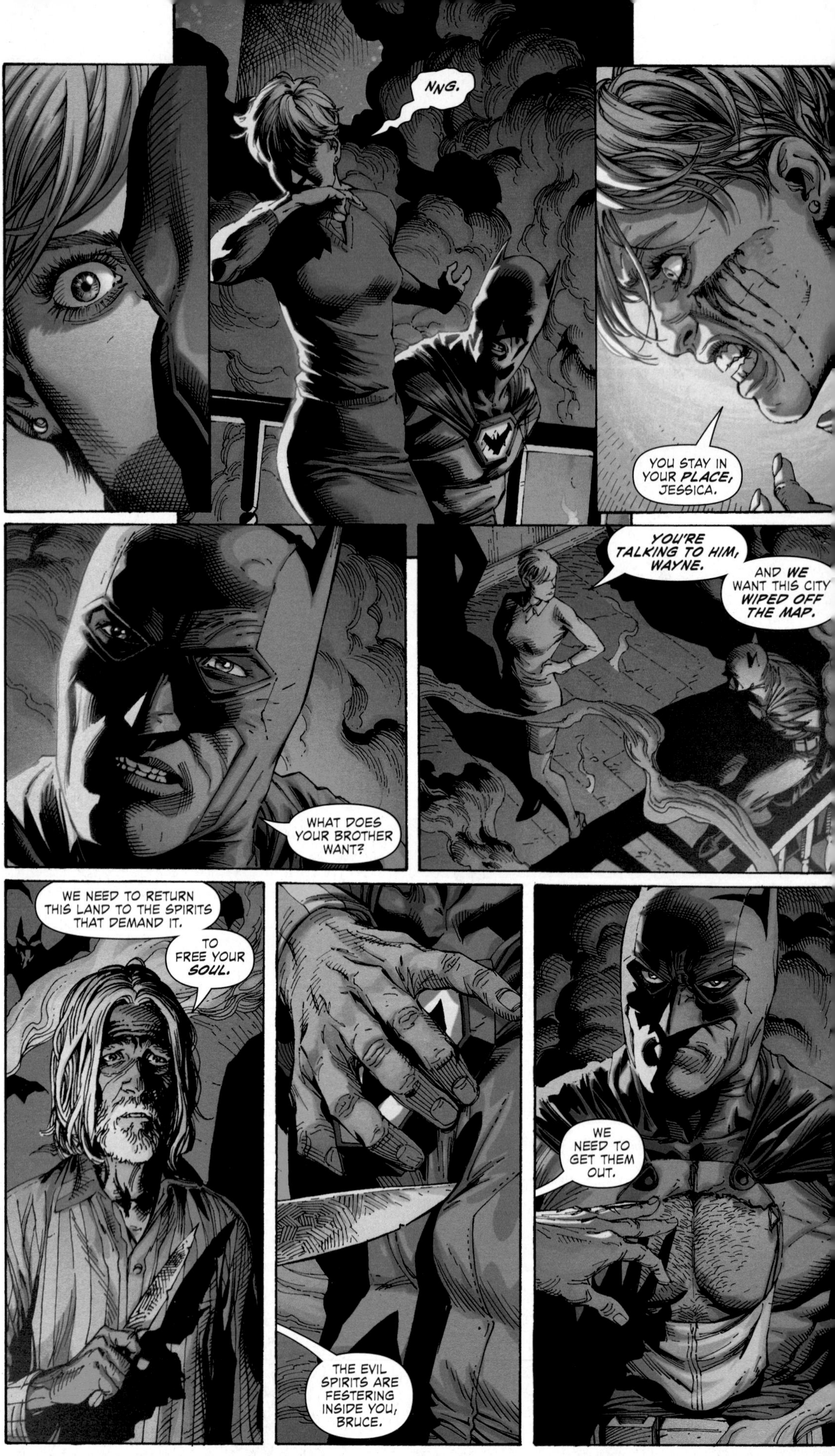
NNG.
YOU STAY IN YOUR PLACE, JESSICA.
WHAT DOES YOUR BROTHER WANT?
YOU'RE TALKING TO HIM, WAYNE.
AND WE WANT THIS CITY WIPED OFF THE MAP.
WE NEED TO RETURN THIS LAND TO THE SPIRITS THAT DEMAND IT.
TO FREE YOUR SOUL.
THE EVIL SPIRITS ARE FESTERING INSIDE YOU, BRUCE.
WE NEED TO GET THEM OUT.

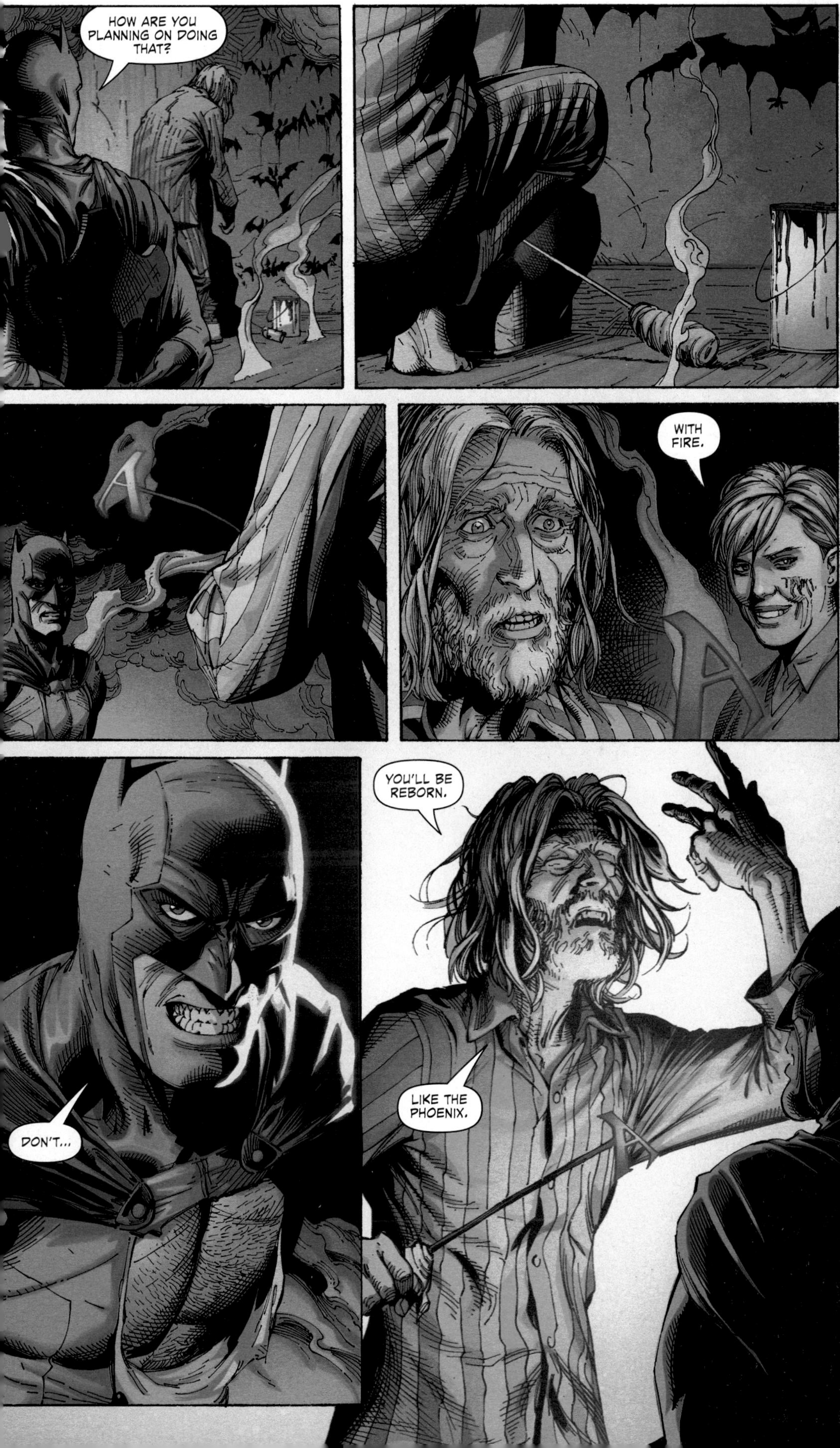
HOW ARE YOU PLANNING ON DOING THAT?
WITH FIRE.
YOU'LL BE REBORN.
DON'T...
LIKE THE PHOENIX.

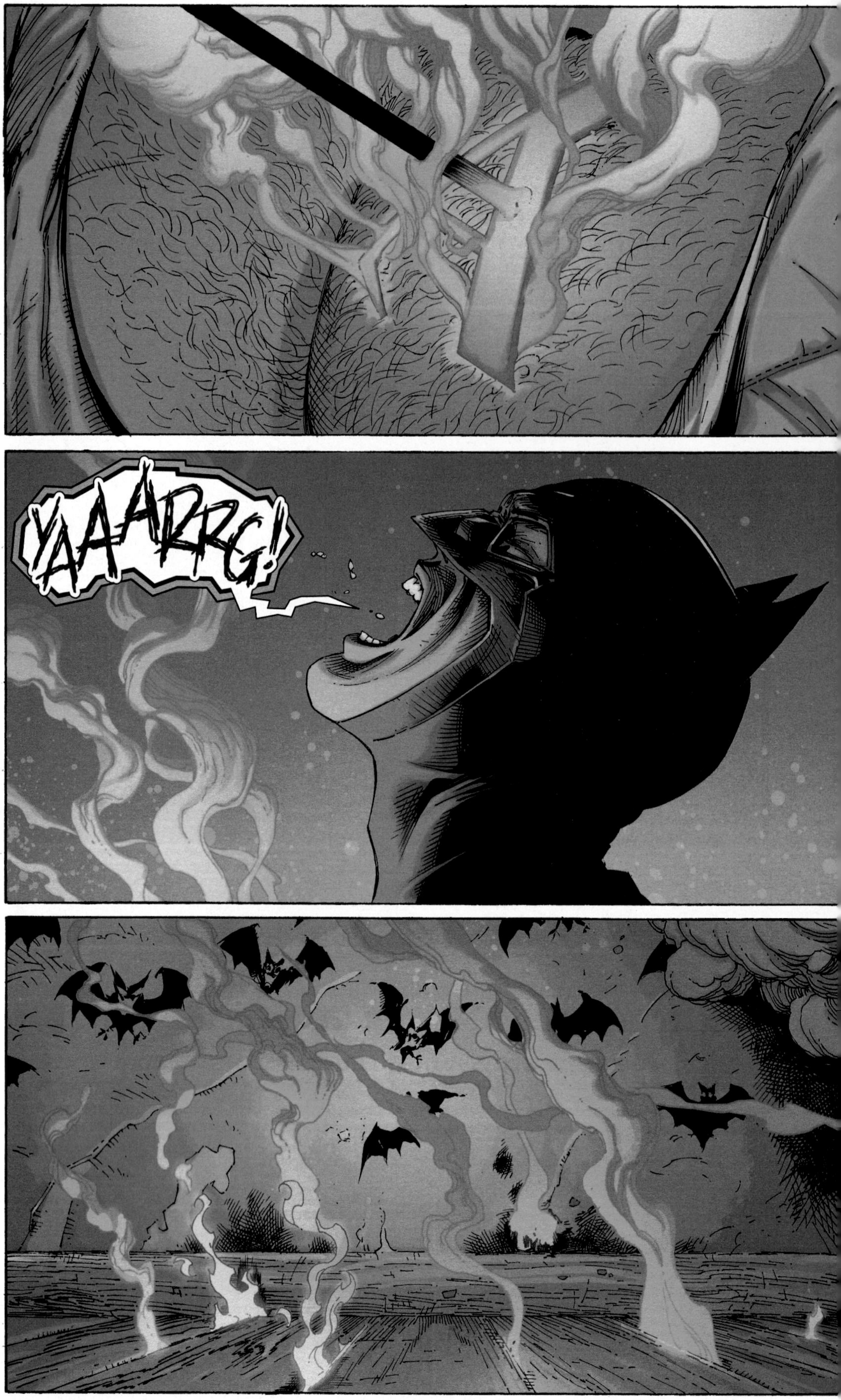
YAAARRG!

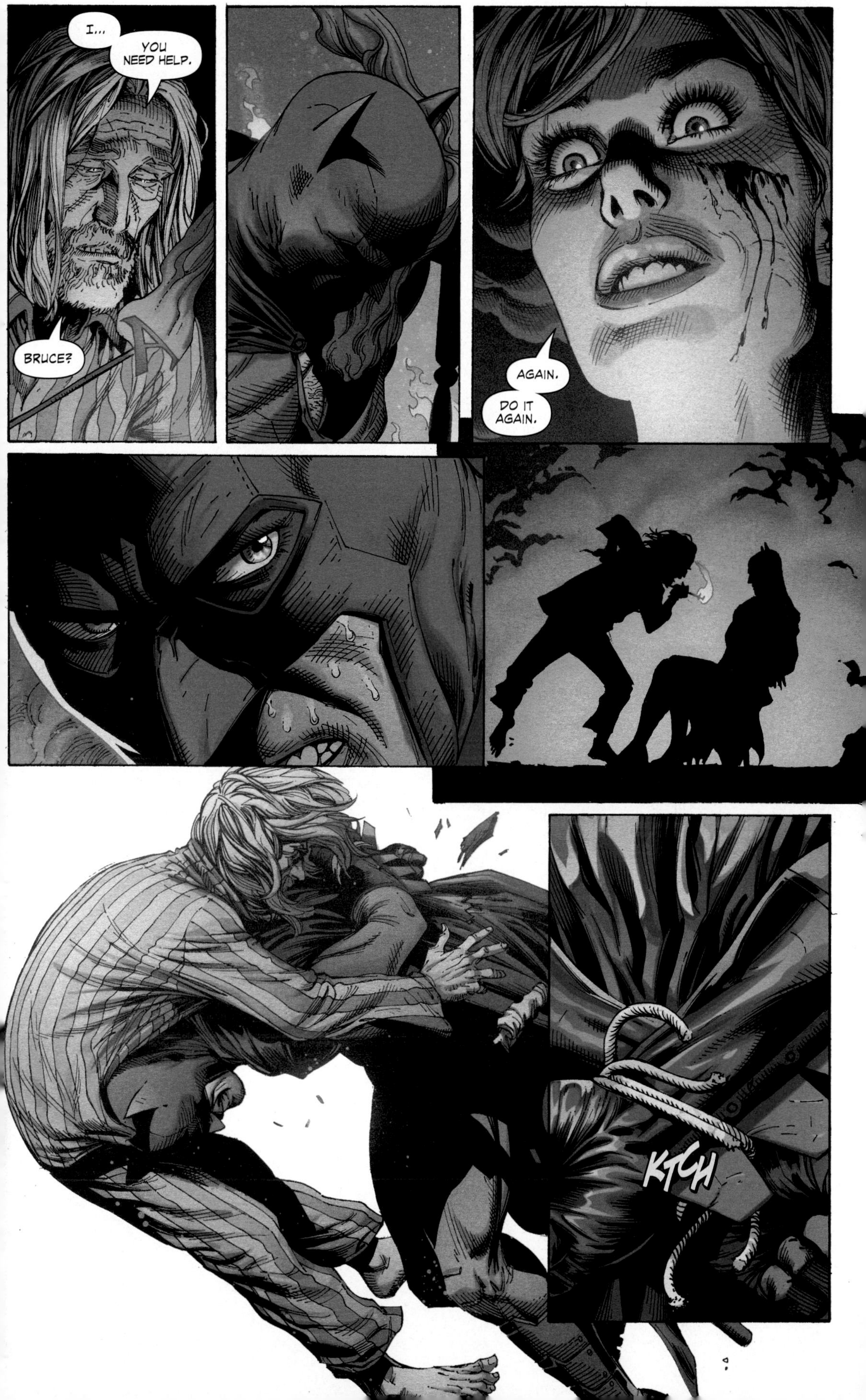
I...
YOU NEED HELP.
BRUCE?
AGAIN.
DO IT AGAIN.
KTCH

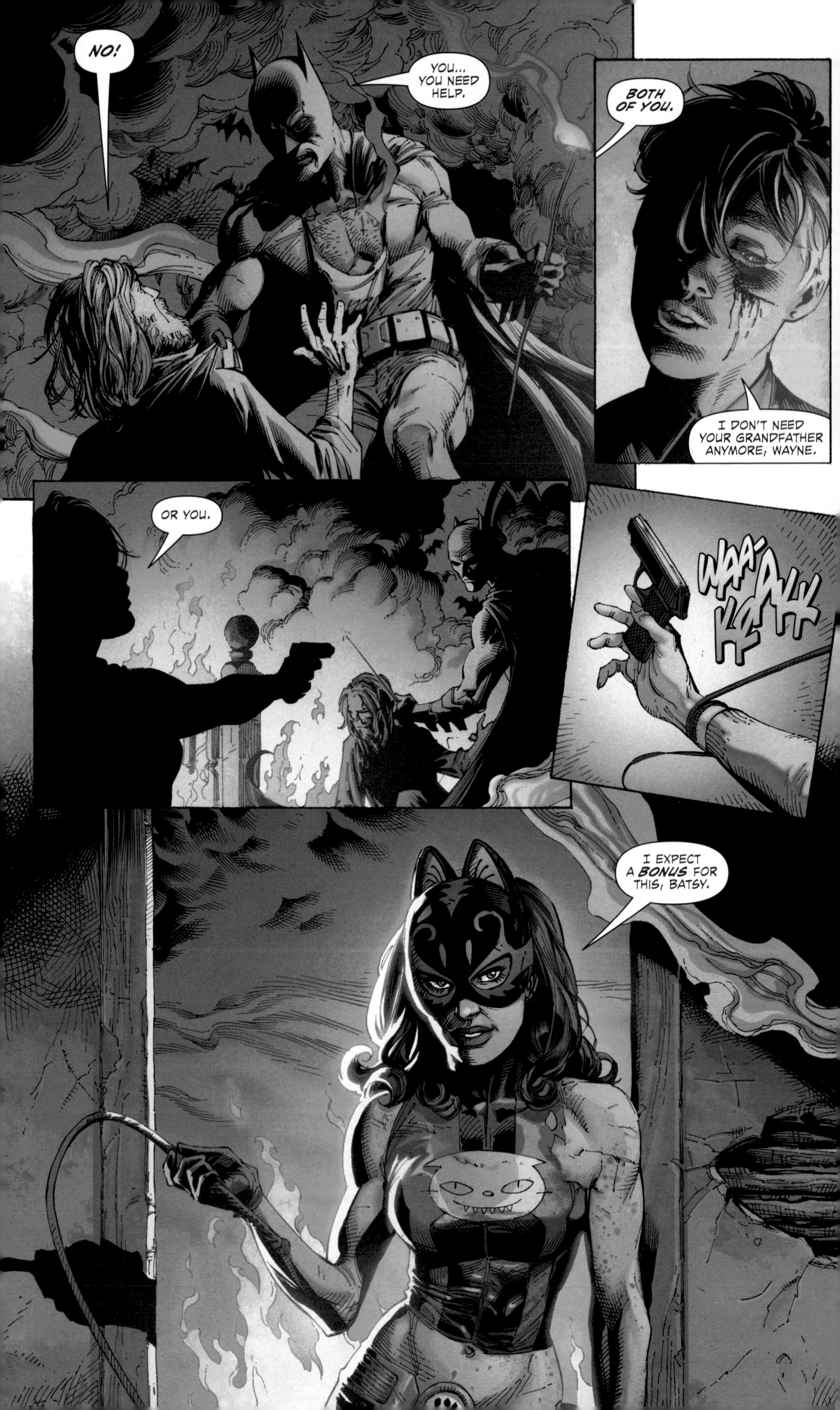
NO!
YOU... YOU NEED HELP.
BOTH OF YOU.
I DON'T NEED YOUR GRANDFATHER ANYMORE, WAYNE.
OR YOU.
WAA-PAK KRAK
I EXPECT A BONUS FOR THIS, BATSY.

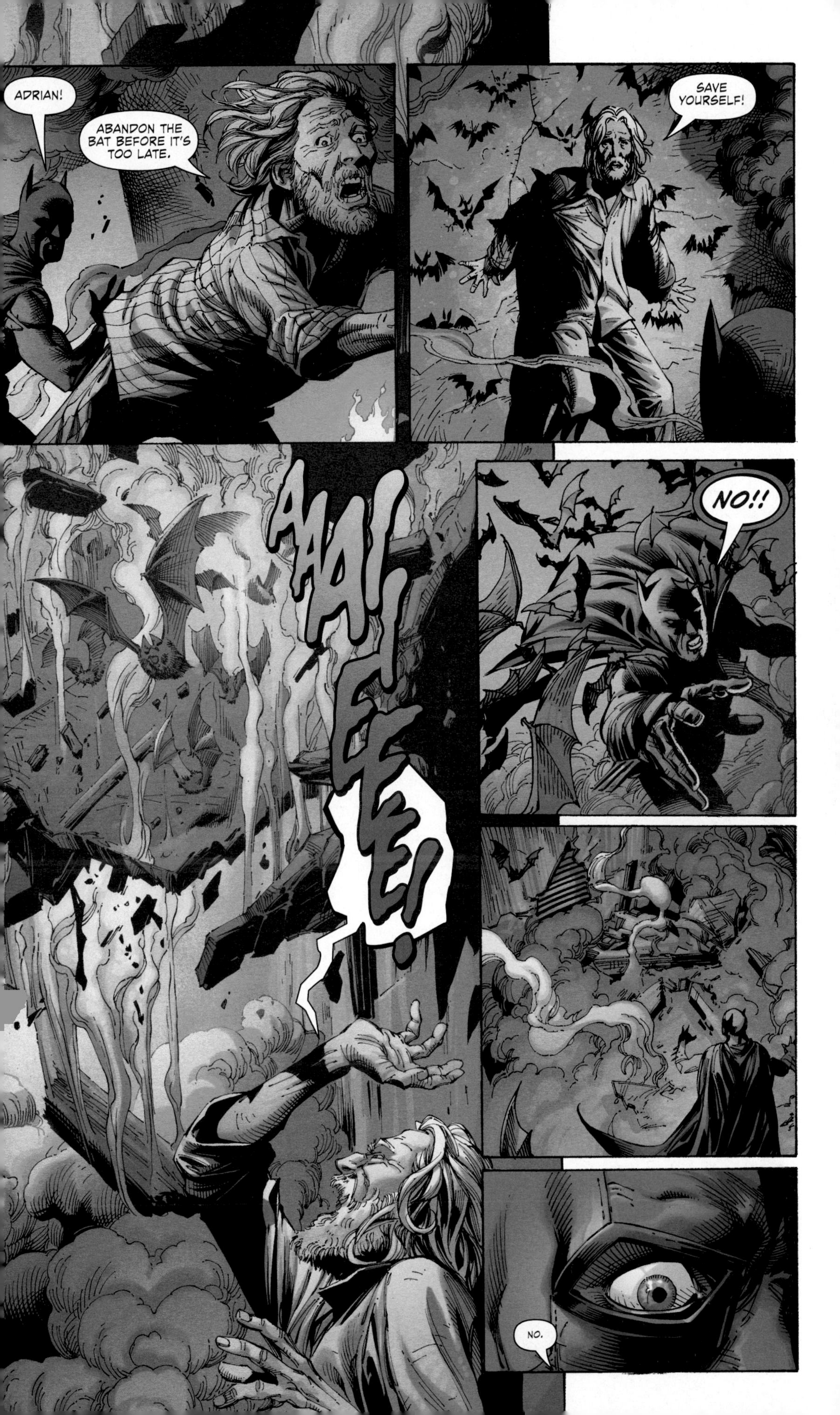
ADRIAN!
ABANDON THE BAT BEFORE IT'S TOO LATE.
SAVE YOURSELF!
AAAIEEEE!
NO!!
NO.

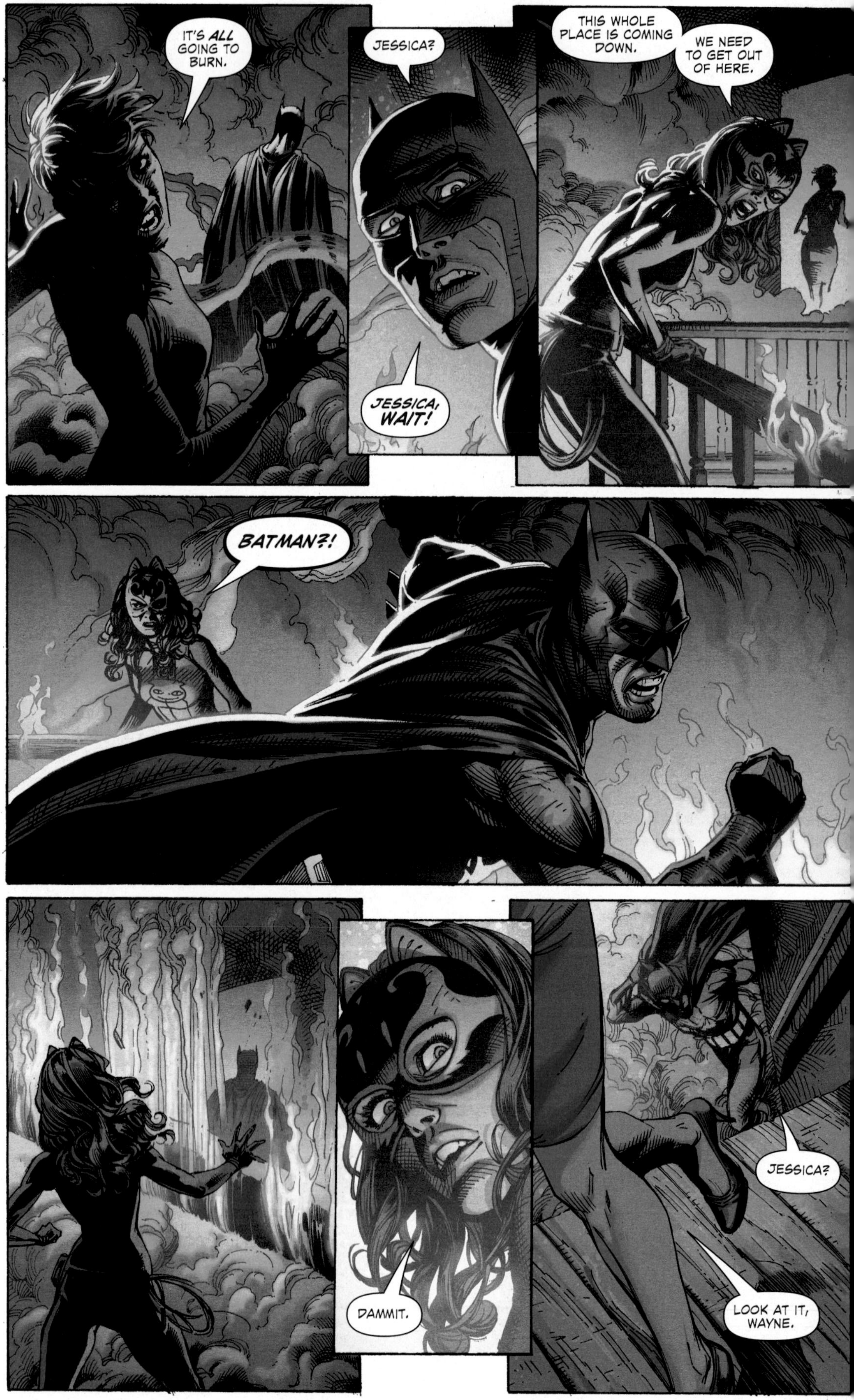

IT'S ALL GOING TO BURN.
JESSICA?
JESSICA, WAIT!
THIS WHOLE PLACE IS COMING DOWN.
WE NEED TO GET OUT OF HERE.
BATMAN?!
DAMMIT.
JESSICA?
LOOK AT IT, WAYNE.

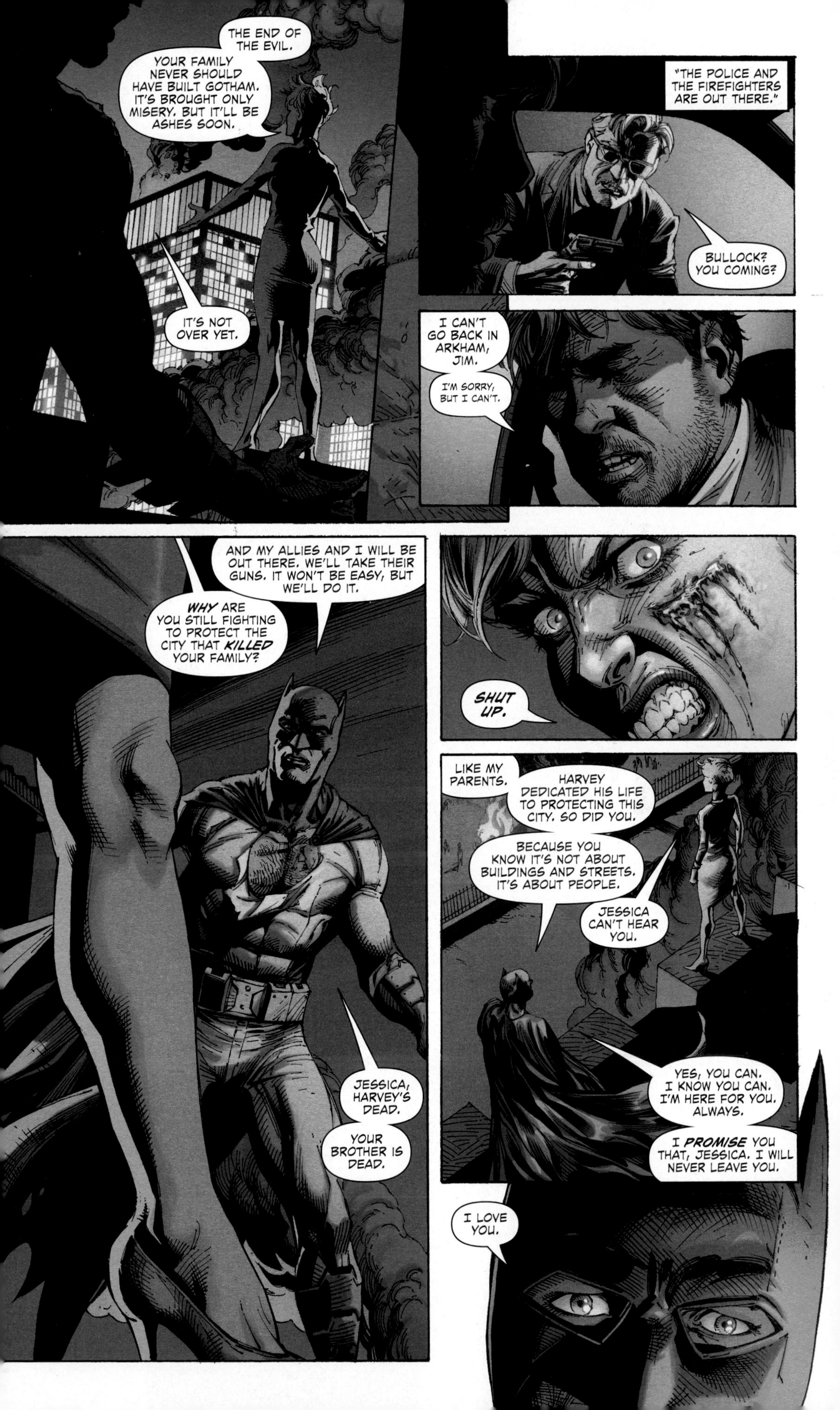

THE END OF THE EVIL.
YOUR FAMILY NEVER SHOULD HAVE BUILT GOTHAM. IT'S BROUGHT ONLY MISERY. BUT IT'LL BE ASHES SOON.
IT'S NOT OVER YET.
"THE POLICE AND THE FIREFIGHTERS ARE OUT THERE."
BULLOCK? YOU COMING?
I CAN'T GO BACK IN ARKHAM, JIM.
I'M SORRY, BUT I CAN'T.
AND MY ALLIES AND I WILL BE OUT THERE. WE'LL TAKE THEIR GUNS. IT WON'T BE EASY, BUT WE'LL DO IT.
WHY ARE YOU STILL FIGHTING TO PROTECT THE CITY THAT *KILLED* YOUR FAMILY?
SHUT UP.
JESSICA, HARVEY'S DEAD.
YOUR BROTHER IS DEAD.
LIKE MY PARENTS.
HARVEY DEDICATED HIS LIFE TO PROTECTING THIS CITY. SO DID YOU.
BECAUSE YOU KNOW IT'S NOT ABOUT BUILDINGS AND STREETS. IT'S ABOUT PEOPLE.
JESSICA CAN'T HEAR YOU.
YES, YOU CAN. I KNOW YOU CAN. I'M HERE FOR YOU. ALWAYS.
I *PROMISE* YOU THAT, JESSICA. I WILL NEVER LEAVE YOU.
I LOVE YOU.

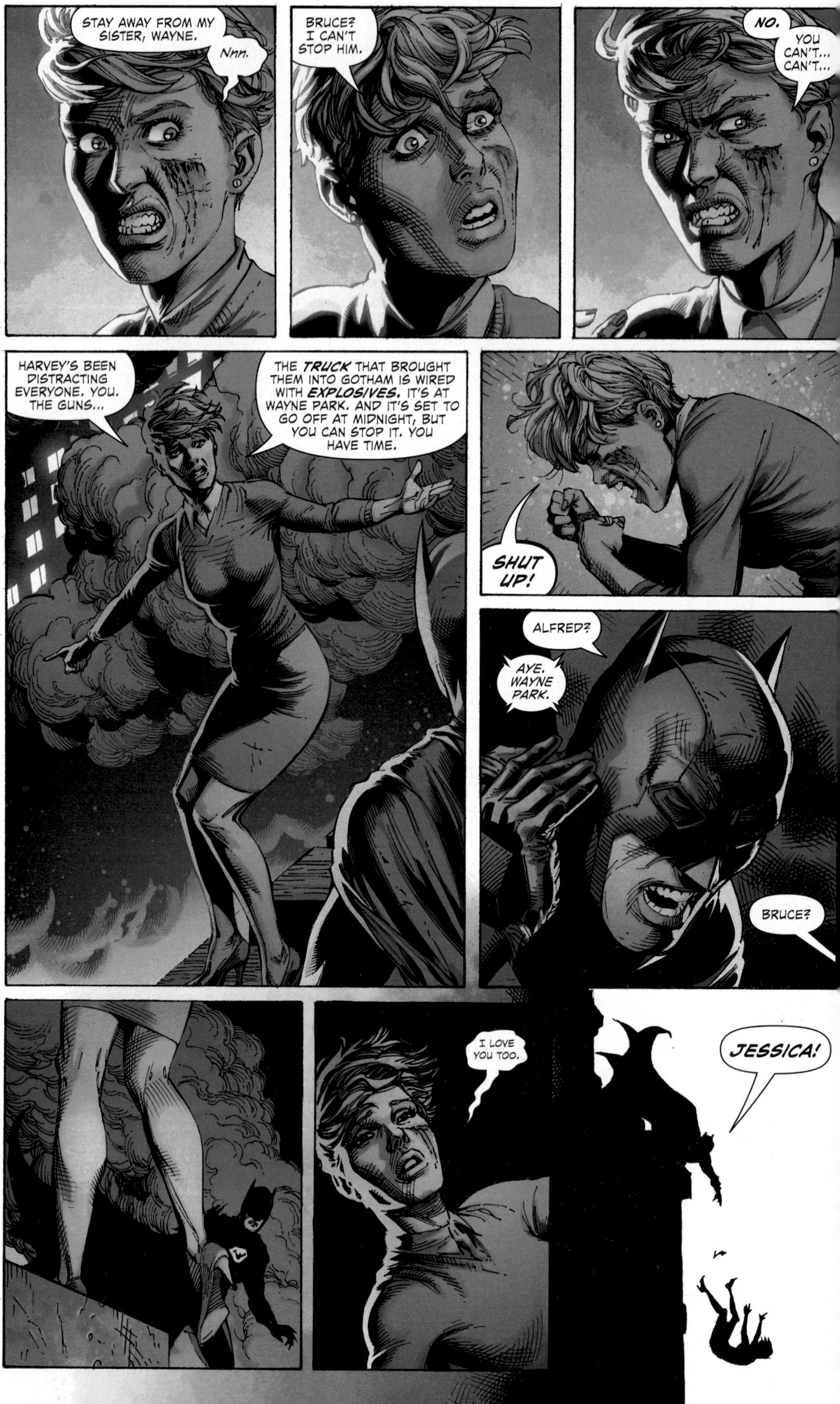
STAY AWAY FROM MY SISTER, WAYNE.
Nnn.
BRUCE? I CAN'T STOP HIM.
NO.
YOU CAN'T... CAN'T...
HARVEY'S BEEN DISTRACTING EVERYONE. YOU. THE GUNS...
THE TRUCK THAT BROUGHT THEM INTO GOTHAM IS WIRED WITH EXPLOSIVES. IT'S AT WAYNE PARK. AND IT'S SET TO GO OFF AT MIDNIGHT, BUT YOU CAN STOP IT. YOU HAVE TIME.
SHUT UP!
ALFRED?
AYE. WAYNE PARK.
BRUCE?
I LOVE YOU TOO.
JESSICA!

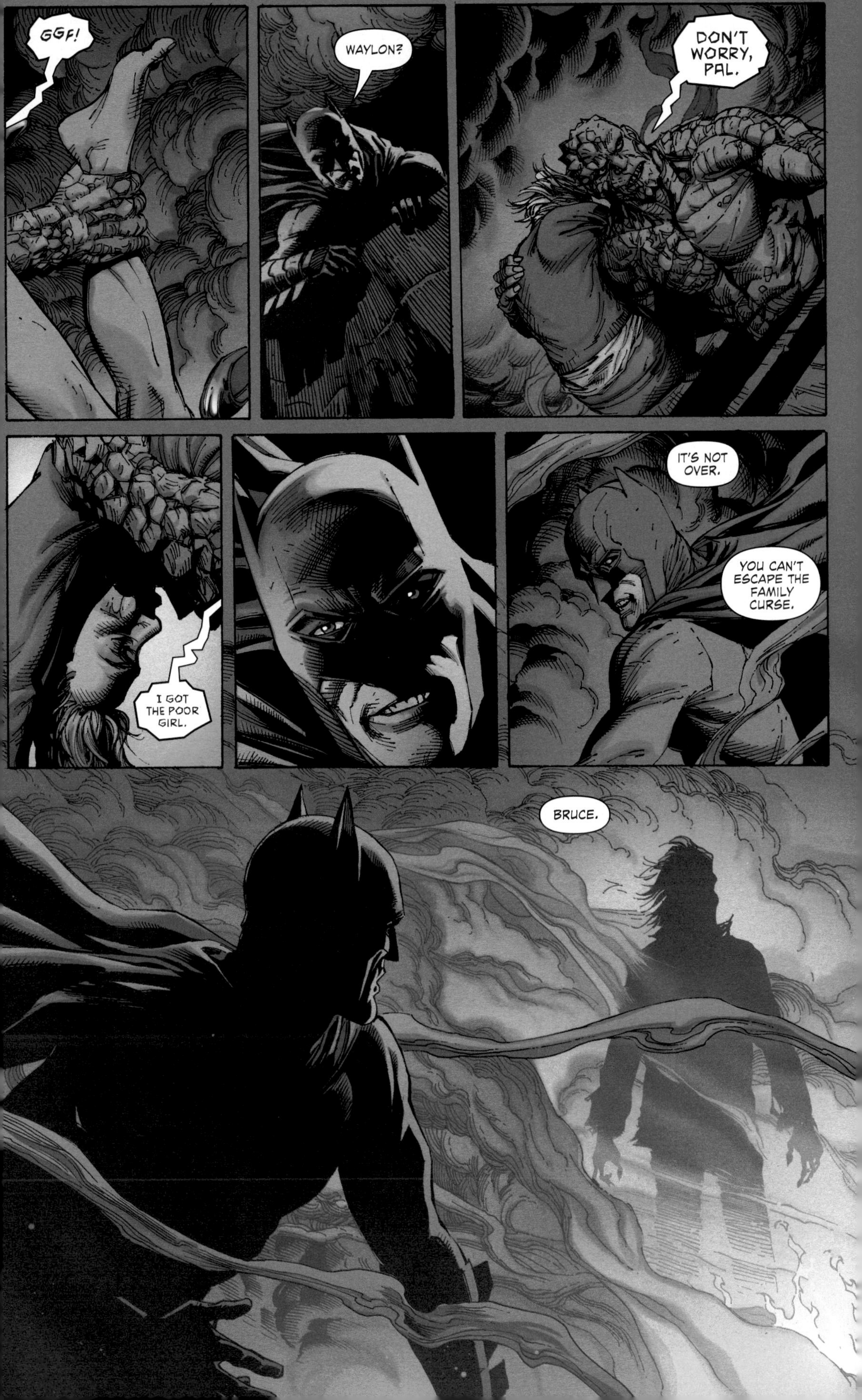
GGF!
WAYLON?
DON'T WORRY, PAL.
I GOT THE POOR GIRL.
IT'S NOT OVER.
YOU CAN'T ESCAPE THE FAMILY CURSE.
BRUCE.

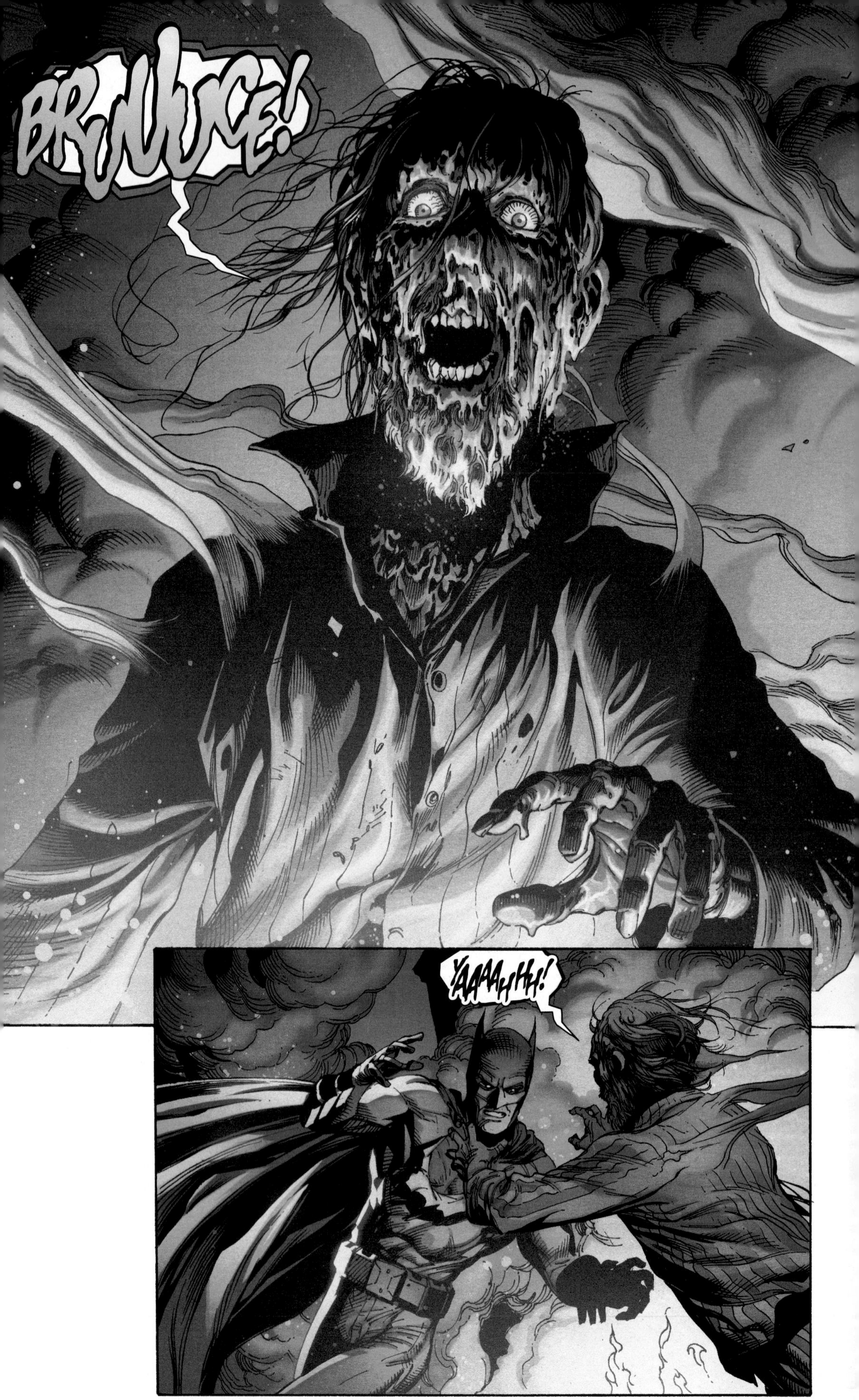
BRUUUCE!
YAAAAHHH!

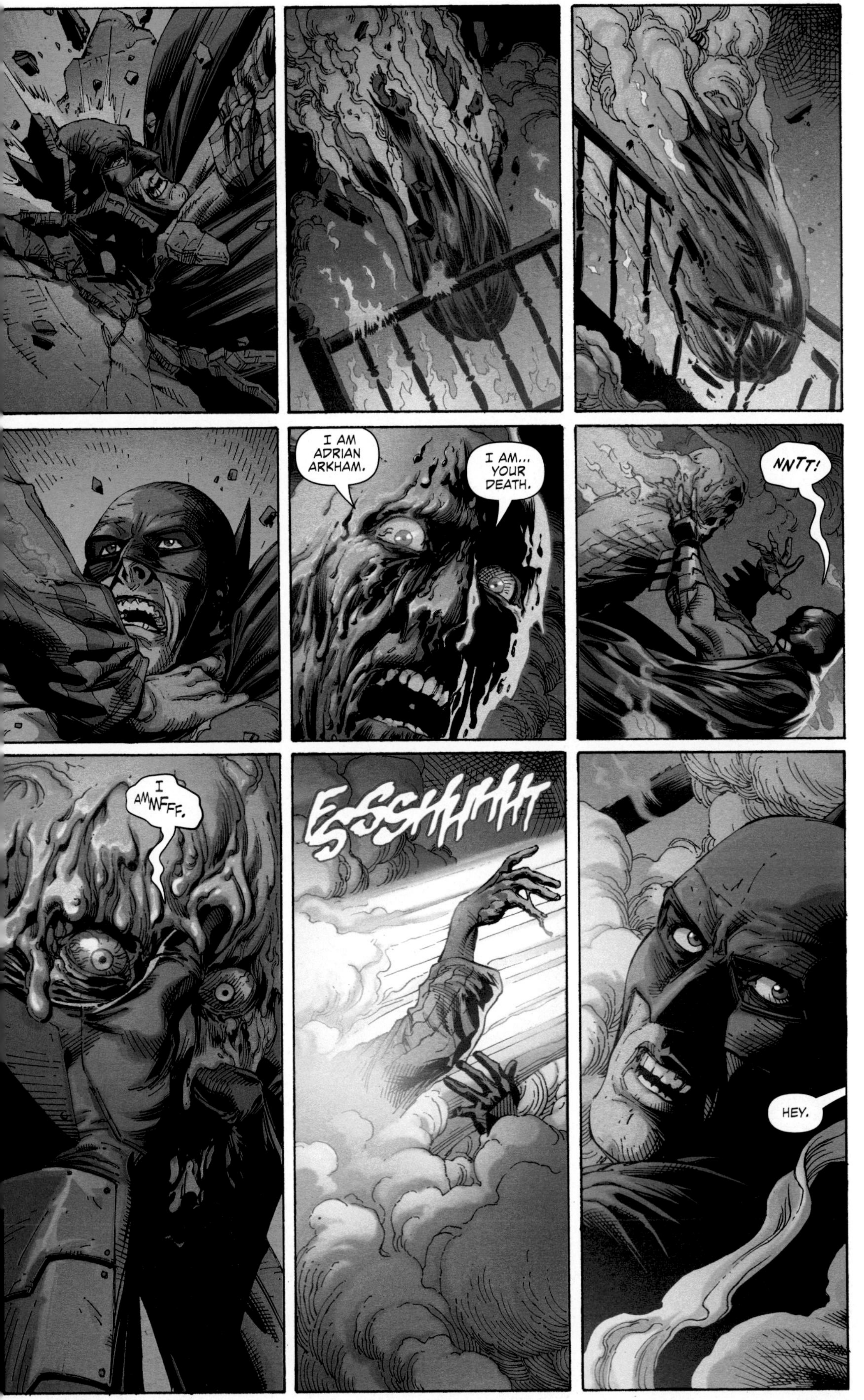
I AM ADRIAN ARKHAM.
I AM... YOUR DEATH.
NNTT!
I AMMFFF.
ESSSHHHH
HEY.

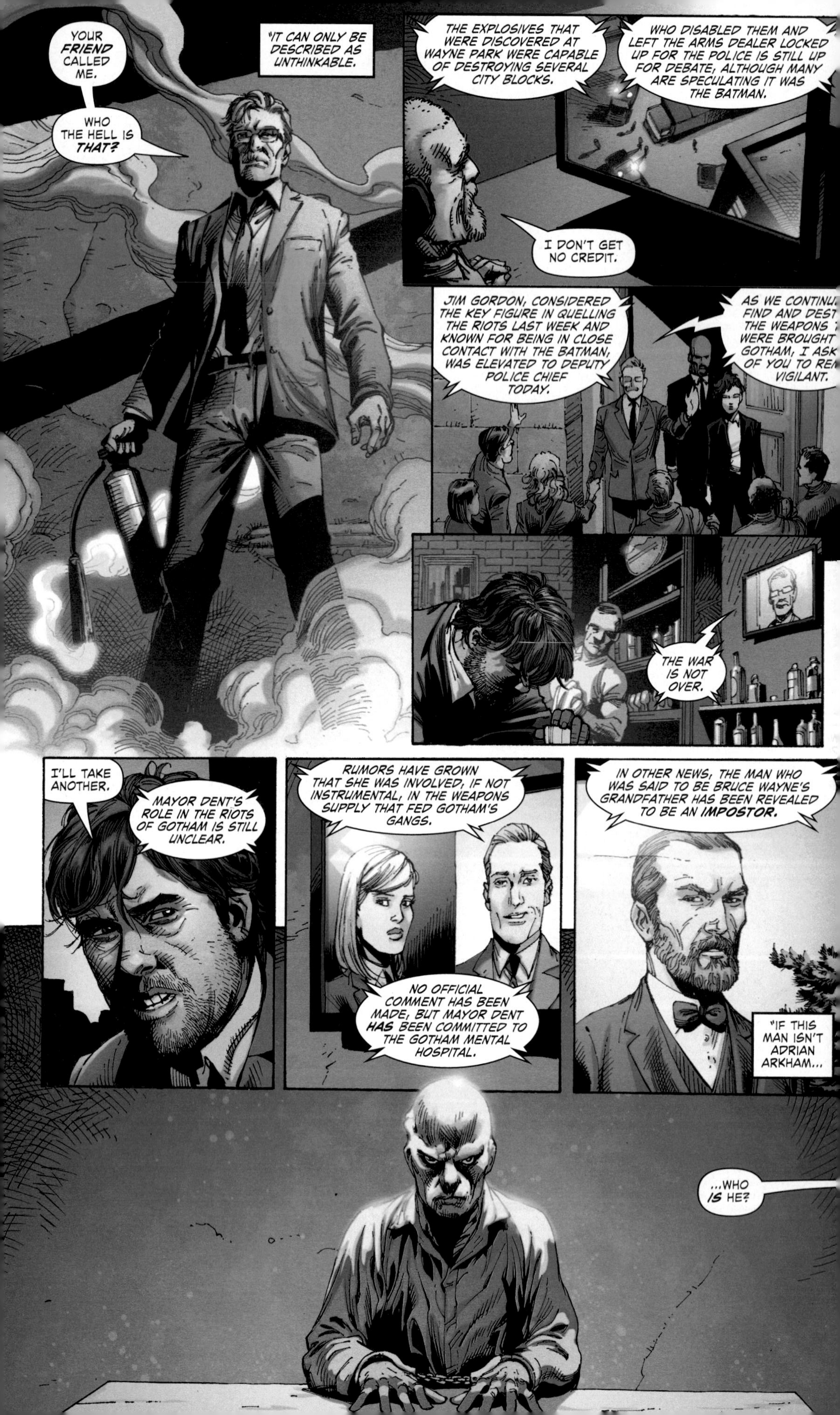
YOUR FRIEND CALLED ME.
WHO THE HELL IS THAT?
"IT CAN ONLY BE DESCRIBED AS UNTHINKABLE.
THE EXPLOSIVES THAT WERE DISCOVERED AT WAYNE PARK WERE CAPABLE OF DESTROYING SEVERAL CITY BLOCKS.
WHO DISABLED THEM AND LEFT THE ARMS DEALER LOCKED UP FOR THE POLICE IS STILL UP FOR DEBATE, ALTHOUGH MANY ARE SPECULATING IT WAS THE BATMAN.
I DON'T GET NO CREDIT.
JIM GORDON, CONSIDERED THE KEY FIGURE IN QUELLING THE RIOTS LAST WEEK AND KNOWN FOR BEING IN CLOSE CONTACT WITH THE BATMAN, WAS ELEVATED TO DEPUTY POLICE CHIEF TODAY.
AS WE CONTINU FIND AND DEST THE WEAPONS WERE BROUGHT GOTHAM, I ASK OF YOU TO RE VIGILANT.
THE WAR IS NOT OVER.
I'LL TAKE ANOTHER.
MAYOR DENT'S ROLE IN THE RIOTS OF GOTHAM IS STILL UNCLEAR.
RUMORS HAVE GROWN THAT SHE WAS INVOLVED, IF NOT INSTRUMENTAL, IN THE WEAPONS SUPPLY THAT FED GOTHAM'S GANGS.
NO OFFICIAL COMMENT HAS BEEN MADE, BUT MAYOR DENT HAS BEEN COMMITTED TO THE GOTHAM MENTAL HOSPITAL.
IN OTHER NEWS, THE MAN WHO WAS SAID TO BE BRUCE WAYNE'S GRANDFATHER HAS BEEN REVEALED TO BE AN IMPOSTOR.
"IF THIS MAN ISN'T ADRIAN ARKHAM...
...WHO IS HE?

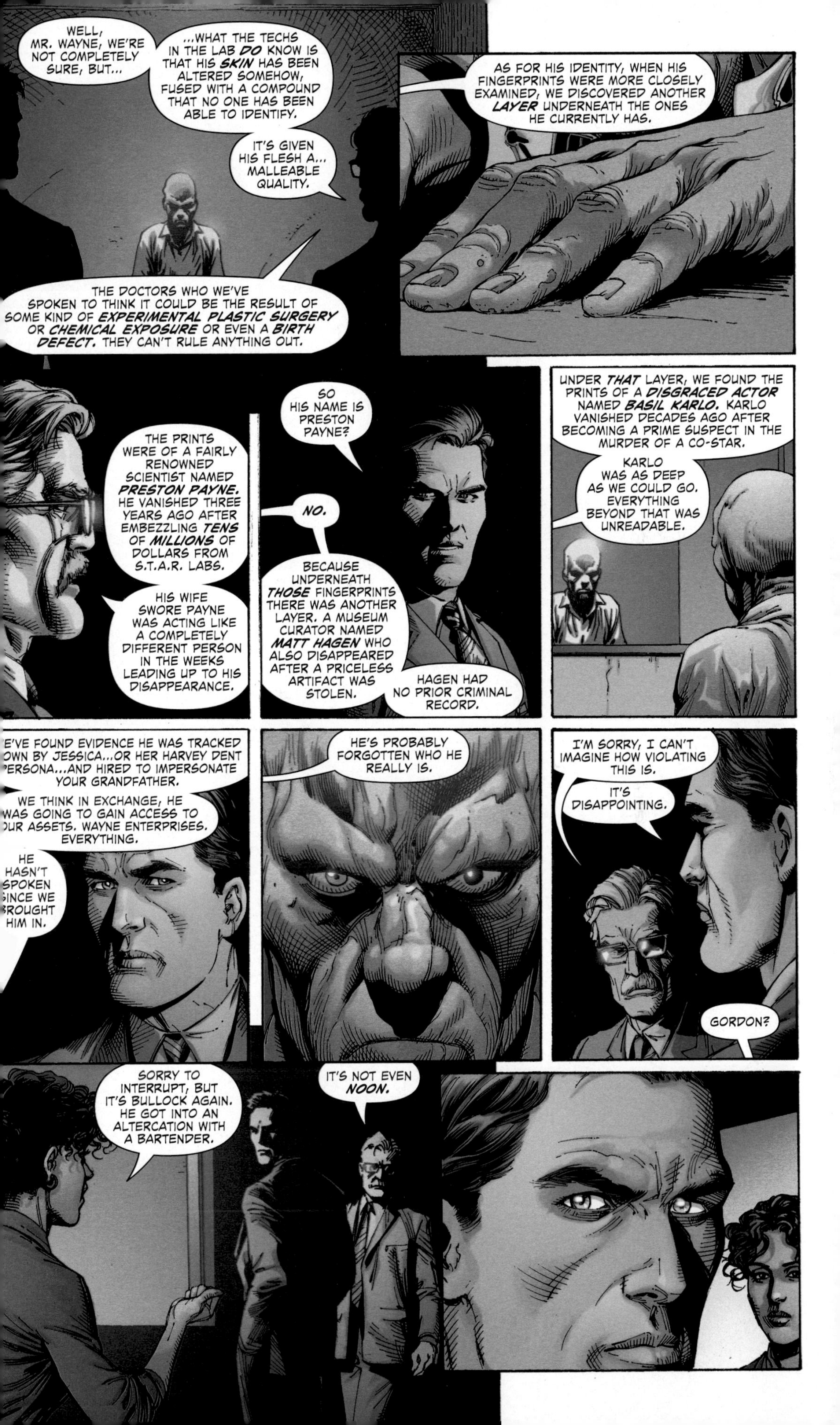

WELL, MR. WAYNE, WE'RE NOT COMPLETELY SURE, BUT...
...WHAT THE TECHS IN THE LAB DO KNOW IS THAT HIS SKIN HAS BEEN ALTERED SOMEHOW, FUSED WITH A COMPOUND THAT NO ONE HAS BEEN ABLE TO IDENTIFY.
IT'S GIVEN HIS FLESH A... MALLEABLE QUALITY.
THE DOCTORS WHO WE'VE SPOKEN TO THINK IT COULD BE THE RESULT OF SOME KIND OF EXPERIMENTAL PLASTIC SURGERY OR CHEMICAL EXPOSURE OR EVEN A BIRTH DEFECT. THEY CAN'T RULE ANYTHING OUT.
AS FOR HIS IDENTITY, WHEN HIS FINGERPRINTS WERE MORE CLOSELY EXAMINED, WE DISCOVERED ANOTHER LAYER UNDERNEATH THE ONES HE CURRENTLY HAS.
THE PRINTS WERE OF A FAIRLY RENOWNED SCIENTIST NAMED PRESTON PAYNE. HE VANISHED THREE YEARS AGO AFTER EMBEZZLING TENS OF MILLIONS OF DOLLARS FROM S.T.A.R. LABS.
HIS WIFE SWORE PAYNE WAS ACTING LIKE A COMPLETELY DIFFERENT PERSON IN THE WEEKS LEADING UP TO HIS DISAPPEARANCE.
SO HIS NAME IS PRESTON PAYNE?
NO.
BECAUSE UNDERNEATH THOSE FINGERPRINTS THERE WAS ANOTHER LAYER. A MUSEUM CURATOR NAMED MATT HAGEN WHO ALSO DISAPPEARED AFTER A PRICELESS ARTIFACT WAS STOLEN.
HAGEN HAD NO PRIOR CRIMINAL RECORD.
UNDER THAT LAYER, WE FOUND THE PRINTS OF A DISGRACED ACTOR NAMED BASIL KARLO. KARLO VANISHED DECADES AGO AFTER BECOMING A PRIME SUSPECT IN THE MURDER OF A CO-STAR.
KARLO WAS AS DEEP AS WE COULD GO. EVERYTHING BEYOND THAT WAS UNREADABLE.
E'VE FOUND EVIDENCE HE WAS TRACKED OWN BY JESSICA...OR HER HARVEY DENT PERSONA...AND HIRED TO IMPERSONATE YOUR GRANDFATHER.
WE THINK IN EXCHANGE, HE WAS GOING TO GAIN ACCESS TO OUR ASSETS. WAYNE ENTERPRISES. EVERYTHING.
HE HASN'T SPOKEN SINCE WE BROUGHT HIM IN.
HE'S PROBABLY FORGOTTEN WHO HE REALLY IS.
I'M SORRY, I CAN'T IMAGINE HOW VIOLATING THIS IS.
IT'S DISAPPOINTING.
GORDON?
SORRY TO INTERRUPT, BUT IT'S BULLOCK AGAIN. HE GOT INTO AN ALTERCATION WITH A BARTENDER.
IT'S NOT EVEN NOON.

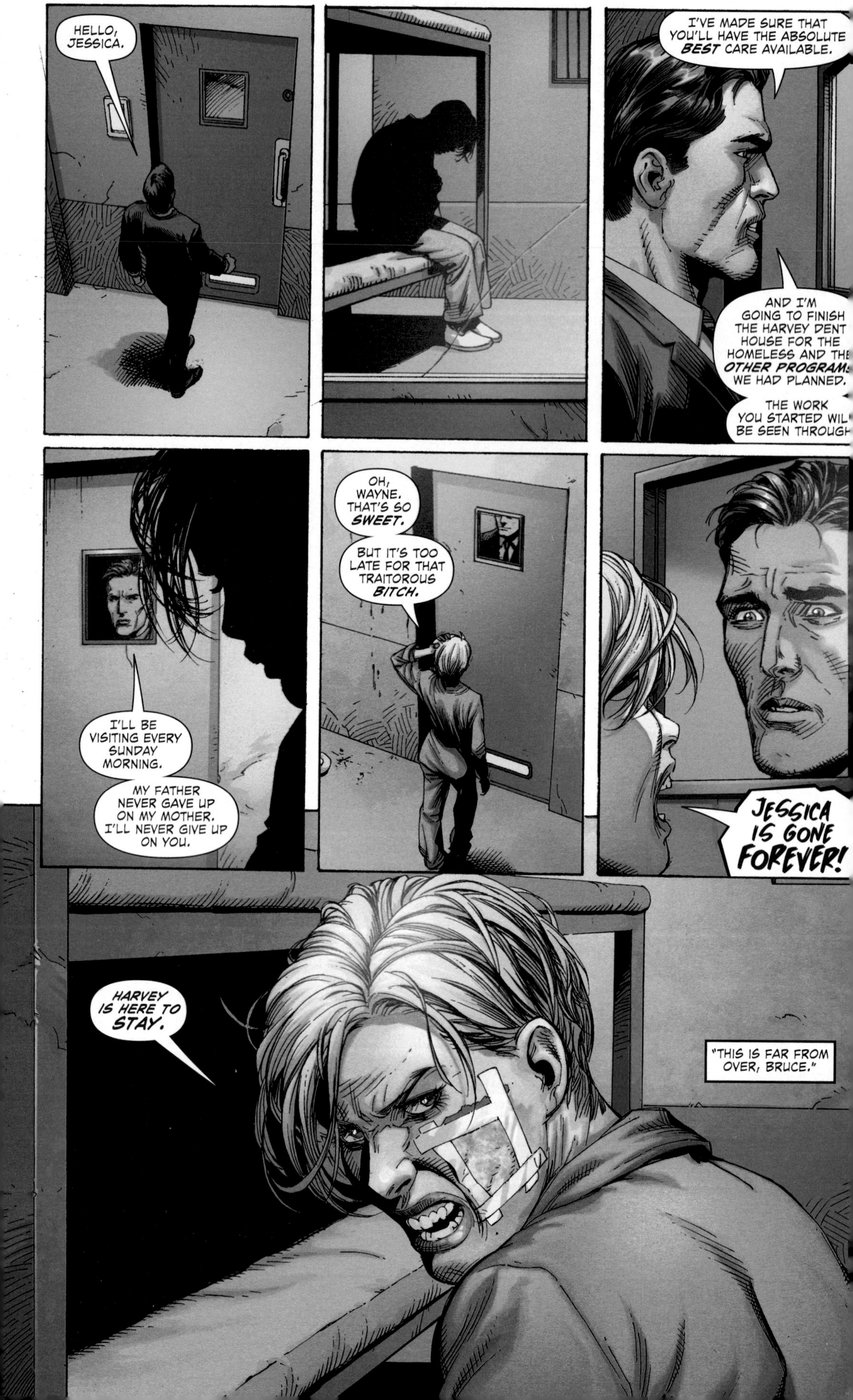
HELLO, JESSICA.
I'VE MADE SURE THAT YOU'LL HAVE THE ABSOLUTE BEST CARE AVAILABLE.
AND I'M GOING TO FINISH THE HARVEY DENT HOUSE FOR THE HOMELESS AND THE OTHER PROGRAMS WE HAD PLANNED.
THE WORK YOU STARTED WILL BE SEEN THROUGH.
I'LL BE VISITING EVERY SUNDAY MORNING.
MY FATHER NEVER GAVE UP ON MY MOTHER. I'LL NEVER GIVE UP ON YOU.
OH, WAYNE. THAT'S SO SWEET.
BUT IT'S TOO LATE FOR THAT TRAITOROUS BITCH.
JESSICA IS GONE FOREVER!
HARVEY IS HERE TO STAY.
"THIS IS FAR FROM OVER, BRUCE."

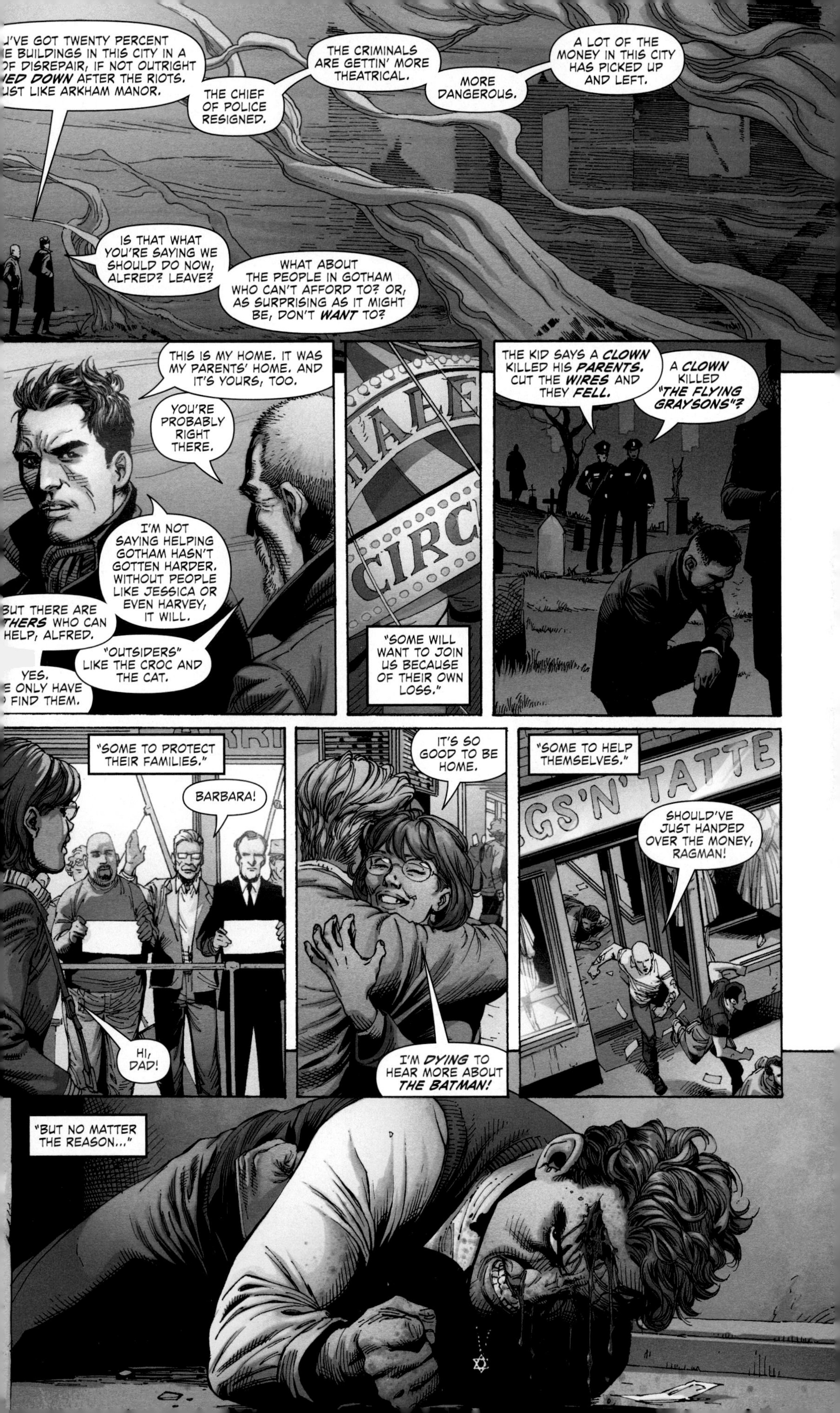

U'VE GOT TWENTY PERCENT
E BUILDINGS IN THIS CITY IN A
OF DISREPAIR, IF NOT OUTRIGHT
IED DOWN AFTER THE RIOTS.
UST LIKE ARKHAM MANOR.
THE CHIEF OF POLICE RESIGNED.
THE CRIMINALS ARE GETTIN' MORE THEATRICAL.
MORE DANGEROUS.
A LOT OF THE MONEY IN THIS CITY HAS PICKED UP AND LEFT.
IS THAT WHAT YOU'RE SAYING WE SHOULD DO NOW, ALFRED? LEAVE?
WHAT ABOUT THE PEOPLE IN GOTHAM WHO CAN'T AFFORD TO? OR, AS SURPRISING AS IT MIGHT BE, DON'T WANT TO?
THIS IS MY HOME. IT WAS MY PARENTS' HOME. AND IT'S YOURS, TOO.
YOU'RE PROBABLY RIGHT THERE.
I'M NOT SAYING HELPING GOTHAM HASN'T GOTTEN HARDER. WITHOUT PEOPLE LIKE JESSICA OR EVEN HARVEY, IT WILL.
BUT THERE ARE
THERS WHO CAN
HELP, ALFRED.
"OUTSIDERS" LIKE THE CROC AND THE CAT.
YES.
E ONLY HAVE
FIND THEM.
"SOME WILL WANT TO JOIN US BECAUSE OF THEIR OWN LOSS."
THE KID SAYS A CLOWN KILLED HIS PARENTS. CUT THE WIRES AND THEY FELL.
A CLOWN KILLED "THE FLYING GRAYSONS"?
"SOME TO PROTECT THEIR FAMILIES."
BARBARA!
HI, DAD!
IT'S SO GOOD TO BE HOME.
I'M DYING TO HEAR MORE ABOUT THE BATMAN!
"SOME TO HELP THEMSELVES."
SHOULD'VE JUST HANDED OVER THE MONEY, RAGMAN!
"BUT NO MATTER THE REASON..."

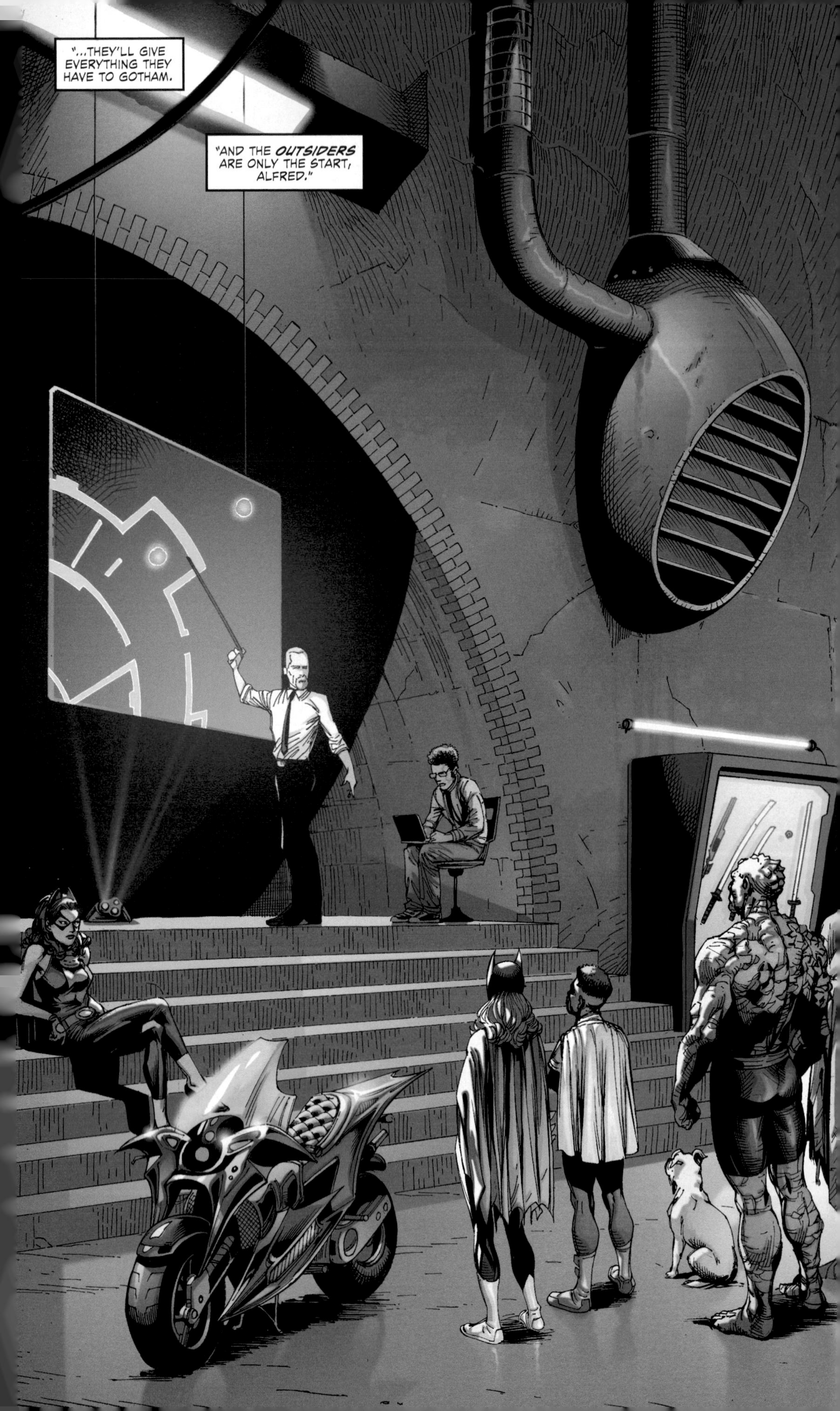
"...THEY'LL GIVE EVERYTHING THEY HAVE TO GOTHAM.
"AND THE OUTSIDERS ARE ONLY THE START, ALFRED."

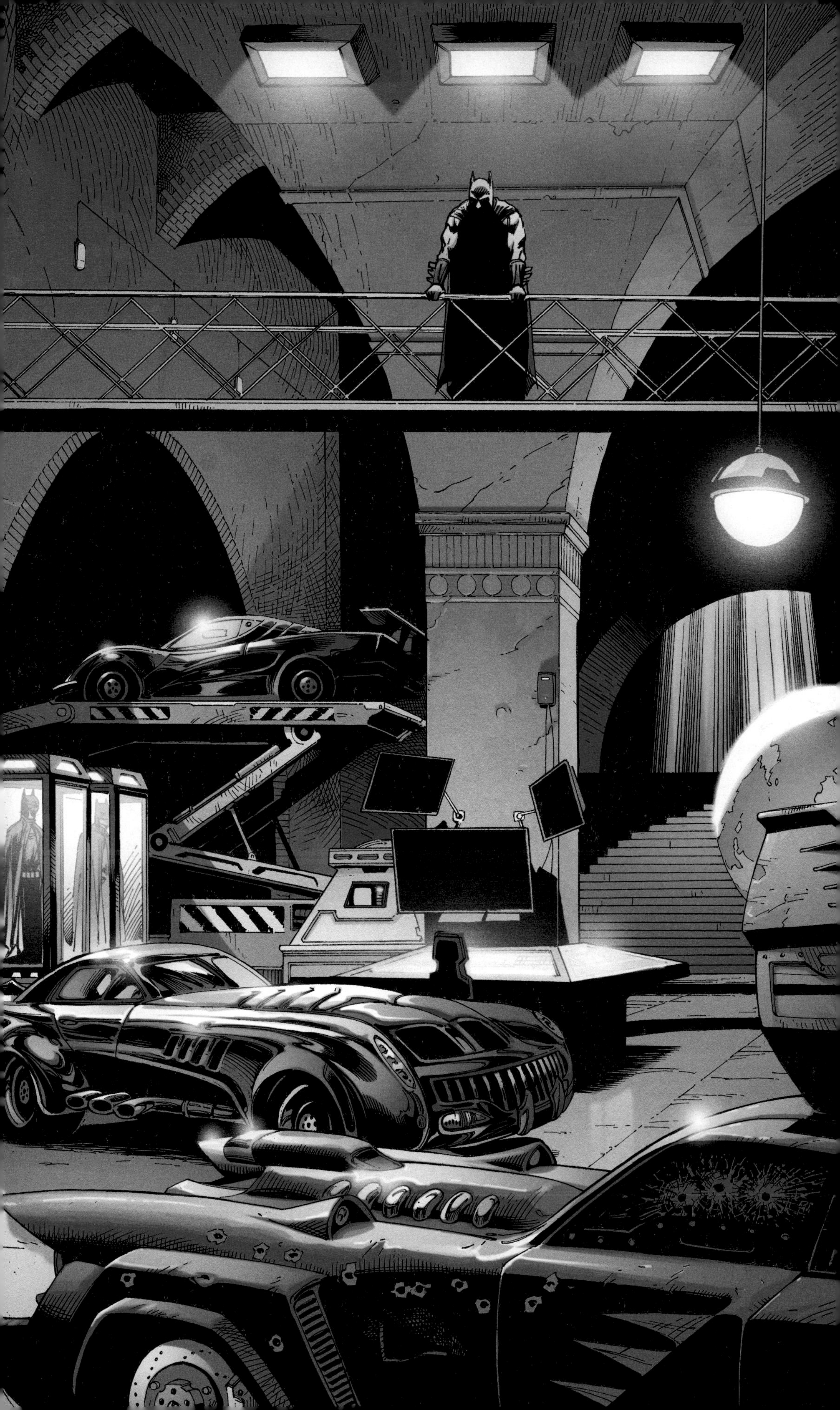

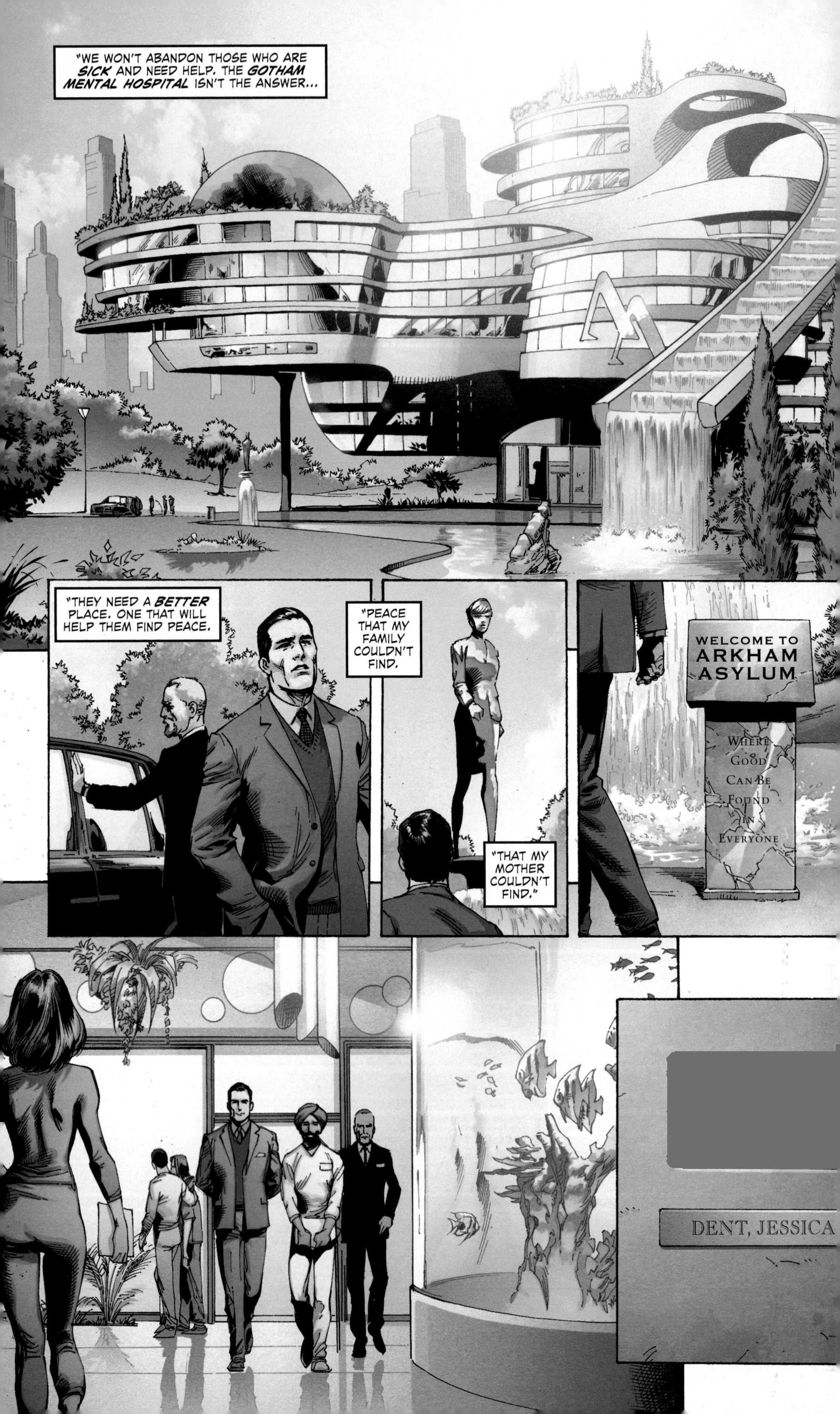
"WE WON'T ABANDON THOSE WHO ARE *SICK* AND NEED HELP. THE *GOTHAM MENTAL HOSPITAL* ISN'T THE ANSWER...
"THEY NEED A *BETTER* PLACE. ONE THAT WILL HELP THEM FIND PEACE.
"PEACE THAT MY FAMILY COULDN'T FIND.
"THAT MY MOTHER COULDN'T FIND."
WELCOME TO ARKHAM ASYLUM
WHERE GOOD CAN BE FOUND IN EVERYONE
DENT, JESSICA

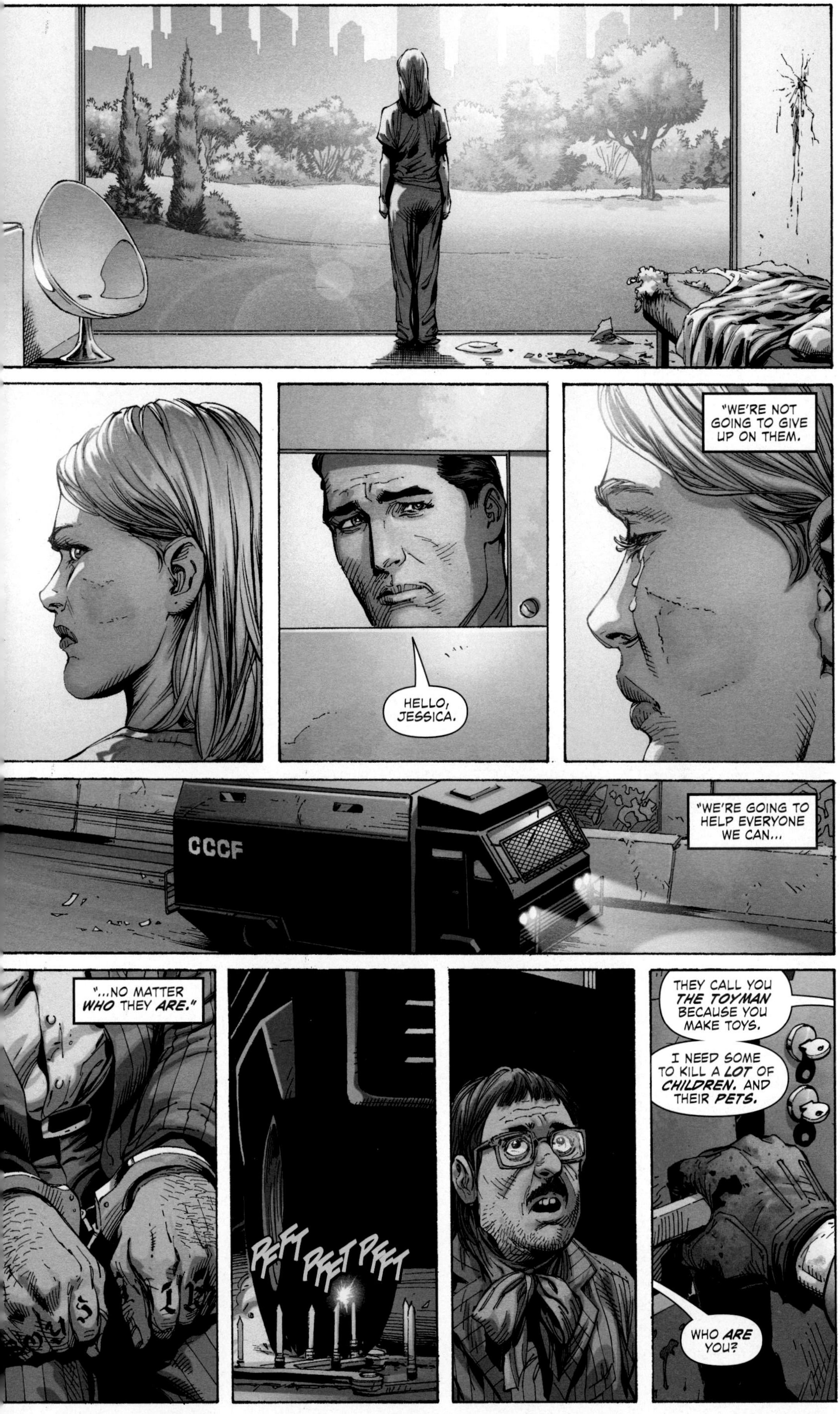
HELLO, JESSICA.
"WE'RE NOT GOING TO GIVE UP ON THEM.
"WE'RE GOING TO HELP EVERYONE WE CAN...
"...NO MATTER WHO THEY ARE."
PFFT PFFT PFFT
THEY CALL YOU THE TOYMAN BECAUSE YOU MAKE TOYS.
I NEED SOME TO KILL A LOT OF CHILDREN. AND THEIR PETS.
WHO ARE YOU?

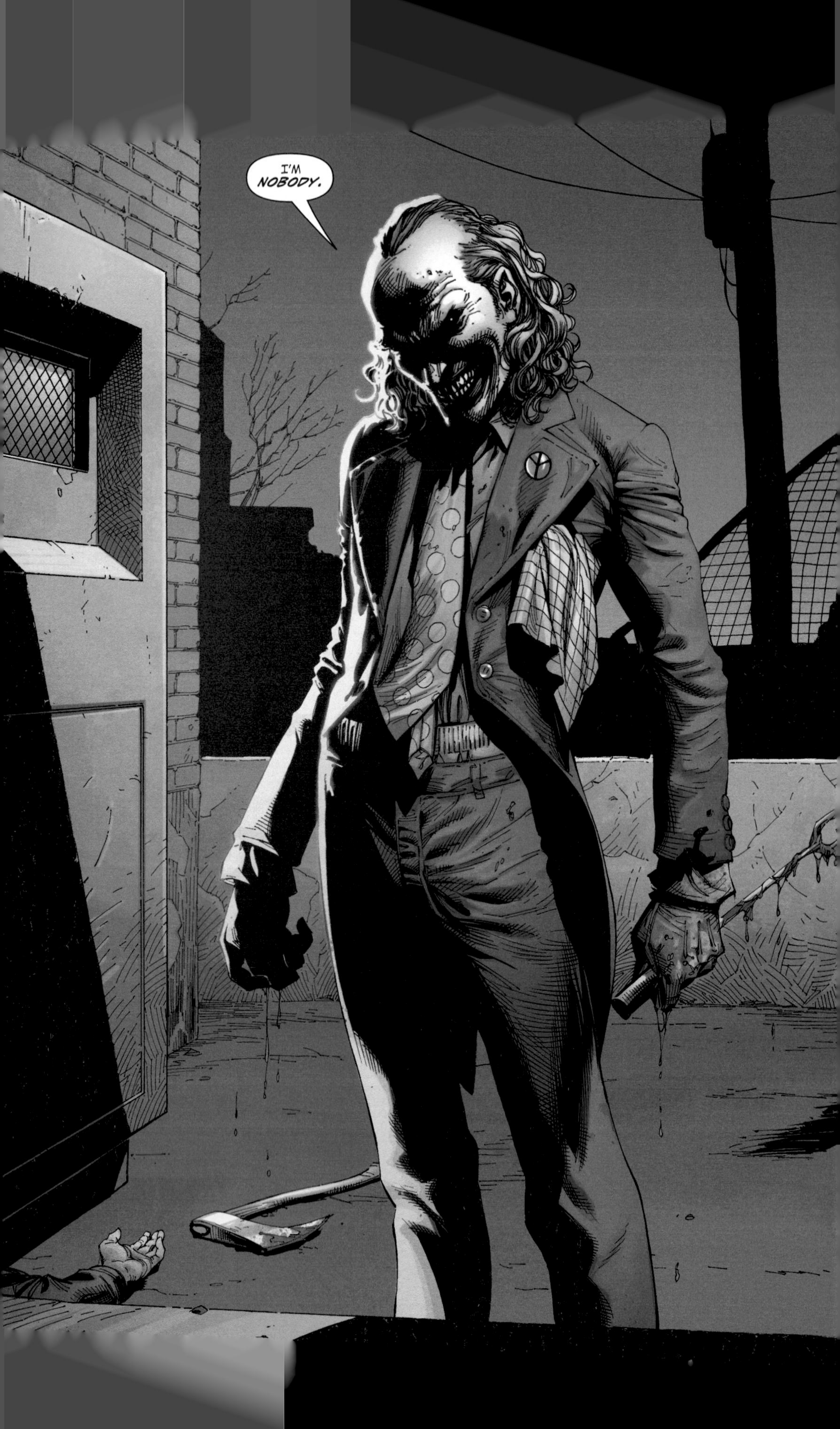
I'M NOBODY.

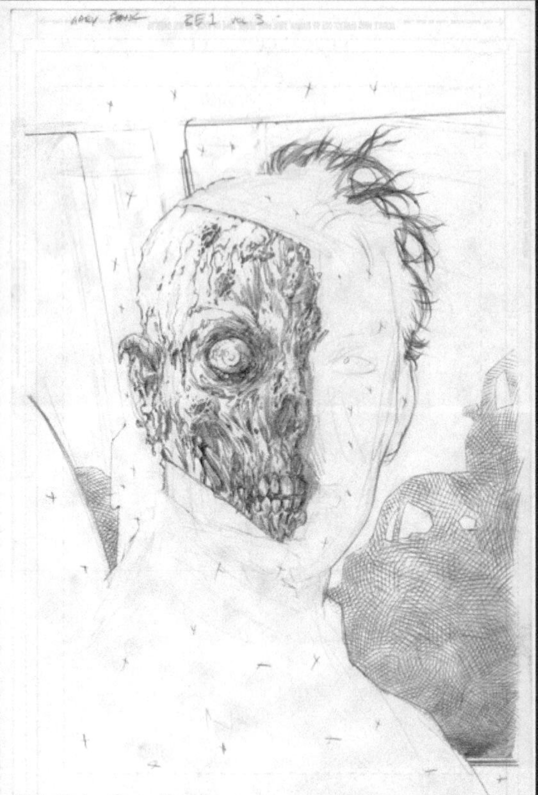

Pencils by **Gary Frank**

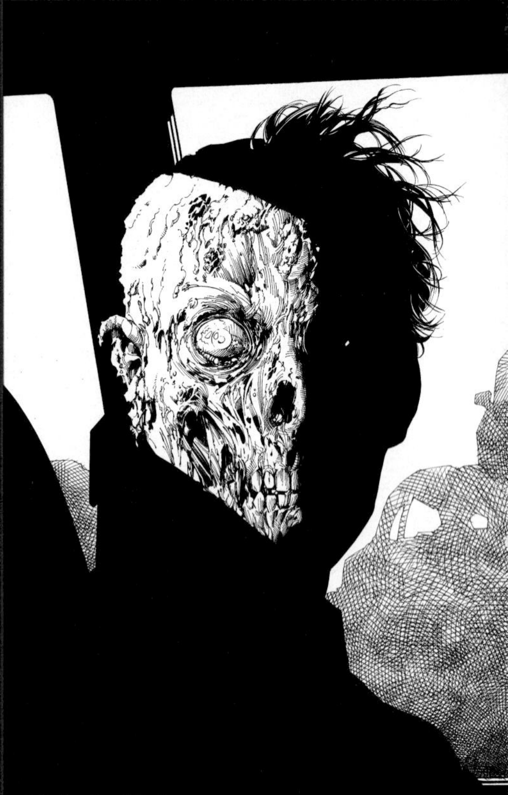

Inks by **Jon Sibal**

...WHAT JESSICA SAW.

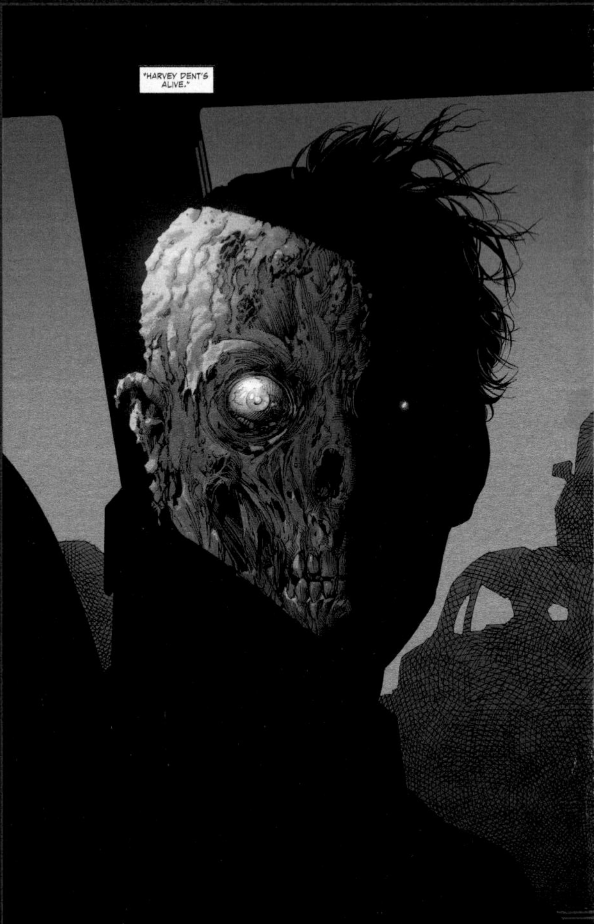
"HARVEY DENT'S ALIVE."

Colors by **Brad Anderson** • Letters by **Rob Leigh**

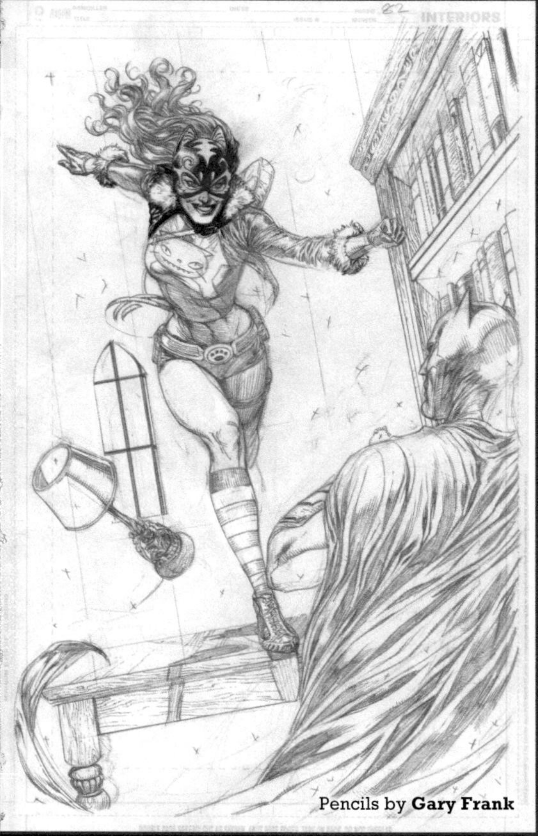

Pencils by **Gary Frank**

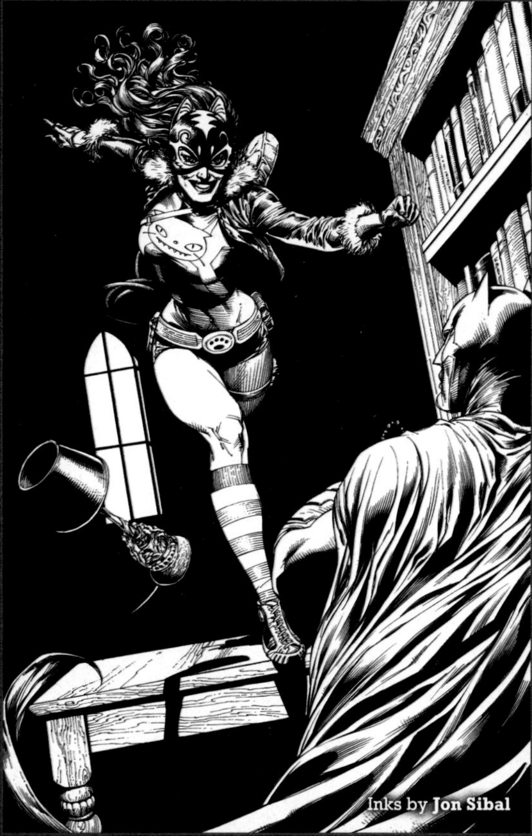

Inks by **Jon Sibal**

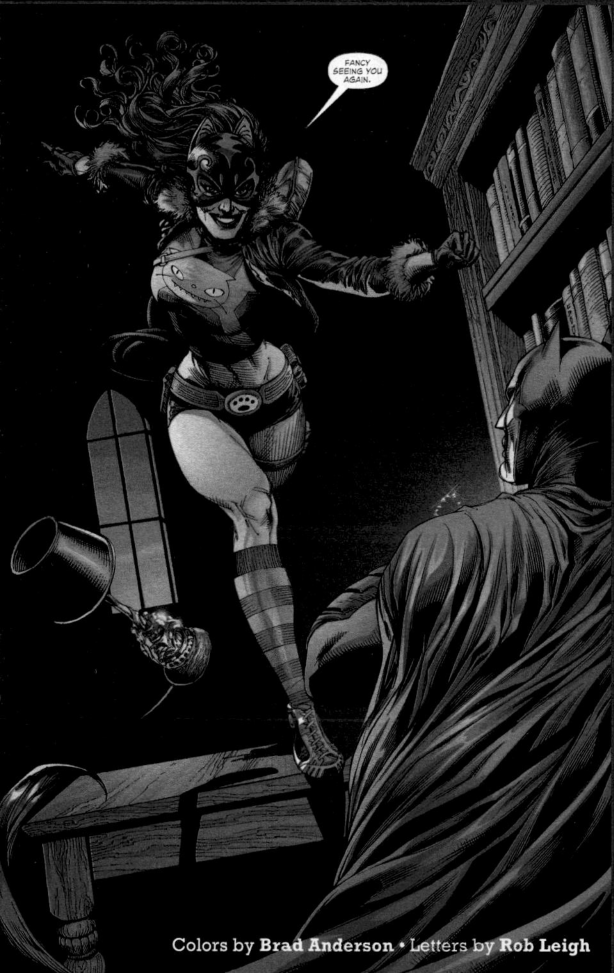
FANCY SEEING YOU AGAIN.

Colors by **Brad Anderson** • Letters by **Rob Leigh**

...THE CAT CAME BACK.

GEOFF JOHNS is an award-winning screenwriter and producer and one of the most successful comic book writers of his time. He has written dozens of *New York Times* bestselling graphic novels, including some of the most recognized and highly acclaimed stories featuring Superman and the Justice League. He has also reinvented lesser-known characters with great commercial and critical success. Under his Mad Ghost Productions banner, Johns is currently in various stages of production on an extensive list of projects in television and film. Among other projects, he wrote and produced *Stargirl* for the DC Universe streaming service and he is writing the anticipated *Green Lantern Corps* feature film. He also produced the second installment of the *Wonder Woman* film franchise, *Wonder Woman 1984*, which he co-wrote with director Patty Jenkins. On the comic book side, he developed the commercial and critical hit *Doomsday Clock*.

GARY FRANK, a native of Bristol, England, began his comics career working on various titles for Marvel UK before entering the American comics scene as the penciller on Marvel's *Incredible Hulk*. Frank then came to DC Comics, where he was the original artist on *Birds of Prey* and pencilled the adventures of Supergirl. He has also worked on WildStorm's *Gen13* as well as on his creator-owned series *Kin*. Frank, along with writer Geoff Johns, has worked on the bestselling titles *Superman: Brainiac*, *Superman and the Legion of Super-Heroes*, *Shazam!*, and the *New York Times* #1 bestseller *Batman: Earth One*, as well as the landmark issue *DC Universe: Rebirth* #1.

BRAD ANDERSON, originally from Kenora, Ontario, began his comics career after attending the Kubert School in 1996. Shortly after returning to Canada, he began painting comics at Digital Chameleon, where he cut his teeth on some of the top comics characters in the business. After leaving his position as art director, he began independently working on *Star Wars: Legacy* at Dark Horse, *Catwoman* at DC, and *Ultimate Hawkeye* at Marvel. Over his more than 22 years in the business, he's worked on such prominent titles as *Justice League*, *Doomsday Clock*, and *Dark Knight III: The Master Race* with Frank Miller, among many others.

ROB LEIGH is a graduate of the Kubert School. His lettering first received critical notice in 1972, when he was sent home with a note for writing a four-letter word on the blackboard of Miss Tuschmann's second-grade class. An avid outdoorsman, when not at his computer lettering, Leigh can be found wandering his natural habitat: the woods, water, and mountains.